D1334394

ENGLISH PLACE-NAME SOCIETY. VOLUME LI
FOR 1973–1974

GENERAL EDITOR
K. CAMERON

THE PLACE-NAMES OF BERKSHIRE

PART III

The Society gratefully acknowledges a bequest towards the
publication of the Berkshire Survey received in 1944 from
Mr A. E. O. Slocock of Newbury

ENGLISH PLACE-NAME SOCIETY

The English Place-Name Society was founded in 1923 to carry out the Survey of English Place-Names, undertaken with the approval, encouragement, and support of the British Academy. The Society has published the following volumes:

Communications regarding the Society should be addressed to:
The Hon. Secretary, English Place-Name Society,
Department of English Studies, University of Nottingham,
Nottingham NG7 2RD.

THE SURVEY OF ENGLISH PLACE-NAMES
UNDERTAKEN WITH THE APPROVAL AND SUPPORT OF
THE BRITISH ACADEMY

THE PLACE-NAMES OF
BERKSHIRE

BY

MARGARET GELLING

PART III: I

THE OLD ENGLISH CHARTER BOUNDARIES OF BERKSHIRE

PART III: II

INTRODUCTION TO 'THE PLACE-NAMES OF BERKSHIRE'
AND ANALYSES OF MATERIAL IN PARTS I AND II

NOTTINGHAM

ENGLISH PLACE-NAME SOCIETY

1995

Published by the English Place-Name Society
(Registered Charity No. 257891)
Department of English Studies
University of Nottingham NG7 2RD

© English Place-Name Society 1976

Library of Congress Catalogue Card Number: 72-75303

ISBN: 0 904889 00 9

First published 1976
Reprinted 1995

M0234685 BU

The collection from unpublished documents of material for all the
Berkshire volumes has been greatly assisted by generous
grants received from the British Academy

Originally printed at the University Press, Cambridge
Reprinted by Woolnough Bookbinding, Irthlingborough, Northants.

THE SHAKESPEARE CENTRE
STRATFORD-UPON-AVON

CONTENTS

MAPS

I THE OLD ENGLISH CHARTER BOUNDARIES OF BERKSHIRE

INTRODUCTION TO THE CHARTER BOUNDARIES

EPNS volumes have not in the past dealt systematically with the complex problems presented by the boundary surveys incorporated in pre-Conquest land-grants. The Old English surveys have not usually been printed in full, although starting with *The Place-Names of Worcestershire* (1927) the individual boundary-marks have mostly been treated somewhere in the volumes, either in the field-name sections of the various parishes within which they were considered to lie, or in a footnote under the heading of the parish to which the grant referred. In *The Place-Names of Wiltshire* (1939), however, names from charter boundaries appear only to be treated if they can be identified with names on modern maps or in Tithe Awards. Discussion of Old English bounds in a footnote, as seen e.g. in *Worcestershire* and *Surrey* (1927, 1934), had the virtue of quoting the names in the order in which they occurred in the OE survey. The treatment of the individual boundary-marks as field-names arranged in alphabetical order, which was first used in *The Place-Names of Oxfordshire* (1953–4), was more closely related to the plan of the volumes, but had the disadvantage of breaking up the order of the original bounds. An attempt was made to counteract this disadvantage by printing the Old English surveys in an Appendix, with page references to the treatment of the names in the volumes. This treatment was followed in *The Place-Names of Gloucestershire* (1964–5), but the text of the bounds was not printed, its place being taken by a *List of Anglo-Saxon Charters and References* (Gl 4 217–22), which is complicated to use, but enables the determined student to find the charter-names in the text of the volumes. The nearest precedent for the treatment adopted here for the Berks bounds is the Appendix to *The Place-Names of Middlesex* (1942), in which the bounds of Hendon, Hampstead and Westminster were discussed in detail.

The charter material for Berkshire is very extensive, and a more detailed study than is usually undertaken for place-name purposes was necessary in order for it to be properly utilised for the place-name survey. It was originally intended that this study of the Berkshire charter-bounds should be published separately (if a publisher could be found), but Professor Cameron decided that it should be incorporated in *The Place-Names of Berkshire*. Among other advantages this made it unnecessary to print the charter-names in Berks **1** and **2**, except where they were needed as documentation for names recorded in later sources. It is hoped that material in the following pages which is not directly concerned with the linguistic interpretation of Old English boundary-marks will be of interest to readers of the place-name volumes. All the problems discussed are so closely interrelated that it is difficult to see how the names in the bounds can be treated satisfactorily in isolation. It is necessary to know where the boundary-marks are, and this depends on a decision as to the nature of the land-unit in the grant, which may depend on the later history of the estate as recorded in the Domesday Survey. The dating of the linguistic material may depend on a decision (difficult in some cases) as to the authenticity of the Latin charters to which the surveys are attached. The sections of the work which deal with these matters are a new feature in a place-name survey, but they are certainly not irrelevant to place-name studies.

The last comprehensive study of Berkshire charter boundaries was contained in a series of articles by G. B. Grundy in *The Berks, Bucks and Oxon Archaeological Journal* between 1922 and 1928. These studies were part of his extensive work on Anglo-Saxon charter bounds in the whole country. Grundy's work, pioneering in its time, remains of great value, and has been constantly consulted for the purpose of the present study. It does not, of course, satisfy modern standards as regards charter criticism or linguistic analysis. It would have been tedious to refer constantly to Grundy's studies of individual charters whenever his suggestions are either adopted or rejected. He is only mentioned when his comment is particularly necessary to the development of an argument, and precise references to his articles are not given, but it should be easy for the interested reader to find Grundy's discussion of a particular set of bounds in the run of journals referred to above.

The present study makes extensive use of maps for presenting identifications of boundary-marks. This departs from the tradition established by Professor H. P. R. Finberg of identifying the marks by giving Ordnance Survey grid references. Mapping of the type undertaken here may not be generally appropriate to these studies. It is so in Berkshire partly because many of the surviving surveys relate to clusters of parishes, so that a particular mark often occurs in a number of sets of bounds, and one inscription on a map fixes it more concisely than a written description. The maps were drawn by Mrs Brenda Timmins over a period of years, before the method of publication was settled, and some slight differences of style between maps are to be ascribed to this long period of preparation. I am most grateful to Mrs Timmins, whose feeling for this curious type of mapping has produced a pleasing visual effect. I was not sufficiently skilled to be able to provide much topographical detail, and the absence of contours or height-shading may be considered a disadvantage, but the maps should in any case be used in conjunction with the relevant Ordnance Survey ones. The original tracings were taken from the O.S. $2\frac{1}{2}''$ series, the printed maps being 1:50,000, as in the new O.S. popular series.

The clustering of the surviving surveys has enabled them to be treated in groups (A–G), which are loosely connected with the hundredal organisation of the county. The index map should make this arrangement clear.

There are 74 surviving Old English surveys for Berks. All these are edited in the following pages. Where more than one text survives, selection has usually been made of the earliest copy, but the major variant readings are noted. Only in two cases, the Glastonbury charter for Ashbury (C VIII) and the Sotwell charter (G VII) in the Liber de Hyda, have texts been taken from a printed edition. All the others are from a MS source. There is no systematic discussion of those charters relating to Berkshire which do not incorporate a boundary clause. A complete handlist of Berkshire charters will be provided in my forthcoming book *Early Charters of the Thames Valley*, in the series published by Leicester University Press.

THE AREAS DESCRIBED BY THE OLD ENGLISH SURVEYS

Only 4 of the sets of boundaries edited here describe areas which cannot be identified with much precision. These relate to Barkham, Buckland, *Cern* (? in Pusey) and Wittenham. Of the remaining sets, it seems fair to say that at least 36 can be identified exactly with the area of a modern parish, or a group of parishes, or a portion of a parish which has had a separate identity, e.g. that of a distinct estate in the Domesday Survey. Most of the remainder, nearly the same number as the 'precisely identified' bounds, can be said to have some relationship to modern parishes. The material does not lend itself to exact statistical analysis, but some examples may make clear the difference between these two categories. In the first category, where the line of the Old English survey can be shown to follow modern parish boundaries precisely, may be instanced the wonderful survey of the 100-hide estate at Blewbury (G IV). This includes the five modern parishes of Blewbury, both Astons and both Moretons; the estate was later split into several administrative units, but the outside boundary remains intact. Exact correspondences with units which have not been split or amalgamated can be seen in the surveys of Shellingford and Watchfield (C IX and X). In the surveys which fall into this category there are many instances where sections of the Old English bounds correspond to the line of a modern boundary in startling detail, such as the account of the west boundary of Chieveley (B (a) II) between points 19 and 30, or the part of the East Woolstone survey (C II) which runs from the Manger over Dragon Hill and 'always along the edge' to Uffington Castle. In the second category, which comprises surveys of which the general area is clear but the details cannot all be elucidated, there are some bounds such as those of Cumnor (E VI) where the boundary-marks are too widely spaced for precision. In others, such as those of Benham (B (b) V), most of the survey (for Benham the S., W. and N. sides) fits modern boundaries well, but there is one stretch which defies identification. In this category also belong some of the grants of part of a modern parish, e.g. that of Hawkridge in Bucklebury (A (b) III), which is said to be a wood. The bounds refer twice to the R. Pang, and as Hawkridge Ho, Fm and Wd lie within a right-angle bend of the river, the location is clear enough, though none of the ten boundary-marks other than the Pang can be located. There are also a number of surveys, such as those of Bessels Leigh (E II) and Drayton (D XI, XII), which describe an area slightly larger or smaller than the modern parish.

While a distinction should be observed between these two categories of precisely located and generally identified surveys, it is absolutely clear that only in a very small proportion are we seriously uncertain about the identity of the estate and its general area. In the case of Barkham (A (b) I) and *Cern* (D II), it is not certain that the surveys relate to places in Berkshire. In the case of Buckland (D XIV) there is no doubt about the identity, as Gainfield is mentioned, but only one boundary-mark can be located and there is no way of judging how much of Buckland parish is involved. The survey of Wittenham (G I) is probably a defective text.

The estates disposed of in Anglo-Saxon charters do not always consist of a single unit of land; it is fairly common for such an estate to have a piece of woodland or meadow, recognised as a distinct unit, sometimes adjacent but sometimes at a considerable distance. This phenomenon is not particularly well evidenced in Berks, but the following instances may be noted. Separate meadow is mentioned in the Waltham survey (A (a) I), and this can be located by the Thames at Cookham, over 5 miles away. The Bayworth survey (E IV) has bounds of two pieces of detached meadow by the Thames, and hay was still carted from one of these to farms in Wootton (included in the Bayworth estate) in the present century. Brightwell and Harwell (G V and IX) have contiguous meadow which seems to have been regarded as distinct from the main estates. Separate woodland is surveyed for Farnborough (B (b) VIII), where it constitutes a projecting corner of the modern parish, and Chilton (G XIII) has a detached wood which is probably near the Farnborough one. The name *Wealcottes leahe* in the Oare survey (B (a) IV) probably denotes wood belonging to Wawcott in Kintbury. The gift of a wood at Hawkridge in the N. of Bucklebury parish to Abingdon (A (b) III) denotes a similar arrangement. These pieces of woodland lie fairly close together, S. of the Downs. There are no similar indications of detached woodland in the area of Windsor Forest, or in the wooded area of Hormer Hundred.

Mills outside the main estate are referred to in the Leckhampstead charter (B (b) II), and in the Sparsholt survey (C VI), the last being 12 miles away from the estate and having some arable land with it. The only mention of urban properties occurs in the Brightwell survey (G V), which refers to property in Wallingford, the town which adjoins the estate. A house in Oxford is granted with the portion of W. Hanney in F VIII, but it is not certain that this is an appendage of the estate.

The identification of points in charter boundaries is, of course, closely linked with the work of compiling the County place-name survey. Confirmation of the line of a set of bounds is constantly provided by minor p.ns. or f.ns. which can be identified with the Old English boundary-marks. Many instances of this will be found in the following pages, and references are given in the notes to the later material in Pts 1 and 2. Later p.n. evidence may be particularly helpful for the location of detached parts of estates. The meadow attached to Waltham is located partly by the occurrence of a f.n. *Le Stond* in Cookham, and the second of the two meadows attached to Bayworth is located by later p.n. evidence (Pt 2 456). In Berks, as in O (*v.* O xxviii–xxix), there are many instances of names which occur as boundary-marks in charters and are then not heard of again until they appear in recognisable form in a Tithe Award. This survival of boundary-marks as minor ns. or f.ns. is generally a reliable guide, but it is sometimes necessary to be on one's guard against too confident an identification of a later name with an OE one. The greater one's experience of p.n. work the greater one's awareness of the possibility of coincidental conjunctions of similar or even identical names. Cf., e.g., the proximity of *croh hamme* (A (b) II n.10) to the village of Crookham. If an apparent p.n. clue seems to prevent a reasonable interpretation of a charter survey, it is always advisable to ask whether the resemblance of p.ns. compels identification. The survey of Leverton (B (b) X) has a boundary-mark *Eadgife gemære* which might reasonably be expected to be on the boundary of Eddington ('Ēadgifu's estate') which lies E. of Leverton. The bounds only work, however, if *Eadgife gemære* is assumed to be W. of Leverton, and there is nothing improbable in the assumption that two women called Ēadgifu owned estates in this area, perhaps at different dates. Similarly, it is sometimes reasonable to assume that the name of a boundary-mark was that of an extensive feature, so that its appearance in later sources need not be a guide to the exact position of the point in the Old English survey. The second Waltham survey (A (a) II) refers to a *hwitan pearruc*, which is to be connected with the n. *Witeparroch*, *White-Paddock* in later sources; but the later forms refer to a wood and it is reasonable to postulate that this covered a wide area, which gives more room for manœuvre in the interpretation of the bounds. A similar view is taken here of the name *wærnan hyll* in the Longworth survey (D III), which need only be on the same ridge as the *Warnhill* of the Tithe Award, not necessarily at the same spot.

The high proportion of the boundaries of these Old English surveys which can be shown to have remained in existence to the present day will come as no surprise to anyone who has used G. B. Grundy's pioneer work. The present study offers solutions of some boundaries which defeated Grundy, notably of the *Æscesbyrig* group (C I, II, V), also of the Chieveley and Beedon group (B (a)). These solutions are based on the identification of the charter boundaries with those of later administrative units, the new suggestions being due to a more careful consideration of the nature of the land-units involved and of the recorded history of the estates. For others, such as Waltham (A (a) I–II), *Cern* (D II), Longworth (D III–IV), Appleton (E I), Cumnor (E VI), alternative solutions to Grundy's are proffered, without any claim that they are proved to be correct.

The present study is far from definitive; local historians with more time to give and greater knowledge of Berkshire topography and history will certainly be able to solve some of the problems left unsolved here, and with this probability in mind, something may be said about two points likely to influence future work on these charters. One is the extent to which these problems may be solved by field-work, the other is the feasibility of tracing precisely the line of an Old English survey which does not correspond to a known administrative boundary.

Some field-work has been undertaken for the present study, and the results are incorporated in the notes on some of the sets of bounds. Perambulation of charter boundaries is always illuminating to the person who undertakes it, but it is not certain that it contributes to the solution of problems proportionately to the time and energy, and in recent years the expense, which it involves. Some nice details were found in Berks, such as the *sand gewyrpe* in Appleford (G II) and the sequence 'white hollow way–stony way' in Aston Upthorpe (G XII). There were some possible correlations of visible ridge and furrow with 'headlands' and such in the charter bounds, and one possible trace of a group of tumuli (*þrymbeorgum* in Hendred, F VII), though on the whole the search for tumuli was disappointing, as L. V. Grinsell had previously established. More work of this kind should ideally have been done, but at no point did I feel that the line of a set of bounds was proved or disproved by what was seen on the ground. For the identification of an Old English boundary-mark with an existing feature of the landscape to be proved it is necessary to have at least three conditions fulfilled; if only two are present, the argument is not conclusive. For instance, if there is a valley at the point where the investigator is looking for an Old English boundary-mark with a name in cumb or denu, this constitutes two factors, but it can only be conclusively demonstrated that this is *the* valley if some third point tallies. The third point may be that the valley has the same name (e.g. Tadcom Pt **1** 153, which is *tottencumbe, totan cumbe* in G III (b) and

G IV), or it may be that the valley lies on a parish boundary between two other points which can be located in the survey. As regards survival of the old name, however, it is necessary to remember that names of woods, valleys, rivers and some hills may not give an indication of the exact point. Unless the name is a very distinctive one and is that of an object, such as a stone or tree, which must be in one spot, name correspondence will seldom be precise enough to prove the exact line of a survey, though it often helps to pin down the general direction.

My own experience suggests that unless an Old English survey is following a known administrative boundary it is not advisable to try to establish its line too precisely, and this principle has been adhered to in the present study. If the line is following a known boundary, then perambulation will throw light on various details, but will not seriously affect the interpretation. This is only a personal view, however, and it is hoped that local historians will do a great deal more field-work on these bounds, on those of which the line is uncertain, as well as on those which are following modern parish boundaries.

In accordance with the conclusion that precise interpretation of the line of an Old English survey should only be attempted when it clearly corresponds to a modern boundary, the only boundaries shown on the maps are those of the civil parishes traced from the $2\frac{1}{2}''$ O.S. maps of 1948–52, and in one instance (Sotwell G VII) from the 6''. The only exception is a Tithe Award boundary for Curridge (B (a) III). All firmly identified place-names are shown, and the notes to each survey endeavour to make it clear when the Old English boundary is not the modern one, so that the reader may form his own conclusion about the line it takes.

The high incidence of connection between the Old English estates described by these boundaries, the Norman manors of the Domesday Survey, and the ecclesiastical and (in Berks) the civil parishes of modern times, may be regarded as proved. In some counties more reliance would have had to be placed on the ecclesiastical parishes of the Tithe Awards, but in Berkshire, particularly in the W. where most of the Old English surveys lie, the civil parishes of modern O.S. maps are not substantially different from the earlier units. How far these estates may be considered to antedate the period of the Old English charters is a problem discussed elsewhere in this volume (pp. 807 ff).

THE DATE AND NATURE OF THE OLD ENGLISH SURVEYS

Two sets of bounds, Charney Bassett (D I) and one of the sets for
Abingdon (E VII) cannot be dated. Of the remaining 72, 61 are
attached to charters dating from between A.D. 930 and A.D. 985, 42 of
them falling within the narrower limits of A.D. 940–60. There are
only 11 Berks surveys attached to charters earlier or later than 930–85.
These are W. Woolstone (C I) A.D. 856, Wittenham (G I) A.D. 862,
Lockinge (F I) A.D. 868, Appleford (G II) c. 895, Basildon, Hagbourne and Cholsey (G III a–c) c. 895 (or so purporting), Hardwell
(C III) A.D. 903, Waltham St Lawrence (A (a) II) A.D. 1007, Chilton
(G XIII) A.D. 1015, W. Hanney (F VIII) A.D. 1032. The date of the
charter is not, of course, necessarily the date of origin of the boundary
survey, which may be a traditional account of the bounds, perhaps
orally preserved until a written version was required for incorporation
in a charter. This is an interesting field for speculation, which it is not
proposed to explore in detail here. There is in the Berks material one
piece of evidence which suggests that some of the surveys attached to
mid-10th-century charters would have been much the same if they
had been written down a century earlier. This lies in the degree of
coincidence between the surveys of the estates at W. and E. Woolstone
(C I–II), dated 856 and 958 respectively. They have one boundary in
common, and 5 boundary-marks are repeated exactly in the later
survey, including the *æþenan byrigels* (which seems more likely to
have been a tradition than a visible monument). Some slight changes,
such as *brembæl hyrnan* in 856 becoming *bræmbel þyfelan* in 958, and
ealdan hola becoming *foxhola*, serve to emphasise the stability of the
boundary-marks. In other instances of a shared boundary, however,
such as the Longworth and Kingston Bagpuize surveys (D III–VI),
different boundary-marks are used in sets of bounds much closer
together in date. There is no marked difference in the general style of
the bounds between the earliest (W. Woolstone) and the latest (part
of W. Hanney), though the dates of the charters are 856 and 1032
respectively. It seems likely that most of these surveys took a traditional form over several centuries, though some (such as Padworth
A (b) IV) were idiosyncratic, and others (such as Blewbury G IV)
were exceptionally precise.

The bounds for Charney Bassett and Abingdon, which cannot be
dated, indicate either that sets of boundaries were sometimes written
down for other purposes than inclusion in a charter, or that the

boundaries could be preserved without the charter for which they were commissioned. Such detached bounds exist for estates in other counties.

The study of a large number of charter bounds in one operation enables some statistics to be provided about the starting points of the surveys. Most starting places are in the S., and there is a marked preference for a corner. 18 surveys start at a S.E. corner, 18 at a S.W. one. Another 7 start on the S. boundary, but not at a corner. Aston Upthorpe (G XII) starts at the S. tip. 7 surveys start at points on the W. boundary of the estate, 4 at points on the E. 7 start at a N.E. corner, 7 at a N.W. corner. Garford (D X) starts on the N. boundary, Waltham (A (a) II) at the N. tip. In 3 instances (Barkham A (b) I, *Cern* D II, Buckland D XIV) the starting point cannot be ascertained. Only one of the 71 surveys which can be followed runs anti-clockwise, this being the Appleford survey, G II.

There is a great range between the most detailed surveys (such as Blewbury G IV) and the most sparsely provided with boundary-marks (such as Cumnor E VI). Sometimes the boundary-marks are fairly evenly spaced (as for Brimpton A (b) II), but in a number of surveys they are bunched in one part of the circuit with long gaps in others. The Hagbourne survey G III (b) has one very long gap, and the E. side of the Drayton surveys D XI–XII is very unsatisfactory, as is the S. part of the Waltham bounds A (a) I–II. It is probably a mistake to try to solve charter bounds by allocating a mathematical proportion of boundary-marks to each stretch.

References to points of the compass are clearly not intended to be precise. At the beginning of the Farnborough bounds (B (b) VIII), the direction *west* refers to a stretch of boundary which runs due W., but this is followed by *suð*, for a stretch which runs S.W., and this latter use is more typical. Care is often taken to indicate whether the bounds proceed up or down a river, but *andlang*, if not qualified, may refer to either. When a topographical feature lies athwart a boundary this is sometimes indicated by the term *þwyres* (as in *þwures ofer wrestles hyll* in Leckhampstead B (b) II), and *ofer* sometimes has the same sense (as in *ofer beocumb* in Farnborough B (b) VIII). The term *rihte* sometimes indicates a particularly straight stretch of boundary, as in *norð rihte* in Brightwalton B (b) I. Care is often taken to indicate from which direction the survey approaches a feature, and such terms as *ufewearde, suðewearde, norðewearde, estweardne, westeweardne* are used with precision.

THE BOUNDARY-MARKS

The types of objects used as boundary-marks may be observed in the section *Old English Words in the Boundary-Marks of Berks Charters*, pp. 769 ff. It has seemed advisable to do a separate list for the charters, rather than treat this material in the general *List of Elements in Place-Names and Field-Names*, pp. 848 ff. The separate list of elements for the charters, linked as it is to a detailed topographical study, may be of special use to students of charter bounds in other areas. Another reason for keeping the list of terms in charter boundaries separate from the list of elements in Berks place-names and field-names is that the boundary-marks in the charter surveys are not always true place-names. This distinction was pointed out by Mats Redin in 1919 (Redin p. iv, n.1) – 'It is obvious that we are not concerned here with real place-names but with indications made for the occasion. It seems desirable that investigators of place-names should notice the difference between such formations and stabilised place-names . . .' The vast quantity of material published since 1919 shows that a surprising number of these 'indications made for the occasion' did become 'real place-names', and the Berks instances in which this can be shown to have occurred are all included in Pts 1 and 2, and analysed in the List of Elements on pp. 848 ff. For the rest, although many of them probably had a longer currency than that of the survey in which they are recorded, it seems more precise to compile a separate list of elements.

It may be useful here to draw attention to some categories of objects, man-made or otherwise, which are well represented in these surveys.

The terms *æcer*, *andhēafdu*, *forierð*, *furh*, *furlang*, *gāra*, *hēafod*, *hēafod-æcer*, *hēafod-land* are of special interest because they relate to details of the field-systems in use in Berks in the 10th cent. A recent discussion of the light thrown by such boundary-marks on the problems connected with Anglo-Saxon farming is to be found in Professor H. P. R. Finberg's section of *The Agrarian History of England and Wales*, vol. I, part II, pp. 487–93, but this is not, of course, linked to a detailed topographical study of a body of charter boundaries such as is presented here. The details of field-systems are not strictly within the competence of a toponymist, and it is hoped that more expert scrutiny will be made of these boundaries by historians and geographers specialising in this subject. It seems necessary, however, to offer some suggestions here about the use of the terms listed above.

In the Berks surveys, *æcer* seems to denote something like the pre-enclosure strip, i.e. the long piece of ground, sometimes to be identified with a single ridge in the ridge and furrow of open-field ploughing, which was the unit of ownership, but not the unit of cultivation. The *fif and sixti æccera* in the common land which belonged to the estate at Curridge (B (a) III) were probably strips, and the *seouan æcera* of E IV 23 and the *six æcerum* of B (a) II 26, which lay beside the boundaries of Chieveley and Wootton, were probably blocks of strips forming the units called furlongs, which were the units of cultivation. The term *furlang* is used in this sense at least twice in Berks boundaries, in the Hardwell survey (C III) which runs 'crosswise over a furlong', and in *þæt longe furlang* in Harwell (G IX).

The terms *andhēafdu*, *hēafod* and *gāra* are related to the ploughing of the furlongs. The strips of the furlongs were ploughed in such a way as to create a series of parallel ridges, but while this was being done strips had to be left at both ends so that the oxen could turn, and these were eventually ploughed so as to make ridges lying at right-angles to the others. These are the 'headlands' referred to by the terms *andhēafdu*, *hēafod*, *hēafod-æcer*, *hēafod-land*, and when surveys go 'along' these it is to be presumed that the boundary runs alongside a furlong, or between two furlongs which belong to different estates. The laying out of rectangular furlongs in an irregularly shaped field sometimes left a roughly triangular piece of land in a corner, which would be ploughed separately. This is the *gāra* or *gār-æcer* of some of these surveys (though *gāra* could have other meanings). Professor Finberg takes *forierð* to be another term for a headland, but *v.* p. 685 n. 12.

When the surveys pass along headlands, outside acres, to a gore-acre, etc., it is likely that a field-system more ancient than the estate boundary lay athwart the division, and that the estate boundary was drawn so as to pass between the furlongs. It cannot be proved that the field-system lay on both sides of the boundary, but if the arable had ended at the boundary a surveyor would probably have used some phrase such as 'north of the ploughed land' (as in G IV 31) rather than mentioning the details of the furlongs. In some instances where these terms occur in the charter surveys, the modern parish boundary can be seen from the Maps to have a characteristic 'step' pattern, which presumably results from going along the edges of rectangular furlongs. Particularly clear instances may be seen on the W. boundary of Chieveley, where the survey (B (a) II) runs 'to a headland' and 'outside six acres', and on the boundary between E. Hagbourne and S. Moreton, where the Blewbury survey (G IV) twice runs 'along the headlands'. Cf. also the zig-zag line of the footpath N. of the Ridge Way in Compton Beauchamp, which may be the ancient boundary of Hardwell and has been marked on Map C; field-system terms are thick in the portion of C III which relates to this stretch. It should be noted, however, that the pre-English field-systems which have sometimes remained visible on downland are made up of rectangular blocks of irregular size, and the outside edge of one of these systems would have just such a 'step' pattern, v. Introd. 845–6.

Less easy to understand than the references to headlands and gores (which would lie at the edges of the furlongs) are the instances in which the boundaries run 'along the furrow'. These are listed under **furh** on p. 776. The furrow is presumably the hollow between the ridges, but it is not quite clear what a boundary is doing running along a furrow, if the furrow does not mark the outside edge of a furlong. The direction in C IV 'by the west furrow of the head acre' is clear enough, as the head acre would be a ridge with furrows on either side, and the west furrow of the headland is a clearer statement than 'along the headland'. But in two instances the references to furrows or furlongs imply that a furlong is bisected by a boundary. These are the phrases 'over the crosswise furrow' (which follows *be heafd æceres west furh*) in C IV, and 'crosswise over a furlong' in C III. These suggest the possibility that furlongs could be split by a late boundary; and the 'deep' furrow of D IV 11 and the 'driven' furrow of C VII 22 may refer to adjustments in the ploughing made to mark an estate boundary which ran through a furlong in which the strips lay parallel to the boundary.

Whether these late estate boundaries ran through or round the furlongs of established field-systems, the surveyors obviously had a difficult task describing such sections, and two of the Berks surveys, C III (Hardwell) and F VII (Hendred) are good instances of endeavours to cope with this problem.

The Berks surveys include references to the artificial terraces known as 'strip lynchets'; *ruwan hlync* in G IV 14 and *ealdan bece* in G XIII 14 refer to terraces still to be seen. This is of some importance, as the date of origin of these terraces is disputed.

The references to strips and furlongs in Berkshire bounds are predominantly a feature of the N.W. of the county. They are most numerous in the Hundred of Shrivenham, and all but one of the surveys dealing with estates in this Hundred contain terms referring to this type of field-system. Such terms are well represented in the valley of the Ock, and in the parishes bordering the Thames from Buckland to Appleton. There are other groups in Wantage and Moreton Hundreds, and sporadic instances in the Hundred of Hormer. In the S.W. of the county, the only certain references to this type of farming occur in the surveys of Chieveley. None has been noted in E. Berks.

Special interest attaches also to the boundary-marks which refer to enclosing fences or hedges. In Berks the term *haga* clearly denoted a fence suitable for marking a boundary in wooded country. Some land-units in E. Berks seem to have had this type of enclosure running right round their boundaries, apart from stretches along a river. The E. boundary of Padworth (A (b) IV) is defined only by the phrase *seo east mearc eal se haga scæt*, and there was a *haga* running along part, at least, of the W. boundary. The *haga* which marked part of the boundary of Barkham (A (b) I), however, had a definite *ende*, as did one of the two mentioned in Brimpton (A (b) II). The wood at Hawkridge (A (b) III) was partly surrounded by a *haga*, and the phrase *a be hagan* suggests that it was of some length; the *cinges hagan* of W. Chieveley (B (a) II 17) extended between three boundary-marks. Oare (B (a) IV) has *andlang hagan* twice, and the phrase is used once in Brightwalton (B (b) I) and in Basildon (G III (a)). Some of the references (i.e. *grægsole hagan andlang hagan to hagena gemyðum – on tichan stedes hagan* A (b) VI, *westleas hagan on ceawan hrycges hagan* A (b) V 16) suggest that the enclosure was a feature expected of an estate in this terrain, and this is the implication of the phrase *cinges hagan* in B (a) II 17, and *gemær hagan* in E II 3 and E VIII 43. One might imagine something fairly slight, such as boards or ropes fixed from tree to tree, but against this there is the *ealdan wulfhaga* of the Bessils Leigh survey (E II 13), which must have been very solid. Whatever the exact structure, this way of marking an estate boundary in woodland must have required a good deal of labour for its erection and its maintenance.

Other terms for fences or hedges are *hæcce, (ge)hæg, hecge, hege, hege-ræw*; and some instances of *geat* and *stigel* probably indicate a standing enclosure.

In open country, estate boundaries were sometimes marked by ditches, and *dic* is one of the commonest terms used in these surveys.

The ditches mentioned are of various kinds. A few are prehistoric earthworks or geographical features (such as *langen dic, sceortan dic* C IV 29, 30), but most probably fall into the two large categories of drainage ditches (which may be straightened watercourses) and dry ditches dug to mark the boundary between estates. Many of the examples listed on pp. 773–4 cannot be identified with sufficient certainty to be classified. Among those which are likely to be ditches dug to mark an estate boundary the following may be instanced: *abbodes dic* E VIII 3, *ælfðryþe dic* D VII 7, *cyninges dic* G III (b) 12, *Kingges-dych* C VIII 27, *dic þære se æþeling mearcode* G IV 33, *þa ealdan dic þæ lið betwux wigbaldincgtune and æppelforda* G II 6. Ditches sometimes occur in woodland surveys, e.g. A (b) III 2, E IV 18, E IX 23; but more of them are in unwooded country, many in marshy areas. In the two instances of gærs-tūn in these surveys there is reference to the ditch which presumably surrounded the paddocks.

Objects placed to mark a boundary include stones (listed under hān and stān), posts (listed under stapol) and crucifixes (cristel-mæl, cristesmæl). There are 4 instances of hēafod-stoccas. Pits and hollows are relatively frequent, but not always artificial. In hrung putt C I 28 pytt refers to a natural hollow, but in the 3 instances with lām it refers to an artificial feature. Quarries are referred to in the 19 instances of crundel, and in *cealc seaþas* C V 7.

Another large category of man-made objects consists of the tumuli and burial-places referred to by the terms beorg, hlāw (hlǣw) and byrgels. The relationship of some of these to the estate boundaries is probably significant, *v.* Introd. 807. Roads and river-crossings feature conspicuously, and instances are listed under brycg, ford, herepæð, gelād, pæð, strǣt, wænweg and weg. One of the commonest of all terms in these boundaries is weg. The relationship of parish boundaries to the more ancient roads of the area is discussed in Introd. 808 ff.

Buildings are very rare as boundary-marks. There are 3 instances of cot, 2 of cot-stōw, one of scypen and one of wīc (*heal wicum* A (a) I 11, named from its position in an angle of a parish, *v.* Pt 1 71–2). It is surprising to find a hāmstede (*mules hamstæde* G III (a) 7, which may be the site of a settlement antecedent to Moulsford, Pt 2 527–8). Since buildings do not normally lie on these boundaries, some interest attaches to the boundary-marks listed under tūn on p. 789. Some of these can be explained as references to the modern village, such as the direction *andlang mores to æppeltune* in D IX, where the modern village lies very near the boundary, but is not actually on it, or they are to features specified as lying east or west of the tūn. In 2 instances, however, there seem to have been settlements, now lost, lying on the boundary. These are referred to in *þurh þone tun* B (a) II 38 (W. Chieveley and Beedon) and *be mersce to þam tune* B (b) VII 15 (Boxford). These two tūns are lost; but some modern villages in Berks lie across boundaries. Kingston Bagpuize spreads over the W. boundary of the parish, and the charter-survey (D V) implies that the 10th-cent. boundary went through the tūn. Aston Upthorpe and Aston Tirrold are two ends of the same village, lying athwart a modern parish boundary, and it appears from the evidence of G IV and G XII that Aston Upthorpe became a separate estate between A.D. 944 and A.D. 964. The village of Woolstone lies athwart the boundary of the two estates granted in C I and C II, and although the name Woolstone dates from the mid-10th cent. the village, under an earlier name, perhaps *Æscesbyrig*, may have been a centre for the administration of the area before it was divided. The phenomena of the occasional lost tūn on a boundary, and of existing villages lying athwart present-day or earlier boundaries, are related to the division of large, ancient estates which is discussed in Introd. 810.

There are 4 instances of **wyrð** and one of **wyrðig**, but, as explained on pp. 917–18, these terms probably do not indicate buildings.

The boundaries themselves, which must also be classified as man-made features, are referred to generally by the term **(ge)mǣre**, this and **weg** being the commonest terms of all. The alternative word, **mearc**, is much less common, but is well represented. Of particular interest is the casual association of **gemǣre** and **mearc** with personal names or terms like **cing**, **ealdormann**, referring to the ownership of the neighbouring estate. These compounds must be remembered in any consideration of the historical significance of the '*x*'s tūn' type of place-name, and this important question is discussed in Introd. 822 ff. Sometimes the boundaries are identified as those of a neighbouring community, and these instances are listed under -hǣma- and -inga-.

Among the natural features mentioned as boundary-marks, valleys, hills and rivers are all frequent. The terms used for valleys are **cumb**, **denu** and **slæd**, and these are employed with some degree of precision, though there is not an absolute distinction between them. The features listed under **cumb** on p. 773 can mostly be located on the map, and they are generally the short, relatively straight type of

valley which gives rise to major and minor ns. in cumb in this county
(*v.* 925). An exception is *humbracumb* G IX 6, which is a long,
twisting valley, of the type usually called denu in Berks; and it is
interesting that when it reappears in 1628 and 1840 the n. has been
transformed into *Humberden, Humberdean* (Pt 2 484). Of the features
for which denu is used, at least half are of the elongated, twisting type,
but at least 3 (*acdene* B (b) I 2, *cawel dene* A (a) I 9, *holan dene* E VII
34) can be identified with short valleys of the type more usually called
cumb. The third term for a valley, slæd, is used more frequently in
these bounds than its incidence in the p.ns. of the county would lead
one to expect. There are 13 instances, 2 being the compound with
wæter which occurs 6 times as a f.n. Where the boundary-marks can
be precisely located, slæd usually refers to a very slight hollow; but
in 2 instances, *brochylle slæd* G XII 9 and *fearnhilles sled* C III 18,
it refers to well-marked valleys.

The use of dūn in Berks p.ns. (*v.* 925) suggests that it is more likely
to refer to a massif than to a small, abrupt, isolated hill, though it may
sometimes be used of a relatively isolated knob on the edge of a larger
block of high ground. This last use is well illustrated by *bleo byrig dune*
G XII 11 (Blewburton Hill), and *ealdan dune* G XI 8, *waddune* G
XIII 1 (both of which probably refer to Hagbourne Hill). The *hean
dunæ* of C II 31 is one of the highest points on the Downs. Sometimes a dūn appears to be a ledge on the side of a hill, as in *mules dune*
B (a) II 40. The *weardan dune* of B (b) II 14 is the end of a low ridge.
The phrase *betweonan mæde and dune* E IV 43 is noteworthy; here
dūn appears to be used of a ledge of very slightly raised ground
formed by the 175' contour following the curve of the R. Thames.
Similar to this is *mordune* C IV 47, which is a low ridge in marshy
ground. There are fewer boundary-marks in hyll than in dūn, and not
all of them can be firmly located. Judging from the position of those
that can, it does not look as if there is much distinction between the
two terms in charter boundaries. The two ridges called *fearnhill* and
hæsl hyll (C III 18, C VII 20) could equally well have been described
by the term dūn. The ridge between the R. Thames and R. Ock is
called *wærnan hylle* in D III 5, and the *wrangan hylle* of G IV 8 and
the *wrestleshylle* of B (b) II 9 are both long, narrow ridges.

As regards words for streams and springs, brōc and w(i)ell are both
common, as in p.ns. and f.ns., but burna is rare. The term ēa is only
used of major rivers. The term lacu is better represented than its
incidence in Berks p.ns. would lead one to expect, but rīð, rīðig and

sīc are rare, as in surviving ns. and f.ns. There are 3 instances of flōde.

Names in lēah are well evidenced in Hormer Hundred, where there are 5 in the bounds of Wytham and Hinksey (E V), 2 in Wootton and Sunningwell (E IV), and one each in Abingdon (E VII), Appleton (E I), Cumnor (E VI) and Wootton (E IX). The other Hundred in which they are particularly numerous is Faircross: here, Brightwalton (B (b) I) has 3, there are one each in Chieveley (B (a) II), Curridge (B (a) III) and Oare (B (a) IV), and the uncompounded term lēah occurs twice in Welford (B (b) III). Farnborough (B (b) VIII), with 2 ns. in lēah, is adjacent to Faircross Hundred; and the woodland belonging to Chilton (G XIII), the survey of which has 3 ns. in lēah, was probably near Farnborough. In Moreton Hundred there are 2 ns. in lēah in Basildon (G III (a)), and one each in Aston Upthorpe (G XII), Harwell (G IX), and Blewbury (G IV). In the E. of the county, the bounds of Winkfield (A (b) V) has 3 ns. in lēah, and there is one example in Wokefield (A (b) VI) and one in Hawkridge (A (b) III). Elsewhere, the only instance is the isolated leacumb in Kingstone Lisle (C VI 10). (Some of the ns. in lēah in charter bounds are not counted here, as they survived as p.ns. and are therefore listed and analysed with the p.n. els. on pp. 888, 935 f.)

The occurrence of boundary-marks in lēah in Hormer and Faircross Hundreds accords well with the distribution of p.ns. in lēah shown on Distribution Map III. The occurrence of a number of instances in Moreton Hundred, on the other hand, together with other evidence from these bounds, suggests the presence of woodland in Moreton and Compton Hundreds which is not mentioned in other p.ns. One of the 4 instances of *rod[1] is in Chilton (G XIII) in Moreton Hundred, the other 3 being in estates in Faircross. The term hangra, besides examples in Hormer and Faircross, occurs in Basildon (G III (a)), Blewbury (G IV) and Cholsey (G III (c)), all geographically in Moreton Hundred. The only instance of holt in Berks charter bounds is *bullanholt*, also in Cholsey, and both instances of trēow-steall are in the Blewbury survey.

The term wudu occurs twice in Hormer Hundred and twice in Faircross. The *ealdan wudu weg* of C III 6 (Hardwell) suggests the presence of some woodland near the crest of the Downs. Examples of grāf are in Hormer or Faircross, with the single exception of *cearna graf* D IV 3, in Longworth. (Here again, ns. which survived and are therefore discussed in Pts 1 and 2 are not counted in this analysis.)

The word trēow occurs 10 times in these surveys, and it is compounded with the gen. of a pers.n. in at least 7 of these. The meaning is probably 'tree on the boundary of *x*'s estate', and this usage (like that in the '*x*'s boundary' ns. mentioned *supra*) is important for an evaluation of the significance of pers.ns. in p.ns. A number of types of tree are also mentioned (āc, æsc, alor, elebēam, ellen, hæsel, mapuldor, peru, plūme, sealh, syrfe, þorn and þyrne, welig and wiðig), but only ellen and þorn are frequent, the latter being very common. All but one of the elders are stumps.

References to open, uncultivated land in these bounds involve the terms hǣð and feld. The compound hǣ ð-feld occurs 4 times, and in 3 instances it refers to modern Commons – Brimpton, Wokefield and Snelsmore Commons in A (b) II 22, A (b) VI 12 and B (a) II 20. The term hamm occurs in two senses. The meaning 'river-meadow' is well evidenced, but there are some instances where this is not possible, and the meaning appears to be 'enclosure', sometimes an enclosure for a particular crop. The series of ns. in hamm in B (b) III and IV come into this last category, and another clear instance is *stigel hammas* B (b) II 5. This sense occurs in some surviving ns., *v.* 929.

There are 9 instances of the term *wyrtwala* 'root', none of the synonymous *wyrtuma*. Five examples are in Group A, which means they are in E. Berks. Of the others, 2 are in the N.W., one in the S.W. In 5 instances the bounds run 'by' the *wyrtwala*, and it seems clear that here, as in other counties, the term refers to a linear feature. Suggestions can only be offered for 3 of the instances: in E VII 17, the *wyrtwala* might be the edge of Bagley Wd, in A (b) VI 7 it might be a stretch of Sulhamstead Bannister boundary which follows the 150' contour, and in G IV49 it might be the W. edge of Cholsey Hill.

WORK ON CHARTER BOUNDARIES BY SWEDISH SCHOLARS

Tribute should be paid to the patient learning displayed by Swedish scholars, in particular Erik Tengstrand and Rune Forsberg, who have written theses based on a selection of material from Old English charter bounds. Dr Tengstrand, in his fundamental contribution to the grammar of place-name formation, *A Contribution to the Study of Genitival Composition in Old English Place-Names*, Uppsala 1940, treated many names in Berkshire bounds in which the first el. is in the genitive. His book was not the *vade mecum* it should have been while my own work was taking shape, as a copy has only recently come into my possession. My treatment is far from exhaustive from the linguistic point of view (or, indeed, from any other); and interested readers may be referred to Dr Tengstrand's work (if they can obtain it) for a more thorough and subtle discussion of all names with a genitival construction. In the main, Dr Tengstrand's discussions of individual names, while of great value in their own right, do not add significantly to the understanding of each set of bounds as a whole. An instance of this is his discussion of *on stocwylle broc* (G IX 21) and *to stoccæs wælle* (G III (b) 10) on pp. 157-9. All that is said in these three pages of the nature of the stocc and its relationship to the wiell is excellent, but this type of consideration in depth of individual landmarks is not possible within the framework of a county survey.

Dr Forsberg's work, *A Contribution to a Dictionary of Old English Place-Names* (Uppsala 1950), treats all names in charter bounds beginning with the letter *l*. I was able to study this book at the time of its publication, and hope that Dr Forsberg's conclusions have entered adequately into my own briefer discussions of individual names.

The main contribution of Swedish scholarship to the present undertaking has been the vetting of the typescript by Professor Matthias Löfvenberg. This has been of immense value; it has saved me from a number of errors in grammar and syntax, has curbed my rasher speculations about the meaning of obscure terms, and has enabled me to put forward some inspired suggestions of Professor Löfvenberg's own. I have also had the great benefit of Dr Olof von Feilitzen's comments on the personal names. I am humbly aware that my competence in Old English falls a long way short of Swedish standards; but I hope that this study will be of value as an attempt to treat the bounds in their context of time and place, and to provide a balanced mixture of historical, topographical and philological information. I should be happy for it to be seen mainly as a way of making the material more conveniently available for further study.

A (a) WALTHAM ST LAWRENCE,
SHOTTESBROOKE AND WHITE WALTHAM

The later version of the Abingdon Chronicle, *ClaudiusBvi*, contains two charters granting land at *Wealtham*. The earlier of these, BCS 762, is a grant of 30 hides. The boundaries are brief for an area of this hidage, and there is room for difference of opinion about the area of the grant. Grundy thought it referred to White Waltham and Shottesbrooke. It seems to me highly probable, however, that the area described comprises the modern parishes of both Walthams, and that of Shottesbrooke, which lies between them. This interpretation accords well with the later history of the places, and it seems probable that the area of the three parishes was originally a single land-unit. The shape of Shottesbrooke, especially its extraordinary E. boundary, clearly suggests that it is a land-unit of late origin, carved out of a larger estate. The fact that the two Walthams have the same name might mean that one was a daughter settlement of the other, but is compatible also with this whole area being originally one estate known as *Wealtham*. The hidage of the grant (30) is very close to the 28 hides which was the combined assessment TRE of the four estates described by DB in these three parishes. My interpretation of the bounds of BCS 762 assumes, therefore, that the three parishes were a single estate in 940. They were all in the Hundred of Beynhurst in 1086.

The area had been split up into smaller estates by 1007, the date of the second charter (KCD 1303). This is a grant of 8 hides, and as the royal estate at Waltham St Lawrence described in DB was assessed at 8 hides TRE, it seems reasonable to assume that the parish of Waltham St Lawrence was the land granted by this charter. Grundy, however, thought that this referred to Shottesbrooke.

The bounds of these two charters present considerable difficulties whether my interpretation or Grundy's is adopted. These difficulties are explained in the notes, and it should be emphasised here that no degree of certainty is claimed for my interpretation of these two sets of bounds. The charters are –

I. BCS 762, A.D. 940, an Abingdon charter, only copied in *Claudius-Bvi*, by which King Eadmund gives to Ælfsige 30 hides at Waltham. The bounds probably describe the modern parishes of

Waltham St Lawrence, Shottesbrooke and White Waltham. At
the end of the bounds there is mention of 12 *mæð æceras*, 'mowing
acres'or (if *mæð* is a side-form of mǣd) 'meadow acres', which
were probably in Cookham.

II. KCD 1303, A.D. 1007, an Abingdon charter, only copied in
ClaudiusBvi, by which King Æthelred grants to Ælfgar 8 hides at
Waltham. The bounds probably describe the modern parish of
Waltham St Lawrence.

These two sets of bounds are not very informative as regards the
nature of the land surveyed. There were two man-made enclosures
for which the term **pearroc** is used, and this word occurs again in the
bounds of Winkfield (646), a few miles away. There are two places
with names in lēah, and these are close together, in the northern tip
of the area surveyed, which may indicate that clearing and settlement
was mostly in the northern part. The sparseness of boundary-marks
for the southern part of Waltham St Lawrence parish gives a similar
impression. The obstacle to settlement in this area may have been
marsh, rather than forest.

A (a) I THE BOUNDS OF WALTHAM ST LAWRENCE, SHOTTES-
BROOKE AND WHITE WALTHAM: 940 (C. 1240) BCS 762

ærest of wassam hamme[1] on gerihte to ceaggan heale[2]. þonne of
ceaggan heale to dyrnan garfan[3] of dyrnan grafan to weg cocce[4]
þonne of weg cocce to godan pearruce[5]. of godan pearruce to hild
leage[6] of hild leage to swæfes heale[7]. þon of swæfes heale to wulfa
leage[8]. of wulfa leage to cawel dene[9]. of cawel dene to þære syrfan[10].
þonne of þær syrfan to heal wicum[11]. of heal wicum eft to wassan
hamme. þonne heafþ eadmund cing gebocad ælfsige feowertyne hida
binnan þam þritigum hidum land gemæro[12] ofer wudu ofer feld ofer
ecen læse and to ecan urfe and xii mæð æceras at þære standan[13]
buton þam land gemærum.

NOTES

1 *wassan hamme*, at the end of the bounds, is probably the correct
version of this name. The meaning may be 'meadow of the
marsh' (*v.* wæsse, hamm), and the name probably referred to a
considerable area of marshy ground along the stream which
traverses the three parishes (*v.* map). It may later have been transferred from the meadowland to the stream. There are two bridges

on the stream with names which suggest this; one is Wane Bridge, Pt **1** 117, in Warfield, which was *Wambridge* 1841 *TA*, and the other (Pt **1** 115) is recorded as *Wom Bridge* 1822 OS, *Wombridge* 1839 *TA*, *Womb Bridge* 1846 Snare, near Beenham's Heath in Waltham St Lawrence. *Wam-* and *Wom-* may be contractions of *wassan hamm*, later ?**Washam*. I take this boundary mark in the present survey, and in KCD 1303, to refer to the crossing by this stream of the E. boundary of Waltham St Lawrence. Both surveys deal sparsely with the long stretch of Waltham St Lawrence boundary between this and *godan pearruce*. Professor Löfvenberg points out that the first el. of *wassan hamm* may be the pers.n. **Wassa* as in Washington Sx. He does not accept the postulated connection between the charter form and the bridges, and considers that the bridge-ns. may contain a r.n. **Wann* or **Wanne* 'the dark one'.

2 'nook of gorse', *v.* ceacga, h(e)alh.

3 Possibly 'hidden ditch', *v.* d(i)erne, grafa[1]; grāfe 'grove' does not seem appropriate with d(i)erne.

4 'hillock by the road', *v.* weg, cocc[1]. The name survives in Weycock Hill, *v.* map.

5 'good paddock', *v.* gōd[2], pearroc or 'Gōda's paddock'; the bounds of KCD 1303 start at this point, which may have been at the northern tip of Waltham St Lawrence parish.

6 *hild leage* is Littlewick Green, *v.* map. The charter-form is probably a mistake for *hlid leage*, 'gate clearing' or 'slope clearing', *v.* Pt **1** 72.

7 'Swǣf's nook', *v.* h(e)alh.

8 'wolves' clearing'; this is Woolley Green, *v.* map and Pt **1** 73.

9 'colewort valley', *v.* cāl, cāwel, denu. This is represented by *Calden Field* in the *TA* for White Waltham, *v.* Pt **1** 74. The position in the *TA* suggests that the valley is the shallow one followed by the N.E. boundary of White Waltham, to the E. of Heywood Lo.

10 'service-tree', from OE *syrfe*.

11 This boundary-mark can be precisely located, *v.* map and Pt **1** 71. A wood at *Halewik* and one at *Lidlegewik* (n. 6) are associated with White Waltham in KCD 844.

12 I do not know what is meant by this statement. BTSuppl suggests that *ecen læse* in the following phrase is an error for *etenlæse* acc. of *etenlǣs* 'common pasture'.

13 Forsberg, p. 112 n. 2, supplies a convincing explanation of this. He takes *standan* to be the oblique case of a noun *stande, probably meaning 'pond'. There was a pond in Cookham called *Le Stond(e)*, *v.* Pt I 87. In KCD 844, a spurious writ of Edward the Confessor granting an estate in Waltham to Chertsey Abbey, mention is made of 20 acres of meadow at Cookham, and this traditional association of meadow at Cookham with an estate at Waltham strongly suggests that the *standan*, which is said to be outside the bounds of the present survey, is identical with *Le Stonde* in Cookham. For *mæð æceras v.* p. 636.

A (a) II THE BOUNDS OF WALTHAM ST LAWRENCE: 1007 (C. 1240) KCD 1303

ærest æt godan parruce[1] of godan parruce on ecgeles stiele[2] on hwitan pearruc[3]. of hwitan pearruce on þane greatan stoc[4]. of þan greatan stocce on wassanham[5]. of wasanhamme on bibban þorn[6]. of Bibban þorne on ceaggan heal[7]. of ceaggan heale on wifeles wyll[8]. of wifeles wylle þæt eft on godan pearruc.

NOTES

1 *v.* p. 637, n. 5.
2 '*Ecgel's stile', *v.* stigel.
3 'white paddock'. Paddock Wood (*v.* map) in White Waltham is referred to by Hearne in his account of the bounds of White Waltham in 1711 as *White-Paddock*, and it is probably the wood of *Witeparroch* referred to in Richard I's reign, *v.* Pt I 72–3. This is the same name as *hwitan pearruce* in the present survey, but the position of the wood is different. If my interpretation of the Waltham charters is correct, the survey is travelling down the E. boundary of Waltham St Lawrence. It is possible that Paddock Wood is the remnant of a much larger wood which extended across the parishes of White Waltham and Shottesbrooke. Grundy thought that the present survey referred only to Shottesbrooke, and he located *hwitan pearruce* on the E. boundary of Shottesbrooke, which also precludes identification with the modern Paddock Wood.
4 'great tree-stump or log of wood', *v.* grēat, stocc.
5 *v.* p. 636, n. 1. I am assuming that *wassan hamm* refers in this survey, as in the preceding one, to the point where the stream crosses the E. boundary of Waltham St Lawrence, *v.* map.

'*Bibba's thorn-tree'.

v. p. 637, n. 2.

'spring or stream of the beetle' or 'of a man named Wifel'. This is probably *Wyvils*, *Hither Wyvils* in the *TA* for Wargrave, which adjoins Waltham St Lawrence on the N.W. The lack of boundary marks on the W. boundary is surprising.

A (b) ISOLATED SURVEYS

It is convenient to consider as a group six charters relating to land in Barkham, Brimpton, Hawkridge (in Bucklebury), Padworth, Winkfield and Wokefield. These places are all in the S. of the county, in well-wooded country; the grants all date from the mid-10th century, and the six surveys have a good deal in common. The charters are –

I. BCS 895, A.D. 952, by which King Eadred grants to Ælfwine 3 hides at Barkham. This is copied in the later version of the Abingdon Chronicle, but not in *ClaudiusCix*. There is another copy, probably from an original charter, in MS *C.C.C.C. cxi*, and the text of the bounds has been taken from this. The area described may well be that of the modern parish of Barkham, but none of the landmarks can be identified. It is not, in fact, certain that the grant refers to Barkham in Berkshire, but it is copied into *ClaudiusBvi* as one of a group of Berkshire charters, and unless the survey can be positively located elsewhere it seems best to accept the identification. Previous investigators (Grundy and Forsberg) have located it in Finchampstead, south of Barkham, on the grounds that one of the roads described as *stræt* is likely to be the Roman road known as the Devil's Highway. This does not seem to me sufficient reason for placing the estate outside Barkham, however, and the whole question is best left open. As no boundary-marks can be identified, no map has been drawn for this set of bounds.

II. BCS 802, A.D. 944, copied only in the later version of the Abingdon Chronicle, by which King Eadmund grants to Ordulf 8 hides at Brimpton. The bounds describe the modern parish.

III. BCS 919, A.D. 956, an Abingdon charter copied (with some abbreviation in *ClaudiusCix*) in both versions of the Chronicle, by which King Eadwig gives to Abbot Æthelwold a wood at Hawkridge. The dimensions are given as a little more than 60 *jugera*, and the purpose of the gift is to provide building material for the church of St Mary at Abingdon. The wood is given 'cum suis campis'. In *ClaudiusCix* the bounds are headed 'Nem' heafochrig his limitibus circumgiratur'. Hawkridge is in the N. of the modern parish of Bucklebury, but there is no reason to suppose that the bounds of the piece of woodland coincide at all with those of the parish, and it has not seemed worth while to draw a map for this survey. The charter is almost certainly genuine; Sawyer (*Anglo-Saxon Charters*, R.Hist.S. 1968, p. 212) says it was condemned by Stevenson, but this misrepresents Stevenson's comment. The date was mistakenly given between inverted commas in Pt **1** 16.

IV. BCS 984, A.D. 956, copied twice in *ClaudiusBvi* but not at all in *ClaudiusCix*, by which King Eadwig grants to Eadric 5 hides at Padworth. The description of the estate in the boundary clause is unusual; the surveyor is concerned mainly with securing the part N. of the River Kennet, and gives only a cursory reference to the *haga* which marks the boundaries S. of the river. It is not certain that he is describing the whole of the modern parish; there were two estates in Padworth in 1086.

V. BCS 778, A.D. 942, an Abingdon charter, copied (with omission of most of the witnesses in *ClaudiusCix*) in both versions of the Chronicle, by which King Eadmund grants to a nun, named Sæþryþe, 11 hides at Winkfield and Swinley. Eleven *segetes* of meadow at *Hoceshamm* are said to belong to the estate. *ClaudiusCix* omits the mention of Swinley, both in the text of the charter and in the heading to the bounds. The survey is not a detailed one, and (as is often the case in forest territory) not many of the place-names have survived. Enough points can be identified, however, to make it probable that the area described is the modern parish of Winkfield, which includes Swinley Park. *Hoceshamm* has not been identified, and is not certain to be in Winkfield; on the analogy of the meadow attached to Waltham (p. 638, n. 13) it may have been near the Thames.

VI. BCS 888, A.D. 950, copied only in the later version of the Abingdon Chronicle, by which King Eadred grants 3 hides at *Weonfelda* to Ælfgar. The bounds appear to describe the modern parishes of Wokefield and Sulhamstead Bannister. The connection between the names *Weonfeld* and Wokefield is a very difficult problem, which is discussed Pt **1** 227–8. Exact correspondence between the survey and the modern boundaries of Wokefield and Sulhamstead Bannister is perhaps unlikely, but it is at any rate quite clear from the mention of three identifiable points, *grægsole* (i.e. Grazeley), Foudry Brook, and the boundary of Burghfield, that the estate included these modern land-units. The parishes in this area were re-arranged in the 19th cent., and it is probably rash to assume that any of the modern boundaries correspond to ancient ones.

Although all these charters were copied in the Abingdon Chronicle, the Abbey owned only one of the estates in 1086, that at Winkfield (said in Abingdon I 429 to have been given to the Abbey by a lady named Eadfled); here the DB assessment of 10 hides corresponds closely to the 11 hides of the charter (V). Hawkridge (III) is not mentioned in DB, and no property at Bucklebury belonging to Abingdon appears there. Barkham (I) was assessed at 3 hides TRE and in 1086, and this coincidence with the charter hidage might be considered to support the identification discussed *supra*. At Brimpton, DB records two estates, one of $4\frac{1}{2}$ and the other of $3\frac{1}{2}$ hides TRE, and the total of these corresponds exactly with the 8 hides of the charter (II). In Padworth also there were two estates in 1086, one of $2\frac{1}{2}$ hides TRE and the other described as containing $7\frac{1}{2}$ hides, but paying geld for $5\frac{1}{2}$. This latter may correspond to the 5-hide estate of IV. It had $2\frac{1}{2}$ mills and 48 acres of meadow, and the smaller estate had half a mill and 16 acres of meadow. Presumably all the mills and the meadow were by the Kennet, and it may have been the existence of two estates with shares in this property by the river which led to the pre-occupation of the charter surveyor with this part of the survey. At Wokefield there were two estates in 1086, both assessed at $1\frac{1}{2}$ hides TRE, and it is tempting to identify these with the 3-hide estate of the *Weonfeld* charter (VI).

The salient feature which these six surveys have in common is the frequent use of the term *haga* (*v.* 628) which seems in some cases to refer to a fence round a land-unit. This appears particularly clearly in the *Weonfeld* charter (VI). *wyrtwala* is comparatively common. The Brimpton bounds contain a name in *snād*, which seems to mean a detached piece of woodland, and this is the only occurrence of the el. noted in Berks. There are two instances (in II and VI) of *hǣðfeld*, referring to areas which were later Commons. The only reference to cultivated land is the *flex æcyras* of III, and the general impression given by the group of charters is of forest and uncultivated heath. The Padworth charter, however, has a careful description of meadowland by the Kennet.

A (b) I THE BOUNDS OF BARKHAM: 952 (16TH) BCS 895

ærest of ceollanwylle[1] and lang riþe[2] to yge[3] to þæs hagan end[4] þonne andlang hagan to cnottinga hamme[5] þonne of cnottinga hamme forþ be wyrtwalan[6] and lang slades[7] to hwitan stane[8] þonne from hwitan

stane andlang stræt[9] to Loddera stræt[10] þonne of Loddera stræt eft to
ceollanwylle[1].

1 'Ceolla's spring or stream', v. w(i)ell.
2 'stream', v. rīð.
3 'island', v. īeg.
4 'end of the enclosure', v. 628.
5 Final element hamm 'river-meadow'. This appears to be a n. of
   the same type as Buckingham, formed from a pers.n., -inga- and
   hamm. The meaning would be 'river-meadow of the people of
   *Cnotta'. *ClaudiusBvi* has *Cnotanga hamme*, however, and the
   -*ingahamm* formation, although it appears more than once in major
   p.ns., is not altogether likely in a lost minor n.; the text may be
   corrupt at this point.
6 v. 633.
7 'valley', v. slæd.
8 'white stone', v. hwīt, stān.
9 'street', v. stræt.
10 'street of the beggars', v. loddere, stræt. There is no known
   Roman road in Barkham, but the road from London to Silchester,
   known as the Devil's Highway, runs through Finchampstead, less
   than a mile S. of the south boundary of Barkham. There is no
   evidence, however, that the Devil's Highway was ever known as
   loddera stræt, and it does not seem to me safe to identify either of
   the streets of this survey with it.

A (b) II   THE BOUNDS OF BRIMPTON: 944 (C. 1240), BCS 802

Ærest on heafd beorh[1] þonne on wyrt walan[2] on þæs hagan ende[3].
þonne andlang hagan þær fisces burna[4] and alaburna[5] to gædre scotaþ.
þonne of alaburnan ut on herred snad.[6] and swa norþ to herpaþe[7]
andlang herpaþes to þære efisc.[8] þonen eft on wyrt walen[9] to croh
hamme[10] þonne on hunnes wylle[11] þonne west be yfre[12] þæt hit sticaþ
on weala brucge[13] þonne þær ut on cynetan[14] andlang cynetan on myþ
ford[15] þonne on middel ea[16] þæt swa on befer ige[17] þonne on fyrs ige[18]
of dune andlang ea. þær ala burna scyt on cynetan.[19] þonne up
andlang alaburnan on scealdan ford[20] þonon andlang hagan[21] ut on
heaþ felda[22] swa to herpaþe[23] andlang herpaþes to imman beorge[24] of
imman beorge eft on heafod beorge.[1]

NOTES

1 'head tumulus', v. beorg; hēafod is probably used in the sense 'chief'. There is a group of tumuli in the S.E. of the parish, one of which, shown by the 2½″ map as the biggest, is at the S.E. point of the boundary, v. map.

2 v. 633.

3 'end of the enclosure', v. 628.

4 'fish stream', v. fisc, burna, and map for probable identification.

5 'alder-stream'; alaburna (Auborn on Rocque's map of 1761) was the name of the R. Enborne. Confusion with the name of the village of Enborne is recent, v. Pt I 9.

6 Second el. snād, 'detached piece of woodland'; first el. possibly the pers.n. Herred.

7. 'army path', v. here-pæð, possibly the road leading W. from Brimpton, which the boundary follows for some distance.

8 'edge', possibly of a wood.

9 v. 633.

10 croh hamme is probably not Crookham, v. map and Pt I 189. The second el. of the n. is hamm 'river-meadow' and the first is probably croh[1] 'saffron'.

11 Second el. w(i)ell 'spring' or 'stream', first el. uncertain.

12 'west by the brow of the hill', v. yfer; this is an excellent description of the stretch of boundary along Manor Lane, between the 200′ and 225′ contours, v. map.

13 'bridge of the Welshmen', v. w(e)alh, brycg.

14 R. Kennet, v. Pt I 11–12.

15 'ford by the river-junction', v. (ge)mȳðe, ford.

16 'to mid-river', v. ēa.

17 'beaver island', v. beofor, īeg.

18 'furze island', v. fyrs, īeg.

19 'where the Enborne joins the Kennet'. This river-junction (v. map) is now some distance E. of the boundary of Brimpton. but it is an area in which river-courses are likely to have shifted.

20 'shallow ford'; the name survives as Shalford, v. map and Pt I 240.

21 'enclosure', v. haga and 628.

22 'heath field', v. hǣð, feld; this probably refers to Brimpton Common, v. map.

23 'army path', v. here-pæð.

24 'Imma's tumulus', v. beorg.

A (b) III THE BOUNDS OF HAWKRIDGE WOOD: 956 (C. 1200)
BCS 919

Ærest on panganburnan[1]. þæt on ða dic[2]. þæt a be dic on ðæne hagan[3]. þæt on cristen mælbeam[4]. þæt andlang hagan on ða þornihtan leage[5]. þæt forð on brycg ford[6]. þæt a be hagan on stan wege[7]. of stan wege a be weortwalan[8] on þa fleax æcyres[9]. þæt a be weortwalan on masan mere[10]. of þam mere on cuðulfes cotstowe[11]. of þæm cotstowum on panganburnan[1]. þæt up midstreame eft on ða dic[2].

NOTES

1 R. Pang, v. Pt I 16; this flows across Bucklebury parish, S. of Hawkridge.
2 'ditch', v. dīc.
3 'enclosure', v. 628.
4 'tree or post with a crucifix', v. cristel-mæl, bēam.
5 'thorny wood or clearing', v. þorn, -iht, lēah.
6 'bridge ford', v. brycg, ford.
7 'stone way', v. stān, weg.
8 v. 633.
9 'flax acres', v. fleax, æcer; Flex Field occurs in the TA for Marlston, which adjoins Hawkridge, v. Pt I 159.
10 'pond of the tit-mouse', v. māse, mere.
11 'Cūðwulf's cottage-sites', v. cot-stōw.

A (b) IV THE BOUNDS OF PADWORTH: 956 (C. 1240) BCS 984

Ærest of ælflæde gemæra[1] norð on þone hagan[2] andlang hagan on standan[3] þon' on þa dic[4] þæt þon' on þa ea[5] andlang ea on ðone mulen ger[6] þonan andlang ðære mylen dic[7] eft on þa ea andlang ea. oþ þa byrcg[8]. and se mylen stede[9] and þæt land be norþan ea. þe þær to hyrð. and þara oxena wic[10]. and seo mæd on tun ege[11] þe þær midrihte to gebyreð and seo east mearc eal se haga scæt[12] est on ælflæde mearce[1] and swa wer bæra[13] and seo mead be norþan ea[14] and þa hammas[15] þa þer midrihte to ge byriað.

NOTES

1 'Ælflæd's boundaries', v. (ge)mære; Ælflæd was presumably the owner of the estate to the S. This is referred to as ælflæde mearce (v. mearc) later in the survey.
2 'enclosure', v. 628.

3 'pond', *v.* 638, n. 13.

4 'ditch'; there is an earthwork called Grim's Bank running across the parish, but this ditch seems more likely to be a drainage channel near the R. Kennet.

5 'river', i.e. the Kennet, *v.* ēa.

6 'enclosure by a mill for catching fish', *v.* myln, gear.

7 'mill-ditch', *v.* myln, dīc, and *v.* map for position of Padworth Mill.

8 'bridge', *v.* brycg.

9 'mill-stead', *v.* myln, stede. Here the surveyor ceases to describe boundaries, and gives instead a list of the properties of the estate N. of the river.

10 'farm of the oxen', *v.* oxa, wīc.

11 'the meadow on the island belonging to the estate', *v.* tūn, īeg, mǣd; *tun ege* survives as Towney (Bridge and Lock, on the Kennet and Avon Canal), *v.* map and Pt 1 214.

12 'and the east boundary just as the enclosure runs'; *est* following this phrase is a mistake for *eft* 'again'.

13 'pastures by the weir', here the surveyor is making another list of properties; *swa* should probably be *twa* 'two'. *v.* wer, bǣr[2].

14 'the meadow north of the river', *v.* mǣd, ēa.

15 'the water-meadows', *v.* hamm.

A (b) V   THE BOUNDS OF WINKFIELD: 942 (C. 1200) BCS 778

Ærest of þam gemænan treowe[1] on bogeles pearruc[2]. of begeles pearruce on hritmes mere[3]. of hrytmes mere on þone blacan mor[4]. of þam blacan moran on imbelea[5]. of imbelea on wernan wille[6]. of wernan wille on gyrdford[7]. of gyrdforda on æcgstanes stan[8]. of æcgstanes stane on Gunredesford[9]. Of Gunredesforda on seofan acon[10] on hylneslea[11]. of hylneslea on braccan heal[12]. of braccan heale on ruwanbeorh[13]. of ruwanbeorhe on teappan treow[14]. of teappan treowe. on westleas hagan[15]. of westleas hagan on ceawan hrycges hagan[16]. of Ceawanhricges hagan. eft on þæt gemene treow.

NOTES

1 Literally 'common tree', though the phrase may have been felt as equivalent to 'boundary tree', *v.* (ge)mǣne, trēow.

2 Second el. pearruc 'enclosure', first el. uncertain, if *begeles* is correct, probably a pers.n. *Bǣgel*.

3 Second el. mere 'pool'; the first is obscure.

4 'black marsh'; this is represented by Blackmoor Stream (v. map and Pt 1 7), and is the first identifiable boundary-mark.

5 'clearing where bees swarm', v. imbe, lēah.

6 Probably 'spring or stream of the wren', v. wrenna, wærna, w(i)ell; the same compound occurs in Wrenwell D 523. Professor Löfvenberg points out that wrǣna 'stallion' or a pers.n. are possible first els.

7 'rod ford', probably a ford marked off with stakes, v. gyrd, ford.

8 'Ecgstān's stone.'

9 Identical with *Gundrichesforde* 1327 in a perambulation of the Sr Forest (ArchJ 36, 120). Professor Löfvenberg points out that in the 1327 form -*d*- is intrusive and -*ch*- is for -*th*-, and that a pers.n. *Gunred* would be an anglicisation of ON *Gunnrøðr*.

10 'seven oaks', v. seofon, āc.

11 Second el. lēah; the first is obscure.

12 Now Bracknell, v. map and Pt 1 116. h(e)alh in this n. probably refers to land in an angle of the parish.

13 'rough hill or barrow', v. rūh, beorg.

14 'Teappa's tree', v. trēow.

15 'the enclosure of west clearing', v. west, lēah and 628. The fact that the place had a haga may indicate that it is a lost administrative unit, in which case Westley Mill in Binfield Pt 1 78 is not too far away to contain the same n.

16 'the enclosure of Chawridge'; v. map and Pt 1 37.

A (b) VI   THE BOUNDS OF WEONFELD (WOKEFIELD AND
SULHAMSTEAD BANNISTER): C. 950 (C. 1240) BCS 888

Ærest on hunda leage[1] on grægsole burnan[2] andlang burnan on grægsole hagan[3] andlang hagan to hagena gemyðum[4] of þen gemyþun on tichan stedes hagan[5] andlang hagan ut to felda[6] þæt a be wyrtwalan[7] oþ hit cymð ut on fulan riþe[8] andlang riþe ut on doccena ford[9] of þan forda west be more[10] oþ hit cymð on þone licgendanstoc[11] of þan stocce andlang hagan ut to heaðfelda[12] to beorhfeldinga gemære[13] to þen hagan. andlang hagan bur[14].

NOTES

1 'wood or clearing of the dogs', v. hund, lēah.

2 'Grazeley Brook', v. map; this stream (now known as Burghfield Brook) runs across Wokefield and Grazeley parishes. Grazeley means 'badgers' wallowing-place', v. Pt 1 166.

3 'Grazeley enclosure', *v.* 628.

4 'the meeting of enclosures', *v.* haga, (ge)mȳðe, and map for suggested position.

5 *tichan stedes* may be a corrupt form for a n. in hāmstede, with an uncertain prefix, perhaps ticcen, ticce 'kid', cf. *tycc hám stede* BCS 377 (Ha). Since this place had a haga, it may have been a land-unit, like Grazeley.

6 'open land', *v.* feld.

7 *v.* 633, the reference here may be to the 150′ contour, to which a stretch of modern boundary runs very close, *v.* map.

8 Foudry Brook, *v.* map and Pt I 10. The name means 'dirty stream'. The boundary probably followed the brook for only a very short stretch, and the course of the stream may have altered.

9 'dock ford', *v.* map for suggested position, where a road crosses Foudry Brook, *v.* docce, ford.

10 'marsh', *v.* mōr.

11 'lying tree-stump', *v.* stocc, possibly the roots of a fallen tree, which might remain in position for a long time.

12 *v.* hǣð, feld; as elsewhere in these surveys, the term refers to land which became a Common, in this case Wokefield Common, *v.* map.

13 'boundary of the people of Burghfield', *v.* map and Pt I 204–5.

14 The text appears to be corrupt at the end of the survey, but as the junction of Wokefield and Burghfield boundaries is close to *grægsole burnan* the circuit is virtually complete.

B (a) CHIEVELEY AND BEEDON

These two modern parishes represent four 10th-century estates, Stanmore, Chieveley, Curridge and Oare, the first two of which were given to the thegn Wulfric. Wulfric lost all his estates temporarily, and they were restored to him in A.D. 960 (BCS 1055). The restoration included Stanmore and Chieveley, but it is possible that not all of the Chieveley estate was restored, as Beedon was given to Abingdon in 965 by a charter (BCS 1171) which states that the bounds of the area granted are included in the survey attached to the Chieveley charter. This implies that Abingdon had the major part of Wulfric's estate at Chieveley by 965; the date of his death is not known. The modern parochial arrangements presumably date from after the acquisition by Abingdon of most of the land in these four estates. The charters are all copied in the Abingdon Chronicle, and no. II is also in MS *C.C.C.C. cxi.*

I. BCS 866, A.D. 948, copied only in *ClaudiusBvi*, by which King Eadred grants to Wulfric 'bis quinas' (presumably meaning 10) hides at Stanmore. This estate was probably roughly two-thirds of the modern parish of Beedon.

II. BCS 892, A.D. 951, copied (with some abbreviation in *Claudius-Cix*) in both MSS of the Abingdon Chronicle, and in MS *C.C.C.C. cxi* (p. 155), by which King Eadred grants to Wulfric 25 hides at Chieveley. The estate is given 'with the pasture which is held on a certain hill', a phrase which may refer to Stanmore, already in Wulfric's possession, and included in the bounds. The survey describes the western part of Chieveley (excluding Oare and Curridge) and Beedon (including Stanmore). A later charter, BCS 1171, A.D. 965, by which King Edgar grants 5 hides at Beedon to Abingdon, states that the bounds of this charter lie in the Chieveley charter, which shows that the Chieveley survey was understood to include Beedon.

III. BCS 900, A.D. 953, only copied in *ClaudiusBvi*, by which King Eadred grants 5 hides at Curridge (in Chieveley) to Ælfric. The bounds probably correspond to those of Curridge given in the Tithe Award (p. 655, n. 1).

IV. BCS 1225, A.D. 968, copied (with omission of the witnesses in

ClaudiusCix) in both MSS of the Abingdon Chronicle, by which King Edgar grants 10 hides at Oare (in Chieveley) to Abingdon. The survey describes an area of Chieveley parish which includes Oare and Bradley.

DB records that the estate of Abingdon Abbey at Beedon was assessed at 15 hides until King Edward reduced it to 11. Stanmore is not mentioned in DB, so it is possible that the 10 hides there described in I, and the 5 hides at Beedon conveyed in BCS 1171, are all included in the DB estate of Beedon; this would give an exact correspondence with the hidage before King Edward reduced it. Chieveley was assessed at 27 hides TRE, which is close to the 25 hides of II. Oare is not mentioned in DB, but at Curridge there were two estates, one of 7 and the other of 2 hides. These assessments cannot be linked up with the 5 hides at Curridge of III, or the 10 hides at Oare of IV.

These four sets of boundaries provide much information about the nature of the 10th-cent. landscape. The Chieveley survey encounters arable land S.W. of Chieveley village. It is probable that this extended some way to the E., and a statement at the end of the Curridge survey suggests that this set of open fields was continuous with that belonging to Curridge (*v.* 626). This arable was bordered by heath to the S.W. (cf. *lytlan hǣþfeld*, p. 653, n. 20) and by woodland to the E.; S.E. of Chieveley there are references to a *haga* (*v.* 628), and there was another N. of Oare. There are several lost names ending in lēah, and near Bradley there was a wood with the interesting name *Cilte*. In the N.W. of this block of land there were wolves, or at any rate a memory of them, giving rise to the name *wulfora* (p. 651, n. 9). Particularly interesting is the suggestion conveyed by the name *wealcottes leah* (p. 656, n. 6) that surrounding estates had detached woodland in this area. Ancient monuments, most of which survive, are frequent boundary-marks on the W. boundary of Chieveley and Beedon, and the area was well covered by roads, two of which (*stræt* and *ealdan weg*) had a reputation for antiquity, and one of which qualified for the term *herepæð*. The boundaries mention six chalk-pits. The most mysterious item is the *tūn*, which apparently stood on the boundary between Beedon and Peasemore (p. 654, n. 38), but this stretch of the Chieveley survey is difficult to follow, and not certain to correspond to the modern boundary.

B (a) I THE BOUNDS OF STANMORE: 948 (C. 1240) BCS 866

Ærst of þan crundelun[1] þær to stræte[2] andlang stræte to aþulfes
þorne[3] þonnon on fyrd hammas[4] anlang stific weges[5] þon' on cat
beorh[6] þon' on ælfheages gemære[7] þonon andlang mære weges[8] on
wulforan[9] þonon andlang gemæres to ines dene ufewearde[10] þæt
þonon on stiele[11] þon' andlang gemæres þæt on lic hangan[12]. of lic
hangan on pocging rode[13] þonnon on dunan wyrþe[14] þonon on loceres
weg[15] andlang weges on þa ealdan stigele[16] of þære stigele þwers ofer
rammes hrycg[17] þonnon on þone ealdan hyrne weg[18] þonnon on beden
weg[19] on beden weg suþe wearde innan andlang hecgan onbutan hunes
dune[20] þæt eft on þa crundelas besuþan haran grafas[21].

NOTES

1 'chalk-pits', v. crundel.
2 This is Old Street Lane, v. map.
3 'Aðulf's thorn-tree.'
4 Possibly 'ford meadows', from fyrde (a variant of ford) and
hamm, but Professor Löfvenberg points out that fyrde is not
otherwise evidenced as a first el. There is no stream on the W.
boundary of Beedon, but it is possible that the stream from which
Winterbourne is named once rose some distance further N. than its
present source.
5 'tree-stump way', v. map and styfic, weg. This road is also mentioned in the bounds of Farnborough (p. 673, n. 30).
6 'cat hill'; this is the starting-point of the Chieveley survey (p. 653,
n. 1), and appears to have been at the N.W. corner of Beedon
parish, at the S. end of a ridge.
7 'Ælfhēah's boundary', v. map; a man named Ælfhēah was given
Farnborough, which adjoins Beedon, in 931 (BCS 682).
8 'boundary way', v. (ge)mǣre, weg.
9 'wolf slope'; this name survived in Woolvers Barn in East Ilsley,
v. map and Pt 2 503.
10 'the upper part of Ine's valley', v. denu. The survey has probably
left the N. boundary of Beedon, and is describing a line between
Stanmore and Beedon which cannot be precisely defined.
11 'stile', v. stigel.
12 lichanga is obscure, the second el. may, as suggested by Forsberg
(193–4) be an error for hagan (v. haga), cf. lychaga KCD 1309
(Do), which may contain *lycce 'enclosure'.

13 Second el. rodu 'clearing'; *pocging* may, as suggested D 350, be a pers.n. *Pocg(a)* + -ing-.

14 'Duna's enclosure', v. worð, wyrð.

15 'shepherd's way', v. lōcere, weg.

16 'old stile', v. eald, stigel.

17 'crosswise over raven's or ram's ridge', v. Pt I 233; Grundy notes a modern f.n., Great Ram Ridge, just S. of Beedon village (v. map), and concludes that the ridge was the one which runs across the parish from its N.W. corner to the hamlet of Beedon Hill. The charter-bounds presumably cross it W. of Beedon. The boundary-marks between 9 and 17 are surprisingly numerous.

18 'the old corner way', or 'the old way to the place called Hearn'. The *TA* for the adjacent parish of Peasemore mentions a field called The Hearn, which is *Le Heron, Le Herron* in a survey of 1547, v. Pt I 263.

19 'Beedon way.'

20 'the hedge round Hūn's down', v. hecge, dūn.

21 'boundary groves', v. hār[2], grāf.

B (a) II THE BOUNDS OF WEST CHIEVELEY AND BEEDON
(INCLUDING STANMORE): 951 (16TH) BCS 892

Ærest of catbeorge[1] andlang weges on aþelunes þorn[2]. þonon andlang weges on seal hangran estweardne[3]. þonon andlang weges on þa byrgelsas[4]. þonon andlang byden hæma gemæres[5] on þa haran apoldre[6] þonon on orhæme gemære[7] andlang þæs gemæres on ciltewudes gemære[8] to þam stane[9]. þonon west andlang weges to þam hæcce[10] þonon andlang gemæres to þam crundle[11]. þonon andlang gemæres to þam oþrum crundle[12] þonon to þam won stocce[13] and þær to wuda[14]. þonon on þa syrfan[15]. þonon ofer hean hrycg[16]. þonon on þæs cinges hagan[17]. þonne þær west andlang hagan on hnæfleage suþewearde[18] þonon andlang hagan to þam bæce[19]. of þam bæce þær norþ utan þone lytlan hæþfeld[20] þonon andlang weges be winterburninga gemære[21] be westan þære ealdan byrig[22] on þone stanihtan weg[23] of þam wege to þam stan cystlum[24]. þonon on þa andheafda[25] þonne þær west oþ þone burnan buton six æcerum[26]. þonne þær norþ an furlang[27] þonne þær west ofer þa twegen beorgas[28] to þam hearpoþe[29]. norþ andlang herpoþes on bradan ford[30] þær west andlang burn stowe[31] to ibban stane[32] þonne þær east andlang weges on stan dene[33] þonon west to þam wyrtwalan[34] þonon norþ on sceaphammes[35]. þonon on gerihta þær tun wegas ut sceotaþ[36]. þonon on gerihta to þære haran apoldre[37]. of þære haran apoldre þurh þone tun[38] to þam ruwan crundle[39]. þonon andlang gemæres on þone lytlan beorh. up on mules dune[40]. of þam beorge andlang gemæres on hrycgweg[41] andlang hrycgweges oþ catmeres gemære[42]. þonne þær east andlang gemæres on puttan pyt[43]. of þam pytte andlang gemæres eft on catbeorh[1].

NOTES

1 v. p. 651, n. 6.
2 'Æðelhūn's thorn-tree', v. þorn.
3 'the east part of sallow hanger', v. s(e)alh, hangra.
4 'the burial-places', v. byrgels.
5 'the boundary of the people of Beedon' (as opposed to the boundary of Stanmore), v. hǣme, (ge)mǣre.
6 'the boundary apple-tree', v. hār², apuldor.
7 'the boundary of the people of Oare', v. hǣme, (ge)mǣre.
8 'the boundary of *Cilte* wood', this may be an earlier name of the wood at Bradley. *Cilte* is obscure but related to a number of other names which are discussed Gl 2 101–2.
9 'stone', v. stān.
10 'gate', v. hæcc; perhaps in the fence mentioned in the bounds of Curridge, v. p. 655, n. 2, which appears to have marked the boundary between Curridge and Chieveley S.W. of Prior's Court.
11 'chalk-pit', v. crundel.
12 'the other chalk-pit.'
13 'crooked tree-stump', v. wōh, stocc.
14 'wood', v. wudu.
15 'service-tree', OE *syrfe*.
16 'high ridge', v. map and hēah, hrycg.
17 'king's enclosure', v. cyning, haga and map; the S. boundary of Chieveley is the N. boundary of Shaw cum Donnington, both of which places are said in DB to have belonged to the King before the Conquest.
18 'the south part of *hnæf* wood or clearing', v. lēah, Professor Löfvenberg suggests that *hnæf* is connected with Old Norse *hnafa* 'to hew, cut'.
19 'back', v. bæc, here used of the bank of a linear earthwork; v. map for the Black Ditch, which crosses the parish boundary.
20 'outside the small heath', Snelsmore Common is W. of this stretch of boundary. *hǣðfeld* is several times used in Berkshire bounds of land which was later a common.

21 'boundary of the people of Winterbourne', *v.* (ge)mǣre.

22 'west of the old camp', *v.* map, the fort is now known as Bussock Camp, *v.* Pt I 245.

23 'stony way', *v.* stāniht, weg.

24 'heaps of stones', *v.* stān, second el. *ci(e)stel, from ceastel.

25 'headlands', *v.* 626.

26 'west to the stream outside the six acres', *v.* map.

27 'north one furlong', *v.* map.

28 'west over the two barrows', *v.* beorg and map; ploughing has spread these into one mound.

29 'army path', *v.* map and here-pæð, this is the southern continuation of Old Street Lane.

30 'broad ford', *v.* brād, ford and map; this is where the boundary encounters for the second time the stream which gives name to Winterbourne, and the $2\frac{1}{2}''$ map marks the ford. The survey from 19 to 30 is a remarkably clear description of the present W. boundary of Chieveley.

31 Elements 2 158 translates burn-stōw 'bathing-place'. Sandred (98) suggests 'watering-place for cattle.'

32 'Ibba's stone.'

33 'east along the way to the stone valley', *v.* stān, denu; this portion of the survey can be reconciled with the boundary of Chieveley by assuming that 'east along the way' covers a long stretch, all going N.E. or due E., the final part of it running along Gidley Lane. There is a *standene* in the bounds of Leckhampstead (p. 662, n. 12), which probably refers to a more westerly branch of the same valley.

34 *v.* 633.

35 'sheep meadows', *v.* scēap, hamm; the bounds of Stanmore (I) have *fyrd hammas* further N. on this stretch of boundary. Both boundary-marks may suggest the former presence of streams here.

36 'straight on where the farm ways branch off.'

37 'boundary apple-tree', *v.* hār[2], apuldor.

38 'through the farm'; there is no settlement on the parish boundary now, and the situation is an unusual one for a farm, *v.* 630.

39 'rough chalkpit', *v.* rūh, crundel.

40 'the little barrow on Mūl's down', *v.* lȳtel, beorg; there is a tumulus on Barrow Hill, very close to the boundary, *v.* map. 'Mūl's down' overlooks the valley called *mulescumb* in B (b) VIII (p. 672, n. 16).

41 'ridge way', *v.* hrycg, weg, part of Old Street Lane, *v.* map.
42 'the boundary of Catmore', *v.* (ge)mǣre and map.
43 'Putta's pit' or 'pit of the kite', *v.* *putta, pytt. *ClaudiusCix* has
   weg in mistake for *pyt*.

B (a) III   THE BOUNDS OF CURRIDGE: 953 (C. 1240) BCS 900

ǣrest on mær weg[1] on lang mær weges on þa heccan[2] andlang heccen
on þa haran þyrnan[3] of þære þyrnan on cyneeahes treow[4] þæt andlang
heorpaþes[5] on quenan dene[6] þon' andlang þæs ealdan weges[7] on
linleahe[8] þæt ondlang heccan[9] on þa haraṇ crundol[10] þæt ofer þone
hric[11] eft on merweg[1] and on þan gemanan lande gebyrað þarto fif and
sixti æccera[12].

NOTES

1 'boundary way', *v.* (ge)mǣre, weg. Grundy (ArchJ 33) quotes an
   account of the bounds of Curridge given in the *TA*, and it seems
   reasonable to suppose that these correspond, perhaps exactly, to
   the bounds in the charter. The line described in the *TA* is marked
   on the map. No points in the charter survey can be identified with
   certainty, but a reasonable correspondence with the map can be
   obtained by starting in the S.W. corner, E. of Snelsmore East
   Common.
2 'fence', *v.* hæcce and p. 653, n. 10.
3 'boundary thorn-bush', *v.* hār[2], þyrne; this may be where the
   survey turns S.E.
4 'Cynehēah's tree', *v.* trēow.
5 'army-path', *v.* here-pæð; the bounds of Curridge in the *TA*
   touch the road marked on the 1″ map as Old Street, and this is
   probably the road referred to in the charter survey, *v.* map.
6 *v.* denu, probably the valley in which the village of Hermitage is
   situated. BCS prints *grenan dene*, but the MS has *quenan dene*,
   apparently 'woman's valley', *v.* cwene. *qu-* is a rare spelling in OE,
   but is found occasionally instead of *cw-*.
7 'old way', probably the road from Newbury to Hampstead Norris,
   which the boundary follows for nearly a mile, *v.* (e)ald, weg and
   map.
8 'flax clearing', *v.* līn, lēah.
9 'fence', *v.* hæcce.
10 'chalk-pit', *v.* crundel; *haran* 'boundary', is dotted for omission
   in the MS.

11 'ridge', *v*. hrycg; this is probably the ridge from which Curridge ('Cusa's ridge', Pt **1** 242) is named.

12 *v*. 626 for a discussion of this statement.

B (a) IV   THE BOUNDS OF OARE: 968 (C. 1200) BCS 1225

Ærest of wintermere[1] andlang riht gemeres on hærgraf[2]. þonan andlang hagan[3] utðruht bradanlea[4]. þæt on þa heafod stoccas[5] þonan on wealcottes leahe norðewearde.[6] þonan andlang hagan[3] on santan dene[7]. ðanon on biscopes weg[8]. andlang weges eft on winter mere[1].

NOTES

1 'winter pool', *v*. winter, mere, the survey probably starts N. of Hermitage, where there are a number of pools (*v*. map).

2 'grove by the rock', *v*. hær, grāf; Grundy thought that this must be identical with the *haran grafas* in the Stanmore survey (p. 652, n. 21), but neither the spellings in the texts nor the probable course of the surveys supports this.

3 'enclosure', *v*. 628.

4 Bradley ('broad wood or clearing') is a surviving p.n., *v*. map and Pt **1** 242.

5 'head-stumps', *v*. hēafod-stocc, for other instances *v*. p. 779.

6 'the north part of Walcot's wood', *v*. lēah. This may have been a detached piece of woodland belonging to Walcot in Kintbury, about 7½ miles away, *v*. Pt **2** 317–18. There was another piece of detached woodland in this area which belonged to Chilton (p. 768, n. 19), and the gift of a wood at Hawkridge, in Bucklebury, to Abingdon (A (b) III) indicates a similar arrangement.

7 *ClaudiusBvi* has *sandan dene*; second el. denu 'valley', Professor Löfvenberg suggests that the first is a reduction of *sandihtan* 'sandy'. The valley runs S.W. from Hampstead Norris.

8 'bishop's way', *v*. biscop, weg, probably the northward continuation of the 'old way' of the Curridge survey, *v*. p. 655, n. 7.

B (b) FAIRCROSS HUNDRED, EXCLUDING CHIEVELEY AND BEEDON, WITH FARNBOROUGH (COMPTON HUNDRED) AND LEVERTON (KINTBURY EAGLE HUNDRED)

All the charters in this group were copied into the Abingdon Chronicle. Nos. I–IX are concerned with land-units which form a block of six contiguous modern parishes. Nos. X and XI, which refer to Leverton in Hungerford, have been treated as part of this group as Leverton is fairly close to this block. It has, however, been necessary to provide a separate map for Leverton. The charters are –

I. BCS 753, A.D. 939, copied only in *ClaudiusBvi*, by which King Athelstan grants to Eadlufu, a nun, 15 hides at Brightwalton. The bounds describe the modern parish.

II. BCS 789, A.D. 943, copied only in *ClaudiusBvi*, by which King Eadmund grants 10 hides at Leckhampstead to Eadric. The charter adds to the grant a mill on the R. Lambourn, which must have been outside the estate. The bounds, which describe the modern parish, are copied in *ClaudiusCix*.

III. BCS 877, A.D. 949, surviving in a contemporary parchment, and copied in *ClaudiusBvi*. An exchange by which King Eadred gives to Wulfric 18 hides at Welford for land at Pendavey in Egloshayle, Cornwall. The bounds are copied in *ClaudiusCix*. They are easy to follow for the first 13 landmarks, which describe the E. boundary of the modern parish as far as the R. Lambourn. The rest of the bounds can be interpreted as describing the area of the modern parish, but some difficulties arise from an attempt to correlate them with those of IV.

IV. BCS 963, A.D. 956, copied in both versions of the Abingdon Chronicle, by which King Eadwig grants 22 hides at Welford to Eadric. Welford does not appear in BCS 1055, by which a number of forfeited estates were restored to Wulfric (who obtained Welford in 949). The bounds are similar to those of III, but with some extra boundary marks. One of these, in the S.E. of the area, suggests that the survey has somehow moved into the E. of Speen parish. As the hidage of IV is slightly greater than that of III, one might have suggested an extra piece of land here. But this charter is of the same date as V, and as that appears to be granting the whole of Speen to a different man, there is no room for manœuvre.

V. BCS 942, A.D. 956, copied only in *ClaudiusBvi*, by which King Eadwig grants 25 hides at Benham to Ælfsige. The bounds are copied in *ClaudiusCix*. They coincide with the modern parish of Speen on the S., W. and N., but the eastern boundary cannot be identified. The hidage suggests that the whole of Speen was involved, *v.* 660. Benham is one of the places restored to Wulfric in BCS 1055, A.D. 960, so Ælfsige's tenancy was a brief one.

VI. BCS 1022, A.D. 958, copied only in *ClaudiusBvi*, by which King Eadred (?a scribal alteration of Eadwig) grants 10 hides at Boxford to Wulfric. The bounds, which describe the modern parish of Boxford, are identical with those of VII. Boxford was one of the places restored to Wulfric in 960.

VII. BCS 1227, A.D. 968, copied in both versions of the Abingdon Chronicle, by which King Eadgar grants 10 hides at Boxford to Ælfwine. The bounds are identical with those of VI. *ClaudiusCix* has these bounds at the end of the MS, and it is not possible to say whether the scribe took them from this charter or from VI. He did not include VI in his text.

VIII. BCS 682, c. A.D. 935, copied in *ClaudiusBvi*, and in *C.C.C.C. cxi* and *Cotton Vitell. Dvii*, by which King Athelstan grants 10 hides at Farnborough to Ælfheah. The bounds are copied in *ClaudiusCix* and this text has been used. They give a very full, description of the modern parish. The south-eastern extension of the parish, which is joined to the main area by a narrow strip, is surveyed as a separate piece of woodland.

IX. KCD 762, A.D. 1042, a possibly spurious charter copied in both versions of the Abingdon Chronicle, by which King Harthacnut grants 10 hides at Farnborough to the Abbey. The bounds are the same as those discussed under VIII. *ClaudiusCix* may have taken the bounds from this charter, as VIII is not included in the MS.

X. KCD 1282, A.D. 984, copied only in *ClaudiusBvi*, by which King Æthelred grants to Brihtric 8 hides near the R. Kennet. The bounds are identical with those of XI, and the scribes of the Abingdon Chronicle considered that the land-unit was Leverton in Hungerford. Hungerford (which is not in DB), consists of several earlier estates. Five of these (*Charlton*, *Calcot*, Standen, Eddington and Leverton) are in DB. Eddington and Leverton are both on the north bank of the R. Kennet, and one would expect that the two estates comprised roughly the eastern and western halves of the part of the modern parish which lies N. of the river. The bounds of X and XI can be fitted quite well to the north-western part of Hungerford. The only difficulty lies in the boundary-mark *Eadgife gemære*. One naturally wishes to associate this with Eddington, which means '*Ēadgifu*'s tūn'. But the bounds will not work unless *Eadgife gemære* is assumed to be W. of Leverton, and as Eddington lies E. of Leverton it is necessary to assume that the boundary-mark and the settlement-name arise from two different women both called Ēadgifu.

XI. KCD 792, A.D. 1050, probably a spurious charter, copied in both versions of the Abingdon Chronicle (twice in *ClaudiusBvi*), by which King Edward grants to Abingdon 8 hides near the R. Kennet. The bounds are identical with those of X. In *ClaudiusCix*, and in *ClaudiusBvi* before the second copy of the charter, there is an introductory statement that this land is called *Leofwartun*, i.e. Leverton. It is possible that Leverton and a number of the other estates in Hungerford were carved out of a large land-unit known by the name of the R. Kennet.

Brightwalton is stated in DB to have been held by Earl Harold as 10 hides, but to have paid geld for 15 hides under the thegn who held it before Earl Harold. This agrees with the 15 hides of I. Leckhampstead is recorded in DB as part of the Abingdon estate at Welford, and is stated to consist of 10 hides, which is the hidage of II.

This satisfactory agreement between charter and DB hidages does not occur in the case of Welford. The TRE hidage of Welford is recorded as 50 hides. Leckhampstead, Weston and Boxford are held as separate estates within the manor, assessed respectively at 10, 4 and 2 hides. Leckhampstead and Boxford were separate estates in the 10th cent., so 12 hides can be deducted from the 50 to allow for these two units. This only reduces the total to 38, however, which is very different from the 18 hides of the first Welford charter (III) and the 22 hides of the second (IV).

The estate at Benham, which is the subject of V, appears to be more or less the modern parish of Speen. DB records five estates here.

There are three separate manors called Benham, assessed respectively at 2, 5 and 2 hides TRE. Speen is said to have been 10 hides TRE, and there is a separate account of Bagnor which quotes a TRE assessment of 3 hides. This gives a total of 22 hides, which is quite close to the 25 hides of V.

Boxford is mentioned twice in DB, once as an estate of 9 hides TRE, and once as a 2-hide holding in the large estate of Welford. This gives 11 hides, which is very close to the 10 hides of VI and VII. Farnborough appears in DB as a single estate, assessed TRE at 10 hides, which is the hidage of VIII. Leverton was assessed at 6½ hides TRE, a slight reduction on the 8 hides of X and XI.

No clear picture of the 10th-cent. landscape emerges from the bounds of this group of charters. Woodland is well represented, but does not appear to be predominant. The Farnborough estate has a wood attached to it, which suggests that such provision was desirable in the area. On the other hand, there are few specific mentions of other types of landscape. The Boxford survey mentions a *hæðfeld*, and the bounds of the Farnborough woodland run *ut on þone feld*. References to arable land are confined to the Farnborough survey, which mentions a furrow and headlands, but a special feature of this set of bounds is the use of the word *hamm*, apparently not referring to river-meadows, and possibly denoting enclosures for agricultural purposes. Flax is mentioned in Welford and in Boxford, and in Curridge (B (a) III). References to pits are particularly common. Most of these were probably for chalk, but some were for stone or loam. Boundary-stones are common, and there are several tumuli.

B (b) I THE BOUNDS OF BRIGHTWALTON: 939 (C. 1240) BCS 743

Ærst of curspandic[1] up on acdene[2] of acdene to wigferþis leage[3] of wigferðis leage to pippes leage[4] of pippes leage norð andlang hagan[5] to þan brandan stane[6] of þam stane to dunian mere[7] þ'onen þonon norð rihte to hæsel lea[8] of hæsel lea west rihte to borsenan beorge[9] of ðam beorge west riht on þone haranstan[10] of ðan stane norð rihte to stan crundele[11] þonnan andlang weges to þam langan treowe[12] of þam trowe andlang weges to mærfloden[13] þonne giet andlang weges þæt eft on cyrspan dic[1].

NOTES

1 Possibly 'the curly ditch'. The bounds begin at the S.E. corner of the modern parish. An elongated, twisting hollow was clearly visible in 1961 in a field immediately W. of road B 4494, S. of the boundary, v. map. The ditch is mentioned in the bounds of Leckhampstead (p. 662, n. 8) and the name occurs as *Cripsedich* in 1239–40 in that parish, v. Pt 1 255.

2 'oak valley', v. map and āc, denu. The boundary of Brightwalton runs up a small valley.

3 'Wīgfrið's wood or clearing', v. lēah; this occurs also in the bounds of Leckhampstead, p. 662, n. 6, v. map for probable position.

4 This was probably another clearing, v. lēah, the first may be a pers.n. *Pipp*, cf. *pippanleah* BCS 1235 (Wo).

5 'enclosure', v. 628.

6 v. stān; *brandan* is probably an error for *brādan* 'broad'.

7 Dunmore Pond, v. map and Pt 1 237.

8 'hazel wood', v. hæsel, lēah; this was probably at the end of the N.–S. stretch of the W. boundary.

9 Possibly 'broken barrow' or 'hill where there has been a landslip', v. beorg; *borsenan* may be a mistake for *borstenan* 'burst'. Alternatively, Professor Löfvenberg suggests an adj. **borsen* from **bors, 'spiky plant'.

10 'boundary-stone', v. hār², stān.

11 'stone quarry', v. crundel and map. Grundy (1923) said that a trench from which stone had been dug was visible there.

12 'tall tree', v. lang, trēow.

13 'intermittent spring on the boundary', v. (ge)mǣre, flōde. Grundy gives a good account of this occasional stream which runs down the E. side of the parish.

The boundary-marks after Dunmore Pond are sparse for the distance covered. The probable positions of some of them are shown on the map. Nos. 10–13 occur also in the survey of Farnborough (VIII). The *weg* along which the boundary travels to reach its starting-point is the road from Wantage to Newbury (B 4494), and Grundy's account of the *mǣrflōde* makes it clear that it ran down the same valley as the road.

B (b) II　THE BOUNDS OF LECKHAMPSTEAD: 943 (C. 1200)
　　BCS 789

Ærest on dene pyt[1]. of þam pÿtte on þone hnottan þorn[2]. of þam
þorne on wines treowe[3] of wines treowe on þa readan hane[4]. þon' on
stigel hammas.[5] of stigel hammum on wigferðes leage norðewearde[7].
þon' on acdene[7]. of acdene on crypsan dic[8]. þon' þwures ofer
wrestleshylle[9] on buccan crundel[10]. of buccan crundle on ða haran
apeldre[11]. þon' andlang standene[12] oð gyddan dene[13] þweores
ofer weardan dune[14] oð ða dene[15] andlang þære dene eft on dene
pyt[1].

NOTES

1　'pit in the valley', v. denu, pytt. The valley is a clearly marked one
　　which changes direction from S.S.E. to due E.; the pit may have
　　been in the angle so formed, v. map, and cf. p. 669, n. 3.
2　'bare thorn-tree', v. hnott, þorn.
3　'Wine's tree'; this is mentioned also in the bounds of Boxford and
　　Welford (p. 666, n. 1, p. 669, n. 1), both of which start at this
　　point, so it can be precisely located at the junction of these three
　　parishes, v. map.
4　'red stone', v. rēad, hān, for later references v. Pt 1 276.
5　'enclosures with a stile', v. stigel; hamm can hardly mean 'river-
　　meadow' here, so it probably refers to man-made enclosures, v.
　　p. 663, n. 5.
6　'north part of Wīgfrið's clearing', v. p. 661, n. 3 and map.
7　'oak valley', v. p. 661, n. 2.
8　'curly ditch', v. p. 661, n. 1.
9　the boundary crosses the tip of a ridge which runs to the N.E., v.
　　map. *Wræstel was possibly the name of this ridge. It may derive
　　from *wrǣst 'something twisted or knotted'. *wrǣst and
　　*wrǣsel are derivatives of wrāse 'knot, lump'. The precise sense
　　is uncertain, but these, and other related words, may be used as
　　hill-names.
10　'goat's quarry', v. crundel; alternatively, Bucca may be a pers.n.
11　'boundary apple-tree', v. hār², apuldor; several of these are
　　mentioned in charter bounds in this area.
12　'stone valley'; the E. boundary of Leckhampstead runs down a
　　small valley, v. map, and cf. p. 654, n. 33.
13　'Gydda's valley', v. denu and map. The standene joins another

small valley coming from near Gidley Fm in Peasemore, which is probably named from the same man, v. Pt 1 262.

14 'hill of the beacon' from OE *wearde, v. Löfvenberg 219, or 'Wearda's hill'. The parish boundary here crosses the tip of a low ridge, v. map. *Worndown* in Peasemore *TA* is near here and probably preserves the name, v. Pt 1 263.

15 This is the valley described in n. 1.

B (b) III THE BOUNDS OF WELFORD: 949 (CONTEMPORARY) BCS 877 (BMFACS III 16)

ærest of wines treowe[1] andlang dene[2] þæt up on þone weg[3] þonon on bradan leage norþe weardre[4] on anne ham[5] and þonne þurh ut þone lea[6] on anne ham suþe weardne[7] on þa ealdan hege ræwe[8] in on wopig hangran[9] of þam hangran on scilling hangran[10] þonon on bradan ham westeweardne[11] on þam hamme on cardan hlæw[12] on þam hlæwe on lámburnan[13] þonon up on deoran treowe[14] of þam treowe on þone elebeam styb[15] þonon on ceolbaldes wylle[16] of þam wylle on cyta sihtes ford[17] of þam forda to wulfrices gemære[18] þonon to hord hlince ufeweardum[19] of þam hlince on sihtre mæde norþe weardre[20] swa forþ on cenelmes stan[21] of þam stane on þone grenan weg[22] on þam wege to rige hamme[23] þonon ut on þa lam pyttas[24] on þane crundel[25] of ðam crundele on þone æsc[26] þonon forþ ofer burnan[27] andlang mylen paþes[28] on þa þrie þornas[29] and swa forþ andlang hlinces[30] on cardan ham[31] of þam hamme ut þurh þone lea[32] on grenan beorh[33] of þam beorge on ecgunes treow[34] of þam treowe on mearc weg[35] þonon on þa dene[36] and swa forþ to þam þrim gemærum[37] of þam gemærum eft on wines treow[1].

NOTES

1 v. p. 662, n. 3 and map.

2 'valley', v. denu, this stretch of boundary follows a narrow valley, v. map.

3 'way', v. weg; the boundary follows a footpath which climbs the western side of the valley, v. map.

4 'the north part of the broad wood or clearing'; the name survives in Bradleywood Fm in Boxford Pt 1 234, v. map.

5 v. hamm. The series of names in hamm, some with a distinguishing first el., which occurs in this group of charters is discussed in M. Gelling, 'The Element hamm in English Place-Names', *Namn och Bygd* 48 (1960), p. 152. In this part of Berks and in an area of

N. Ha the el. seems to have developed a meaning 'close'. In most of the names in this group the commoner meaning 'river-meadow' is not likely.

6 *v*. lēah; it is impossible to say whether the word refers to a wood, in which case the *hamm*s were presumably fenced-off clearings, or to a large clearing, in which the *hamm*s would be individual enclosures.

7 'the south part of a *hamm*.'

8 'old hedge-row', *v*. eald, hege, rǣw.

9 Second el. hangra 'wood on a slope', which may indicate that the survey has reached the point where the land begins to slope down to the R. Lambourn. The first el. may be the OE **wōp* postulated for *Wopland* in Inkpen f.ns. (Pt 2 313), perhaps a bird-name, joined to hangra with a connective -ing-. The later survey has *poppinghangran* (p. 666, n. 7). *Wopig* may be a mistake for *popig*, but this does not seem a likely place for poppies to grow.

10 Apparently 'shilling hanger', but this may be another example of the mysterious el. which is discussed p. 753, n. 2.

11 'the west part of the broad enclosure', *v*. n. 5 *supra*. Although the survey is now approaching the R. Lambourn, the ground is not typical river-meadow.

12 'Carda's tumulus', *v*. hlǣw. The pers.n. is not on record, but *v*. DEPN s.n. Cardeston, Cardley. The following phrase should probably be *of þam hlæwe*.

13 R. Lambourn, *v*. map.

14 'Dēora's tree', *v*. trēow.

15 Apparently 'olive-tree-stump', *v*. stybb, but the word *elebeam* occurs fairly frequently in charter bounds, and was presumably used of some native tree.

16 'Cēolbald's spring', *v*. w(i)ell; O.S. maps mark a number of springs on the parish boundary, *v*. map.

17 This is *cytan seohtresford* in the later bounds of Welford (p. 667, n. 18). It is presumably where the boundary comes down to the R. Kennet. The river-valley is very marshy, and the name probably contains a masc. or neuter form of seohtre 'drain'. The first el. is probably cӯta 'kite'. There was apparently a p.n. *cytanseohter*, and *ford* was added to the gen. of this.

18 'Wulfrīc's boundary.' This is presumably where the boundary leaves the R. Kennet, and turns N. along the boundary of Kint-bury. A man named Wulfric is associated with land at Inkpen and

with a monastery at Kintbury in BCS 678 (the will of Wulfgar),
which is about 10 years earlier in date than the present charter.

19 'the top part of treasure linchet', v. hord, hlinc, presumably a
cultivation terrace where a piece of jewellery or a hoard of coins
was once found.

20 'the north part of drain meadow', v. seohtre, mǣd.

21 'Cyn(e)helm's stone.'

22 'green way', v. grēne, weg.

23 'rye enclosure', v. ryge, hamm and n. 5 supra.

24 'loam pits', v. lām, pytt. The phrase ut on pa lam pyttas might
indicate that the boundary has now changed direction from due
N. to almost due W., v. map.

25 'chalk-pit', v. crundel.

26 'ash-tree', v. æsc.

27 burna refers to the R. Lambourn, which the survey here crosses
for the second time, v. map.

28 'mill path', v. myln, pæð.

29 'three thorn-trees', v. þrēo, þorn.

30 'linchet', v. 627.

31 'Carda's enclosure', v. notes 5 and 12 supra.

32 'wood' or 'clearing', v. lēah and n. 6 supra.

33 'green hill or barrow', v. grēne¹, beorg.

34 'Ecghūn's tree', v. trēow.

35 'boundary way', v. weg; mearc is an unusual word in Berks, v.
630.

36 'valley', v. denu; the boundary here descends into the valley of
n. 2.

37 'three boundaries', v. þrēo, (ge)mǣre; this is probably the point
at which the parishes of Leckhampstead, Chaddleworth and
Welford meet, v. map.

B (b) IV THE BOUNDS OF WELFORD: 956 (C. 1200) BCS 963

Ærest of wines treowe¹ andlang weges² on þone holen weg³. andlang
weges of þam holan wege on bradanlea norðeweardne⁴ on ænne ham⁵.
of þam hamme andlang hegerewe⁶ innan popping hangran⁷. of
poppinghangran innan scilling hangran⁸ on ænne ham⁹. of scilling
hangran on bradanham westeweardne¹⁰. of bradan hamme on Cærdan
hlæw¹¹. of Cærdanhlæw ut on lamburnan¹² on Eoccenford¹³. of
Eoccenforda on ðyran treow¹⁴. of ðyran treowe on ylfing dene¹⁵. on
ænne Elebeam¹⁶. of þam Elebeame on cælboldes wylle¹⁷. of cælboldes

wylle on Cytan seohtresford[18]. of cytanseohtresforda andlang hricgges[19] on syntri mæde norðewearde[20]. of syntrimede on flexhammes[21]. of flexhamman on minthammas[22] on cylman stane[23]. of cylman stane on ðone þryscytan crundel[24]. of þam crundele on þone ruwan crundele[25] þurhut Clodhangran[26]. of þam hangran andlang rode[27] ut on mulesdene[28]. andlang dene utan landburnan[29] andglang burnan on weter weg[30]. of þam weterwege on weterhammas[31]. of þam hamma on grenan beorh[32]. of þam beorhe andlang hæccan[33] on eccunes treow[34]. of þam treowe andlang gæmeres[35] to wines treowe[1].

NOTES

1 v. p. 662, n. 3 and map.
2 'way', v. weg.
3 'hollow way', v. hol[2], weg; this may be the 'way' of the first Welford bounds (p. 663, n. 3) by which the boundary climbs out of a small valley.
4 v. p. 663, n. 4 and map.
5 v. p. 663, n. 5.
6 'hedge-row', v. hege, ræw. These bounds have only one *hamm* between *bradanlea* and the first *hangra*, where the earlier set mentions two.
7 v. p. 664, n. 9.
8 v. p. 664, n. 10.
9 This *hamm* may have been wrongly inserted here; its correct position was probably between 5 and 6, v. n. 6 *supra*.
10 v. p. 664, n. 11.
11 v. p. 664, n. 12.
12 R. Lambourn.
13 This name presents grave difficulties. As regards identification with later spellings it is tempting to associate it with the first part of *Ukkefordysmede* 1476, *Ucford Meadow* 1591, which occurs among the f.ns. of Speen, v. Pt 1 270. This meadow seems from the context to have been in the E. of the parish, near Speen and Woodspeen. If the charter survey is following the modern parish boundary of Welford, however, we are nowhere near that area (v. map). As regards etymology, *Eoccenford* is apparently identical with *Eoccenforda* near Abingdon Pt 2 400, which was named from the R. Ock (Pt 1 14–15), *Eoccen* being a Celtic r.n. derived from a word meaning 'salmon'. If the el. is a r.n. in the Welford survey, then it must be either an older name of the Lambourn or (if we

abandon the attempt to fit the survey to the parish of Welford) of the stream from which Winterbourne is named. The O.S. maps mark a ford where this last stream joins the Lambourn, *v.* map, but (as explained on pp. 657–8) it is difficult to see how land in this area could have been included in the Welford grant. If Ock was an earlier name of the Lambourn, it is perhaps just possible that two fords on it, about 3 miles apart, were each called *Eoccenford.*

14 Probably a poor spelling for *dyran treow = deoran treowe* in III, *v.* p. 664, n. 14.

15 Possibly 'elf valley', from WSax ylf (*v.* elf) (which may be a pers.n.) and denu, with a connective -ing-. This is an extra boundary-mark to those in the earlier Welford survey.

16 *v.* p. 664, n. 15.

17 *v.* p. 664, n. 16.

18 *v.* p. 664, n. 17.

19 'ridge', *v.* hrycg; this replaces the *hord hlinc* of III.

20 *syntri mæd* is an error for *sihtre mæd* in III, *v.* p. 665, n. 20.

21 'flax enclosures', *v.* fleax, hamm.

22 'mint enclosures', *v.* minte, hamm; these two *hamm*s are extra boundary-marks to those in the earlier survey.

23 *v.* p. 665, n. 21, *Cylma* may be a short form of *Cynehelm.*

24 'three-cornered chalkpit', *v.* crundel, first el. OE *þriscȳte* 'triangular'.

25 'rough chalkpit', *v.* rūh, crundel; the earlier survey mentions only one *crundel* on this stretch.

26 *v.* clodd 'lump of earth', hangra 'wood on a slope'.

27 'clearing', *v.* rodu.

28 'Mūl's valley', *v.* denu; the W. boundary of Welford runs down a marked valley to the Lambourn, *v.* map.

29 *landburnan* is an error for *lamburnan.* The modern boundary crosses the R. Lambourn, but does not run along it, as the next phrase makes this survey run.

30 'water way', *v.* wæter, weg.

31 'water enclosures', *v.* wæter, hamm.

32 *v.* p. 665, n. 33.

33 'fence', *v.* 628.

34 *v.* p. 665, n. 34.

35 'boundary', *v.* (ge)mǣre.

B (b) V THE BOUNDS OF BENHAM: 956 (C. 1200) BCS 942

Ærest of Cynetan[1] on þa mærdic[2]. of þære dic on hæddeswyl[3]. of þam wylle on Clænan crundel[4]. of þam crundele on ða readan hane[5]. of þære hane on wigmundes swelgende[6]. of þam swelgende upan ðone hryc[7]. andlang hrycces to ællanstapole[8]. of þam stapole on accange-fyrðæ[9] of þam gefyrhðe on meosbroces ford[10]. of þam forda on screget[11]. of þam gete on holan broces heafod[12]. þon' on þæt hæcget[13]. þon' on ða rode eastewearde[14]. of þære rode on mærlace[15]. of þære lace on stapolford[16] ut on cynetan[1]. þon' up andlang healfan streame[17]. eft on mærdic[2]. and codan mæd þær to[18].

NOTES

1 R. Kennet, v. map and Pt I 11–12. The survey probably begins at the S.W. corner of the parish of Speen.
2 'boundary ditch', v. (ge)mǣre, dīc.
3 'Hæddi's spring', v. w(i)ell.
4 'clean chalk-pit', v. clǣne, crundel; O.S. maps show a chalk-pit near the W. boundary of Speen, v. map.
5 'red stone', v. rēad, hān.
6 'Wīgmund's deep place', v. swelgend. The meaning of this term seems to vary from name to name. There are a number of springs marked near the N.W. corner of Speen, and the Boxford survey describes this area as 'the marsh' (p. 670, n. 14), so the reference in this instance may be to a bog-hole.
7 'ridge', v. hrycg; Wickham Heath (v. map) is on this ridge.
8 'Ælla's post', v. stapol. This is mentioned also in the Boxford survey (p. 670, n. 12), and was probably at the point where the N. boundary of Speen changes direction from S.E. to N.E., v. map.
9 '*Acca*'s wood', v. (ge)fyrhðe.
10 'the ford of marsh-brook', v. map and p. 670, n. 11. The ford may have been a crossing-place on the R. Lambourn near where *meosbroc* flows into it. The first el. is mēos which is replaced by *Mersshe-* in a later spelling, v. Pt I 270. This is the last landmark in the survey which can be identified.
11 v. geat; first el. probably corrupt.
12 'head of hollow brook', v. hol[2], brōc. The boundary of Speen parish follows the stream from which Winterbourne is named, but this cannot be the 'hollow brook', as its head is far away to the N. After leaving this brook the modern parish boundary travels down

a small valley which takes it to the R. Lambourn. The 'hollow brook' could have flowed down this.

13 *v.* hæcc-geat; assuming the survey is now following the Lambourn, as the modern boundary does, this may be a floodgate on the river.

14 'the east part of the clearing', *v.* rodu.

15 'boundary stream', *v.* (ge)mǣre, lacu.

16 'ford marked by a post', *v.* stapol, ford; this is presumably where the survey approaches the R. Kennet, but the name did not survive and the spot cannot be identified.

17 'along half the stream'; this takes the survey W. along the Kennet to its starting point.

18 '*Coda's mead', *v.* mǣd; this piece of meadow, possibly outlying from the main estate, has not been identified.

B (b) VII THE BOUNDS OF BOXFORD: 968 (C. 1200) BCS 1227

Ærest æt wines treowe[1]. þæt andlang herpaðes[2] to dene pytte[3]. þanon up on æsc meres hammas suðewerde[4]. of þam hammum andlang mearce[5] ut on þone hæðfeld easteweardne[6]. þæt ut on lindene norðeweardne[7]. þanon andlang mearce[5] on weoccan ðorn[8]. of þam ðorne. þæt andlang mearce[5] on lamburnan[9]. on clatford[10]. of clatforda on meos broces heafod[11]. þæt þanon to allan stapule[12]. þanon andlang herpaðes[13] ut on þone mersc[14]. þæt a be mersce to þam tune[15] on þa hege ræpe[16]. þæt on þa dic ut on þa burnan[17]. þonan up on þa blacan grafan[18]. of þære grafan on rinda crundel[19]. of þam crundle to þrim þornon[20]. þæt andlang weges[21]. eft on wines treowe[1] þær hit ær onfenge.

NOTES

1 *v.* p. 662, n. 3 and map.

2 *v.* here-pæð; the term is surprising here, as there is not even a footpath along the northern boundary of Boxford, and the Leckhampstead survey (II) does not refer to a road here.

3 *v.* p. 662, n. 1 and map.

4 'the south part of the enclosures of the ash-pool', *v.* æsc, mere, hamm and p. 662, n. 5. Grundy notes a f.n. Ashmore Coppice, *v.* map and Pt 1 236. There was a lost place called *Æscmere* in Ha, from which Ashmansworth (earlier *Æscmeresweorð*) was named. Ashmansworth is about 11 miles S. of this, so there is probably no connection between the Berks and Ha names.

5 'boundary', *v.* mearc and 630.

6 'the east part of the heath', v. hǣð, feld; this does not appear to
have survived as a common, but hǣð occurs in some Boxford
f.ns., v. Pt 1 236. Boxford Common lies a little to the s.

7 'the north part of flax valley', v. līn, denu and map. The valley
curves to the S.E., away from the parish boundary. Leonard's
Plantation Pt 1 235 may have the same first el.

8 Possibly 'wick thorn-tree', with wēoce 'wick of a lamp or candle'
as first el. The other versions of these bounds have weocan instead
of weoccan. The reference may be to the shape of the tree. Dr von
Feilitzen prefers a pers.n. Weocca, a short form of names in
Wīoh-, Wēoh-.

9 R. Lambourn, v. map.

10 'burdock ford', v. clāte, ford.

11 'the head of marsh brook', v. hēafod and p. 668, n. 10. The valley
in which it ran is clearly marked on O.S. maps. There are 16th-
cent. spellings for the name, v. Pt 1 270.

12 v. p. 668, n. 8 and map.

13 v. here-pæð and map; there is a road along the parish boundary
here, but it is not the Roman road, Ermin Street, which ran a
short distance to the N. (v. Margary 121–2).

14 'marsh', v. mersc; the O.S. maps show a number of springs in
this area, and it may have been marshy in spite of being on top of
a ridge.

15 'farm'; this is one of several instances in Berks charters of a tūn
on an estate boundary, v. 630. Upper Fm (v. map) is very close to
the boundary, and may be on the site of the tūn.

16 'hedge-row', v. hege, rǣw; rǣpe should be rǣwe.

17 'to the ditch out to the burn', i.e. R. Lambourn, v. map.

18 'black grove'; there are two surviving instances of this name in
Berks, v. Pt 2 334.

19 v. crundel; Professor Löfvenberg suggests that the first el. is the
gen.pl. of OE rind 'bark', which is often used in the pl., and that
the reference may be to a bark-pit in which hides were steeped for
tanning.

20 'three thorn-trees.'

21 'way', v. weg and map; the boundary is here following a road
which also forms the N.E. boundary of Welford, v. p. 666, n. 2.

B (b) VIII THE BOUNDS OF FARNBOROUGH: C. 935 (C. 1200)
BCS 682

Ærest of fearnbeorhge[1] west on þone weg to þam stanum[2]. of þam
stanum suð on ðone weg on þa andheafda[3]. of þam andheafdum on
ða hlinc rewe[4] ut to þære dic be norðan stodfaldon[5]. þonne forð on
ða dic to mær flodan[6] be æstan lilling lea[7]. þonne forð andlang þes
suðeran weges[8] oð þæt lange treow[9]. þonne forð west on þone weg
ofer beocumb[10] to þam stancrundele[11] þon' norð on ðane smalan
weg[12] wið eastan brocenan beorg[13] to þam wege þæ þær east ligð[14].
þon' forð on ðone weg to cytel flodan[15] be westan mulescumbes[16].
þær ða weges twisligað[17]. þon' forð to scyldmere[18]. þon' forð on ða
furh[19] to furcumbe[20]. andlanges furcumbes middeweardes to þære
dene[21]. þon' forð on ða dene to þære wega gemyþan[22]. þon' forð to
þam hwitan wege[23] to þam haran þornan[24]. þon' of þam hwitan wege
on fearnbeorhg[1].

and se leag be eastan catmere[25] þæ þær to gebyræð. þæt is on ðone
weg þæ ligð to stanleage[26]. þon' forð syððan suð on þone stanihtan
weg[27]. of stanmeringa gemere[28] þon' forð on þone smalan weg[29] to
þam fulan wege. se hatte stific weg. þæt is catmeringa gemære and
þes landes to fernbeorhgan[30]. þon' ford andlang ðæs weges ut on þone
feld[31]. and þonne ealle þa hangran be tweonan þam wege and þam þe
to stanleage ligð. gebyriað ealle to fearnbeorgan[32].

NOTES

1 'fern hill'. The spellings of the parish name in the texts of the
Farnborough charters show that the n. was plural (v. Pt 2 501),
but the boundary mark is singular. Farnborough village stands at
the centre of a ridge which has a number of spurs jutting from it;
probably these were known collectively as the 'fern hills'. The
spur due E. of the village may be the 'fern hill' of the bounds, v.
map. Alternatively, the parish-name may refer to tumuli, of which
this boundary-mark is one.

2 'west to the way to the stone', v. weg, stān; the parish boundary
runs W. for a short stretch, v. map.

3 'south to the way to the headlands', v. 626; the boundary is
actually running S.S.W.

4 'linchet row', v. hlinc, ræw and map; in 1961 there was a small
bank on the boundary here, between the field to the N. and the
wood to the S.

5 'the ditch north of the horse enclosures', *v.* stōdfald.

6 'boundary spring', *v.* p. 661, n. 13 and map.

7 The name survives as Lilley, *v.* map and Pt **2** 497. The actual lēah may be Lilley Copse.

8 'the southerly way', *v.* map. This takes the survey for a long stretch, and the phrase *suðeran wege* may be a warning against taking the right-hand fork where a road branches off to the N. due S. of Farnborough village.

9 'tall tree', *v.* lang, trēow; this occurs also in the bounds of Brightwalton (p. 661, n. 12), *v.* map for probable position.

10 'west to the way across bee-valley', *v.* bēo, cumb. This is a well-marked valley in which Coombe Fm in Brightwalton is situated, *v.* map and Pt **1** 238.

11 'stone quarry', *v.* stān, crundel; this occurs also in the bounds of Brightwalton (p. 661, n. 11), *v.* map.

12 'narrow way', *v.* smæl, weg.

13 the *brocenan beorg* which lies W. of the narrow way could be a disturbed tumulus, or the name could mean 'uneven hill', cf. Brokenborough, W 53–4. The Farnborough name survived in the f.n. Broken Berry which occurs in the *TA*, and was near the N.W. corner of the parish, *v.* Pt **2** 502.

14 'the way which leads east from there'; the boundary turns from N.E. to S.E. at this point (*v.* map), and the survey treats these directions as 'north' and 'east'.

15 'intermittent spring resembling a kettle', *v.* cytel, flōde. Grundy has an excellent note on this spring, which, when he was writing (1928), sometimes flowed from lower down the valley than the point at which it appears to be mentioned in the survey. It is not certain in what sense cytel is used in spring-names, but it may refer to the spring bubbling up.

16 'Mūl's coomb', *v.* cumb and map; the boundary turns N.E. here, and the *cumb* turns off to the E. It is probably only a coincidence that there is a *mules dene* in Welford (p. 667, n. 28). The high ground to the S.E. is called *mules dun* in II (p. 654, n. 40).

17 'where the ways fork.'

18 'shield-shaped pool', *v.* p. 742, n. 1, and see map for approximate position.

19 'furrow', *v.* 627.

20 'furrow coomb', *v.* furh, cumb; the boundary enters a valley here, *v.* map.

21 'along the middle of furrow coomb to the valley', *v.* **denu**. The *furcumb* runs at right angles into Ilsley Bottom.

22 'meeting of ways', *v.* **weg**, (ge)mȳ ðe; this is the point called Lands End on O.S. maps, where several tracks meet, *v.* map.

23 'white way', *v.* **hwīt, weg**; this is the road known as Old Street, *v.* map. In 1961 the surface was very rough and covered with grass, but chalk was still visible in places.

24 'boundary thorn-trees', *v.* **hār², þorn**.

25 *v.* **lēah**; 'the wood east of Catmore' which belongs to the estate is the south-eastern extension of the parish, *v.* map. It is still largely wooded.

26 'the way which leads to stone-wood', *v.* **stān, lēah**; *stanleage* may be identical with *stanlege* which occurs in the bounds of a piece of woodland which belonged to Chilton, *v.* p. 768, n. 19. The survey of the Farnborough *lēah* probably begins at its northern, pointed end.

27 'stony way', *v.* **stāniht, weg**.

28 'boundary of the people of Stanmore', *v.* (ge)mǣre; Stanmore was a separate estate, in the 10th cent., comprising roughly two-thirds of the modern parish of Beedon, *v.* p. 649.

29 'narrow way', *v.* **smæl, weg** and map; this probably ran along the short S. boundary of the *lēah*.

30 'the foul way which is called tree-stump way which is the boundary between the people of Catmore and the land which belongs to Farnborough'; *v.* map and p. 651, n. 5.

31 'along the way out to the open land', *v.* **feld**; this takes the boundary along the W. side of this piece of land.

32 The sloping wood (*v.* **hangra**) between the way of 31 and the way which led to *stanleage* cannot be precisely located.

B (b) X THE BOUNDS OF LEVERTON IN HUNGERFORD: 984 (C. 1240) KCD 1282

Ærest on Cynetan[1] æt Scoelles eald cotan[2] þæt up andlang streames oð Eadgife gemære[3] swa norð innan Hydene[4] ðanon norð on lamburninga mearce[5] swa est andlang mearce oð ælfwiges gemære[6] swa suð andlang gemæres on Hyddene[7] swa suð begemære þat eft innan Cynetan strem[1].

NOTES

1 R. Kennet, *v.* map and Pt **1** 11–12. The starting point is probably between the villages of Leverton and Eddington.

2 The later version of these bounds, in KCD 1050, has *Sceolles ealdcotan, v.* eald, cot. Dr von Feilitzen suggests that the first el. is the gen. of a pers.n. *Sceolh*, originally a byname meaning 'squinter'.

3 'Ēadgifu's boundary'. This is probably where the survey leaves the Kennet, and it must be W. of Leverton, so cannot be associated with Eddington, although that name (Pt **2** 303) means 'Ēadgifu's tūn'. The line is probably that of the county boundary, *v.* map. South of the R. Kennet the county boundary is of late 19th-cent. origin (*v.* 845), but N. of the river it may coincide with Old English boundaries.

4 'valley with a landing-place'; the name survives as Hidden (Pt **2** 304), in Great, Little and North Hidden Fms. Great and Little Hidden Fms are on a hill N.E. of Hungerford. North Hidden Fm is in a valley which is a side-branch of a long valley running from the county boundary, 4 miles N.W. of Hungerford, down to the Kennet at Kintbury. It is named on O.S. maps as Wiltshire Bottom, Old Hayward Bottom, New Hayward Bottom and Radley Bottom, *v.* map. This was the *hȳð-denu*, named from a landing-place at Kintbury. Great and Little Hidden Fms derive their name from it although they are actually situated on a hill overlooking it.

5 'boundary of the people of Lambourn', *v.* map. This is where the survey turns E. For mearc as opposed to gemære, *v.* 630.

6 'Ælfwīg's boundary', *v.* (ge)mære; Ælfwīg may have been the 11th-cent. owner of Eddington.

7 The survey crosses the *hȳð-denu* of n. 4 for the second time on its course from the N. boundary of the estate to the Kennet.

C SHRIVENHAM HUNDRED, WITH
SHELLINGFORD (GANFIELD HUNDRED)

The charters dealing with land in Shrivenham Hundred were preserved at Winchester, Abingdon and Glastonbury. The three grants of land at *Æscesbyrig* (I, II and V) have been misunderstood by previous authors, as it has not been recognised that *Æscesbyrig* is not Ashbury, but the Old English name of Uffington Castle. A correct appreciation of the surveys attached to those grants brings to light several interesting facts about the land-units which later comprised the parishes of Woolstone and Uffington. The area of these two parishes appears to have been a single estate, known as *Æscesbyrig*. This was subdivided in 856, when a narrow strip of land which later comprised the western half of Woolstone parish was given to a man named Aldred. This land was acquired by the thegn Wulfric in 944, and in 958 Wulfric was granted an adjacent strip of land, also carved out of the unit called *Æscesbyrig*, which later comprised the eastern half of Woolstone parish. These two strips of land became known as Woolstone, 'Wulfric's estate', and it is noteworthy that the actual village of Woolstone straddles the boundary between the two. The remaining portion of *Æscesbyrig* was still known by that name in 953, but appears to have been re-named 'Uffa's estate' soon after that, probably in response to the new name which had become current for the western part of the original unit.

The main interest of this group of surveys lies in the identification of *Æscesbyrig* with Uffington Castle, but other surveys in the area are of great value, particularly the one of Hardwell. The charters are –

I. BCS 491, A.D. 856, a Winchester charter by which King Æthelwulf grants 20 hides at *Æscesbyrig* to Aldred. The bounds describe the western half of the modern parish of Woolstone. Substantially the same survey, with the omission of the last two boundary-marks, occurs in BCS 796, A.D. 944, also a Winchester charter, by which King Eadmund grants 20 hides at *Æscesbyrig* to Wulfric.

II. BCS 902, A.D. 958, a Winchester charter by which King Eadred (?scribal substitution for Eadwig) grants 20 hides at *Æscesbyrig* to Wulfric. The bounds describe the eastern half of the modern parish of Woolstone. This survey and that of I have a boundary in common.

[675]

III. BCS 601, A.D. 903, an Abingdon charter, which is only copied in *ClaudiusBvi*, although *Cix* has the boundaries. The charter is a difficult one; King Edward grants to a vassal, whose name is given as *Tata Æthehumflo* (? for *Æthe*[*l*]*huni filio*), 3 hides at Hardwell, and the text appears to be saying that the estate was originally the subject of a grant by the king's grandfather, King Æthelwulf, but the earlier charter has become illegible through being immersed in water ('liber antiquus submersus est, quo paene nihil in eo apertum videbatur'). The survey, which describes the eastern part of Compton Beauchamp parish, is very detailed, and should be dated 903, since it could hardly have been copied from the earlier damaged charter. It is extremely important for its frequent references to arable features. It has one boundary in common with I.

IV. BCS 687, usually dated c. A.D. 931. This is not, strictly speaking, a charter. It is an account, copied into both versions of the Abingdon Chronicle, of a ceremony by which Æthelstan, the ealderman of East Anglia who was known as 'Half King', gave Uffington to the Abbey. As presented by the scribe of *ClaudiusBvi*, the account consists of a statement in Latin, beginning 'Ego Æthelstan senator', which describes the ceremony, then the bounds of the land, then a description of the ceremony in Old English. The Old English account is not in the first person, but begins 'Æthelstan ealderman gebocade this land'; otherwise it corresponds very closely to the Latin account. In both, the gift is said to have been made in the days of King Æthelstan, and in the presence of a large assembly. The reference to the days of King Æthelstan suggests that the record was composed later than the king's death in 939, and the evidence of V (*infra*) suggests a date after 953. The date of the bounds is therefore uncertain; they describe the modern parish of Uffington, and have one boundary in common with II.

V. BCS 899, A.D. 953, an Abingdon charter copied only in *ClaudiusBvi*, by which King Eadred grants to Ælfsige and his wife Eadgifu 33 hides at *Æscesburh*. The bounds describe the same area as those of IV, i.e. the parish of Uffington. In view of the story told in IV, it is curious that Uffington was the subject of a royal grant in 953. It may be tentatively suggested that Ealdorman Æthelstan's gift of the estate to Abingdon c. 931 failed to take effect, and that the Abbey laid claim to the land after 953, compiling the record which constitutes BCS 687 in support of their claim. They seem to have been successful, as BCS 899 appears in their Chronicle, and they owned Uffington TRE. An interesting question arises as to the date at which Uffington ceased to share with Woolstone the name *Æscesbyrig*. Woolstone obviously acquired its modern name ('Wulfric's estate') after 955, since Wulfric was granted one estate there in 944, and the other in 955. One would expect that Uffington ('Uffa's estate') was renamed about the same time. This postulates an owner named Uffa, perhaps the heir of Ælfsige and Eadgifu, who was in possession between 953 and the unknown date at which the land passed to Abingdon. The problems posed by these two Uffington grants have not hitherto been recognised, as it has not been realised that the two estates (one called *Uffentune* and the other *Æscesburh*) are identical; for a discussion of the first grant *v.* HistAb 34–6, ASCharters 44, 299–300.

VI. BCS 1121, A.D. 963, an Abingdon charter by which King Eadgar grants to Æthelsige 10 hides at Sparsholt, and one hide at Balking. There is mention of 12 *agri* at Balking, and of a mill at *Hurgrove* (in Steventon, some 12 miles away) to which belong another 12 *agri*. The charter and the bounds are copied in both versions of the Chronicle, twice in *ClaudiusBvi*, but *ClaudiusCix* omits the witnesses. The bounds are difficult to follow, but probably describe the western half of the modern parish of Kingston Lisle. There were three estates in Sparsholt in 1086 (*v. infra* 679), which seem to correspond to Fawler, Kingston Lisle and Sparsholt. The Abingdon estate corresponds to Fawler. The bounds have one boundary in common with the Uffington surveys (IV and V)

VII. BCS 908, A.D. 955, an Abingdon charter copied only in *Claudius-Bvi*, by which King Eadred grants 8 hides at Compton Beauchamp ('æt Cumtune, iuxta montem qui vocatur Æscesdune') to Ælfheah. The bounds describe the western part of the parish, excluding the Hardwell estate which is the subject of III.

VIII. BCS 828, A.D. 947, a Glastonbury charter by which King Eadred grants 20 hides at *Aysshedun* to Edric. There is an earlier Glastonbury charter, BCS 431, by which King Athelwulf gives 10 hides at *Asshedoune* to Duda, but this has no bounds. GlastonCh identifies both grants with Ashbury. The bounds of BCS 828 may describe the modern parish of Ashbury, or they may describe only the western half, excluding Odstone, which did not belong to Glastonbury in 1086.

IX. BCS 683, A.D. 931, an Abingdon charter, by which King Æthelstan grants 12 hides at Shellingford to the Abbey. The charter is
discussed HistAb 38. Stenton considers that it is to some extent a
12th-cent. fabrication, but that the compiler had before him an
earlier record of the gift. The text is copied in both versions of the
Chronicle, but there are no bounds in *ClaudiusBvi*. The surveys
at the end of *ClaudiusCix* include one of Shellingford, which is
assumed to belong to this charter, and which gives a remarkably
clear description of the bounds of the modern parish.

X. BCS 675, A.D. 931, an Abingdon charter by which King Æthelstan
grants to Ælfric 20 hides at Watchfield. The charter is only copied
in *ClaudiusBvi*, but both versions of the Chronicle have the boundaries, which give a very clear description of the modern parish.

The long, narrow land-units which run athwart the escarpment of
the Downs were in some cases even narrower in the 10th cent. Compton Beauchamp and Woolstone were both divided by a line running
from N. to S., and Fawler was similarly separated from Kingston
Lisle. Some of these narrow estates were characterised by remarkably
high hidages, and comparison with the corresponding estates as
described in DB reveals drastic reductions. Woolstone appears in DB
as a single estate belonging to the Bishop of Winchester. Since BCS
491 and 902 are both in the Winchester cartulary, it is reasonable to
assume that the 1086 estate includes both the charter ones. The combined assessment of the two charter estates was 40 hides; this had been
reduced to 20 TRE, and to 10 in 1086. Uffington, assessed as 33 hides
in V, was 40 hides TRE, but only 14 in 1086. Shellingford and Watchfield, in the Vale of White Horse, are parishes of different shape, but
they share this characteristic of reduced hidage. Shellingford is given
as 12 hides in IX, and was still 12 TRE, but had been reduced to 2
hides one virgate in 1086. Watchfield, given as 20 hides in X, was still
20 TRE, but only 10 in 1086.

In the case of Compton Beauchamp, there are two estates to be
considered. Nos III and VII refer to estates within the modern
parish, one (Hardwell) of 3 hides, the other of 8. In 1086 there were
still two estates, one called Compton and the other Knighton, the
combined assessment of which was 10 hides TRE, though Knighton
had been reduced from 5 hides to 2 virgates and 2 parts of a virgate
in 1086.

In the case of the Sparsholt estate granted in VI, there seems to be little change in the assessment. There were three estates at Sparsholt in 1086, one claimed by Abingdon, one held by the King TRE and after the Conquest, and a third held in 1086 by the King, but in the hands of three freemen TRE. The Abingdon estate, which was assessed at 10 hides TRE and in 1086, is likely to correspond to the land granted in VI, which is an Abingdon charter. The land in question appears to have been the western part of Kingston Lisle, the actual village being Fawler; Fawler appears by that name t. William and t. Hy 1 Abingdon. Balking, which does not appear in DB, may have consisted simply of the 'an hid landes' which belonged to this estate. The DB estate at Sparsholt which had belonged to Edward the Confessor should probably be equated with Kingston Lisle.

Comparison of the DB and charter hidages for Ashbury is difficult, as it is not certain whether the whole parish or only the western half is referred to in VIII. The charter hidage is 20. In 1086 there were two estates, Ashbury and Odstone. Ashbury had the remarkably high assessment of 40 TRE, but only 16 hides 2½ virgates in 1086. Odstone was 10 hides TRE, 5 in 1086.

This group of boundaries is distinguished by frequent references to ancient monuments – the hill-forts and tumuli of the Berkshire Downs – and to arable land. It is clear that the field-systems of some of these estates extended to the 10th-cent. estate boundaries, and the Hardwell survey appears to be negotiating its way through a field-system which straddles the boundary. As explained *supra*, some of the land-units of these charters represent divisions of larger units, such as *Æscesbyrig*, which included Woolstone and Uffington, and Sparsholt, which included Kingston Lisle, so it is not surprising that the arable land was already laid out across the lines of the later boundaries. A number of stones are mentioned, and these had perhaps been moved from the arable for use as boundary-marks. The Kingston Lisle survey begins at *sunemannes wyrðige*, perhaps only an enclosure, but possibly another instance of a farm on an estate boundary, of which there are several in the Berks surveys, *v.* 630. Beans are mentioned twice, in *bean furlong* in Kingston Lisle and *bean broc* in Watchfield. There are relatively few chalkpits, and very few trees. With the exception of *Lippanstubbe* in Ashbury and an alderbed in Hardwell, such trees as do occur are thorn or elder; the *leacumb* in Kingston Lisle may refer to a precious belt of trees. The *hyrdewic* and the land at *hyrde grafe* which are outlying properties of Kingston Lisle may have been primarily pasture land, since they are named from herdsmen.

3

Shellingford in the valley of the Ock has a survey which resembles those of the northern part of the parishes which extend S. over the Downs.

CI THE BOUNDS OF WEST WOOLSTONE: 856 (12TH)
BCS 491

Ærest on þone garan suþæweardnæ[1]. Ðonnæ and lang wægæs[2] oð þonæ mægen stan[3]. þa non uuon hlinc[4]. And lang hlincæs oð loddæræs sæccinge[5]. Andlang hlincæs oð þonæ brystæ del[6]. þanon and lang fyrh ænnæ æcer[7] to þam hlincæ[8]. ðanon on ða heafda[9] on hrycwæg[10]. of hrycwæge on þonæ þorn styb[11]. þanon on hordwyllæ[12] on þonæ ealdan hord wyllæs wæg[13]. and lang þæs ealdan wægæs. on hrysc slædes bygæ[14]. And lang riðæ on swynbroc[15]. And lang brocæs on bæahhildæ byrigels[16]. þonon on þonæ ealdan wæg[17]. and lang wægæs on þonæ garan norðæ weardnæ[18]. Þonon east and lang wæges on hnottan mæræ norðæ wearðnæ[19]. þanon on ða dic[20]. and lang dic on þæt on bulan mædæ norþæ wærdæ[21]. þonon on þa brembæl hyrnan[22]. of þæræ hyrnan on stan mæræ[23]. þo non to þæn æpænan byrigelsæ[24] on æcocænen[25] upp and lang streamæs on þonæ æwulm[26]. Þonon on wæardæs bæorh[27]. of þam bæorgæ on hrung putt[28]. þonon on þa æaldan hola[29]. of ðam holum æft on þonæ garan suþæ wæardnæ[30]. þonnæ þæt on tættucan stan[31]. of þam stanæ on þa æaldan dic[32]. ðær hit ær onfæng.

NOTES

1 'the south part of the gore', v. 626, possibly the pointed projection in the S.W. of the parish.
2 'way', v. weg.
3 'great stone', v. mægen, stān.
4 'crooked linchet', v. wōh, hlinc; strip linchets are common in the S. of this group of parishes, v. 627.
5 'beggar's pallet', v. loddere, perhaps a stone shaped like a pillow.
6 v. dell; brystæ may be related to berstan 'to burst', v. Tengstrand 107–8. There is a large hollow, of indeterminate age, at approximately the right spot, v. map.
7 'along the furrow one acre', v. 626–7.
8 'linchet', v. hlinc and 627.
9 'headlands', v. 626.
10 Ridge Way, v. map.
11 'thorn stump', v. þorn, stybb.

12 'treasure spring'; there is a spring very close to the boundary here,
   v. map. Hardwell, Pt 2 360–1, is named from the stream formed
   by the group of springs which rise near this spot.
13 'old Hardwell way', also in III, v. map and p. 684, n. 4.
14 'the bend of the rush-hollow', v. rysc, slæd, byge[1] and p. 684, n. 3.
15 'along the stream to pig brook', v. rīð, swīn, brōc and map, the
   brook occurs also in III, v. p. 684, n. 1. After this, no landmarks
   can be precisely identified until the survey reaches the stream
   regarded as the head-stream of the Ock, v. 25 infra.
16 'Bēaghild's burial-place', v. byrgels.
17 'old way', v. eald, weg.
18 'the north part of the gore', possibly the pointed projection of
   Compton Beauchamp parish, v. map and cf. n. 1.
19 'the north part of the pool cleared of bushes', v. mere; 'cleared
   of bushes' is the translation suggested BTSuppl s.v. hnot. DEPN,
   s.n. Nottington, suggest a pers.n. Hnotta from hnot 'bald-headed',
   but an adj. seems suitable for the ns. listed 780.
20 'ditch', perhaps one of the drainage channels which occur in the
   N. of the parish.
21 'the north part of Bula's mead', v. map. bulan mæd occurs in both
   the Woolstone surveys, and in the Uffington ones. It must have
   been a long meadow in the N. of both parishes.
22 'bramble corner', v. brembel, hyrne, this corresponds to 'bramble
   thicket' in II, v. p. 683, n. 12.
23 'stone pool', also in II, p. 683, n. 11; the name occurs as Stanmere
   in 1241, v. Pt 2 384.
24 'heathen burials', also in II, p. 683, n. 9.
25 'Ock', v. Pt 1 14–15. A branch of the Ock rises at the base of the
   hollow called The Manger, and flows through the N. of the parish;
   the division between the two Woolstone estates evidently followed
   this stream, which must have been regarded as the source of the
   Ock, as it was in the 18th century, v. Pt 2 384.
26 'source of the stream', v. æwylm and map. It is called ocenne
   wyllas in II, p. 682, n. 7.
27 'Weard's barrow', v. beorg, also in II, v. p. 681, n. 15.
28 'ring pit', i.e. The Manger, v. map. This name occurs also in the
   East Woolstone and one of the Uffington surveys (II, V), and there
   is no doubt that it refers to the impressive hollow N. of Uffington
   Castle. The two Woolstone surveys go along the W. side of the
   feature, the Uffington one along the E.

29 'old hollows', *v.* **eald, hol**[1], possibly chalkpits, but II has *foxhola*
   'fox's earths' in the same position, *v. infra*, n. 3.

30 'the south part of the gore', cf. n. 1. If this is the same boundary-
   mark as 1, it appears to be misplaced; it should have come after
   31 and 32.

31 'Tættuca's stone'; since this occurs in the East Woolstone and
   Uffington surveys also, the three estates must have run to a point
   there, *v.* map. The name occurs as *Tottingestone* in a document of
   c. 1220–30 relating to Uffington, *v.* Pt 2 381.

32 'old ditch', this is the starting point of the survey of East Woolstone (II), but the two surveys must have touched the ditch at
   different points.

C II THE BOUNDS OF EAST WOOLSTONE: 958
(12TH) BCS 902

Ærest on þa ealdan dic[1] andlang hlincæs[2] on þa foxhola[3]. þanon on
hringpyt[4]. of þam pytæ on weardæs beorh[5]. þonon on þonæ smalan
cumb[6] andlang cumbæs on ocenne wyllas[7]. And lang streamæs on þa
mylne[8]. þonne wænt hit þær up on þone æþænan byrigels[9]. þonon and
lang þæs grænan weges[10] on stan mære[11] þo non to þam bræmbel
þyfelan[12]. þanon on ða mæd norðe weardæ[13] on þone þorn[14] þonnæ
and lang wæges[15] on þonæ ællen stub[16]. þonon utt on baccan mor[17].
þæt imbutæ þonæ mor on bulan mædæ norðæ weardæ[18] on þa dic.[19]
þonnæ utt on þonæ mære[20]. þonon upp on þa and heafda[21] on þonæ
þorn[22]. of þæm þornæ þonnæ on þonæ pyt[23]. þonon on æceles beorh
ufæ wæardnæ[24] of æceles beorgæ a bæ ecgæ[25] on þonnæ beorg[26]. of
þam beorgæ in on þæt norþ geatt[27]. þo non on þæt suð geat[28]. þær utt
andlang dic[29] on scortan dic[30]. þo non on hean dunæ ufæ wæardræ[31]
on þonæ beorh[32] of þam beorgæ on þonæ oþærne[33] þonnæ on tæt
tucæn stan[34] of þam stanæ on þa ealdan dic[1] þær hit ær onfænc.

NOTES

1 *v. supra*, n. 32.
2 'linchet', *v.* 627.
3 *v. supra*, n. 29.
4 *v.* p. 681, n. 28.
5 *v.* p. 681, n. 27.
6 'narrow valley', *v.* smæl, cumb.
7 'Ock springs', now Woolstone Wells, *v.* p. 681, n. 26.

8 'mill', *v.* **myln**; there is a modern mill on this stream (*v.* map), and assuming that the 10th-cent. mill was in the same position, this is where the boundary between the two Woolstone estates leaves the stream.

9 *v.* p. 681, n. 24.

10 'green way', *v.* **grēne¹, weg.**

11 *v.* p. 681, n. 23.

12 'bramble bushes', *v.* **þȳfel**; this corresponds to 'bramble corner' in I, p. 681, n. 22.

13 'the north part of the meadow'.

14 'thorn'.

15 'way'.

16 'elder stump', *v.* **ellern, ellen, stubb.**

17 'Bacca's marsh', *v.* map; this is mentioned also in the bounds of Shellingford (IX), and the modern Bagmore Brook, Pt **1** 7, is named from it. The survey probably turns S. at this point.

18 'the north part of Bula's meadow', *v.* p. 681, n. 21.

19 'ditch', *v.* **dīc.**

20 'pool', *v.* **mere** and p. 690, n. 8.

21 'headlands', *v.* 626; this feature occurs also in V, p. 690, n. 6.

22 'thorn'.

23 'pit', probably the Manger, *v.* p. 681, n. 28.

24 'the top of *eceles* barrow', *v.* **beorg**; this is probably Dragon Hill Pt **2** 379, *v.* map and cf. p. 688, n. 34. Dragon Hill is a natural feature, but the top has been flattened, and it is presumably connected with the complex of natural and artificial features comprising Uffington Castle, the White Horse and The Manger. *eceles* could be the gen. of a pers.n., or it could be **eclēsia**, the British word for a Christian church which occurs in a number of English p.ns.

25 'always along the edge' is an excellent description of the boundary from Dragon Hill to Uffington Castle.

26 'barrow', *v.* **beorg** and map. There is a large tumulus above the modern track round White Horse Hill, above the steep part of the slope into The Manger.

27 'north gate', i.e. of Uffington Castle, *v.* p. 688, n. 31.

28 'south gate'.

29 'ditch'; this is the 'long ditch' of IV (p. 688, n. 30).

30 'short ditch', *v.* p. 688, n. 29.

31 'the top of the high hill', v. hēah, dūn; this is probably where the O.S. maps mark the spot height 782.

32 'barrow', v. p. 688, n. 26.

33 'the other (barrow)', v. p. 688, n. 25.

34 v. p. 682, n. 31.

C III THE BOUNDS OF HARDWELL: 903 (c. 1200)
BCS 601

Ærest on spinbroc[1]. þæt up of spinbroce in on riscslæd[2]. of þes riscsledes byge[3] foran on gean hordwylles weg[4]. þæt andlang þæs weges oð hit cymð to Icenhilde wege[5]. þon' of ðæm wege up on þone ealdan wudu weg[6]. þon' of þæm wudu wege be eastan telles byrg[7] on ænne garan[8]. þon' of þæm garan on ænne gar æcer[9]. þæt andlanges þere furh[10] to anum andheafdum[11] to anre forierðæ[12]. and sio forierð gæð in to þam lande[13]. þon' on gerihte to þam stane on hrig weg[14]. þon' west on anne garan[15] andlanges þære furh[16] to anum anheafodum[17]. þon' of dune on fearnhilles sled[18]. þæt þon' on ane furh an æcer near þæm hlince. þon' on ðone hlinc[19]. þæt of þam hlince on oðærne hlinc æt fearnhylles slæde suðæweardre[20]. of þam hlince on anum heafde[21]. forð þær on ane furh[22] on ane stanræwe[23]. þonon on gerihte on hricg weg[24]. þæt þanone on anne gar æcer[25] on an on hæfde[26]. and se gar æcer in on þæt land[13]. þonone andlanges anre fyrh[27] oð hit cymð to anum byge[28]. þanone of þæm byge forð on ane fyrh[29] oð hit cymð to anre forierðe[30]. and sio forierð in to þam lande[13]. þon' on Icenhilde weg be tellesburh westan[31]. þon' norð ofer Icenhilde weg on sicanwylle[32]. þæt þwures ofer an furlang[33] on gerihte on an ælrbed[34] on hæg hylles broces byge[35]. andlang þæs broces oð hit cymð to twam gar æceron[36]. and þa gar æceras inon þæt land[13]. þon' on ane forierðe[37] on anan heafde[38]. þon' on gerihte on readan clif[39] on spinbroc[1]. þon' andlang þæs broces on þæt riscslæd[2].

NOTES

1 *spinbroc* is an error for *swinbroc*, v. p. 681, n. 15 and map.

2 'rush hollow', v. p. 681, n. 14.

3 v. p. 681, n. 14.

4 'Hardwell way', v. map and p. 681, n. 13.

5 'Icknield Way', v. map and Pt I 5.

6 'old wood way', v. eald, wudu, weg.

7 'east of Tell's camp' (now called Hardwell Camp), *v.* map and Pt 2 361.

8 'gore', *v.* 626.

9 'gore-shaped acre', *v.* 626.

10 'furrow', *v.* 627.

11 'headland', *v.* 626.

12 I consider *forierð* to mean 'projecting piece of ploughland', *v.* 626.

13 The phrases 'gæð in to þam lande', 'in on þæt land' are applied twice in this survey to the feature called a *forierð*, and twice to a *gar æcer*. I take the meaning to be 'belongs to the estate', indicating that the boundary runs outside the features.

14 'the stone on Ridge Way', *v.* map.

15 'gore', *v.* 626.

16 'furrow', *v.* 627.

17 'headland', *v.* 626.

18 'valley of the ferny hill', *v.* fearn, hyll, -es[2], slæd and map. The S.E. part of the boundary of Compton Beauchamp runs along a valley between Woolstone Down and Odstone Down, one of which was presumably called *Fearnhyll* in the 10th cent.

19 'then to a furrow an acre nearer the linchet, then to the linchet', *v.* hlinc and 627.

20 'the other linchet at the south part of the valley of the ferny hill', *v.* map; this is possibly the bank marked on O.S. maps as running along the boundary between Compton Beauchamp and Woolstone.

21 'headland', *v.* 626.

22 'furrow', *v.* 627.

23 'row of stones', *v.* stān, ræw.

24 'Ridge Way'.

25 'gore acre', *v.* 626.

26 'headland', *v.* 626.

27 'furrow', *v.* 627.

28 'bend', presumably some feature of the cultivation strips.

29 'furrow', *v.* 627.

30 *v.* n. 12 *supra*. There is a footpath N. of the Ridge Way leading towards Hardwell Camp which may follow the boundary of this survey from 25 to 30. This has been marked on the map.

31 'west of Tell's camp', *v.* n. 7 *supra*.

32 'Sica's spring'; this will be one of the springs S. of Hardwell Fm, *v.* map.

33 'crosswise over a furlong', v. 626–7.
34 'alder bed', v. alor, bedd.
35 'bend of the brook of the enclosed hill', v. (ge)hæg, hyll, brōc; one of the streams N.W. of Hardwell Fm must have had this name.
36 'two gore acres', v. 626.
37 v. n. 12 supra.
38 'headland', v. 626.
39 'red river-bank', v. rēad, clif.

C IV   THE BOUNDS OF UFFINGTON: N.D. (?p. 953)
        (c. 1200) BCS 687

Ærest of hwyresmere¹. andlang þare lace². in to þare blachelace³. of þere blace lace. innan bulemere⁴. Of bulemere. to buleferðes steorte⁵. Of þam steorte. in to bulen dic⁶. Andlang bulendic. in to ðam þorn stybbe⁷. Of þam þorn stybbe. in to þere halige stowe⁸. Of þere halige stowe. andlang þere heafde⁹. in to ikenilde streate¹⁰. of ikenilde strete. in to ægelwardes mearce¹¹. Of ægelwardes mearce. upprihtes be þam heafde¹². in to hremmesbyriges norðgeate¹³. þurhut þa byrig¹⁴. ut æt þam suðgeate¹⁵. Suðrihte be þam heafde¹⁶. uppen hodes hlæwe¹⁷. Of hodes hlæwe. uppan þa stanhlæwe¹⁸. Of þære stanhlæwe. innan þam hwitan hole¹⁹. Of þam hwitan hole. in to þam readan hole.²⁰ Of þam readan hole. in to þam dunnan hole²¹. Of þam dunan hole. in to dunferðes hnesse²². Of dunferðes hnesse. in to paddebyrig²³. Of paddebyrig. in to Tædduces stane²⁴. Of Tædduces stane. in to hundeshlæwe²⁵. Of hundeshlæwe. in to hafeces hlæwe²⁶. Of hafeces hlæwe. in to þam stodfalde²⁷. Of þam stodfalde. uppan lauercebyrig²⁸. Of lauercebyrig. into sceorten dic²⁹. Of sceorten dic. in to langen dic³⁰. Of lange dic. in to æscæsbyriges suðgeate³¹. and swa ut æt þam norðgeate³². Of þam norðgeate middan. uppan duddenbyrig³³. Of dudden byrig. uppan eceles beorh³⁴. hwyrt ofer dunrihtes in to ikenilde stret³⁵. Syððenes dunrihtes be þes heafd æceres west furh³⁶. dun ofer þa þwyrs furh³⁷. dun rihtes to þam riscbedde³⁸. Of þam hriscbedde. to þam dyrne stane³⁹. Of þam dirne stane. to þam hriscþyfele⁴⁰. of þam hriscþyfele. in to hlippem ham⁴¹. Of hlippen ham. in to þam myle streame⁴². Of þam myle streame. innan þa norðlange dic⁴³. andlanges þurh þa smala þornas⁴⁴. innan bulemed⁴⁵. ofer þa clene med⁴⁶. Of þa clene med. nordward. east rihtes be norðe mordune⁴⁷. on þene grene weig⁴⁸. Of þam grene weige þwyrt ofer þene mor. ⁴⁹. innan þwyrsmere¹ midrihtes.

NOTES

1 *þwyrsmere* at the end of the survey, 'crosswise pool', *v.* mere. For the use of *þwyrs* as first el. of p.ns. Professor Löfvenberg compares the occurrence of *up* and *ūt* as first els. of OE compound nouns. Cf. also n. 37 *infra*. The 'crosswise pool' was probably at the N.E. corner of Uffington parish.

Professor Löfvenberg points out that the adverbs *dunrihtes*, *midrihtes* used in these bounds are not mentioned in the OE dictionaries.

2 'stream', *v.* lacu.

3 'black stream', *v.* blæc, lacu.

4 'Bula's pool', *v.* mere.

5 *v.* steort 'tongue of land'. No. V has *æþelferþes mearce* in this region, and *buleferðes* may be a corruption of *æðelferðes*.

6 'Bula's ditch', also in VI, *v.* p. 692, n. 15.

7 'thorn stump', *v.* þorn, stybb.

8 'holy place', *v.* hālig; stōw often refers to a Christian church or monastery in p.ns. This boundary-mark was near Fawler Pt 2 372–3, where (since the name means 'paved floor') there may have been a Roman building, but nothing is known which would account for the term *hālige stōwe*.

9 'headland', *v.* 626.

10 Icknield Street, *v.* map.

11 'Ægelweard's boundary', cf. p. 690, n. 18.

12 'headland', *v.* 626.

13 'the north gate of Raven's Camp.' This is the outer of the two Iron Age camps on Rams Hill, *v.* map. The modern name only preserves the first part of the Old English name, which should have become *Ramsbury*, as in Ramsbury W; there is another modern example in Bucklebury, Pt 1 155, and an ancient one in Ashbury, p. 696, n. 35.

14 'through the camp', *v.* burh.

15 'out at the south gate', *v.* sūð, geat.

16 'headland', *v.* 626.

17 'Hod's tumulus', *v.* hlǣw; *hodan hlæw* in VI, *v.* p. 691, n. 8, corresponds to this but has a weak form of the pers.n.; the O.S. air-photograph mosaic shows a faint mark south of Rams Hill which could be the remains of this tumulus.

18 'stone tumulus', *v.* stān, hlǣw; as pointed out by Tengstrand

(63), the fem. gender of *stanhlæwe* is unexpected. VI has *bradan stanas* in this position.

19 'white hollow', *v.* hwīt, hol[1].
20 'red hollow', *v.* rēad, hol[1].
21 'dark hollow', *v.* dunn, hol[1].
22 'Dunfriđ's headland', *v.* næss.
23 'toad camp', *v.* padde, burh, presumably a vanished earthwork on the S. boundary of the parish.
24 *v.* p. 682, n. 31. The name occurs in a variant form in this survey, but there is little doubt that it is the same boundary-mark.
25 'hound's tumulus', *v.* hund, hlǣw.
26 'hawk's tumulus', *v.* hafoc, hlǣw, now known as Idlebush Barrow, *v.* map; the two tumuli are still visible. The names given them in the survey are probably nicknames, hound and hawk being thought of as things that went together.
27 'stud-fold', *v.* stōd-fald; the name occurs as *Statfold* t. Eliz, *Stutfall Grounds* 1611–12, *v.* Pt **2** 381.
28 'lark camp', *v.* lāwerce, burh; this corresponds to the 'high hill' of II, p. 684, n. 31.
29 'short ditch', *v.* sceort, dīc; a ditch is shown on O.S. maps at right angles to the parish boundary, *v.* map.
30 'long ditch', *v.* lang, dīc; there is a low cliff, probably geological, running alongside the parish boundary for about 700 yards, *v.* map. The surveyor may have taken this for one side of a ditch. The two ditches of 30 and 31 are mentioned also in II, p. 683, nn. 29, 30.
31 'the south gate of Æsc's camp.' *Æscesbyrig* is Uffington Castle, *v.* map. The boundary between Uffington and Woolstone, which now makes a detour round the camp, went through it until the Enclosure Act of 1777, when the camp became part of Uffington. The three estates of I, II, IV and V were all called *Æscesbyrig* until c. 955.
32 'out at the north gate.'
33 Literally 'Dudda's camp', but *byrig* may be a mistake for beorg; II has beorg at this point (p. 683, n. 26), and there is a tumulus in the right position.
34 Dragon Hill, *v.* p. 683, n. 24.
35 Icknield Street, *v.* map. hwyrt is an error for þwyrt. Professor Löfvenberg suggests that the form with -t is due to ON influence (ON þvert by the side of þvers).

36 'west furrow of the head acre', v. 627.

37 'crosswise furrow', cf. n. 1. *þwyresfura* is recorded in OE as a variant of *þwyrhfero*, v. BT s.v. *þweorh-furh* and 627.

38 'rush-bed', v. risc, bedd.

39 'hidden stone', v. dyrne, stān.

40 'rush thicket', v. risc, þȳfel.

41 Second element hamm 'meadow', the first is obscure, but cf. *lippan dic* Pt 2 461.

42 'mill stream', v. myln, strēam, probably the 'Ock' of I and II. There is a modern mill on this stream, v. map and p. 683, n. 8.

43 'northward ditch.'

44 'narrow thorns', v. smæl, þorn.

45 v. p. 681, n. 21.

46 'clean meadow', v. clǣne, mǣd.

47 'hill in marshland', v. mōr, dūn and map; the n. occurs as *Moredowne* 1569, Pt 2 381, and the hill is called Alfred's Hill on the O.S. maps. The p.n. occurs elsewhere as Morden, Mordon.

48 'green way', v. grēne¹, weg.

49 'marsh', v. mōr; Moor Hill (v. map) is named from this marsh.

CV THE BOUNDS OF UFFINGTON: 953 (c. 1240)
   BCS 899

Ærest in æt þam suð geate¹ and ut æt þan norþ geate² on dude beorh³ and þanne on eceles beorh⁴. and þanne on hring pit⁵. and þanne on þa and heafdu⁶. and þanne on þa cealc seaþas⁷ and þanon on þone bradan meare⁸ and þanon and lang dices⁹ on clǣnan mǣde¹⁰ and þanne on þone bradan weg¹¹ on butan mor dune¹² on ðyre ses lace¹³ and þanon on læcesmere norþe wearde¹⁴ and þanne and lang mores¹⁵ be þan norþ stane¹⁶ and þanne þwyres ofer þone mor¹⁵ on bulan dic¹⁷ and swa andlang dices to æþel ferðes mearce¹⁸. on bulen dices ende on þone þorn styb¹⁹. and þanne on talleburnan²⁰ and þonon to þære halgan stowe²¹ and sua up andlang broces²². to aþelferðes mearce¹⁸ weste wearde and swa andlang mearce to hremnes byrig²³ to þan norþ geate and ut æt þan suþ geate²⁴ on hodan hlǣw²⁵ and þanne on stan hlǣwan²⁶ and þanne to þan redan hole²⁷ and þanne to þan dunnan-hole²⁸ and swa be þan hlide²⁹ and þanne on dom ferðes hest³⁰ on tæt taces stan³¹ and þanne on hundes hlǣw³² and þanne on hafoces hlǣw³³. and þanne on þone scortan dic³⁴. and þanne on þa langen dic³⁵ to æscesbyris³⁶ eft to þan su þan geate.

1 *v.* p. 688, n. 31.

2 *v.* p. 688, n. 32.

3 *v.* p. 688, n. 33.

4 *v.* p. 688, n. 34.

5 *v.* p. 681, n. 28.

6 *v.* p. 683, n. 21.

7 'chalkpits', *v.* sēað; other accounts of this boundary, in II and IV, do not mention these.

8 'broad pool'; this is *mære* in II, *v.* p. 683, n. 20.

9 'ditch', also in II.

10 *v.* p. 689, n. 46.

11 'broad way', *v.* brād, weg; the other surveys of this boundary do not mention this.

12 *v.* p. 689, n. 47.

13 lacu 'stream' is here compounded with an obscure first el.; this feature and 14 do not appear in other accounts of the N. boundary of Uffington.

14 'the north part of the pool of the bog (or of the leech)', *v.* læce, lǣce[2], mere, and cf. Lashford Pt **2** 444.

15 'along the marsh', this area was called *baccan mor*, *v.* map and Pt **1** 7.

16 'north stone', not in IV.

17 *v.* p. 687, n. 6.

18 'Æðelfrið's boundary'; he was presumably the owner at this time of the estate given to Æðelsige in VI. This is 'Ægelweard's boundary' in IV.

19 *v.* p. 687, n. 7.

20 *v.* p. 692, n. 12.

21 *v.* p. 687, n. 8.

22 *v* brōc, this is called *stream* in VI.

23 *v.* p. 687, n. 13.

24 *v.* p. 687, n. 15.

25 *v.* p. 687, n. 17.

26 *v.* p. 687, n. 18.

27 *v.* p. 697, n. 20.

28 *v.* p. 687, n. 21.

29 *v.* hlid[1] 'slope'; the boundary follows the 600' contour for a stretch.

30 A corrupt version of *dunferðes hnesse* in IV, *v.* p. 688, n. 22.
31 *v.* p. 688, n. 24.
32 *v.* p. 688, n. 25.
33 *v.* p. 688, n. 26.
34 *v.* p. 688, n. 29.
35 *v.* p. 688, n. 30.
36 *v.* p. 688, n. 31.

C VI THE BOUNDS OF THE WESTERN PART OF KINGSTON LISLE: 963 (C. 1200) BCS 1121

Ærest æt sunemannes wyrðige[1]. of þam wyrðige on gerihte on þa heafod stoccas[2]. of þam heafod stoccum on þone rugan hlinc niðæwearde[3]. þon' on gerihte on bryxstanes garan suðeweardon[4]. of þam garan on duddes dene[5]. of ðære dene on þone ealdan garan suðeweardan[6]. þonon on gerihte on ða bradan stanas[7]. of ðam stanum on hodan hlæw[8]. of þam hlæwe on hremmesbyrig westeweardon[9]. of hremmesbyrig on leacumb[10]. þon' rihte andlang streames[11]. þæt on tealeburnan[12]. andlang tealeburnan þæt on þa riðe[13]. andlang riðe on þone ðornstyb[14] on bulan dic[15]. andlang dices on ðes cincges scypene[16]. of þam scypenum on þæt riscbed[17]. of ðam riscbedde on ðees cincges þornas[18]. þon' on gerihte on þæt bean furlang[19]. þon' on hsnelles ufeweardan. of snelles hlince[20] þæt eft on sunemannes weorðig[1]. And þer hyrð in an hyrde wic æt baþalacing. and an hid landes. and. xii æceres mede. and an myln æt hyrde grafe. and. xii. æceres landes[21].

NOTES

1 'Suneman's enclosure or farm', *v.* worðig.
2 'head stumps', other instances occur in the bounds of East Hanney (p. 743, n. 2), and Oare (p. 656, n. 5).
3 'the lower part of the rough linchet', *v.* rūh, hlinc.
4 'the south part of Beorhtstān's gore', *v.* 626.
5 'Dudd's valley', *v.* denu.
6 'the south part of the old gore', *v.* 626.
7 'broad stones', *v.* p. 687, n. 18.
8 *v.* p. 687, n. 17.
9 'the west part of Raven's Camp', *v.* p. 687, n. 13, and map.
10 Second el. cumb 'valley'. The first el. is lēah, which can mean 'wood' or 'clearing'; the former is possibly more likely here. The valley (S. of Fawler) is wooded today.

11 'stream', *v.* strēam and map.

12 This is the old name of Stutfield Brook, Pt **1** 17, and occurs also in the bounds of Goosey, *v.* p. 745, n. 2. There must have been a stream near Fawler which was regarded as its head-stream, since comparison with the Uffington surveys makes it clear that this boundary-mark is on the W. boundary of Kingston Lisle, N. of Fawler.

13 'stream', *v.* rīð.

14 This and the next landmark occur also in the Uffington surveys, *v.* p. 687, n. 7.

15 *v.* p. 687, n. 6.

16 'king's cow-sheds', *v.* cyning, scypen.

17 'rush-bed', *v.* risc, bedd.

18 'king's thorns', *v.* þorn; the references to royal ownership in 16 and 18 should be connected with the name Kingston, 'royal estate', *v.* 679. It is not clear at what point the survey turns S.

19 'bean furlong', *v.* bēan, furlang.

20 'Snell's linchet', *v.* hlinc; the text is corrupt at the first mention of this.

21 These appurtenances of the estate are described also in the Latin charter, *v. supra* 677. The 'herdsmen's building' (*v.* hyrde, wīc) at Balking might be the predecessor of Hale Fm, *v.* map. *hyrde graf* (Hardgrove 1655) was in Steventon, *v.* Pt **2** 418.

C VII THE BOUNDS OF COMPTON BEAUCHAMP,
     EXCLUDING HARDWELL, 955 (C. 1240) BCS 908

Ærest of hricg wege[1] on þæt wide geat[2] of þan widan geate on æþelmes hlinc on forwerde dune[3] of æþelmes hlince on icen hilde weg[4]. of icenhilde wege on bican dic[5] of bicandice in on swyn broc[6]. of swyn broce on þone bradan þorn be westan mere[7] of þan þorne on þa readan dic[8] and lang þære dic on hildes hlæw[9]. of hildes hlæwe on blæc pytt[10]. of blæc pytte andlanges þære westran risc ræwe[11] innan swynbroc[12] of swynbroce on read[13]. of ræde on hwittuces hlæwe[14] on icen hilde weg[15]. of icenhilde weg on mæres crundel[16]. of mæres crundelle on dinra beorh[17]. of dinra beorge on hricg weg[18] of hricg wege on fearn hylles slæd[19]. of fearn hylles slade to hæsl hylle suþe weardre[20]. of hæsl hylle west on þone grenan weg[21] andlang weges to þære gedrifonan fyrh[22] andlang fyrh oþ hit cymð on þæt wide geat[2] be eastan welandes smidðan[23].

NOTES

1 Ridge Way, *v.* map; the survey starts on the W. boundary of Compton Beauchamp parish.

2 'wide gate', *v.* wīd, geat; this may be identical with the *widen yate* in Ashbury, p. 696, n. 33. The term also occurs in Appleford (p. 755, n. 3). The meaning is uncertain, but it may describe some feature of the field-system.

3 'Æðelhelm's linchet on the front part of the down', *v.* hlinc. The O.S. maps show banks along the parish boundary on the escarpment here, *v.* map.

4 Icknield Way, *v.* map.

5 'Bica's ditch', *v.* dīc.

6 'pig stream', *v.* swīn², brōc; this is the stream which occurs again in n. 12 *infra*, and in the West Woolstone and Uffington surveys (p. 681, n. 15). The present boundary-mark is near Compton Marsh Fm (*v.* map), indicating that the stream rose to the S.W. of the farm.

7 'the broad thorn west of the pool', *v.* brād, þorn, mere; the charter surveys mention a number of pools in the N. of this group of parishes.

8 'red ditch', *v.* rēad, dīc.

9 'Hild's tumulus', *v.* hlǣw. This was the meeting-place of *Hildeslowe* Hundred, the S. part of the Hundred of Shrivenham, *v.* Pt 2 343.

10 Probably 'black pit', *v.* blæc, pytt.

11 'the more westerly row of rushes', *v.* risc, rǣw.

12 'pig stream', *v.* map and cf. n. 6 *supra*. The survey is now travelling S. down the middle of Compton Beauchamp parish.

13 The Hardwell survey has *readan clif* in this position, *v.* p. 686, n. 39. The text of the present survey is corrupt here.

14 'Hwittuc's tumulus', *v.* hlǣw.

15 Icknield Way, *v.* map.

16 'chalkpit by the boundary', *v.* (ge)mǣre, crundel.

17 'barrow of coins', perhaps a tumulus where coins, or some objects resembling coins, had been found, *v.* beorg, first el. OE *dīnor*. Alternatively the reference could be to a natural hill where a hoard of Roman coins was found.

18 Ridge Way, *v.* map.

19 'valley of the ferny hill'; this is mentioned also in the Hardwell

survey (p. 685, n. 18), but as a landmark on the E. side of the Hardwell estate. The present survey must touch the valley on its western side.

20 'the south part of hazel hill', v. hæsel, hyll.

21 'green way', v. grēne[1], weg.

22 'driven furrow', v. 627. This must have been on the stretch of boundary leading up to the Ridge Way, where there is now a prominent ridge to be seen.

23 'east of Wayland's Smithy' (Pt 2 347), v. map for the position of this neolithic burial-place.

C VIII THE BOUNDS OF ASHBURY: 947 (14TH) BCS 828 (GLASTONCH p. 687)

Erest of Buckansticke[1] west on Buckanmer'[2] to þan Ruancrundele[3] þanon mide ward Burnestowe[4] to þan stone[5] þanen west endlang-smaleweyes[6] on þare crundel[7] bi est' þa Ertheburgh'[8] and so north on riȝt to Hordenestone[9] þane to elden berwe[10] and so endlangdiches[11] north to þan Whytestone[12] þanen to þan stanberwe[13] þare þanen to þe litel berwe[14] þanen endelangmeres[15] to Middildych[16] þanen north to riȝt weye on þan ston on midderiȝtweyes[17] an so to Loppancomb' overward[18] þar forth endlangfurth[19] on riȝt to Merewelle[20] endlang-stremes to Folanruwers[21] over þan ridde[22] to þan stone whytoute þar Irwelond'[23] þar forth to þan beche[24] þanen to Piwanmer'[25] of Piwan-mer on Lippanstubbe[26] þar on Kinggesdych[27] endlangdych to Melanbrok'[28] of Milanbrok' on Lortanbrock'[29] þanen on Lortan-berwe[30] so up endlangfurtz[31] to Mereberwe[32] þanen out to þan wydem yate[33] of þan ȝate to þan horestonford'[34] to Rammesbury[35] yate of Rammesbury so forth endlangweyes to Buckanstick'[1].

NOTES

1 First el. the pers.n. *Bucca*; for the second Professor Löfvenberg suggests sticca 'stick', perhaps used of a tree-trunk. The text of these bounds has been 'modernised' by the 14th-cent. scribe, and is corrupt in a number of places.

2 'Bucca's pool'; v. mere[1]; Crawford, p. 125, describes the site of a pond on Fognam Down at Lambourn Corner, which may be this one.

3 'rough chalkpit', v. rūh, crundel.

4 Possibly 'bathing place', *v.* p. 654, n. 31. There is a valley at
 the S.W. corner of Ashbury parish down which a stream may at
 one time have flowed, *v.* map.

5 'stone', *v.* stān.

6 'along the narrow way', *v.* smæl, weg.

7 'chalkpit', *v.* crundel.

8 'east of the earthwork', *v.* eorðburh; the W. boundary of Ashbury
 does not pass E. of any surviving earthwork, and *est'* may be an
 error for *west'*.

9 '*hordene* stone'; the first el. is obscure.

10 'old barrow', *v.* (e)ald, beorg; this may be *Oldebury*, mentioned
 in 1519, Pt 2 350.

11 'along the ditch', *v.* dīc.

12 'white stone', *v.* hwīt, stān.

13 'stone barrow', *v.* stān, beorg.

14 'little tumulus', *v.* lȳtel, beorg.

15 'along the boundary', *v.* (ge)mære.

16 'middle ditch', *v.* middel, dīc; none of the archaeological features
 mentioned in 10, 11, 13 and 16 is marked on the O.S. maps, but
 perambulation might reveal faint traces of some of them.

17 'north to the Ridge Way to the stone in the middle of the
 Ridge Way'; *riȝt weie* is probably a corrupt copying of *hrycg
 wege*.

18 'the upper part of Loppa's valley', *v.* cumb; the W. boundary of
 Ashbury touches the head of a valley just N. of the Ridge Way,
 v. map.

19 'furrow', *v.* 627.

20 'boundary stream', *v.* (ge)mære, w(i)ell and map. There is a
 stream which rises just N. of the Icknield Way and flows along the
 boundary for some distance. The 1519 survey (*v.* n. 10 *supra*)
 mentions *Marewell* and *Marwellfurlong*.

21 This term is corrupt.

22 This might be a corruption of ryde 'clearing', or rīð 'stream'.

23 'the stone outside the ploughed land'; *Irwelond'* is miscopied
 from *irþland*.

24 'stream valley', *v.* bece[1].

25 This term is corrupt.

26 'Lippa's tree-stump', *v.* stubb.

27 'king's ditch'; the name Kingstone Winslow (*v.* map) denotes a
 royal estate.

28 'mill-stream'; probably the stream which flows through Shrivenham, and is called *mylen broc* in the Watchfield survey, *v.* p. 698, n. 4 and map.

29 'Lorta's brook'; the name is probably connected with Lertwell S.W. of Ashbury village, *v.* map and Pt 2 346. The stream which rises there joins the one described in 28.

30 'Lorta's hill or tumulus', *v.* beorg.

31 'along the furrow', *v.* 627.

32 'boundary hill or tumulus', *v.* (ge)mǣre, beorg.

33 'wide gate'; assuming that this survey describes the whole of Ashbury parish, this will be identical with *wide geat* in the Compton Beauchamp survey, p. 693, n. 2.

34 'boundary stone', *v.* hār, stān, followed by the word *forð* 'forward'.

35 'raven's camp'; the name is identical with that of the camp on Rams Hill, p. 687, n. 13. Assuming that the survey is here travelling down the S.E. boundary of Ashbury, the 'raven's camp' is likely to be on Weathercock Hill. The hill is not actually fortified, but there are two large strip linchets on the E. side of it, which could be mistaken for ramparts. Grundy noted an 'unfinished camp' here, and he (and the Anglo-Saxons) could have been misled by these linchets.

C IX THE BOUNDS OF SHELLINGFORD: 931 (C. 1200) BCS 684

Ærest on eoccen æt sandfordinga gemære[1]. swa ut on gean stream[2] to snitan ige. on norðhealfe þæs igeðes[3]. and swa on baccan mor middeweardne[4]. swa andlang mores on fisclace[5] innan crypeles heale[6]. and þæt andlang fearnbroces[7]. þæt hit sticað up on þa readan dic[8]. swa andlang dic þæt on hlydan[9]. andlang hlydan on bradan mor[10]. Of bradan more to preosthamme[11] up on myos wyllan[12]. of myos wyllen on þene hricg weg[13]. andlang hrycgeweges to þam cristes mæle[14]. þon' suð þæt hit sticoð eft on Eoccen þæt hit onfeng.

NOTES

1 'River Ock at the boundary of the people of Stanford'; *sandfordinga* is an obvious error for *stanfordinga*, Stanford being the adjacent parish to the E.

2 'up-stream'.

3 'to the island of the snipe, to the northern side of the island', *v.* snīte, īeg, īgeð and map.

4 'to the middle of Bacca's marsh', *v.* map and p. 683, n. 17.

5 'fish stream', *v.* fisc, lacu and map.

6 'corner of the burrow', *v.* crypel, h(e)alh; *healh* may refer to the indentation in the S.W. boundary of Shellingford, *v.* map.

7 'fern stream', *v.* fearn, brōc and map, and cf. the name of the neighbouring parish Fernham Pt 2 371.

8 'red ditch', *v.* rēad, dīc; this must have been near the railway, at the S. end of Cole's Pits. The soil is very red on the W. side of the railway here, much less so on the E.

9 'the loud one'; this is a common stream-name, *v.* map. The name survives in Lyde Copse Pt 2 397.

10 'broad marsh', *v.* brād, mōr; this is near the area now called Kitemoor, *v.* map. The name occurs as Broadmoor in the *TA*.

11 'priest meadow', *v.* prēost, hamm.

12 'marsh spring or stream', *v.* mēos, w(i)ella; there is a tributary of the Ock N.E. of the boundary here, which may have risen a little further to the S.W., or there may have been a marshy hollow with a spring on top of the low hill near Bowling Green Fm.

13 'ridge way', *v.* map, obviously the road from Faringdon to Wantage, which forms the N. boundary of the parish.

14 'crucifix', OE *cristesmǣl*; *v.* map for probable position, where the boundary leaves the Faringdon–Wantage road.

CX THE BOUNDS OF WATCHFIELD: 931 (c. 1200)
BCS 675

Ærest on þone stan æt þam hæðenan byrgelsan[1]. þonne ut on pricelles hæssecas ufewearde[2]. þon' on cocbroc[3]. andlang streames. þæt on mylen broc[4]. þon' andlang streames. þæt on lentan[5]. þon' andlang streames. þæt on mærpol[6]. þon' of þam pole on bean broc[7]. þon' andlang streames on heafdon mere[8]. þon' of þam mere on þa lace þær þa brocas twisliað[9]. þon' of þam twislan[10]. on mærbeorh[11]. þon' of þam beorge on þone herpað[12]. þonon andlang hærpaðes. seofan and fiftig gyrda[13]. þon' andlang furh on þone stan beorh[14]. þon' of þam stan beorhe on þone hæðænan byrgels. eft to þam stane[1].

NOTES

1 'the stone at the heathen burial-places', *v.* stān, hǣðen, byrgels; the survey starts in the S.E. of Watchfield parish, and a modern housing estate occupies the probable area of the heathen burial-places.

2 'upper part of the tufts of coarse grass of the point', *v.* hassuc, and map for probable position. OE *pricel* seems to be used of the pointed indentation in the parish boundary.

3 'wild-bird stream', *v.* cocc², brōc and map.

4 'mill-stream', *v.* myln, brōc; probably the modern Tuckmill Brook, *v.* map. This may be the 'mill-stream' of the Ashbury survey, *v.* p. 696, n. 28.

5 *lenta* is the old name of the R. Cole, *v.* map and Pt 1 9.

6 'boundary pool', *v.* (ge)mǣre, pōl, presumably where the parish boundary leaves the Cole. The O.S. maps do not show a pool there now.

7 'bean brook', *v.* bēan, brōc.

8 Professor Löfvenberg suggests emendation to *on heafdo on mere* 'to the headlands situated on the pool'.

9 'to the stream where the brooks fork.' There are three stream-forks on the N. boundary of Watchfield now, but the drainage is likely to have altered.

10 'stream-fork', *v.* twisla, probably where the boundary turns S.

11 'boundary hill or tumulus', *v.* (ge)mǣre, beorg, possibly where the O.S. maps mark a spot height for 360' at an angle in the parish boundary, *v.* map.

12 'army-path', *v.* herepæð and map; this is the road from Faring-don to Shrivenham.

13 'fifty-seven yards along the army-path'; the modern boundary runs along the road for about this distance.

14 'along the furrow to the stone hill or tumulus', *v.* stān, beorg.

D GANFIELD AND OCK HUNDREDS

The area which comprises the S. bank of the R. Thames and the valley of the R. Ock is fairly well covered by surviving charter boundaries, all of which were copied into the Abingdon Chronicle, four of them only into the later MS. Most of the surveys relating to the Hundreds of Ganfield and Ock have been included in this group. They include one of Charney Bassett, published here for the first time, which cannot be linked with a surviving charter. The documents are –

I. The Bounds of Charney Bassett in *ClaudiusCix*. These occur on f. 198b of the MS, with the heading 'Termini. vii. mansarum apud Cernige'. In *ClaudiusCix* all the charter bounds are written at the end of the MS, dissociated from the Latin texts, which are copied into the narrative of the Chronicle. Charney is included in the list of the Abbey's lands in the forged charter of Coenwulf (BCS 366), but neither of the Abingdon cartularies has a specific grant to which these bounds might have been attached. They are not in *ClaudiusBvi*, and they have not previously been published. They describe the modern parish of Charney Bassett, and they are important for the correct identification of the stream which gave name to Charney and to Cherbury Camp.

II. BCS 1035, A.D. 958, an Abingdon charter, only copied in *ClaudiusBvi*, by which King Eadwig grants to Cenric 2 hides at *Cern*. Ekwall and Grundy considered this charter to refer to Charney Bassett, but this seems unlikely, as the bounds do not resemble I *supra*. The survey touches the stream called *cern* at two points, and as the only modern land-unit whose bounds do this is the parish of Pusey, it may be tentatively suggested that BCS 1035 refers to a small estate in the N. of Pusey. Four estates at Pusey are described in DB, and one of these belonged to Abingdon and was assessed at 2 hides.

III. BCS 1028, A.D. 958, an Abingdon charter, only copied in *ClaudiusBvi*, by which King Eadwig grants 20 hides at Longworth to Eadric. The bounds are headed 'þis sint þa land gemære æt wurþe þara þritiga hida', and it is probable that the '20 hides' in the charter text is a mistake. It is not certain whether the

bounds describe Longworth and Draycott Moor, or only Longworth. Grundy took them to refer only to Longworth, his reasons
being that the E. boundary has no marks in common with the
Kingston bounds (708 *infra*), and that Warnhill (formally identical
with *wærnan hyll*) is a modern f.n. on the E. boundary of Longworth. In spite of these points, it seems probable that Draycott
Moor is included in this survey. The E. boundary is specifically
said to be that of Kingston, and although Grundy meets this with
the suggestion that Draycott Moor was part of Kingston, its
historical associations are with Longworth (VCH IV, 466 f.).
There is nothing unnatural about the choice of different-
boundary marks in the Longworth and Kingston surveys. The
occurrence of Warnhill as a modern name on the E. boundary of
Longworth could be explained on the assumption that *wærnan hyll*
was the name of the whole ridge between the Thames and the Ock.

IV. BCS 1047, A.D. 959, for which v. 717. The estate at Longworth
is said to be 30 hides. The survey is more detailed than that in III,
but covers the same area.

V. KCD 1276, A.D. c. 977, an Abingdon charter, copied only in
ClaudiusBvi, by which King Eadweard grants 13 hides at Kingston to Bishop Ælfstan. The bounds describe the modern parish
of Kingston Bagpuize.

VI. KCD 1277, A.D. c. 977, a spurious Abingdon charter, copied in
both MSS, by which King Eadweard grants 7 hides at Kingston
to Abingdon. The bounds are identical with those in V, apart from
some differences in phrasing and spelling.

ClaudiusCix has a defective version of these bounds on f. 200.
One boundary mark is omitted. The heading states that these are
the bounds of the 13 hides at Kingston, but the final portion of
the survey has a separate heading stating that it is the bounds of
the 7 hides at Kingston. This confusion may be due to an attempt
to reconcile the two apparently incompatible charters, both of
which were copied into *Bvi*.

There is another Abingdon charter relating to a place called
Kingston, BCS 1260, A.D. 970, copied only in *ClaudiusBvi*, by
which King Eadgar grants 7 hides at Kingston to Brihtheah. This
has no bounds, and there is no reason why the Kingston bounds
in *ClaudiusCix* should belong to it, though they are printed after
it by Birch (BCS 1261). It is not certain that BCS 1260 refers to
Kingston Bagpuize.

BCS 1262 is an account, taken from the Abingdon Chronicle, of the purchase of 20 hides at Kingston by Abbot Osgar from Ealdorman Ælfhere, who inherited the estate from his brother, Ealdorman Ælfheah. *ClaudiusCix* has an Old English and a Latin version of this, *ClaudiusBvi* only the Latin one. The account is placed in the Chronicle immediately after the two Kingston charters, KCD 1276 and 1277, indicating that the authors believed it to relate to Kingston Bagpuize. The purchase is said to have been ratified at a great moot at Alderbury W, for which the list of people concerned indicates a date between 971 and 980. This moot is discussed by Sir Frank Stenton in HistAb 36–7. It is not certain that the estate was Kingston Bagpuize; Kingston Lisle is just as likely. At Kingston Bagpuize, DB describes two estates of 5 hides each TRE.

VII. BCS 977, A.D. 956, an Abingdon charter, copied only in *ClaudiusBvi*, by which King Eadwig grants 13 hides at Fyfield to Æðelnoð. The bounds describe the southern part of the modern parish.

VIII. BCS 1221, A.D. 968, an Abingdon charter, copied in both MSS of the Chronicle, by which King Eadgar grants 25 hides at Fyfield to Abingdon. There is another copy, of 16th-cent. date and probably from a contemporary parchment, in MS *C.C.C.C.cxi*, f. 167. The bounds describe the whole of the modern parish.

IX. BCS 1169, A.D. 965, an Abingdon charter, copied, with omission of the witnesses in *Cix*, in both MSS of the Chronicle, by which King Eadgar grants 50 hides at Marcham to the Abbey. The boundary-marks are widely spaced, but it seems probable that the accompanying survey describes the modern parishes of Marcham, Frilford and Tubney.

In *ClaudiusBvi* this charter is followed by the statement that 'Frileford, Appeltun, Leoie' were members of Marcham in King Edgar's time. It is not certain that the chronicler had any authority for this statement, and the survey attached to the Marcham charter certainly does not include Appleton and Bessels Leigh. The bounds which follow the statement in *ClaudiusBvi* are those of the woodland attached to Chilton (*v.* 767, n. 15), but the author has given them the heading *Metæ de Leia*, apparently on the erroneous assumption that they relate to Bessels Leigh.

X. BCS 761, A.D. 940, an Abingdon charter by which King Eadmund grants 15 hides at Garford to Wulfric. The charter is only copied in *ClaudiusBvi*, but *ClaudiusCix* has a copy of the bounds, which describe the modern parish of Garford.

XI. BCS 1032, A.D. 958, an Abingdon charter, by which King Eadwig grants 10 hides at Drayton to Eadweald. The charter is only copied in *ClaudiusBvi*, but the bounds occur also in *ClaudiusCix*. The area of the survey cannot be defined with certainty, but it is possible that it is the modern parish of Drayton, with the exclusion of Sutton Wick in the N.E., and of some land on the W. side.

XII. BCS 1058, A.D. 960, an Abingdon charter copied (with omission of the witnesses in *ClaudiusCix*) in both MSS of the Chronicle, by which King Eadgar grants 20 hides at Drayton to Abingdon. This charter contains a difficult sentence giving the former history of the estate. A possible interpretation would be that 10 out of the 20 hides were given to Eadweald by King Eadred, and that Eadweald decided on his deathbed to give these 10 hides to Abingdon. It is far from certain, however, that this is the meaning. The actual charter in favour of Eadweald (XI *supra*) is in the name of King Eadwig, but may be a confirmation of a grant by his predecessor, King Eadred. The bounds are identical with those of XI, with the addition of one boundary-mark. This extra mark possibly indicates the inclusion of the western part of the parish, which may be excluded by the earlier survey. Two later charters, KCD 1280 and 1294, deal with a small estate in Drayton and Sutton, given by King Æthelred to Wulfgar in 983, and by King Æthelred to Abingdon in 1000. There are no bounds, but this probably represents a temporary alienation from Abingdon of land included in the earlier Drayton grants. It seems likely that Sutton Wick is excluded by XI and XII. Though now part of Drayton parish, it must have had earlier connections with Sutton Courtenay.

XIII. BCS 935, A.D. 956, surviving in a contemporary parchment, by which King Eadwig grants 15 hides at Milton to Ælfwine. This charter was copied into both MSS of the Abingdon Chronicle. The bounds describe the modern parish of Milton.

XIV. BCS 1005, A.D. 957, an Abingdon charter, copied (with omission of most of the witnesses in *Cix*) in both MSS, by which King Eadwig grants 10 hides at Buckland to Ælfheah. The bounds cannot be related to the modern map. It is likely that they describe only part of the modern parish, as 10 hides is a low assessment, and there were several estates here in 1086.

XV. BCS 798, A.D. 944, an Abingdon charter, only copied in

ClaudiusBvi, by which King Eadmund grants 6 hides at Lyford to Ælfheah. This contains the statement ' Ðis sint þa landgemæro to Linforda; betweox eccene and cilla riþe'. *ClaudiusCix*, which does not include this charter, has a variant account of these bounds which runs 'Termini vi mansarum ad linford. Be tweox eoccene and cilla riðæ, synd þa land gemæro to linforda.' This perfunctory description probably refers to the area of the modern parish.

Four of these surveys (II, VII, XI, and XIV) describe only part of a modern parish, and the parishes concerned, Pusey, Fyfield, Drayton and Buckland, still contained more than one estate in 1086. Small estates appear to be characteristic of the area, but an exception is provided by Marcham (IX), the survey of which describes the modern parishes of Marcham, Frilford and Tubney. These had become separate estates by 1086, and Longworth and Draycott Moor, probably combined in the 10th-cent. surveys (III and IV) were also separately described in DB.

The description of areas smaller than the modern parish leads in some cases to serious difficulties in relating the bounds to the modern map. In the case of II and XIV, precise location has proved impossible.

There is little correspondence between the charter hidages of these estates and the assessments recorded in DB. Abingdon had a 2-hide estate at Pusey in 1086, which may be identical with the 2 hides described in II. On the whole, comparison of hidages in the charters and in DB suggests that assessments in this area had been reduced before the Conquest, and in some cases they were reduced again after the Conquest. Charney Bassett, 7 hides according to the heading of the Old English survey (I), contained two estates, both assessed at less than 1 hide TRE and in 1086. Fyfield (VIII), which was 25 hides in 968, contained two estates of 10 hides each TRE, one of which had been reduced to 5 hides before the Conquest. Garford (X) was 15 hides in 940, 10 hides TRE, and 6 in 1086. The situation in Marcham and Longworth is harder to judge because the charters probably deal with several estates described individually in DB; but the 50 hides of the Marcham charter (IX) can probably be set against a total of 31 hides TRE for Marcham, Frilford and Tubney, and Marcham itself had been reduced from 20 to 10 in 1086. It is not certain whether the Longworth charters (III and IV) include Draycott Moor: if so, the

30 hides of 958 and 959 had risen to 40 (30 for Longworth, 10 for Draycott Moor) TRE, but Longworth itself had been drastically reduced from 30 to 8 in 1086. Drayton (XII), which was 20 hides in 960, contains two estates in DB, one assessed at 2 hides TRE and nothing in 1086, the other at 3½ hides TRE and 1 hide in 1086. Milton (XIII) and Lyford (XV), however, provide an exception to this general reduction in hidage. Milton was 15 hides in 956, 28 TRE, and 23 in 1086, while Lyford, which was 6 hides in 944, contained two estates of 7 and 3 hides TRE and in 1086.

Several of these estates, especially those in the valley of the Ock, are defined by streams, which in some cases were also drainage channels. Some of the drainage ditches are fulfilling the same function today, the most striking instance being Mere Dike between Drayton and Steventon (p. 712, n. 5). Frequent references to streams and ditches make the survey of this area less informative than some others about vegetation and land use, but there are some references to arable farming. Arable land, which was evidently on the ridge between the valleys of the Thames and Ock, is mentioned in the surveys of Longworth, Kingston and Buckland, and there was a 'rye down' in Fyfield (p. 710, n. 10). The apparent survival till 1816 of the common land called *mænan mor* in Fyfield (p. 709, n. 3) is noteworthy. The area may have been less wooded than it is today. Two groves and one 'hanger' are mentioned, but a number of surveys refer to single trees as if these were an event in the landscape. Thorn-trees, perhaps deliberately planted as boundary-marks, are fairly common.

D I THE BOUNDS OF CHARNEY BASSETT IN
CLAUDIUSCIX

Ærest of eoccen[1] andlanges þara lace[2]. æt stanbrycge[3]. þon' of stanbrycge east andlang þære lace þæ scyt wið cerenburhg westan[4]. þonan norð andlang þære lace æt þam gemyðum[5]. of þam gemyþan andlang þære lace æt cerenforda[6]. of cerenforda andlang lace on eoccen[1]. þon' up andlang eoccen et landbroce[7]. þ' up andlang landbroces on þa mæd dic[8]. þon' up andlang dic. þ' eft on Eoccen[1].

NOTES

1 R. Ock. The ancient course may have been different from the modern one, *v.* p. 745, n. 3.
2 'stream', *v.* map.

3 'stone bridge', *v.* stān, brycg; this name has not survived, but the bridge was probably at the N.W. corner of the parish.

4 'east along the stream which flows past Cherbury from the west', *v.* map. *cerenburhg* is Cherbury Camp (Pt **2** 390).

5 'stream junction', *v.* (ge)mȳðe. This is probably near Race Fm, at the northern point of the parish, though this is actually the point where a stream forks, rather than a junction.

6 This ford may have been where the road from Charney to Longworth crosses the stream, *v.* map. This name and *cearna graf* which occurs in the bounds of Longworth (*v.* 707, n. 3) suggest that *cern* was the old name of the stream which rises N. of Pusey and flows past Race Fm to join the Ock N. of Lyford. For a discussion of the name *v.* Pt **2** 389.

7 Land Brook, *v.* map and Pt **1** 12–13. *et* should probably be *æt* 'to'.

8 'mead ditch', *v.* mǣd, dīc and map for approximate position.

D II THE BOUNDS OF TWO HIDES AT CERN: 958 (c. 1240) BCS 1035

ærest þære lund score broc scyt on cern[1]. þonen of land score broc on þæt ænlipe ellyn[2]. þonne of þan ænlupan ellynne on hodduces hancgran[3]. of hodduces hancgran on þa ænlypan ac[4]. and of þære æce on þæne hearapod[5]. þonon anlang hearpodes oð þere þorn[6] of þær þorne on aniges ham[7] of haniges hamme on cern[1] þonne of cern on þone broc[8]. of þan broce on hæðennan byriels[9]. of þan hæðenan byrielse on heað dune[10] on stod lege get[11]. of þæne gete on þone broc. andlang broces on cern[1].

NOTES

1 'where boundary brook flows into *Cern*', cf. land-scearu, but *score* is the gen. of scoru, an ablaut variant of sc(e)aru. Cf. *supra*, n. 6 for *cern*.

2 'solitary elder-tree', *v.* ānlī(e)pig, elle(r)n.

3 'Hodduc's wood on a slope', *v.* hangra.

4 'solitary oak-tree', *v.* ānlī(e)pig, āc.

5 'main road', *v.* here-pæð.

6 'thorn-tree', *v.* þorn.

7 Apparently 'river-meadow belonging to Hanney', *v.* hamm and Pt **2** 477. The parish of Hanney is separated from Pusey (to which these bounds are here tentatively ascribed) by Charney Bassett.

It is possible that there was an outlying portion of Hanney in Pusey. This apparent reference to Hanney is the main reason for considering this to be a Berks charter.

8 'brook'.

9 'heathen burial-place', v. hǣðen, byrgels.

10 'heath-down', v. hǣð, dūn; a fairly common p.n. which usually becomes modern Haddon.

11 'horse-pasture gate'; stōd-lēah, modern Studley, is a fairly common p.n.

D III   THE BOUNDS OF LONGWORTH, PROBABLY
         INCLUDING DRAYCOTT MOOR: 958 (C. 1240)
         BCS 1028

ærest on stan bricgge[1]. of stan bricgge east onlang temese[2] þæt hit cymð to cing hæma gemære[3] suð ondlang gemæres þæt hit cimð to þam heafud stoccun[4]. of þam heafod stoccun up on wærnan hylle[5] to þam þorne[6]. of þæm þorne ondlang mearce on eccene[7] ondlang stremes oð hit sticað on cearninga gemære[8] ondlang mearce þat hit sticað on heantunninga gemære[9].

NOTES

1 'stone bridge', v. stān, brycg and map.

2 R. Thames.

3 'boundary of the people of Kingston', v. hǣme and Pt 2 412–13.

4 'head stumps', i.e. posts on which criminals' heads were exposed, v. hēafod-stocc.

5 'stallion's hill' or 'wren's hill', v. wrǣna, wrenna; the first el. could also be a pers.n. Wærna. This is possibly an old name for the ridge between the Thames and Ock. If this survey includes Draycott Moor, wærnan hyll cannot be equated with the modern f.n. Warnhill, on the E. boundary of Longworth (Pt 2 395), but the two names occur at the northern and southern edge of the same ridge.

6 'thorn-tree.'

7 R. Ock.

8 'boundary of the people of Charney', v. -ingas and Pt 2 389.

9 'boundary of the people of Hinton', v. Pt 2 392. It is assumed that the Hinton boundary is followed back to the Thames.

D IV THE BOUNDS OF LONGWORTH, PROBABLY
    INCLUDING DRAYCOTT MOOR: 959 (c. 1200)
    BCS 1047

Ærest of eoccen[1] on þa ge mærlace[2]. andlang lace be westan cearna graf[3] be þan andheafdan[4] to eadulfes pytte[5]. þanon andlang sledes[6] to þam heafod æcere[7] norð weardon. þonne andlang æceres to þam andheafdan[4]. þ' to þan hæðnan byrgelse[8] on þa ealdan dic[9]. andlang dic to þam port wege[10]. þonne on þa deopan furh[11]. þonne on þa stanbricge[12] on Temese[13]. andlang temese to þam ðornstybbe æt kingtuninge gemære[14]. þonne to þam hæðenan byrgelse[8]. þonne on þa mærdic be eastan ælsiges cotan[15] andlang dic a to þam paðe[16]. þonne ofer þone mor[17] on þa heafda[18]. þ' on þone wenweg[19]. andlang weges to þam þornstybbe wið þone weg[20]. þonne on Eoccen[1] on þæt morsled[21] easteweard andlang eoccen[1]. þæt eft on þa mærlace[2].

NOTES

1 R. Ock.
2 'boundary stream', v. (ge)mǣre, lacu and map.
3 'grove by the Cern', v. grāf and p. 705, n. 6.
4 v. 626.
5 'Ēadwulf's pit', v. pytt.
6 'valley', v. slæd.
7 v. 626.
8 'heathen burial-place', v. hǣðen, byrgels.
9 'old ditch', v. dīc.
10 'town way', v. port-weg and map, probably so called because it led towards Faringdon.
11 'deep furrow', v. 627.
12 v. p. 706, n. 1.
13 R. Thames.
14 'the thorn-stump at the boundary of the people of Kingston', v. -inga-.
15 'boundary ditch east of Ælfsige's cottages.'
16 'path', v. pæð.
17 v. mōr, which here seems to refer to the top of the Corallian ridge, later known as More or Southemore, v. Pt 2 405.
18 v. 626.
19 'cart way', OE wænweg, v. wægn, weg.

20 'the thorn-stump by the way', v. þorn, stybb.

21 'marsh valley', v. mōr, slæd; it is not clear what 'eastward' means here, but the course of the Ock may have been slightly different from the modern one.

D V THE BOUNDS OF KINGSTON BAGPUIZE:
c. 977 (c. 1240) KCD 1276

Þis sind ða land gemæro æcer under æcere. Ærest of eccene[1] on mere þorn[2]. of mere þorne on þa heafod æceras[3] þanun on swanes ig[4] on þone ealdan garan[5] midde wearde of þam ealdan garan andlang riht gemæres on ælfredes beorh[6] þæt andlang riht gemæres innan Cyngestun[7] andlang riht gerið[8] on þone byt beneoðan Cyngestun[9] swa andlang riht gemæres on þone ðorn[10] þæt ut on Temese[11] andlang Temese on þæt eald gemæra[12] up andlang ge mæres on ælfðryþe stan[13]. of þane stane andlang dice[14] of þære dic andlang riht gemæres þæt eft on eo ccene[1].

NOTES

1 R. Ock.

2 'boundary thorn', v. (ge)mǣre, þorn.

3 v. 626.

4 This refers to land along the small stream on the S.W. boundary of Kingston. Second el. īeg 'island', well-watered land; the first could be swan[1], 'swan' swān[2] 'herdsman', or a pers.n. Swān. The p.n. appears as Swansea 1842 TA (for Draycott Moor), and the first el. probably survives in Swan Bottom 1844 TA (for Kingston Bagpuize).

5 v. 626.

6 'Ælfrǣd's tumulus', v. beorg.

7 This implies that the boundary ran through the village, v. 630.

8 This is probably a mistake for the phrase andlang riht gemæres 'along the lawful boundary', used frequently in this survey. gerið occurs at this point in all three copies of the bounds.

9 KCD prints þyt, but the MS has byt. A word bytt occurs in the bounds of BCS 1285. The meaning is uncertain, but the position of the boundary-mark 'beneath Kingston' may indicate that it lay in the hollow made by the 275′ contour immediately W. of the village.

10 'thorn', v. þorn.

11 R. Thames.

12 'old boundary.'

13 'Ælfðrȳð's stone.'

14 This is called *ælfð ryþe dic* in VII and VIII *infra*. It is named from the same woman as the stone of the preceding boundary-mark. Crawford (p. 240) records that he has seen the remains of this ditch extending along the boundary for approximately ¾ of a mile, *v.* map.

D VII   THE BOUNDS OF THE SOUTHERN PART
        OF FYFIELD: 956 (c. 1240) BCS 977

ærest on ydeles ige[1]. of ydeles ige andlang ge mæres to þat teles wege[2] andlang weges on mearan mores heafod andlang mænan mores heafud[3] on eoccene[4] up mid stræme to hudes lade[5] of hudes lade to þære scortandic[6]. of þære scortan dic on ælfðryþe dic[7]. andlang dic on holan broc[8] andlang holan broces on wasan[9]. andlang wasan eft to ydeles ige[1].

NOTES

1 This corresponds to *cyddesige* in VIII, *v.* p. 710, n. 9.

2 This corresponds to *pættes weg* in VIII, *v.* p. 710, n. 11.

3 The second version of this phrase is the correct one; 'head of the common marsh', *v.* hēafod, (ge)mǣne, mōr, and see map. The name survived as *Minmoor Common* 1816 *EnclA* (Fyfield). It is interesting that the land remained a common.

4 R. Ock.

5 'Hud's river-crossing', *v.* (ge)lǣd; this was probably where the boundary leaves the Ock.

6 'short ditch', *v.* sc(e)ort, dīc.

7 'Ælfðrȳð's ditch', *v. supra*, n. 14.

8 'hollow brook', *v.* hol[2], broc and map.

9 *v.* map and Pt ɪ 15–16; this stream is still known locally as Osse Ditch.

D VIII THE BOUNDS OF FYFIELD: 968 (16TH)
BCS 1221

Ærest of eoccan[1] on seortan dic of sceortan dic[2] on ælfþryðe dic[3] andlang dic on þæne mor[4]. of þam more on ða ealdan dic[5] of þære dic on temese streame[6] on þæt riðig[7] andlang riðiges on ƿase[8] of wasan on cyddesige[9] ofer rigedune[10] on pættes wege[11]. of þæm wege on mæne mor[12]. of ðam more þæt eft on eoccan.

NOTES

1 R. Ock.
2 v. p. 709, n. 6.
3 v. p. 709, n. 14, and see map.
4 'marsh', v. mōr and see map.
5 'old ditch', v. eald, dīc.
6 R. Thames.
7 'stream', v. rīðig and map.
8 v. p. 709, n. 9.
9 'Cyddi's island', v. īeg and see map.
10 'rye hill', v. ryge, dūn and see map. The name survives as Rye-down Plantation on the 6″ map. v. Pt 2 408.
11 'Pætti's way', v. map. The variant readings in VII for this boundary mark and for 9 supra suggest that the original pers.ns. may have been Pættel and Cyddel.
12 v. p. 709, n. 3.

D IX THE BOUNDS OF MARCHAM, FRILFORD AND
TUBNEY: 965 (c. 1200) BCS 1169

Ærest of eoccan[1] on mæne mor[2]. Of mæne more up on hwite more[3]. of hwite more on heafoces hamme[4] on tubba forda[5]. of tubba forda andlang mores[6] to æppeltune[7] on þone broc[8]. of ðæm broce on ðone pæð[9]. of þæm pæðe on ðone ealdan hege[10]. of ðæm hege on pyrtanmore[11]. of pyrta more þæt eft on Eoccen.

NOTES

1 R. Ock.
2 v. 709, n. 3.
3 Grundy notes that land S.E. of Woodhouse Fm is called Wide

Moor, which may be a corruption of *hwite mor* 'white marsh', *v.* map.

4 *v.* hamm 'riverside meadow'; first el. heafoc 'hawk', perhaps used as a pers.n.

5 now Tubworth, *v.* p. 723, n. 5.

6 'marsh', *v.* mōr.

7 Appleton; the N.W. boundary of Tubney passes close to Appleton village.

8 *on þone broc* probably qualifies *æppeltune*. Appleton is beside Osse Ditch, the brook which forms the W. boundary of Tubney.

9 'path', *v.* pǣð.

10 'old hedge', *v.* eald, hege; this may correspond to the *gemærhagan* of the Bessels Leigh bounds, *v.* p. 724, n. 3.

11 Second el. mōr 'marsh'; the first is obscure. Professor Löfvenberg compares Purfleet Ess and other ns. in *Purte-* discussed Ess 130–1. The name is not mentioned in any later source, and the position of the marsh cannot be ascertained. There is, however, a good deal of marshy land along Sandford Brook, which forms the E. boundary of Marcham, and it is just possible that Peat Moor Lane (see map) contains a corruption of the early name.

DX THE BOUNDS OF GARFORD: 940 (c. 1200)
BCS 761

Of Garaforda¹ andlang eoccen² oð ðæt þær cilla riþ³ ut scyt. þonon up andlang cille riðe oð linfordinga gemere⁴. þonon on wintres hlewe⁵. þæt þonna eft ut on Eoccan. þonon andlang eoccen. oð eft on garanforda.

NOTES

1 The ford from which the village is named, *v.* Pt **2** 410, and *v.* map for probable position.

2 R. Ock.

3 Childrey Brook, *v.* map and Pt **1** 8. The following phrase, *up andlang cille riðe*, implies that the stream now known as Nor Brook was regarded as the main course of Childrey Brook in the 10th cent.

4 'the boundary of the people of Lyford', *v.* (ge)mǣre and Pt **2** 413–14.

5 'Winter's tumulus', *v.* hlǣw.

D XI THE BOUNDS OF DRAYTON, PROBABLY EXCLUDING
SUTTON WICK, POSSIBLY EXCLUDING LAND
IN THE WEST OF THE PARISH: 958 (c. 1200)
BCS 1032

Ærest of Englafes forda[1] on dyþmere[2]. þonon on laking[3]. andlang
lacing on cealcford[4]. þonon on mær dic[5]. andlang dic on mide dic[6].
þonon on wanetincg[7] on eoccene[8]. þonone on þa ealdan dic[9]. andlang
dic on englafes ford.

NOTES

1 An error for *eglafes forda* in XII, 'Ecgláf's ford; possibly, as
Grundy suggests, where Drayton East Way crosses Mill Brook, *v.*
map.
2 *v.* mere 'pool'; first el. apparently dȳð 'fuel, tinder', perhaps
describing a pool near which this was gathered. The pool was
probably on Mill Brook.
3 *lacing* is Mill Brook. This r.n. gives rise to the p.n. Lockinge, *v.*
Pt 1 13.
4 'chalk ford', *v.* cealc, ford; the meaning is uncertain, as the soil is
not chalky.
5 'boundary ditch', *v.* map. The name survives as Mere Dike,
marked on the 6″ map, *v.* Pt 2 406, 418.
6 *ClaudiusBvi* has *mydeling* for *mide dic*, and this is almost certainly
the correct reading. For *mydeling v.* p. 713, n. 6. The survey
encounters the brook of this name in Drayton Copse.
7 *v.* Pt 1 17–18. This name is applied in several sets of charter boundaries to the stream which now forms the boundary between East
Hanney and Steventon, and which probably originally flowed along
the boundary between East Hanney and Drayton. It was also the
name of Letcombe Brook, and is the source of the p.n. Wantage.
If the present survey excludes the western portion of Drayton, as
suggested *supra*, the bounds will reach the *wanetinge* shortly before
its junction with the Ock.
8 R. Ock.
9 'old ditch', *v.* eald, díc; this single boundary-mark seems an
inadequate guide to the complicated E. boundary of Drayton, and
the exact line cannot be ascertained. It is probable that it ran W.
of Sutton Wick (which must originally have been connected with

Sutton Courtenay), then N. of Drayton village, then S. to join the present parish boundary.

D XII THE BOUNDS OF DRAYTON, PROBABLY EXCLUDING SUTTON WICK: 960 (c. 1200) BCS 1058

Ærest of eglafes forda[1] on dyþmere[2]. þanon on lacing[3]. andlang lacing on cealcford[4]. þanon on merdic[5]. andlang dic on mydeling[6]. up of mydeling wið norðan hyrde graf[7]. þæt on gerihtan on waniting[8]. andlang waneting on eoccene[9]. þanon on þa ealdan dic[10]. andlang dic on eglafes ford[1].

NOTES

1–5 For these names v. p. 712, nn. 1–5.

6 v. Pt **1** 14; this is a stream-name of the same type as *lacing* and *waneting*. It refers to the stream which crosses the parish roughly parallel with the Wilts and Berks canal. Grundy says there is a field called Middlings beside it, for which v. map.

7 'grove of the herdsmen', v. hirde, grāf. A mill *æt hyrde grafe* is mentioned in BCS 1121, A.D. 963, as an appurtenance to an estate at Sparsholt. *Hurgrove* occurs fairly frequently in records from c. 1270 to 1655 (v. Pt **2** 418), but the exact position is not certain. Grundy says there is a Hulgrove Meadow W. of the Wilts and Berks canal, and this may be a corruption of the name. The 6″ map shows detached portions of Sutton Wick and Sutton Courtenay near here, and *Hurgrove* is mentioned in connection with Sutton Courtenay in several references. This boundary-mark may indicate that the survey includes the whole parish, whereas XI excludes some land in the west.

8 v. p. 712, n. 7. If this survey differs from that in XI, the bounds must be assumed to reach the *waneting* lower down its course. The stream has been much affected by drainage, but its original course probably formed the boundary between East Hanney and Drayton.

9 R. Ock.

10 v. p. 712, n. 9.

D XIII THE BOUNDS OF MILTON: 956 (CONTEMPORARY)
BCS 935

ærest of cealc forda[1] on ealdan lacing[2] þanune on dyðmere[3]. þanune on sceortan mor[4] þanune on þone anlipan beorh[5] þanune on hæsel broc[6] þanune up to gynan bæte[7] þonne to þam stodfalde[8] þanune to seofan þornum[9] þonne to smalan wege[10] and on lacing[2] and syx cotsetlan[11].

NOTES

1 v. p. 712, n. 4.
2 v. p. 712, n. 3; *ealdan* may refer to part of the stream which has been replaced by a drainage channel.
3 v. p. 712, n. 2.
4 'short marsh', v. sceort, mōr.
5 'solitary tumulus', v. ānlī(e)pig, beorg.
6 'hazel brook', v. p. 764, n. 12 and map.
7 *ClaudiusCix* has *grnan bæce*, *ClaudiusBvi gynan bæce*. *bæce* is probably the correct form of the second el., v. bæc 'ridge'; the first el. is obscure, but v. BTSuppl s.v. *gin*. Toller cites two names in charter bounds which may contain an element **gin*, and suggests a meaning 'gaping'. *ginne* 'wide, spacious' is well recorded, but has not been noted in p.ns. There is an ancient causeway in Steventon (Pt 2 418). If this had continued eastward, it might have crossed Milton parish and been described as a bæc in these bounds. Professor Löfvenberg informs us that the word *gin* in BTSuppl is very doubtful.
8 v. stōdfald.
9 'seven thorns', v. seofon, þorn.
10 'narrow way'; a road with this name occurs in the bounds of Harwell (p. 764, n. 4), on the S.W. boundary of that parish. The Milton road could be a continuation of it.
11 'six cottagers': these are part of the property, not a boundary-mark.

D XIV THE BOUNDS OF PART OF BUCKLAND:
957 (c. 1200) BCS 1005

Ærest sprindlesham[1] hyrð to bocland. and eal gamafeld[2] to boclande gemære. of lytlan mores heafde[3] to laurocan beorghe[4]. of laurocan beorghe to kasan ðornne[5]. of kasan ðorne to bradan weg[6]. of bradan wege andlang þara heafod æcera[7] oð fisceras dene[8]. of fisceras dene to þære mæd[9]. of ðære mæde ut to wasan[10]. of wasan ut to æa[11]. andlang æa to healhwere[12]. of healhwere to þam westran wiðige[13]. of ðam wiðige to þam yrðlande[14]. of þam yrðlande on þone hig weg[15]. of þam hig wege þurh bocland[16] to kynnan wylle[17] on þone heafod æcer[18]. of þam hæfod æcere ut on þone steort[19]. of þam steorte on þone yrnendan mor[20]. of þam yrnendan more. on ælfsiges mor[21].

NOTES

1 v. hamm 'river-meadow'; first el. sprindel, which Holthausen translates 'Vogelschlinge'. 'Meadow of the bird-snare' is a possible etymology. The name has not been noted in any later source, and the position cannot be ascertained.

2 gamafeld is the modern Gainfield, v. map. This was the meeting-place of Ganfield Hundred (Pt 2 385), and the name means 'open land of the sports'. eal gamafeld, 'all Gainfield', may be the projecting corner of the parish in which the modern farm is situated.

3 'the head of the little marsh'; it is not known where this survey starts or what area it describes.

4 'lark's tumulus', v. lāwerce, beorg.

5 v. þorn 'thorn'; the first el. is obscure. Dr von Feitilzen suggests a copyist's error for haran.

6 'broad way', v. brād, weg.

7 v. 626.

8 'fisherman's valley', v. fiscere, denu.

9 'meadow', v. mǣd.

10 This is the same name as wasa in Appleton, v. p. 723, n. 4 and Pt 1 15–16. Here it refers to a small stream called Ouse Ditch in the Buckland TA, v. map.

11 v. ēa 'river', here referring to the Thames.

12 'weir in a nook or corner', v. healh, wer.

13 'the more western willow', v. wīðig.

14 'ploughland' v. 626.

15 'hay way', the same name occurs in bounds in Hormer Hundred, *v.* p. 728, n. 15.

16 If 'through Buckland' means that the bounds go through the village, the survey cannot be describing the whole parish, *v.* map.

17 'Cynna's spring or stream', *v.* w(i)ell.

18 *v.* 626.

19 'tongue of land', *v.* steort.

20 'the flowing marsh', *v.* mōr.

21 'Ælfsige's marsh.'

E HORMER HUNDRED, WITH APPLETON WITH EATON (OCK HUNDRED)

The inclusion of I and II in this group of charters is somewhat arbitrary. They deal with two estates in *Earmundes leah*, an area which appears to have included Appleton, Eaton and Bessels Leigh. Both were in Marcham Hundred in 1086, but Appleton is now in Ock Hundred and Bessels Leigh in Hormer. It has seemed advisable to keep the two *Earmundes leah* surveys together, however, and as the one which relates to Bessels Leigh has close links with other surveys of estates in Hormer Hundred, it is convenient to deal with them in this group. By 1086 the land formerly known as *Earmundes leah* was not part of the compact block of estates comprising the Hundred of Hormer, in which the Abbot of Abingdon had probably been granted special judicial rights by Edward the Confessor (ASWrits 125 ff.).

With the exception of Appleton with Eaton, all the estates dealt with in these charters had been acquired by Abingdon Abbey before the Norman Conquest, and all the charters are preserved in the Abingdon Chronicle. With two exceptions, they are copied in both *ClaudiusCix* and *ClaudiusBvi*, but *Cix* usually abbreviates the Latin texts. The charters are –

I. BCS 777, A.D. 942, copied only in *ClaudiusBvi*, by which King Edmund grants 10 hides at Appleton in *Ærmundeslea* to Æthelstan. For *Ærmundeslea v.* Pt 2 443–4. The bounds may describe the modern parish of Appleton with Eaton, but Grundy took them to refer to Appleton only, and no certainty is possible.

II. BCS 1047, A.D. 959, of dubious authenticity, copied (with some abbreviation in *Cix*) in both MSS, by which King Edgar restores to the Abbey 10 hides in Ginge, 15 hides in Goosey, 30 hides in Longworth and 5 hides in *Earmundes leah*. There are bounds of all four places. The bounds of *Ermundeslea*, which are copied twice in *Cix*, refer in the main to the modern area of Bessels Leigh, but the 10th-cent. land-unit seems to have been somewhat larger than the modern one, including part of Appleton with Eaton on the N.W., and possibly part of Cumnor on the N.E.

III. BCS 971, A.D. 956, copied (with omission of the witnesses in *Cix*)

in both MSS, by which King Eadwig grants Kennington to the
priest Beorthelm. No hidage is given. The bounds describe the
modern parish of Kennington with the addition of a small part of
Radley in the S.E. The charter is followed in the Abingdon
Chronicle by an account of an exchange whereby Bishop
Beorhthelm gave the Abbey Kennington in return for Curbridge
O; this is BCS 972.

IV. BCS 932, A.D. 956, copied (with omission of most of the witnesses
in *Cix*) in both MSS, by which King Eadwig grants 25 hides at
Bayworth to Ælfric. The main bounds describe the modern
parishes of Wootton and Sunningwell, and there are surveys of
two pieces of meadow, both by the Thames, one in Kennington
and the other in Radley.

V. BCS 1002, C. A.D. 957, copied (with omission of most of the
witnesses in *Cix*) in both MSS, by which King Eadwig grants 20
hides in Hinksey, Seacourt and Wytham to the Abbey. The bounds
describe the modern parishes of Wytham and North and South
Hinksey. *Bvi* introduces the bounds with the statement 'Ðis
sindon þa land gemæro þæs ge burlandes to abbendune þæt is
gadertang on þreo genamod þæt is hengestes ig. and seofocan
wyrð. and wiht ham.'

VI. BCS 1222, A.D. 968, copied (with considerable abbreviation in
Cix) in both MSS, by which King Edgar grants 30 hides at
Cumnor to the Abbey. The text is said in HistAb 48 to be 'not
above suspicion'. The bounds are short, and Grundy considered
that they referred to Eaton. Probably, however, they describe the
modern parish of Cumnor, though the boundary-marks are too
widely spaced for a precise interpretation to be possible. With this
charter it is necessary to consider BCS 680 and 681, two spurious
charters of King Æthelstan, both dated 931 and largely identical
in wording, which follow each other in both MSS of the Abingdon
Chronicle. The first of these purports to be a grant of 5 hides,
stated in *Bvi* to be at *Swynford*, but in *Cix* to be at *Sandford*, while
the second is a grant of 15 hides, at *Sandford* according to *Bvi*, but
at *Swinford* according to *Cix*. The confusion is increased by the
note *Samford* in the margin of *Cix* against *Swinford* in the second
charter. Both charters contain the words 'Termini vero hujus
præfatæ telluris in libro qui ad Cumenoran pertinet scripta
habentur'. The statement about the bounds being in the Cumnor
charter is reasonable as applied to Swinford, but cannot be

accepted as applied to Dry Sandford. Any genuine record which lay behind these forgeries is, therefore, likely to have referred to Swinford.

VII. BCS 906, a spurious charter of King Eadred, copied in both MSS, which purports to be a grant to the Abbey of the *villa* of Abingdon with outlying estates at Ginge (10 hides), Goosey (10 hides), Longworth (30 hides) and Cumnor (30 hides). In *Bvi* this charter includes a set of bounds headed 'Metæ xx hidarum Abbendoniæ quas Ceadwalla, rex Westsaxonum, Deo et sanctæ Mariæ primitus dedit'. These bounds, with the same heading, occur at the end of *Cix*, with all the other bounds in this MS, and not therefore connected with a charter. A statement at the end of them says that *Æþeleahingwudu, Colmanora* and *Geatescumb* belong to the 20 hides at Abingdon, and the author of *Cix* has turned this statement into Latin near the beginning of his Chronicle. This Latin version is printed as BCS 844, which is a ghost charter. The bounds attached to BCS 906 cannot be dated, but certainly have no connection with Cædwalla, in whose reign (685-9) such a survey was unknown. On linguistic grounds they are unlikely to be later than the mid 10th cent. The area they describe cannot be defined with absolute precision, but includes the modern parishes of Abingdon, Kennington and Radley, and part of St Helen Without. In the Abingdon Chronicle this spurious charter follows the information about Abingdon possessing 40 hides and being given a royal estate of 100 hides in Eadred's reign, which is part of Ælfric's life of St Æthelwold (*v. infra*, pp. 720-21).

VIII. BCS 924, A.D. 956, a charter of King Eadwig, copied in both MSS, by which the king grants to the Abbey 20 hides of land. There is another copy, probably from a contemporary parchment, in MS *C.C.C.C.cxi*, p. 147. *Bvi* has a sentence after the bounds stating that they are the bounds 'to Abbandune', and the copy in *C.C.C.C.cxi* has the title ' Ðis is ðæra XX. hyda bóc æt Abbandune ðe Eadwig cyning gebecte on ece yrfe in to Sancta Marian Cyricean'. The area described by the bounds seems to be identical with that of the survey in VII, but this survey is more detailed and has more boundary-marks in common with those of neighbouring estates.

IX. KCD 1283, A.D. 985, a charter of King Æthelred, granting 10 hides at Wootton to Leofwine. The charter is copied only in *Bvi*, but *Cix* has the boundaries, which describe the modern parish of Wootton.

A close study of these charters throws some light on the history of Abingdon Abbey in the 10th cent. The continuous history of the Abbey begins with the appointment of Æthelwold of Winchester as Abbot by King Eadred, shortly before the king's death in 955. Ælfric's life of St Æthelwold, printed in Abingdon II, pp. 255–66, contains information about the condition and possessions of the monastery at the time of this appointment. Ælfric says that the Abbey, 'poverty-stricken and neglected', possessed forty hides of land, and that the rest of the land 'of this place', which was a hundred hides, was a royal estate. It has been assumed (HistAb 47) that this 100-hide royal estate was the later Hundred of Hormer; it seems possible, however, that it was the Domesday Hundred of *Sutton*, as the monks had a tradition that their Abbey had given King Cenwulf of Mercia 100 hides there (Pt 2 424). It seems probable that the forty hides still owned by the Abbey consisted of the two twenty-hide estates, one of which is described in VII and VIII, and the other in V. Both VIII and V are charters of King Eadwig, the young successor of King Eadred, and they are probably ratifications of an agreement to confirm this property to Abingdon, which had been made by King Eadred but not recorded before his death. Ælfric also says that King Eadred gave Æthelwold the royal property of a hundred hides 'in Abingdon'. Whether this royal property was in Hormer or in *Sutton* Hundred, this gift cannot have been honoured by his successor, as other estates in Hormer Hundred were only acquired by the Abbey in later years, and Sutton Courtenay remained a royal estate.

The charters dealing with the forty hides deserve detailed comment. VII is a clumsy forgery in the name of King Eadred, from whom the monks would naturally feel that they should have a charter. Attached to it is a survey, which obviously antedates the forgery, describing an area which includes the modern land-units of Abingdon, Kennington, Radley and part of St Helen Without. This survey has been provided with a heading, stating that it is the twenty hides granted to the Abbey by King Cædwalla. The connection with Cædwalla is an obvious fiction, but may indicate that the monks believed this land to have been among the Abbey's earliest endowments. VIII is a genuine charter of King Eadwig, dated 956, which grants them substantially the same area, with a revised version of the boundaries. Since this land included most of Kennington, VIII appears inconsistent with III, also dated 956, by which King Eadwig gave Kennington to Bishop Beorhthelm. The Abingdon Chronicle follows this charter, however, with an Old English account (BCS 972) of an exchange by which the bishop gave Kennington to the Abbey, and it may well be that the negotiations about Kennington were part of an agreement designed to confirm for the Abbey the estate described in VII. V is a grant by King Eadwig to the Abbey of twenty hides in Hinksey, Seacourt and Wytham. The survey describes approximately the modern parishes of Wytham and North and South Hinksey, and if these surveys do represent the forty hides mentioned by Ælfric as the surviving possessions of Abingdon, the property was a strip of land running along the east side of Hormer Hundred. Stenton (HistAb 48, n. 2) suggested that Uffington was the 40 hides belonging to Abingdon in King Eadred's time, but it is demonstrated *supra* (p. 676) that Uffington was assessed at 33 hides in the 10th cent., and it was probably not in the Abbey's possession at the date of Æthelwold's appointment. It is noteworthy that the surveys attached to VII and VIII exclude most of the modern parish of St Helen Without, which can probably be roughly equated with the manor of Shippon. The monks claimed to have been in possession of Shippon in the time of Edward the Confessor (Abingdon II 19), but DB expressly states that this was not the case, and it is probable that they acquired it for the first time by the gift of Earl Hugh of Chester, whose charter appears in Abingdon II 20.

King Eadred's gift of a hundred hides in the vicinity of Abingdon cannot have taken effect, as the remaining land-units of Sunningwell, Wootton and Cumnor were acquired later, the two first by means which the monks appear to have forgotten. Wootton and Sunningwell are both included in a grant of 956 (IV) to a private individual, and no authority attaches to the Chronicler's statement (Abingdon I 218) that the grantee gave the land to the Abbey. This is in any case contradicted by IX, which is a grant of Wootton to another private individual. Cumnor, the largest land-unit in the Hundred, is stated in VI to be given to the Abbey by King Edgar. These estates do not amount to a hundred hides, according to the assessments given in the charters, and King Eadred's intended gift may have included more places to the W. of Abingdon, or as stated *supra* it may have been in *Sutton*.

There is no correspondence between the division into land-units revealed in these charters and that recorded in the Domesday account of this area. Domesday describes the Abbey's lands in Hormer

Hundred as being in two main portions, named Cumnor and Barton. Various tenants hold estates within these two divisions, and from the record of these it appears that Barton includes Shippon, Dry Sandford, Bayworth, Sugworth, Sunningwell and Kennington, and Cumnor includes Seacourt and Wytham. It is evident that Cumnor is the northern, and Barton the southern part of the Hundred. Some of the charter estates must, however, have kept their integrity, since it is possible to identify their bounds approximately with those of modern parishes. The Kennington survey (III) describes the modern parish, with a slight alteration in the S.E., and the Wootton survey seems to correspond very closely to the modern land-unit, though neither estate can be recognised from the Domesday account of the Hundred. This is not due in every case to the provision of a parish church for the estate; Kennington was not an ecclesiastical parish until 1936. A remarkable instance of the persistence of the 10th-cent. arrangements is to be seen in the case of the first piece of mead by the Thames attached to the 'Bayworth' estate (IV); hay was still carted from Berry Mead to farms in Wootton in the present century.

The bounds of these charters present some difficulty in detail, but the main outline of the grants is fairly clear. Landmarks and place-names survive less well in forest than in open land, and the difficulties are partly due to the wooded nature of much of the ground. The W. boundary of North Hinksey and Wytham (V), which was probably running through wooded country, has a series of landmarks of which none can be identified, and the northern part of the Wootton survey (IX) is similarly obscure. Much assarting was probably done in these areas after the 10th cent., but it is interesting to note that the extent of Bagley Wood seems to have been the same in the mid-10th cent. as it is today. Several of the surveys mention deer.

In some cases, precise interpretation is prevented by later alterations in the boundaries, as, for instance, in the case of Wootton and South Hinksey, which marched together in the 10th cent. but are now separated by a strip of Cumnor. The topography of the rivers has changed considerably, the mouth of the Cherwell being much further S. than it is now. Considerable detail is given about the course of the Thames, and the names of a number of islands in the river are recorded.

All references to arable land in the boundaries are in the southern half of the area, where the parishes are smaller. *Sceaceling æcer* (p. 726, n. 9) and *rige worð* (p. 725, n. 3) were on the N. and S. edges of

Bagley Wood; there was arable land in Appleton Lower Common (p. 724, n. 8), which must have been in marked contrast to the modern wood there; and a number of open-field features were mentioned on the S. boundary of Sunningwell, E. of Sunningwell Brook (pp. 728–9, nn. 23, 25, 26). There was, presumably, other arable land in the centre of these estates, with which the bounds are not concerned.

E I THE BOUNDS OF APPLETON WITH EATON:
 942 (c. 1240) BCS 777

þis synt þa landemæro to ærmundes lea and oþre namen æt æppeltune ærst up of temese¹ on ða dic æt doccan grafe² þæt on þæt sic þe scyt þurh hæsel lea³ foran ongean þa dic þe scyt to wasan⁴ siþþan andlang wasan þæt hit sticað on tubban forda⁵. þonon on þæt riþig⁶ oþ hit cymð to þære stræte⁷. of þære strete on þa dic þe scyt to þam heafod lande⁸. þonne on west healfe þæs heafod landes. vi. gyrda⁹ be westan yttinges hlawe¹⁰. þonon on þa ræwe¹¹ of þære reawe on temese¹. on þæt in fyrde¹² andlang temese eft on doccan dic².

NOTES

1 R. Thames.
2 'the ditch at dock-grove', v. docce, grāf, shortened to 'dock-ditch' at the end of the survey. I take the survey to run first along the N. boundary of Appleton with Eaton.
3 'the stream which flows through hazel-wood', v. sīc, hæsel, lēah.
4 'the ditch which runs to *wasan*', v. map; *wasan* is the stream which rises S. of Cumnor and flows into the Ock S. of Marcham. It is locally known as Osse Ditch, and the name is a derivative of *wāse* 'mud', v. Pt 1 15–16.
5 '*Tubba*'s ford', named from the same owner as Tubney (Pt 2 425–6). It is mentioned also in the bounds of Marcham (which include Frilford and Tubney), and appears to have been near the junction of Tubney, Fyfield and Appleton parishes. Later references (Pt 2 426) occur under Tubney and Fyfield, and Tubworth Barn in Tubney may preserve the name with corruption of the second el. to worð.
6 The rīðig is the stream which joins Osse Ditch at the junction of Appleton, Fyfield and Tubney parishes.
7 v. stræt; this is the road on which Appleton is situated. The same

term is applied in the bounds of II (*infra* n. 6) to the continuation of this road S. of Cumnor.

8 'the ditch which runs to the headland', *v.* 626. Grundy says this ditch is still clearly marked along the W. side of Appleton Lower Common.

9 g(i)erd is here a linear measure, *v.* Elements **1** 200.

10 For *yttinges hlaw v.* Pt **2** 402–3. The n. survives in Titlar Hill.

11 'hedgerow', *v.* ræw.

12 Toller (BTSuppl) suggests that *in-fyrde* means 'entrance to a ford'. The term occurs again in the bounds of Cumnor (p. 731, n. 3).

E II   THE BOUNDS OF BESSELS LEIGH: '959' (C. 1200)
        BCS 1047

Ærest of Sandforda¹ on þa fulan lace² andlang þæs ge mærhagan³. ut on þam totan⁴. þannon andlang ge mæres on hæseldic⁵. andlang stræte⁶ ut on styrian pol⁷. andlang þere dic east to wasan⁸. þonon on hrocanleage⁹ norðewearde andlang dic on ufewearde hægdune¹⁰. þæt up on snoddes hylle¹¹ ufewearde to þam haran stane¹². þonne to þam ealdan wulfhaga¹³. þonon andlang slædes¹⁴. þæt to læcesforda¹⁵. þonon andlang lucringes¹⁶. eft on Sandford.

NOTES

1 The ford from which Dry Sandford (Pt **2** 438) is named, *v.* map.

2 'dirty stream', *v.* fūl, lacu, and see map.

3 'boundary enclosure', *v.* (ge)mære, haga¹, and 628.

4 The second copy of these bounds in *ClaudiusCix* has *cotan*, and *ClaudiusBvi* has *coten*. *cotan* could be the dat.pl. of cot 'cottage'.

5 'hazel ditch', *v.* hæsel, dīc, perhaps an extension of the third landmark in I *supra*. The survey seems here to have left the modern boundary and to include part of Appleton with Eaton.

6 The 'street' is the northern continuation of the road called stræt in I (*supra*), *v.* map.

7 The position of *styrian pol* (*v.* map) is crucial to the understanding of this survey. It is mentioned again in that of Cumnor (VI, p. 731, n. 1), and a later reference is *Sterepole* 1538 *MinAcc* in Cumnor. O.G.S. Crawford (*Antiquity* IV, 480–3) claimed to have identified *styrian pol* with a narrow rectangular pool beside Osse Ditch, between Lower England's Copse and Bessels Leigh Common, but

this is in Appleton with Eaton, and does not accord either with the charter bounds or with the occurrence of *Sterepole* in a document relating to Cumnor. It was probably an artificial fish-pond (*v.* pōl), with first el. OE *styria*, used of various fishes.

8 *wasan* is Osse Ditch, *v.* p. 723, n. 4 and map.

9 'Hrōca's wood or clearing', *v.* lēah. The name survives in Rockley Heath, Cottages and Copse (Pt 2 444), which the boundary now approaches from the N.

10 'fence hill', *v.* (ge)hæg, dūn, identical with Haydon So.

11 'Snodd's hill', *v.* hyll.

12 'boundary stone', *v.* hār, stān. This may be the *haran stan* of VI (p. 732, n. 9).

13 'the old wolf fence', *v.* wulf, haga¹, and 628. BTSuppl suggests 'an enclosure to protect flocks from wolves'.

14 'along the valley', *v.* slæd. None of the last four boundary-marks can be identified.

15 Probably 'ford of the bog', *v.* Pt 2 444. The name survives in Lashford Lane and the ford was probably where the lane crosses Sandford Brook. The survey may include part of Cumnor, as well as the part of Bessels Leigh which contains Little Bradley Fm.

16 *lucring* was evidently the name of Sandford Brook, *v.* Pt 1 16.

E III THE BOUNDS OF KENNINGTON: 956 (C. 1200)
  BCS 971

Of temese stæde¹ on wulfrices broc² uppan hrige weorðæ³ on ða ealdan dic⁴. of ðere dic ut on rige wurðe heal⁵. þonne on þone rah hege⁶. andlang þes heges on baggan wurðe⁷. efre be efisc⁸ þæt hit cymð on sceaceling æcer⁹. þonne ut on sandford¹⁰. þonne ut on temese on þone igoð¹¹ ðwyres ofer berege¹² on cearewyllan¹³. andlang streames ut æt temese. andlang temese þæt hit cymð on hyrdige¹⁴. þonne ut eft on wulfrices broc².

NOTES

1 'the bank of the Thames'; *stæd* is probably for stæð 'shore, bank'.

2 'Wulfrīc's brook', *v.* map and cf. p. 737, n. 47.

3 'rye enclosure', *v.* ryge and cf. p. 737, n. 44. The second el. is a fem. noun *wyrð*, which existed by the side of masc. or neut. worð. Professor Löfvenberg considers that the -eo- of *weorðæ* may be an inverted spelling.

4 'old ditch', v. eald, dīc and cf. p. 737, n. 45.

5 v. healh 'nook or corner', perhaps referring to the projecting S.W. angle of the parish.

6 'deer fence', v. rā¹, hege; the same fence is mentioned in IV (p. 728, n. 16).

7 'Bacga's enclosure', v. n. 3 supra, named from the same man as Bagley Wood (Pt 2 453) and bacgan broc in VIII (p. 737, n. 41).

8 'edge (of the wood).' The northern boundary of Bagley Wood appears to have been where it is today.

9 v. æcer 'cultivated land'. The first el. might be a derivative in -ing of sceacol, v. Elements 2 98 for a discussion of this el. PN -ing 73 suggests that there was an OE *scacol 'strip, tongue or point of land'. Such a term would be appropriate for the projection of S. Hinksey parish which cuts into the N. edge of Bagley Wd, v. map.

10 ClaudiusBvi has Stanford, which is certainly correct, as it occurs at this point in other surveys (p. 730, n. 2, p. 734, n. 25); 'stone ford', v. stān, ford.

11 These bounds apply the name Thames to the western branch of the river, and Cherwell to the eastern branch, now held to be the main stream of the Thames. The modern boundary goes round a small island which could be the igoð (v. ēgeð). Grundy, however, suggests that it is the island E. of the hospital at Cold Harbour.

12 For a full discussion of this name v. Pt 2 454.

13 v. n. 11 supra.

14 'herdsman island', v. hirde, īeg. The name appears as Herdy Meade, Le Herdey, Hoday Meade, Hard(a)y Meade in a survey of Radley in 1547, and Herd Eyott in Radley TA, v. Pt 2 457 and map. The boundary of Kennington appears to have come further S. than it does today.

E IV THE BOUNDS OF WOOTTON AND SUNNINGWELL: 956 (c. 1200) BCS 932

Ærest of gorgræfan¹ up andlang slades² on þone ðorn³. þonon on þæt crundel⁴ suðe weard. þonon to þam wylle⁵. þonon on lecæs ford⁶. þonon up andlang riðe⁷ on gemærweg⁸. andlang weges on ða dic æt scobban oran⁹. andlang dic on gemær weg⁸. andlang weges on butan wrohthangran¹⁰ on ceobban stan¹¹. forð andlang gemær weges on þone weg æt Cealues wylle¹². forð andlang weges to yfemæstan leage¹³. þonon forð ofer sciteres clif¹⁴ to hig wege¹⁵. up andlang weges

to þam rah hege¹⁶. andlang weges to hæsel dic¹⁷. þon' on wufstanes
dic¹⁸. of þære dic on maduces lea¹⁹. þurh þone lea on þone pyt²⁰. of
þam pytte on ðone ellen styb²¹. þon' on lippan dic²². andlang dic on
seouan æcera²³ westewearde. þonon on þon hæðenan byrgels²⁴. þon'
on þæt scorteland²⁵ suðeweard. þæt andlang fyrh on þone healfan
æcer²⁶. þon' on þæt wiðig bæd²⁷. þon' on dunanford²⁸. of þam forda
andlang sunninga wylle broces²⁹ on wudaford³⁰. þon' andlang
hrycges³¹ on westmor³² in on þone broc³³. up andlang broces on
gorgræfas¹ þær hit ær onfeng.

Et he sunt mete pratorum pertinentium illic
Ærest of þære brycge on beryge³⁴. up andlang midstreames oð foran
on gean þa niwan dic³⁵. up andlang dic. þonon oð midne streame
niðær andlang streames up on þone greatan welig³⁶. þonon andlang
þære hæge ræwe³⁷. ut on þa ea³⁸ oþ midne stream.

Þonne þis synd þa gemæro þære mæde æt ennanbeorgum³⁹
Of þære diceænde⁴⁰ forð on ða ea niðær andlang midstreames. up on
ða won lace⁴¹ oþ foran on gean þone beorh⁴². þær betweonan mæde.
and dune⁴³ eft on þa dic.

NOTES

1 This landmark occurs also in the bounds of Wootton (p. 737, n. 1)
  and its approximate position is clear. The valley in which *gorgræfas*
  was situated is the one in which Honey Bottom now is. The name
  probably means 'mud pits', *v.* gor, græf. The second el. is treated
  as a strong masc. noun at the end of this survey and in that of
  Wootton, so the *-an* of the first reference probably represents the
  dat.pl. ending. Tengstrand (272) takes the second el. to be grāf
  'grove'.
2 'valley', *v.* slæd.
3 'thorn-tree', *v.* þorn.
4 'quarry', *v.* crundel.
5 *v.* w(i)ell, here referring to Sandford Brook.
6 *v.* p. 725, n. 15, and see map.
7 *v.* rīð, this also refers to Sandford Brook.
8 'boundary way', *v.* (ge)mære, weg.
9 'the ditch at Sceobba's slope', *v.* dīc, ōra.
10 *ClaudiusBvi* has *thorn hangran*, but *wrohthangran* must be pre-
   ferred, as it occurs also in the survey of Wootton (p. 738, n. 9).
   v. wrōht 'debate' and hangra 'wood on a slope'. The reference is

probably to a wood of which the ownership has been disputed. This may be Hen Wood (Pt 2 463). The later name means 'wood of the monastic community', and this acquires some significance if the land had been in dispute; it would otherwise be difficult to explain in an area where all the land belonged to Abingdon.

11 'Ceobba's stone' v. stān. This is *Cybban stan* in the Wootton survey (p. 738, n. 10) and in that of Hinksey, Seacourt and Wytham (p. 730, n. 10). The precise course of the present survey from here to *hig wege* (15) is uncertain. This stretch of boundary is identical with that of Hinksey in V, but the two modern parishes do not adjoin, being separated by an extension of Cumnor. The 10th-cent. boundary was presumably somewhere in this portion of Cumnor.

12 *ClaudiusBvi* has *cealfes wulle*. One would expect this to be Chilswell, but the charter name is incompatible with the ME forms, which point to an etymology 'Ceofel's stream' (Pt 2 445–6). The scribe may have misunderstood the name and interpreted it as 'stream of the calf', v. c(e)alf.

13 'highest wood or clearing', v. lēah. If the survey is following the modern boundary of Wootton, this might be E. of Pickett's Heath Fm, where the modern boundary crosses a ridge between the valleys of two streams.

14 v. clif 'bank'. *scitere is probably a stream-name, cf. RN 363, v. map for suggested position.

15 'hay way', v. hēg, weg and map. This road can be identified with certainty, as it occurs also in V (p. 730, n. 6) and VIII (p. 736, n. 37); v. map. Rix (p. 7) gives an account of hay being carted from fields by the Thames to a farm in Wootton.

16 v. p. 726, n. 6.

17 'hazel ditch', v. hæsel, dīc. This occurs also in VIII (p. 736, n. 34).

18 *ClaudiusBvi* has *wulfstanes dic* 'Wulfstān's ditch'.

19 'Maduc's wood or clearing', v. lēah. The pers.n. is PrWelsh *Madōg*. Cf. *Madoch* in DB for Gl, Feilitzen 325.

20 'pit', v. pytt.

21 'elder stump', v. elle(r)n, stybb.

22 Perhaps 'ditch with a lip (OE *lippa*)', but the first el. could be a pers.n. The name occurs as *Luppigediche* 1291 SCD, *Lyppyndyche* 1447 *ib*, in Sunningwell.

23 'seven acres', v. seofon, æcer, indicating arable land, v. 626.

24 'heathen burial-place', v. hǣðen, byrgels.

25 'short land', land probably being an arable strip, v. 626. Nos. 19, 22, 23, 24 and 25 occur in VIII in the reverse order (p. 736).

26 'along the furrow to the half-acre', v. 626 f.

27 'willow bed', v. wiðig, bedd. The likeliest place for this would be the stream junction N. of Northcourt.

28 'Dunna's ford'; this is *dunnanforda* in VIII (p. 736, n. 17), and is named from the same man as Dunmore Fm (Pt 2 438).

29 'Sunningwell brook', v. map. This stream is the S.W. boundary of Sunningwell (Pt 2 459).

30 This is *wuduforda* in VII (p. 733, n. 8), *wudeford* in VIII (p. 736, n. 15), *wudaforda* in IX (p. 738, n. 25); 'ford by the wood', v. wudu, ford and map. Cf. *Wodefordisfurlonge*, f.n. in Abingdon, Pt 2 442.

31 hrycg perhaps refers to a feature of the arable land, v. 626 f.

32 'west marsh', v. mōr.

33 The brōc is Wildmoor Brook.

34 'from the bridge to barley island.' This first piece of mead is in Kennington, probably S. of *Berige*. For *Berige* v. p. 726, n. 12.

35 'new ditch', v. nīwe, dīc.

36 'thick willow-tree', v. grēat, welig, and cf. p. 737, n. 49.

37 'hedgerow', v. hege, rǣw.

38 'river', v. ēa.

39 *ennanbeorgum* should probably be connected with Eney in Radley (v. map), the two names meaning 'Enna's tumuli' (v. beorg) and 'Enna's island' (v. Pt 2 456). *Ennanbeorgum* appears as *Emborowe Eliz RentSur*, a document relating to Sunningwell.

40 'ditch end.'

41 'crooked stream', v. wōh, lacu.

42 'tumulus', v. beorg; there is a tumulus in Radley village, v. map.

43 'between meadow and hill'; dūn may be used of the 175' contour.

E V   THE BOUNDS OF WYTHAM AND NORTH AND SOUTH HINKSEY: C. 957 (C. 1200) BCS 1002

Ærest on mægðæ ford¹. þæt mid stræme on stanford². forð mid streame wið utan cytan igge³ on þa land lace⁴. of þære lace on scecyling æcer⁵. þæt on hiwege⁶ to yfemestan leagæ⁷. þæt on preosta leage⁸. þæt to catleage⁹. þæt to cybban stane¹⁰. of þæm stane on ða þrio gemæru¹¹ ðæt innan ruwanleage¹² to brogan gete¹³. þæt to sundran edisce¹⁴ on þone greatan þorn¹⁵. of þæm ðorne on totan healas¹⁶. þæt in to tiddamcumb¹⁷. of ðæm cumbe on tetan hylle¹⁸. of tytan hylle. to ðæm heafodweg[19] andlang cumbes to þæm hæcce[20]. of þæm hæcce to paðe stocce[21]. þæt to plumleage[22]. þæt on friðelaby-rig[23]. þæt to ydyrleage[24]. of ydyrleage to ðæm stane[25]. þæt on temese æt eanflæde gelade[26]. þæt amidstreame. þæt hit cymð eft on mægðaford[27].

NOTES

1 'maiden ford' or 'mayweed ford', *v.* mægð[1], mægðe, ford. This occurs also in VII (p. 734, n. 26). It may be *Maideford* 1252 InqMisc.

2 'stone ford', *v.* p. 726, n. 10. The position of these two fords cannot be ascertained, and it seems probable that the various water-courses have changed since the 10th cent.

3 'island of the kite', *v.* cȳta, īeg; this is probably *Kidney Mead* 1721 *Bodl*, in a document relating to S. Hinksey, *Kidney Meadow* 1814 S. Hinksey *EnclA*.

4 Probably synonymous with Land Brook (Pt 1 12–13) which forms the boundary between Denchworth and Goosey. 'Boundary stream', *v.* lacu, land being used in the sense 'estate'.

5 *v.* p. 726, n. 9.

6 *v.* p. 728, n. 15.

7 *v.* p. 728, n. 13.

8 'priests' wood or clearing', *v.* prēost, lēah.

9 'cat wood or clearing', *v.* cat(t), lēah.

10 *v.* p. 728, n. 11. The survey here leaves the boundary of the estate described in IV and follows approximately the modern boundary between Cumnor and North Hinksey.

11 'three boundaries', *v.* þrēo, (ge)mǣre.

12 'rough wood or clearing', *v.* rūh, lēah. This is mentioned also in VI (p. 732, n. 8).

13 *v.* geat, first el. apparently OE brōga 'prodigy, monster, terror', perhaps used as a pers.n.

14 *v.* edisc 'enclosed park'. For the first el. Professor Löfvenberg suggests a pers.n. *Sundra* corresponding to ON *Sundri*; it cannot be sundor 'separate', as that is an adverb.

15 'thick thorn-tree', *v.* grēat, þorn.

16 *ClaudiusBvi* has *cotan healas*, which makes the first el. uncertain; it may be the pers.n. *Tōta*. Second el. the pl. of healh 'nook or corner'.

17 *ClaudiusBvi* has *tiddan cumb* '*Tidda*'s valley', *v.* cumb. This may

be the valley in which Tilbury Fm is situated. Grundy mentions a modern name Titcomb Hill, $\frac{1}{3}$ mile S.W. of N. Hinksey village. This would correspond well enough to the charter name, but the survey is almost certainly a good deal further N. at this point.

18 'Tȳta's hill', *v.* hyll.

19 *v.* hēafod 'head', weg.

20 'gate', *v.* hæc(c).

21 'tree-stump by the path', *v.* pæð, stocc.

22 'plum-tree wood or clearing', *v.* plūme, lēah.

23 '*Friðela*'s fort', cf. Frilford (Pt 2 407). Wytham Hill would be a likely place for a fortification. Ramparts here might have led to the belief recorded in *ClaudiusBvi* (Abingdon 1, 8) that a fort was built here during the war between Offa of Mercia and Cynewulf of Wessex – 'factum erat castellum super montem de Witham'. *v.* burh, byrig.

24 *v.* lēah, first el. obscure.

25 'stone', *v.* stān.

26 'Ēanflǣd's crossing-place', *v.* (ge)lād and map. The county boundary follows first the modern Thames, then a rivulet, then Seacourt stream and (roughly) Hinksey stream. Seacourt stream may have been regarded as the main stream of the Thames in the 10th cent.

27 *ClaudiusCix* repeats a number of boundary-marks before the final phrase *eft on mægðaford*. This is an obvious error, and has not been reproduced here.

E VI THE BOUNDS OF CUMNOR: 968 (c. 1200)
BCS 1222

Ærest of stirigan pole[1] to þære dic[2]. andlang dices to infyrde[3] a be mære on temese[4]. andlang temese on wadleahe[5]. of wadleahe ðet on þa ealdan dic[6]. andlang þere dic on feower gemæra[7]. of feower gemæra on ruhan leahe[8]. of ruhan leahe on þone haran stan[9]. of þam stane þæt on wase[10]. of wase eft on styrigan pole[1].

NOTES

1 *v.* p. 724, n. 7.

2 'ditch', *v.* dīc.

3 This term occurs also in I, *v.* p. 724, n. 12, referring to a point some 2 miles upstream.

4 R. Thames.

5 'wood or clearing where woad grows', v. wād, lēah. This was probably on the Wytham–Cumnor boundary, and might have been the name of Wytham Great Wood.

6 'old ditch', v. eald, dīc.

7 'four boundaries', v. fēower, (ge)mǣre.

8 'rough wood or clearing'; this is mentioned also in V, v. p. 730, n. 12.

9 'boundary stone', possibly identical with the one mentioned in II (p. 725, n. 12).

10 Osse Ditch, v. p. 723, n. 4 and map.

E VII THE BOUNDS OF TWENTY HIDES 'AT ABINGDON': n.d. (c. 1200) BCS 906

Ærest on eoccenforda[1]. up andlang eoccenes[2] to abbedes dic[3]. þet to cealdenwulle[4]. þæt to mearcforda[5] andlang broces oð þene grenen weig[6]. andlang weges to broce[7]. þæt to wuduforda[8]. þæt adune be broce oð pyppel riðiges ut scyte[9]. þæt þurhð ðene mor[10] a beriðige[11]. to guman grafe[12]. þæt to pyppel bricge[13]. þæt on ðene sic æt þere fulan æc[14]. þæt to hæglea[15] on ðæne bradan mere[16]. þæt a be wyrt walan[17] to bromcumbes heafod[18]. þæt on gerihtum to abbendune[19]. to þere port strete[20]. þæt andlang stret on hiwege[21]. þæt to ecgunes wyrðe[22]. þenne on bacgan leah[23]. þæt on scæceling æcer[24]. þæt ut on stanford[25]. þæt to mægþeforda[26]. andlang lace[27]. ut on temese[28]. þæt on forð mid streame wið ufan micclanige[29] on cearewyllan[30]. eft wið neoðan berige[31] on temese[28]. þæt þer up be streame. þæt on bacgan broc[32]. þæt on heafoces oran[33]. þæt on holan dene[34]. þæt on tidewaldes wille[35]. andlang broces ut on temese[28]. þæt forð mid streame oð geafling lace[36]. andlang lace eft ut on temese[28]. þæt up be streame on occenes gerstun dic[37]. þæt a be dic on eoccen[2]. þæt þer up eft on eoccenforda[1]. Æðeleahing wudu[38]. colmanora[39]. and geatescumb[40]. hyren into ðys twentigum hydum. þa ic sylf studum gerad. studum gereow. and rumoðlice gescarode[41] me sylfum. and minum foregengum. and eftyrgengum to ecumrymete. for gode and for worulde.---

NOTES

1 This is the ford from which Ock Hundred (earlier *Ocford Hundred*) was named (Pt 2 400). Ock Bridge is on the site of the ford.

2 R. Ock.

3 'abbot's ditch', v. abbod, dīc; Shippon, which lies to the W. of

this boundary, was not acquired by the Abbey till after the Norman Conquest (*supra* 721).

4 'cold stream or spring', *v.* ceald, w(i)ell; this is the stream, now Wildmoor Brook, from which Cholswell (Pt **2** 438) is named.

5 'boundary ford', *v.* mearc, ford.

6 'green way', *v.* grēne[1], wēg.

7 'brook', probably the *sunninga wylle broc* of other surveys (*v.* p. 729, n. 29).

8 'wood ford', *v.* p. 729, n. 30 and map.

9 'pebble-stream's outfall', *v.* papol, pyp(p)el, rīðig, and see map.

10 *Bvi* has *þurh ðæt dene mor*, which is probably correct, 'valley marsh', *v.* denu, mōr.

11 'always by the stream', i.e. *pyppel riðig*.

12 Apparently 'man's grove', *v.* grāf; *guma* may be a pers.n.

13 'pebble bridge.'

14 'to the stream at the diseased oak', *v.* fūl, āc. There are a number of drainage ditches in the area, and the sīc may be one of these.

15 'enclosure wood or clearing', *v.* (ge)hæg, lēah.

16 'broad pool', *v.* brād, mere.

17 wyrtwala sometimes means 'foot of the slope', which does not seem appropriate here. Perhaps 'edge of the wood', with reference to Bagley Wood, *v.* 633.

18 'the head of broom valley', *v.* map; Brumcombe and Brumcombe Copse (Pt **2** 459) preserve the name of this valley.

19 The occurrence of *abbendun*, the OE form of Abingdon (Pt **2** 432–4), as a boundary-mark is difficult to explain. It seems probable that the name is comparable to *Æscesdun*, the OE name for the Berkshire Downs (Pt **1** 2–3), and that it originally denoted all the high ground between Abingdon and North Hinksey, of which Boar's Hill is one of the highest points. The bounds are here ascending the eastern tip of Boar's Hill. The story told in *Claudius-Bvi* of a migration by the earliest monks from this place to the later site by the river was probably invented on the basis of these bounds. For a detailed discussion of the problem *v.* M. Gelling 'The Hill of Abingdon', *Oxoniensia* XXII (1957), pp. 54–62.

20 This term means 'road leading to a market town', *v.* port, strǣt. The identification is a matter of some difficulty. Possibly the *port strǣt* and the *hig weg* are identical, cf. p. 766 for another example of a road which has different names for various stretches of the route.

21 'hay way', *v.* p. 728, n. 15.

22 'Ecghūn's enclosure', *v.* worð, wyrð.

23 Bagley Wood (Pt **2** 453). The 10th-cent. wood seems to have been of similar extent to the modern one.

24 *v.* p. 726, n. 9.

25 *v.* p. 726, n. 10.

26 *v.* p. 730, n. 1.

27 'stream', *v.* lacu.

28 R. Thames; the name is applied in charter bounds to the western branch of the river, see map.

29 'big island', *v.* micel, īeg; perhaps the northern part of the land between the two arms of the Thames. In the bounds of Kennington (III), *berege* seems to be used of this same ground (p. 726, n. 12).

30 R. Cherwell, used in these bounds of the eastern branch of R. Thames, *v.* map.

31 *v.* p. 726, n. 12. *berige* seems here to be used of the southern portion of the land between the arms of the Thames.

32 'Bacga's brook', *v.* map for suggested identification. The survey has travelled upstream to reach this, and is probably excluding the first piece of mead land described in IV, which belonged to the Bayworth estate.

33 'hawk's slope', *v.* heafoc, ōra.

34 'hollow valley', *v.* hol², denu. This may be the valley in which Little London is situated.

35 'Tīdweald's spring or stream', *v.* w(i)ell; this may be an earlier name of *Wulfrices broc*, p. 725, n. 2.

36 This stream (*v.* map) forms the modern county boundary. The name is probably a derivative in ing of geaf(e)l 'fork'.

37 'ditch of the paddock by the Ock', *v.* gærs-tūn, dīc. This was probably an enclosure S. of the R. Ock.

38 'Æðelhēah's wood', with connective -ing, *v.* Pt **2** 462. No later reference has been found to this.

39 Mentioned in IX, p. 738, n. 12.

40 'Gēat's valley' or 'valley of the gate', *v.* geat, cumb. Yatscombe in Sunningwell (Pt **2** 460) preserves the name.

41 This is a curious addition to the survey; *ic* is presumably intended for the grantor, who is made to say that he has perambulated the bounds, sometimes (reading *stundum* for *studum*) riding and sometimes rowing. An anathema in OE follows the text given here.

E VIII THE BOUNDS OF TWENTY HIDES 'AT ABINGDON':
956 (c. 1200) BCS 924

Ærest on temese[1] besuðan fordwere[2] ðær up on ða dic on occenes
gærstun[3] suðeweardne. þonne andlang dic to eoccen[4]. andlang
eoccenes to abbodes dic[5]. andlang dic to cealdan wylle[6]. of cealdan
wylle on þæt risc slæd[7] middeweard oð torhtwoldes mor[8]. þæt þær
on ða dic[9]. andlang dices to mearcforda[10]. þonne up andlang broces[11]
oð hyt cymð to emnes þam ealdan læghrycge[12]. þonne on gerihte be
tweoh porteles treow[13] on þone ellen styb[14]. ðæt þær on wudeford[15]
on sunningawylles broc[16]. andlang broces to dunnanforda[17]. þæt þær
on þæt wiðig bed[18]. þonne on ðone heafan æcer[19] norðeweardne.
þonne andlang furh[20] to þam heafdan[21]. þæt þær suð ofer ðone heafon
æcer[19]. þæt þær east on ða furh[20]. ðæt to ðam sceortan londe[22]. þær
on ðone hæðænen byrgels[23]. þonne þær on þa seofen æceres[24] weste
wearde. þæt þær norð to lippan dic[25]. andlang dic þurh suggan graf[26].
þet on þone ellen styb[27]. ðonne on ða brembel ðyrnan[28] on ða dic[29].
andlang dic to horo pytte[30]. þonne þurh madoces leah[31] on ða ealdan
dic[32]. ðonne on þa æcer dic[33]. ðonne on hæsel dic[34]. of hæsel dic on
ðone gemærweg[35] on beganwyrðe[36]. andlang weges to hig wege[37].
andlang hiweges to Ecgunes wyrðæ[38]. þonon on Bacganleah[39]. þæt
a be wirtwalan[40]. þæt on Bacganbroc[41]. of bacganbroce on hafeces
oran[42] andlang ðes gemær hagan[43]. þæt ut on ryge wyrðæ[44] westeweardne on ða ealdan dic[45]. þonne andlang dic to perhangran[46].
ðonne on Wlfrices broc[47]. þonne on gerihte ofer hyrdyige[48] to þam
greatan welige[49]. þet ðær ut on temese[1]. ðonne andlang temæse. þet
eft on eoccenes gerstun dic[3] suðeweardne.

NOTES

1 R. Thames.
2 'weir by the ford', v. ford, wer.
3 'the ditch round the southern part of Ock paddock', v. p. 734, n.
37.
4 R. Ock.
5 v. p. 732, n. 3.
6 v. p. 733, n. 4.
7 'rush valley', v. risc, slæd.
8 'Torhtweald's marsh', v. mōr.
9 'ditch', v. dīc.
10 v. p. 733, n. 5.

11 It is not certain, here or in the corresponding passage of VII, which 'brook' is meant; it is probably Wildmoor Brook.

12 'alongside the old fallow ridge', *v.* eald, lǣge, hrycg.

13 *potteles treow* Bvi and *C.C.C.C.cxi*; *v.* trēow, the same landmark is *Pottenes treow* in IX (p. 738, n. 26). The first el. is uncertain. *treow* is probably acc. pl.

14 'elder stump', *v.* ellen, stybb.

15 *v.* p. 729, n. 30, and map. *C.C.C.C.cxi* has *wuduford*.

16 *v.* p. 729, n. 29.

17 *v.* p. 729, n. 28.

18 *v.* p. 729, n. 27.

19 *healfan æcer* Bvi, *C.C.C.C.cxi*, and also in IV, *v.* p. 729, n. 26.

20 'furrow', *v.* 627.

21 'headlands'. *v.* 626.

22 *v.* p. 729, n. 25.

23 *v.* p. 729, n. 24.

24 *v.* p. 729, n. 23.

25 *v.* p. 729, n. 22.

26 'Sucga's grove', named from the same man as Sugworth in Radley and Sugnell Copse in Sunningwell (Pt 2 456, 460). *C.C.C.C.cxi* has *sucgan graf*.

27 'elder stump', cf. n. 14 *supra*. This stump is mentioned also in IV, p. 728, n. 21.

28 'bramble thorn-bush', *v.* brēmel, þyrne.

29 'ditch.'

30 'dirt pit', *v.* horu, pytt; the pit is mentioned in IV, p. 728, n. 20.

31 *v.* p. 728, n. 19.

32 'old ditch', this is *wulfstanes dic* in IV, p. 728, n. 18.

33 'acre ditch', *v.* 626.

34 *v.* p. 728, n. 17.

35 'boundary way', *v.* (ge)mǣre, weg.

36 Bayworth, *v.* Pt 2 459. The bounds do not go very near Bayworth, and 35 is presumably the boundary way which either belongs or leads to that settlement.

37 *v.* p. 728, n. 15, and map.

38 *v.* p. 734, n. 22.

39 *v.* p. 734, n. 23.

40 *wyrtwala* 'root', appears in this instance to mean the northern edge of Bagley Wood, cf. p. 733, n. 17.

41 *v.* p. 734; n. 32; this survey, unlike VII, has not run out to the Thames.

42 *v.* p. 734, n. 33.

43 'boundary enclosure', *v.* (ge)mǣre, haga[1], and 628.

44 *v.* p. 725, n. 3.

45 *v.* p. 726, n. 4.

46 'pearwood on a slope', *v.* peru, hangra.

47 *v.* p. 725, n. 2, and map.

48 *v.* p. 726, n. 14, and map.

49 *v.* p. 729, n. 36, and map.

E IX   THE BOUNDS OF WOOTTON: A.D. 985
        (c. 1200) KCD 1283

Ærest æt gorgrafes slede[1] on þæt crudel. of ðam crundelle[2] on læccesford[3]. on þone mor[4]. of þam forda[5] on ceobban hangran[6]. of ðam hangran on þæt weterslæd[7]. of ðam slæde on sceobbanoran-wylle[8]. of sceobbanoran wylle on prohthangran[9]. of prohthangran on Cybban stan[10]. of þam stane on þone hrycg weg[11]. andlang weges on Colmenoran[12]. of Colmenoran. on wendlescumb[13]. of þam cumbe. on ðone swan weg[14]. of þam wege. on riscleahe[15] ufewearde. of riscleahe. on þone rugan weg[16]. of þam wege. on þone lam pyt[17]. of þam pytte. on þescumbes heafod[18]. of þæs cumbes heafode. on þone port weg[19]. oð ðone greatan ðorn[20]. of þam ðorne. on foxholacumb[21] ufeweardne. of þam cumbe to blacan graue[22] ufeweardan. on ða dic[23]. andlang dic. to heorthamme[24]. of heorthamme. to wudaforda[25]. of wudaforda. on wottenes treow[26]. of þam treow. andlang gemæres. on þone mor[27]. þæt up andlang broces[28] on Cealdan wyl[29]. of cealdan wylle. to þære ðorn rewe[30]. Of þære ðorn ræwe. þæt eft in on gorgraues slæd[1].

NOTES

1 *v.* p. 727, n. 1, and map. The grammatical forms of this group of ns. raise some problems, *v.* Tengstrand 272.

2 *v.* p. 727, n. 4.

3 *v.* p. 725, n. 15, and map.

4 'marsh', *v.* mōr; the precise line of the boundary is uncertain, as are those of neighbouring surveys.

5 'ford.'

6 'Ceobba's wood on a slope', *v.* hangra, named from the same man as *Cybban stan* (n. 10 *infra*).

7 'water valley', *v.* wæter, slæd.

8 'the spring on Sceobba's slope', cf. p. 727, n. 9.

9 *ClaudiusBvi* has *wrohthangran*, which is doubtless correct, *v.* p. 727, n. 10.

10 *v.* p. 728, n. 11.

11 'ridge way', *v.* hrycg, weg; probably a road along the top of Boar's Hill.

12 'coalman's slope', *v.* ōra. This was one of the three appurtenances to the 20-hide estate at Abingdon described in VIII (p. 734, n. 39). A 'coalman' may have been a charcoal burner, but Professor Löfvenberg points out that *coleman* is not on record as an occupational surname.

13 '*Wendel*'s valley', *v.* cumb. This archaic pers.n. occurs also in Kingston Winslow (Pt 2 345–6).

14 'herdsman way', *v.* swān², weg.

15 'rush clearing', *v.* risc, lēah.

16 'rough way', *v.* rūh, weg.

17 'loam pit', *v.* lām, pytt.

18 'the top of the valley', *v.* hēafod, cumb.

19 'town way'; *v.* port-weg. Mrs G. M. Lambrick considered this to be the road on which the Fox Inn stands.

20 'thick thorn-tree', *v.* grēat, þorn.

21 'fox-hole valley', *v.* fox-hol, cumb. Foxcombe Heath and Hill (Pt 2 459–60) preserve the name. This is the first certainly identifiable point in the survey since 3. If Mrs Lambrick's identification of 19 is correct, the reference here is to a descent into the valley on its E. side.

22 'black grove', Blagrove Fm (Pt 2 462) preserves the name, *v.* map.

23 'ditch', *v.* dīc.

24 'river-meadow frequented by deer', *v.* heorot, hamm. The name occurs as *Hertham* 1447 SCD, in Sunningwell.

25 *v.* p. 729, n. 30, and map.

26 *ClaudiusBvi* has *Pottenes treow*, *v.* p. 736, n. 13.

27 *v.* mōr; this is marshy ground by Wildmoor Brook.

28 *v.* brōc, the streams in this area may not correspond exactly to those of the 10th cent.

29 *v.* p. 733, n. 4.

30 'thorn hedgerow', *v.* þorn, rǣw.

F WANTAGE HUNDRED

All the charters dealing with land in this Hundred are preserved in the Abingdon Chronicle; they are –

I. BCS 522 and 523, A.D. 868, by which Queen Æðelswið of Mercia grants 15 hides at Lockinge to a minister named Cuðwulf. The charter is copied in both MSS, but no bounds are copied with it. There is, however, a set of bounds of a 15-hide estate at Lockinge at the end of *ClaudiusCix*, and these (which are printed as BCS 523) are assumed to be connected with the charter. The lack of detail in the survey suggests that it is earlier than the 10th cent. It probably describes the modern parish of Lockinge, but with so few boundary-marks no certainty is possible.

II. BCS 949 and 950, A.D. 956, by which King Eadwig grants to his adopted relative Ælric 20 hides in Hanney. The scribe of *Claudius-Bvi* gives two versions of this, with slight variations of the wording, and both versions include the bounds. *ClaudiusCix* has the bounds but not the charter. The survey refers to East Hanney, though the correspondence with the modern parish is not exact.

III. BCS 1224, A.D. 968, by which King Eadgar grants an estate at Hanney to Abingdon. The charter is copied in both MSS. In *ClaudiusCix* the hidage is three times stated to be 10; in *Claudius-Bvi*, the heading and text of the charter give it as 20, but in the text *viginti* is written over an erasure. The survey is different from that in II, but describes the same area.

IV. BCS 833, A.D. 947, by which King Eadred grants 5 hides at Denchworth to Wulfric. The bounds describe the modern parish of Denchworth. BCS 1034, A.D. 958, is a grant by King Eadwig of 5 hides at Denchworth to Wulfric, apparently a repetition of the grant of 947, with the same bounds. Both charters are copied only in *ClaudiusBvi*. *ClaudiusCix* has a single set of boundaries for Denchworth, headed *Mete Denceswrðe. v. mansarum sunt hec*, and this text is used *infra*. BCS 1172 (A.D. 965) is a grant to Abingdon of 2 hides at Denchworth, but there are no bounds. Possibly this is North Denchworth (*v.* no. VIII).

V. BCS 1047, A.D. 959, for which *v.* 717. One of the places restored to Abingdon by King Eadgar in this charter is a 15-hide estate at

Goosey. The bounds of Goosey at the end of *ClaudiusCix* presumably relate to this charter, but J. Stevenson (Abingdon 1, 15) has inserted them misleadingly after the Chronicler's statement that Goosey was originally given to the Abbey by King Offa. This has caused Birch to print them as BCS 907. The survey describes the modern parish.

VI. BCS 981, A.D. 956, by which King Eadwig grants 10 hides at Ginge to Abingdon. This is copied in both MSS. It was considered spurious by W. H. Stevenson (*English Historical Review* XXIX, 1914, p. 695 n. 33, p. 700 n. 49). The survey cannot be followed precisely, but it is clear that it describes roughly the southern part of the modern parish of Ardington, which includes West Ginge. The same survey appears again in BCS 1047 (cf. V *supra*) to describe the 10-hide estate at Ginge which is one of the places restored to Abingdon by this charter.

VII. BCS 1142, A.D. 964, by which King Eadgar grants 10 hides at Hendred to Abingdon. This was considered 'suspicious' by Napier and Stevenson (*The Crawford Collection of Early Charters and Documents*, p. 118, n. 1). It is copied in both MSS, and the survey describes the northern part of the parishes of East and West Hendred. There are two more Abingdon charters relating to Hendred: BCS 975, A.D. 956, is a grant (only copied in *Claudius-Bvi*) by King Eadwig to Brihtric of 10 hides there, and BCS 1095, A.D. 962, is a grant (copied in both MSS) by King Eadgar to Abingdon of 3 hides. The copy of BCS 975 has a heading *Metae de Hannerithe*, but there are no bounds, only a statement in Old English that this is the charter of the 10 hides of common land. BCS 1095 has the statement 'þises land gemæra syn gemæne sua þæt lið æfre æcer under æcer' where the bounds should be.

VIII. KCD 746, A.D. 1032, copied (with omission of most of the witnesses in *ClaudiusCix*) in both MSS, by which King Cnut grants to Abingdon 2 hides at Lyford and some property in Oxford. The bounds are followed by a statement (in Old English in *ClaudiusBvi*, in Latin in *Cix*) that Æðelwine bequeathed this piece of land, and the house in Oxford which he himself occupied, to Abingdon. If the property were really acquired in this way, Cnut's charter could be explained as a confirmation of the bequest. The land described by the bounds of this charter is not now in Lyford; it is the projecting portion of the modern parish of West Hanney which lies between Lyford and Denchworth, and which

includes North Denchworth Fm (*v.* map). This may be the 2-hide
estate given to Abingdon by BCS 1172 (*v.* no. IV), but if so the
Abbey had lost it between 965 and 1032.

This group of charters provides eight surveys covering seven
estates, four of which (Lockinge, East Hanney, Denchworth and
Goosey) correspond to modern parishes. Of the remaining three
surveys, two (Ginge and part of West Hanney) describe small estates
now incorporated in larger units, and the third (Hendred) describes
the northern part of the two modern parishes.

Comparison of hidage assessments in the charters with those in DB
shows only two possible exact correspondences; the 10-hide estate at
Ginge (VI) may be identical with the Abingdon estate there which was
assessed at 10 hides TRE, and Walter Gifard's 2-hide estate at West
Hanney may represent the 2 hides at Lyford described in VIII.
Goosey (V) was 15 hides in 959, 17 hides TRE; and Lockinge (I),
assessed at 15 hides in 868, contained two 10-hide estates TRE. (It
should be noted that E. and W. Lockinge have been separate parishes,
and are shown as such on the 6″ map.) No comparison is possible in
the case of Hendred, as the estate of 956 cannot be equated with the
various estates in East and West Hendred in 1086, and similar difficulties arise in the case of Hanney. The most surprising apparent
change in assessment is that at Denchworth, where there was a 5-hide
estate in 947; DB describes three estates there, assessed at 7, 6 and 5
hides, and even if one of these is North Denchworth, which is now in
West Hanney, the hidage seems high for the area.

References to arable land are relatively frequent in this group of
surveys. There are 'headlands' in East Hanney, and the bounds of
Hendred run 'along the headland(s)' seven times; 'furrows' are mentioned in Goosey and Ginge, and there are 'loam pits' in West
Hanney. Communal farming is also referred to in the grant of 5 hides
at Charlton (in Wantage) in 988, KCD 1278, which has no bounds but
a statement in Latin after the anathema stating 'the aforesaid land is
not demarcated on all sides by clear bounds because to left and right
lie acres in combination one with another'. In Hendred, where the
survey has frequent references to headlands, there is a possible
correspondence between the charter references to these features and
the visible ridge and furrow. Another Hendred charter, BCS 1095,
two years earlier in date than the one with the survey, and referring
to a smaller area, has for boundary clause the statement (in Old

English) that 'the bounds of this land are common so that acre lies
ever under acre'.

Streams, drainage ditches and roads are frequent boundary-marks,
and there are a number of tumuli. There is a remarkable absence of
reference to trees, in fact a total absence with the single exception of
the 'thick thorn-stump' in Hendred.

F I THE BOUNDS OF LOCKINGE: 868 (c. 1200)
BCS 523

Æn westeweardum and on suðeweardum sceldmere[1]. þon' of
sceldmere on smalan weg[2] and ðanon on gemærbeorg[3]. and of gemær
beorge on werð welle[4]. of werð welle feower æcras be norðan
lakincg[5].

NOTES

1 Probably 'shield-shaped pool', v. Journal I 34 and mere. Grundy
 has an excellent note on this. It occurs also in the Farnborough
 survey (B (b) VIII), so can be roughly located; v. map for probable
 position. Grundy (1926) says it is a few yards in diameter, usually
 dry, but full when an intermittent spring (the *cytelflodan* of the
 Farnborough bounds) is running. There was no sign of it in Sep-
 tember 1961. It may have been more extensive in A.D. 868 than in
 1926, since the survey refers to its western and its southern part.
2 'narrow way', v. smæl, weg.
3 'boundary tumulus', v. (ge)mǣre, beorg.
4 'marsh spring', v. wer(e)ð. The name suggests a location in the N.
 of the parish, near Pinmarsh Fm and Ardington Marsh Lock (v.
 map).
5 *lakincg* is Lockinge Brook (v. map). The survey is curiously
 expressed here, and the text may, as Grundy suggested, be corrupt.

F II THE BOUNDS OF EAST HANNEY: 956 (c. 1200)
BCS 949

Ærest of ðæs cinges gemære[1] on wanontinge broc[2]. andlang streames
þæt hit cymð ut on cyllanrið[3]. þæt þonne andlang riðe þæt hit cymð
ut on Eoccenne[4]. ðæt andlang Eoccene þæt hit cymð to wulfmæres
mylne[5]. þæt þonon suð on þone ealdan broc[6]. andlang broces þæt hit
cymð to snoddan fleote[7]. of þæm fleote to þæm bradan hærpaðæ[8].
andlang hærpaðæs þæt hit cymð eft to ðæs cinges gemæres[1].

NOTES

1 'king's boundary' (*v.* cyning, (ge)mǣre and map). This is the N. boundary of Grove, which appears to be a land-unit of post-Conquest origin. Assuming that Grove was earlier part of Wantage, 'king's boundary' refers to the West Saxon royal estate there.

2 Letcombe Brook, *v.* map and Pt 1 17–18. This is the stream from which Wantage is named.

3 Childrey Brook, *v.* Pt 1 8. This brook does not now form the boundary between E. and W. Hanney. This survey, like that of Garford (p. 711, n. 3), implies that Nor Brook was regarded as the main course of Childrey Brook in the 10th cent.

4 R. Ock.

5 'Wulfmǣr's mill', *v.* map. Marcham Mill is in this position today.

6 *v.* map and p. 744, n. 7.

7 'Snodda's small stream', *v.* flēot. The topography is obscured by the Wilts and Berks canal. The Steventon f.n. *Snogeflete* (Pt 2 423) may be a corrupt version of this n.

8 'broad army-path', *v.* brād, here-pæð and map. There is a track along the boundary here.

F III   THE BOUNDS OF EAST HANNEY: 968 (c. 1200)
BCS 1224

Ærest on ða ealdan dic¹ æt þam heafod stoccan². andlang dic on wanating³ þæt andlang stremes on þone readan meare⁴ on cille riðe⁵. þonne went hit ðær east. þæt andlang streames oð hit scyt on Eoccene⁶. þæt andlang eoccene oð hit scyt on ealden wanatiting⁷. þonne went hit þær west andlang streames oð hit scyt on snoddan fleot⁸ middeweardne. þonne went hit þær west on þa heafda⁹ þæt hit cymð on þone smalan weg¹⁰. þæt andlang weges oð hit geeið eft on þa ealdan dic¹.

NOTES

1 'old ditch', *v.* eald, dīc; this corresponds to the 'king's boundary' of II.

2 'head-stumps'; there is good literary evidence to suggest that a hēafod-stocc was 'a post on which the head of a beheaded criminal was exposed'.

3 Letcombe Brook, *v. supra*, n. 2.

4 'red pool', *v.* rēad, mere; *ClaudiusBvi* has *mære*.

5

5 Childrey Brook, *v.* p. 743, n. 3.

6 R. Ock.

7 'old Wantage.' This corresponds to *ealdan broc* in II, and the same stream is called 'Wantage' in the bounds of Drayton (p. 712, n. 7) and Hendred (p. 748, n. 7). The distinction made by the present bounds between 'Wantage' (Letcombe Brook) and 'old Wantage' suggests that in 968 Letcombe Brook was felt to have the better claim to the name. *v.* map.

8 *v.* p. 743, n. 7.

9 'headlands', *v.* 626.

10 'narrow way', *v.* smæl, weg. This corresponds to the *bradan hærpaðæ* of II, but this survey takes a very different view of the road's status.

F IV THE BOUNDS OF DENCHWORTH: 947 (c. 1200)
BCS 833

Ærest on cilla riðe¹. þæt west on muttic² on ða dic³ on Ordulfes gemære⁴ to ceawan hlewe⁵ andlang dic on landbroc⁶ andlang broces to þam norðran deneceswyrðe⁷. þonon east rihte eft on cillan riðe. þonne ðær suð ðær we ær onfengon. þonne licgað þær þa þreo hida on þam norðran deneceswyrðe undælede⁸.

NOTES

1 Childrey Brook, *v.* Pt 1 8–9.

2 This term is obscure; it occurs in both MSS.

3 'ditch'; the *muttic* of 2 may be a corrupt version of the name of this ditch.

4 'Ordwulf's boundary', presumably referring to a former owner of East Challow.

5 'Ceawa's tumulus', *v.* hlæw; E. and W. Challow (Pt 2 292–3) are named from this. A perambulation of the boundary in 1953 revealed no trace of it.

6 Land Brook, *v.* map and Pt 1 12–13; the name probably means 'boundary brook'.

7 The copy of BCS 1034 in *ClaudiusBvi* has *to þam norþarn deneces-wurþe gemæra* 'to the boundary of the northern Denchworth', which seems appropriate though Tengstrand (204) considers it an error; *v.* map for position of North Denchworth Fm, which is now in the parish of W. Hanney.

8 At a later date there was a separate estate at North Denchworth, which is the subject of no. VIII *infra*. The statement that the 3 hides at North Denchworth lie unseparated may have some connection with this. Possibly the sentence means that the 3 hides in question, though recognised as part of the land of North Denchworth, have not been split off as part of the 2-hide estate there, but remain part of the main estate of Denchworth. Professor Finberg (*The Agrarian History of England and Wales* I, 11, 492–3) suggests, however, that *undælede* means that the 3 hides are not divided into open-field strips.

F V THE BOUNDS OF GOOSEY: 959 (c. 1200) BCS 1047

Ærest on þa mærdic[1]. eastewearde. þæt innan Tealeburnan[2]. andlang tealeburnan þæt innan eoccen[3]. andlang eoccen þæt innan þa merdic[4]. of þam mærdic þæt innan þa furh[5]. of þa furh þæt innan þæt riðig[6]. of þam riðig þæt innan lanbroc[7]. andlang landbroces ford on butan þone ham[8]. eft on þa mærdic[1] eastewearde.

NOTES

1 'boundary ditch', *v*. (ge)mǣre, dīc and map. The survey starts at its eastern end.
2 Stutfield Brook, *v*. map and Pt I 17.
3 R. Ock. Two other surveys, Charney Bassett (p. 704, n. 1) and part of W. Hanney (p. 749, n. 1), refer to the Ock in this region, and none of the three is easy to follow on the modern map. It seems possible that the Ock has changed its course somewhat, and that it flowed some distance to the S. of the present main channel.
4 'boundary ditch', cf. n. 1.
5 'furrow', *v*. 627.
6 'stream', *v*. rīðig.
7 Land Brook, *v*. Pt I 12–13 and map.
8 'round the water-meadow'; the hamm was probably at the S.E. corner of the parish. *ford* is probably an error for *forð*.

F VI THE BOUNDS OF WEST GINGE: 956 (c. 1200) BCS 981

Ærest of lillanhlæwes crundele[1] middeweardan to loddere beorge[2]. þanon to grenan hlince[3] westeweardan. of þam hlince to Earnesdune[4] westewearde. þanon to holan dic[5] eastewearde. andlang þere dic twa furlanc norðweard. þanon east be hæfdan[6] twa furlang andlang fura[7] on lytlan wil[8]. andlang wylles on lacing broc[9]. Andlang broces eft on Gæing broc[10]. andlang broces on þa æwylma[11]. þanon andlang hearpaþes[12] on frigedæges treow[13]. of þam treow. andlang weterdene[14]. west to þere deopan dene[15] to þam readan stane[16]. of þam stane eft on lillanhlæwes crundele[1].

NOTES

1 'chalkpit of Lilla's tumulus', v. hlǣw, crundel; Lilley (Pt 2 497, 'Lilla's wood') in Catmore may be named from the same man.
2 'beggar hill or tumulus', v. loddere, beorg. If the survey includes part of Lockinge (v. n. 4 infra) this may refer to a tumulus on the Ridgeway, v. map. O.S. 6" map XX NE shows a boundary between E. and W. Lockinge, which the survey could be following.
3 'green linchet', v. 627.
4 'eagle's hill' or 'Earn's hill'. It is tempting to associate this with Arn Hill in Lockinge (Pt 2 487), v. map. This survey does not correspond with a modern land-unit. Grundy thought its western boundary ran through the middle of Ardington, and this may be so. If, on the other hand, the association with Arn Hill be correct, it runs through Lockinge, and may correspond to the boundary between E. and W. Lockinge shown on 6" maps, v. n. 2. There is a chalkpit in Lockinge (v. map) which could be the crundel of 1.
5 'hollow ditch', v. hol[2], dīc.
6 'headlands', v. 626.
7 'furrows', v. 627.
8 'small spring' or 'stream', v. lȳtel, w(i)ell and see map for probable position; it is mentioned also in the bounds of Hendred (p. 747, n. 1).
9 Lockinge Brook, v. Pt 1 13 and map.
10 Ginge Brook, v. Pt 1 10 and map.
11 'sources', i.e. of Ginge Brook, v. ǣwielm and map.
12 'army-path', v. here-pæð, evidently a road down the E. boundary of Ardington, v. map.

13 'Friday's tree.' It is suggested in Elements, s.v. **Frīgedæg**, that this referred to a solitary tree which was associated with the Crucifixion. The tree may have been at the S.E. corner of Ardington.

14 'water-valley', v. **wæter, denu**.

15 'deep valley', v. **dēop, denu**.

16 'red stone', v. **rēad, stān**.

F VII THE BOUNDS OF THE NORTH PART OF HENDRED: 964 (c. 1200) BCS 1142

Ærest on ðone litlan wil[1]. of þam wylle on rupelmes hlau[2]. of ðam hlawe andlang heafda[3]. pæt hit cymð on ðet hæfod land on weasthealf drymbeorgum[4]. þonne of ðam heafodlande on ðom gretan ðornstyb[5]. of ðæm stybbe on læce mere[6]. of ðæm mere on wanetingc broc[7]. andlang broces ðæt hit cymð to ðere dic[8] to stifingc hæma gemære[9]. andlang heafdan[10] eastweardan þæt hit cymð to ðes ealdormonnes gemere[11]. þonne syð andlang heafdu[10] þæt on risc broc[12]. þwires ofer risc broc andlang heafdan[10] þæt hit cymð on lacingc broc[13] on ðone lytlan wyl[14]. andlang broces on ðone oðereie wil[15]. þonon suð andlang heafda on babban byorh[16]. andlang heafda on blacan hylle[17] suðe-wearde. Of þære hylle west twa furlang to þæm hæfod lande. andlang heafod þæt hit sticað on ðere dic on lacingc broce[18]. west andlang broces eft on ðone litlan wyl[1]. þer ic onfeng. Seo med is on westhealf waneting þe gebyreð ing to þæm. x. hidan[19].

NOTES

1 The survey covers the northern part of East and West Hendred parishes, and this 'small spring' or 'stream' (v. **lȳtel, w(i)ell**) is probably the one mentioned in the bounds of Ginge (p. 746, n. 8), v. map.

2 v. **hlāw** 'tumulus', which is probably combined with an unre-corded pers.n., a compound in -*helm*. Dr von Feilitzen considers the first el. corrupt.

3 'headlands', v. 626. The visible ridge and furrow is here running parallel to the boundary, however, and *furh* would have seemed more appropriate.

4 'the headland on the west side of the three barrows' (*ClaudiusBvi* has *ðrym*- for *drym*-). In 1955 there was a visible headland W. of the boundary, running E. and W., and opposite it three bumps

with tree-stumps (recently cut down) on them, which were probably the three barrows, *v.* map.

5 'thick thorn-stump', *v.* grēat, þorn, stybb.

6 'leech (or bog) pool', *v.* lǣce[2], lǣce, mere.

7 *v.* map and Pt **1** 17–18; this is the brook referred to as *ealdan broc* in the first, 'Old Wantage' in the second, survey of E. Hanney (p. 743, n. 6, p. 744, n. 7).

8 'ditch', *v.* dīc.

9 'boundary of the people of Steventon', (Pt **2** 417–18), *v.* map.

10 'headlands', *v.* 626.

11 'ealdorman's boundary', *v.* ealdormann, (ge)mǣre; this suggests the existence of another land-unit in Steventon.

12 'rush brook', *v.* map for probable position. The name survived as *Rushe Brooke*, mentioned in 1628 (Pt **2** 485).

13 The lower part of Lockinge Brook, now called Ginge Brook, *v.* Pt **1** 10, 13 and map.

14 'small stream or spring', *v.* map for probable position. This is distinct from the stream of n. 1, which has the same name.

15 'the other spring or stream', *ClaudiusBvi* has *oðerne.*

16 'Babba's hill or tumulus', *v.* beorg.

17 'black hill', *v.* blæc, hyll, probably identical with *Blacknell Hill* 1607, *Blacknells* 1840 (Pt **2** 484).

18 This is the part of Lockinge Brook now called West Hendred Brook. The survey has crossed E. Hendred to reach this point, but the precise line is not known.

19 The 'mead on the west side of *waneting*' (*v.* mǣd) is the N.W. corner of West Hendred parish, *v.* map.

F VIII THE BOUNDS OF PART OF WEST HANNEY:
1032 (c. 1200) KCD 746

Ærest of eoccen[1] east andlang þære ealdan dic[2] on ða lam pyttas[3]. of ðam pyttan east be gemere on byttaman dic[4]. of ðære dic east be gemere on cyllriðæ[5] andlang cyllriðæ to bottanige[6]. of bottanige be leofrices gemere[7] to winegares stapule[8]. of þam stapule to wihtlufe hamme westweardon[9]. eft on eoccan[1].

NOTES

1 R. Ock. These bounds describe an area adjacent to, but outside, the modern parish of Lyford, although the charter relates to that place. The northern boundary of the grant is approximately the southern boundary of Lyford, but the starting point was perhaps a little further N., where Land Brook joins the Ock.

2 'old ditch', *v.* eald, dīc and map for approximate position.

3 'loam pits', *v.* lām, pytt.

4 *ClaudiusBvi* has *byttman dic*, possibly 'ditch of the head of the valley', *v.* bytme, but this must refer to a very slight feature here.

5 Childrey Brook, *v.* map and Pt **1** 8.

6 '*Botta*'s island', *v.* īeg; Botney Meadow appears in the *TA* for West Hanney (Pt **2** 478), *v.* map for position.

7 'Lēofrīc's boundary', *v.* (ge)mǣre.

8 'Winegār's post', *v.* stapol. Lēofrīc and Winegār were probably the owners of adjoining estates.

9 'the west part of Wihtlufu's river-meadow', *v.* hamm. From 7 to 9 the boundary may be following the present N. boundary of Denchworth.

G MORETON HUNDRED, WITH CHOLSEY (READING HUNDRED), APPLEFORD AND WITTENHAM (OCK HUNDRED) AND CHILTON (COMPTON HUNDRED)

Except for Streatley, Wallingford and Ashampstead, the whole of this area is covered by charter boundaries. A number of surveys include several modern parishes, some of the land-units having apparently been subdivided after the mid-10th cent. The charters, which are preserved in the Abingdon Chronicle, the Codex Wintoniensis and the Liber de Hyda, are –

I. BCS 504, 505, A.D. 862, an Abingdon charter by which King Æthelred I of Wessex grants 10 hides at Wittenham to Æthelwulf. The date probably indicates that Æthelred shared the rule before his brother died, v. M. A. O'Donovan in *Anglo-Saxon England* II, p. 108. The charter has been copied twice in *ClaudiusBvi* (Abingdon I, 41–2, 134–6) the two texts differing in some details, and the second one having a different set of witnesses. The bounds occur in the second copy. The first copy occurs in *ClaudiusCix*, and the bounds are written in *Cix* at the end of the MS with the other boundaries. There is no doubt that the survey refers to Wittenham, but the bounds will not fit either or both of the modern parishes of Long and Little Wittenham, and the way in which the scribe of *ClaudiusBvi* has copied them (*infra* 753–4) suggests that the original was defective or illegible. It is also possible that *wigbaldincgtune* (Pt 2 429) was a land-unit comprising the western part of Long Wittenham, which would account for some of the difficulties presented by the W. boundary of this survey.

II. BCS 581, c. A.D. 895, an Abingdon charter by which King Alfred gives Deormod 5 hides at Appleford in exchange for land at Horn Down. This is copied in both texts of the Abingdon Chronicle, but the version in *ClaudiusBvi* includes a statement in Old English that Deormod bought the 5 hides with 50 mancuses of gold, and this and most of the witnesses are omitted in *ClaudiusCix*. The bounds describe the modern parish of Appleford.

III. BCS 565, a Winchester document which records an exchange

between King Alfred and the Bishop of Winchester, whereby the
King obtains 100 hides at Cholsey, with the two villages of Hagbourne and *Bæstlæsford*. The authenticity of this is defended by
Finberg (*The Early Charters of Wessex*, n. 28, *Lucerna*, p. 135), but
Professor Whitelock considers it spurious. There are three sets of
bounds, one describing the modern parish of Basildon, one describing both Hagbournes with Didcot, Upton and (probably)
Chilton, and the third describing Cholsey with Moulsford. It is
possible that the Basildon survey includes part of Ashampstead.

IV. BCS 801, A.D. 944, an Abingdon charter, only copied in *Claudius-
Bvi*, by which King Edmund grants 100 hides at Blewbury to a
bishop called Ælfric. The grantee is Ælfric I, Bishop of Ramsbury
(HistAb 46). The date is not perfectly accurate. The bounds,
which are exceptionally precise, describe Blewbury with both
Astons and both Moretons.

V. BCS 810, A.D. 945, a Winchester charter of doubtful authenticity,
by which King Eadred grants 30 hides at Brightwell to Æthelgeard. The charter says that Brightwell constitutes 10 of the hides,
Sotwell 15 and Mackney 5, and the bounds describe this whole
area. The text also refers to 36 acres of ploughland and 10 acres of
meadow to the N. of Wallingford, and a statement at the end of
the bounds repeats this and adds that there is a mill N. of the *port*
and some property inside the *port*, and 7 houses and 3 churches
outside it.

VI. BCS 830, A.D. 947, a Winchester charter by which King Eadred
grants 10 hides at Brightwell to Æthelgeard. The bounds describe
Brightwell without Mackney, which is the southern part of the
modern parish.

VII. BCS 988, A.D. 957, a Winchester charter (preserved in the Liber
de Hyda) by which King Eadwig grants 15 hides at Sotwell to
Æthelgeard, with bounds which describe the modern parish of
Sotwell. The hidages in VI and VII agree with those in V.

VIII. BCS 864, A.D. 948, a Winchester charter which appears to contain a garbled version of some of the transactions in V–VII. It
purports to be a grant of Eadred to Æthelgeard of 10 hides, 5 in
Mackney, 5 in Sotwell, and for bounds it has the statement ‘Ðis
synt þa fif hida æt Maccanige þe gibhild seo lacu eallan butan
bæliÐ on ælce healfe’, followed by a repetition of the information
about the 36 acres of ploughland and 10 of meadow, and property
in Wallingford, given in V. *Gibhild* is Kibble Ditch, *v.* Pt 1 12.

IX. BCS 1183, A.D. 956, a Winchester charter by which King Eadgar (probably a scribal substitution for Eadwig) grants 7 hides at Harwell to Ælfstan. The bounds describe the modern parish of Harwell, and a piece of meadow which was probably N. of Didcot.

X. BCS 1292, A.D. 973, a Winchester charter by which King Eadgar grants 7 hides at Harwell to Ælfric. The bounds are substantially the same as those in IX.

XI. KCD 648, A.D. 985, a Winchester charter by which King Æthelred grants 17 hides at Harwell to Æthelric. The text says 'xvii cassatos segetibus mixtis'. The bounds have only two points in common with those of IX and X, but it seems probable that they are also describing the modern Harwell. They do not describe the meadow, which appears to be included in the area surveyed.

XII. BCS 1143, A.D. 964, an Abingdon charter (only copied in *ClaudiusBvi*) by which King Eadgar grants 10 hides at Aston to his queen, Ælfthryth. The bounds describe the modern parish of Aston Upthorpe.

XIII. KCD 1310, A.D. 1015, an Abingdon charter by which King Æthelred grants 5 hides at Chilton to Bishop Beorhtwold. The bounds are in both versions of the Chronicle, but the text is only in *ClaudiusBvi*. The survey describes the modern parish of Chilton, and a piece of woodland which may have been near West Ilsley. Abingdon had another charter (KCD 796, A.D. 1052) with the same bounds, by which King Edward gave this estate to the Abbey; this is probably spurious.

If the hidages of these charters are compared with the TRE assessments of the corresponding estates in DB, there are some exact correspondences. Aston Upthorpe is given as 10 hides in both sources, and Appleford as 5 hides. Brightwell and Sotwell had a total of 30 hides TRE, as in BCS 810, though these were distributed differently between the two places. Harwell (for which the correct figure is probably the 17 hides of KCD 648) contained three estates, one of which was assessed at 15 hides TRE. This belonged to the Bishop of Winchester, so is probably the estate of nos. IX–XI. The Cholsey estate is said to be 100 hides in BCS 565, and all the estates in Basildon, Hagbourne, Cholsey, Upton and Chilton described in DB had a total of 88 hides TRE. The separate charter for Chilton (XIII) gives the hidage as 5, whereas there were two estates of 5 hides each TRE. The greatest difference lies in the assessment of the component parts of the Blewbury estate, given as 100 hides in BCS 801. The various estates in Aston Upthorpe and Tirrold, North and South Moreton and Blewbury mentioned in DB were assessed at a total of 55 hides TRE, the most surprising figure being that for Blewbury, where there were two estates of only 3 and 2 hides respectively. This low assessment may reflect the status of the place as royal demesne.

These sets of boundaries described two contrasting types of land: the broad belt of marshy ground in the great angle of the Thames between Abingdon and Cholsey, and an area at the eastern end of the Downs. The surveys of estates near the Thames refer to marshland, drainage ditches and islands of raised ground such as *Meldanige*, Mackney and the hill from which Cholsey is named. The downland surveys refer frequently to ancient monuments, such as Grim's Ditch, The Ridgeway, Icknield Street and numerous tumuli. This part of the Downs was clearly not well wooded in the 10th cent. Individual trees are frequently mentioned, the Blewbury survey refers to two plantations, one of which was on the Downs, and Chilton, which is a downland parish, had a piece of woodland in another part of the county. Only the Basildon survey suggests the presence of woods, and in this respect the whole landscape of this region was probably much as it is today, except that there was a wood on Lollingdon Hill.

References to arable land (two in the Blewbury survey and one each in the Appleford, Harwell, Sotwell and Wittenham bounds) are all in low, marshy ground. The Chilton survey mentions a *bræce* ('land newly broken up for cultivation') on the Downs, near Grim's Ditch.

G I THE BOUNDS OF AN ESTATE AT WITTENHAM:
    862 (c. 1240) BCS 505

Ærest æt gateclife[1]. op be scillinges broce[2] þæt on caberes bec[3] ---[4] weard þæt andlang ---[4] headdan ---[4] weste wardan þonnon on þa niwan furh[5] andlang þære furh þæt þueres ofer crawanbroc[6] on þa niwan furh[5] andlang þære furh on hig weg[7] andlang þæs weges on tamese on norþe warde west wær[8].

NOTES

1 'goat's cliff', *v.* gāt, clif, identical with Gatley Ch.
2 Grundy identified this stream with the one which runs along the E. side of Little Wittenham Wood, which he was told was known locally as Shilling's Spring Brook. Shillingford, *Schillyngwurthe* (O 139)

and *scillinges broc* form a group of names for which no probable etymology can at present be suggested. If the O names contain a group-name **Sciellingas*, the form of the Berks name is corrupt.

3 *caberes bec* corresponds to *gafer bice* in the Brightwell survey, *v.* p. 762, n. 6. The boundary here crosses a col between the two peaks of the Sinodun Hills.

4 *ClaudiusBvi* has gaps of about half a column in the text at these points.

5 'new furrow', *v.* 627. The repetition of this landmark may be erroneous.

6 'crow's brook', *v.* crāwe, brōc.

7 'hay way', *v.* hēg, weg; as the bounds run along this way to the Thames, they can hardly be following the modern boundary of either Long or Little Wittenham, both of which run along small streams to the Thames. They may be following the E. boundary of *wigbaldincgtune* (*v.* 755, n. 6).

8 'the north side of west weir', *v.* west, wer.

THE CORRESPONDING BOUNDS IN CLAUDIUSCIX

Ærest æt gata clife up be scillinges broce. ðet on caberes bæc easteweard. ðæt andlang gemæres to beaddan treowe westeweardan ðornan on ða niwan furh. andlang ðære furh. ðæt ðueres ofer crawan broc on þa niwan furh. andlang ðære furh on hig weg. andlang ðæs weges on temese on norðe weardne west wer.

G II THE BOUNDS OF APPLEFORD: c. 895 (c. 1200)
BCS 581

Ærest on þa lace þæ lið be westan dyrnan gelade[1] andlang lace up on ane furh[2]. þæt on widan geat[3]. and swa andlang dic[4]. þæt on þone mor ðe lið betwux suðtune and wittanhamme[5]. and swa forð be more. þæt on þa ealdan dic þæ lið betwux wigbaldincgtune and æppelforda[6]. and of þære ealdan dic to dices wyllan[7]. of dices wyllan to sand ge wyrpe[8]. and of sand ge wyrpe þæt utan temese[9].

NOTES

1 'the stream which lies west of the hidden river-crossing', *v.* lacu, derne, dierne, (ge)lād; *v.* map for the stream. The (ge)lād was possibly a crossing-place on the Thames. The survey runs anti-clockwise.

2 'furrow', *v.* 627.

3 This may be identical with the *widan geat* in III (b), p. 756, n. 8; *v.* map and p. 693, n. 2.

4 'ditch', *v.* dīc.

5 'the marsh which lies between Sutton and Wittenham', *v.* mōr.

6 'the old ditch which lies between Willington and Appleford'. This is Moor Ditch, *v.* map. *wigbaldincgtune* survives in Willington's Fm, Willington's Down Fm and possibly Wigbald Fm (Pt 2 429), and may originally have been a land-unit comprising the western part of Long Wittenham. It was a separate estate in 1086.

7 'the stream of the ditch', *v.* dīc, w(i)ell and map.

8 'gravel-heap'; this is a hillock beside the junction of Moor Ditch and the Thames, which appears from surface indications to consist of fine gravel, and has been quarried into in various places. OE sand is recorded with the meaning 'gravel'.

9 R. Thames.

G III (a)   THE BOUNDS OF BASILDON (BÆSTLÆSFORD):
c. 895 (12TH) BCS 565

cæccam wæl[1] ðonon andlang hagan[2] on ealden halh[3] ðonon on lid geat[4] ðonon to wæst legæ[5] ðonon to rah slede[6] ðonon to mules hamstæde[7] ðonon to hiorotlege[8] ðonon to blacan mære[9] ðonon to cylf hongran[10] ðonon eft to temæse on wiredes wær[11].

NOTES

1 Probably connected with *Ceacca wylles heafde* in the bounds of Whitchurch O, *v.* O 45.

2 *v.* 628.

3 *v.* h(e)alh 'nook or corner'; first el. either the pers.n. *Ealda* or eald 'old'. The *halh* might be the sharp angle made by the parish boundary halfway along the southern side.

4 'swing gate'. *v.* hlid-geat.

5 'west wood or clearing', *v.* west, lēah.

6 'roe valley', *v.* rā, slæd.

7 'Mūl's homestead', cf. Moulsford Pt 2 527–8.

8 'hart wood or clearing', cf. Hartley Ct Pt 1 104. Hartridge Fm in the adjacent parish of Ashampstead has the same first el. It is possible that this survey includes part of Ashampstead, which is not described separately in DB, though Hartridge is a DB estate.

9 'black pool', *v.* blæc, mere.

10 *cylf* should possibly be scylf which would give a meaning 'wood on a ledge', *v.* hangra, but an el. *cylfe 'hill' has been postulated for Kilve So.

11 'Wīgrǣd's weir', *v.* wer.

G III (b) THE BOUNDS OF HAGBOURNE, DIDCOT, UPTON AND CHILTON: c. 895 (12TH) BCS 565

ðonon of haccebroce[1] on ealdan lace[2] ðonon to tottencumbe ufeweardon[3] ðonon to burgilde treowe[4] ðonon to drægeles bæce[5] ðonon andlanges drægeles bæce to gemær weige emb cylda tun[6] ðonon flecges garan suðe wardan[7] ðonon to widan geate[8] ðonon to eadulfes mære[9] ðonon to stoccæs wælle[10] ðonon of stocces wylle on wittan mære[11] of wittan mære on cyninges dic[12] of cyninges dice on hæðbyrg[13] ðonan of hæðbyrge on haccaburnan[1] emb mortun[14].

NOTES

1 The stream from which Hagbourne is named, *v.* Pt 1 10–11.

2 'old stream', *v.* eald, lacu, probably a drainage channel.

3 'the top of Totta's valley', *v.* cumb; Grundy has identified this with a place now called Tadcombe, *v.* map and Pt 1 153.

4 'Burghild's tree', *v.* trēow, cf. Bucklebury Pt 1 154.

5 Grim's Ditch, *v.* Pt 1 6 and map.

6 'the boundary way round Chilton', *v.* (ge)mære.

7 'the south part of *flecges* gore'; the gāra is probably the pointed projection of Harwell parish (*v.* map), referred to as *ferngaran* in the Chilton bounds p. 767, n. 13. *flecg* is a term of obscure meaning which occurs again in *flecgestane* in the bounds of Chilton (p. 767, n. 12) near this point. Professor Löfvenberg suggests a pers.n. *Flecg* cognate with ON *fleggr* 'giant'. Holthausen suggested a noun meaning 'piece of land'.

8 *v.* p. 755, n. 3; if this is the same 'wide gate', the survey has a long stretch with no boundary-marks.

9 'Ēadwulf's boundary', *v.* (ge)mære.

10 'spring or stream of the tree stump', *v.* stocc, w(i)ell. This is mentioned also in the bounds of the mead attached to Harwell, *v.* p. 765, n. 21.

11 'Witta's boundary', *v.* (ge)mære, i.e. the boundary of Wittenham, *v.* Pt 2 427.

12 'king's ditch', *v.* cyning, dīc. This is on the boundary of the estate granted by King Edmund in IV.

13 'heath fortification', v. hǣð, burh, byrig. This was near Hadden
   in Didcot (Pt 2 518) of which the first el. is also hǣð.
14 Moreton, v. Pt 2 524.

G III (c) THE BOUNDS OF CHOLSEY AND MOULSFORD:
           c. 895 (12TH) BCS 565

ofer sunesforda¹ upp on grenan dune² ðonon on higran hongran norðe
weardne³ þonon on bullanholt⁴ on diopan wei⁵ ðonon on marge wei⁶
and grim gelege⁷ ðonon on romes leg⁸ on stanwei⁹ ðonon andlang
dices on west welle¹⁰ ðonon andlang mores on tibbælde lace¹¹ ðonon
on maccan eige¹² andlang mores ðonon on ðone ealdan dic¹³ est to
temæse æt welingaforda¹⁴.

NOTES

1 Near Runsford Hole, Pt 2 531–2, v. map. The mistake in the first
   letter shows that the scribe was copying an OE original.
2 'green hill', v. grēne¹, dūn.
3 'the north part of magpie's hanger', v. higera, hangra; it is not
   certain what kind of bird *higera* denotes.
4 'Bulla's wood', v. holt.
5 'deep way', v. dēop, weg.
6 v. weg, the first el. may be corrupt.
7 Grim's Ditch, v. Pt 1 6.
8 'wild garlic wood', v. hram(e)sa, lēah, and cf. the Blewbury
   bounds, p. 759, n. 3; the wood was probably on Lollingdon Hill.
9 'stone way', v. stān, weg, and cf. the Blewbury bounds, p. 759,
   n. 4.
10 Amwell, Pt 1 6–7, v. map.
11 v. Pt 1 12 and map. The first part of *tibbælde lace* is obscure, but it
   is probably a different n. from *gybhilde*, p. 762, n. 19.
12 Mackney, Pt 2 516.
13 'old ditch', v. eald, dīc; the modern boundary follows streams to
   the Thames, but these may have been thought of primarily as
   drainage channels. *andlang mores* means 'through the marsh', v.
   mōr.
14 Wallingford, Pt 2 516.

G IV THE BOUNDS OF BLEWBURY, ASTON UPTHORPE AND TIRROLD, NORTH AND SOUTH MORETON: 944 (c. 1240) BCS 801

Đis sindon þa land gemæro to bleobyrig. Ærest on easte wardum þam lande æt amman welle[1] þæt swa suð on gerihte on wæter slædes dic[2] þæt andlang dic oþ þone suð ende on þæt riht land gemære þæt up to þam miclan beorge beneoþan hrameslea[3] þæt of þam beorge up andlang stanweges[4] to þam langan cyrstel mæle æt hafurc þorne[5] þonne of hafuc þorne to þan langan þorne æt ichenilde wege[6] þæt swa to þan þriddan þorne æt wirhangran[7] of þam þorne to þam feorþan þorne on wrangan hylle fore weardre stent[8] þæt swa forþ to þam fiftan þorne[9] to þam elebeame[10] þæt west andlang þæs lytlan weges[11] up to þon þorne[12] up to teonan hylle[13] þæt swa west on þone ruwan hlync[14] andlang þæs rowan linces to þon hæþenum byrgelsum æt þære ealdun dic[15] þæt andlang oþ þæt treow steall[16] þonne of þan treow stealle on ge rihte to þon bradan beorge be eastan wrocena stybbe[17] þæt swa to wrocena stybbe þonne of wrocena stybbe on meoces dune[18] on þone byrgeles[19] of þam byrgelse to þære flodan æt swin weges slo æt þære wege gelæton[20] þæt up to þam eorþ geberste[21] to foxes beorge[22] of þam beorge west andlang drægeles bæces[23] oþ þone hricg weg[24] andlang weges oþ þa readan hane[25] of þare hane norþ andlang þæs smalan weges[26] to totan cumbe æt þam beorge[27] þæt swa norþ on gerihte andlang þæs smalan weges to þon here page[28] þæt to þæs linces ende[29] þæt swa forþ norð andlang weges oþ ordstanes dic[30] þæt andlang dic of þære dic wiþ norþan þæt yrþland[31] þonne bi þam yrþlande to þære lace þe lið on stoc welle[32] þonne of stoc wylle norþ andlang broeces to þære dic þære se æþeling mearcode[33] þæt andlang dic to þære sceap wæscan on haccan broc[34] þonne andlang haccan broces to huddes igge[35] þæt swa forð norþ andlang broces wiþ westan hunddes ig þæt up andlang þære and-heafda[36] to þære lytlan dice ende[37] and þam norð andlang þara andheafda to þan langan cyrstel mæle æt hæþ dune[38] þæt swa norð andlang þæs smalan paþes[39] on þa dic sticcea[40] to þon stodfalde[41] þæt swa eaþ andlang þære ealdan dic[42] oþ æþelstanes treow steal[43] to þare dice byge[44] þæt swa suþ east andlang dic be byrgwylla gemære[45] þat swa suð est ofer þone mor[46] to mæringes þorne[47] of mæringes þorne to sulgeate[48] of sulgeate be wyrt walan[49] to þon read leafan mapuldre[50] of þam mapuldre on þa lace[51] þæt on gerihte on west wylle þen on oþre naman hæt æt amman wylle[52].

NOTES

1 Amwell, Pt **1** 6–7, *v.* map.
2 'ditch of the water valley', *v.* wæter, slæd, dīc, probably a drainage channel.
3 'the large barrow beneath wild garlic wood', cf. p. 757, n. 8. This was probably a wood covering Lollingdon Hill, which is to the E. of the parish boundary. There is now no sign of the barrow.
4 'stone way', *v.* stān, weg; this is the road shown on O.S. maps W. of Lollingdon Hill along which the boundary runs for a short stretch, *v.* map. It has now been ploughed up, but the part which ran along the boundary of Aston Tirrold is marked by a large bank.
5 'the tall crucifix at hawk thorn', *v.* lang, cristel-mæl, h(e)afoc, þorn.
6 'the tall thorn-tree at the Icknield Way', *v.* lang, þorn and map.
7 'the third thorn-tree at bog-myrtle hanger', *v.* wīr, hangra.
8 'the fourth thorn-tree which stands on the front part of the crooked hill', *v.* wrang, hyll, and map.
9 'the fifth thorn-tree.'
10 *elebēam* 'olive tree', must be used in charter bounds of some native tree.
11 'little way', *v.* lȳtel, weg.
12 'thorn-tree', *v.* þorn.
13 OE *tēona* means 'harm, trouble', and if this is the first el. the name would mean 'hill of trouble'.
14 'rough bank', *v.* rūh, hlinc; this is an example of the banks which C.S. and C.S. Orwin call 'lynchet terraces', *v.* 627.
15 'the heathen burial-places (*v.* hæðen, byrgels) at the old ditch.' This phrase may refer to the archaeological remains on Lowbury Hill, where there is a Roman camp, and several tumuli. There is, however, no ditch at all round the earthwork now.
16 'plantation', *v.* trēow, st(e)all.
17 'the broad barrow east of *wrocena* tree-stump', *v.* brād, beorg, stybb. There is now no trace of the barrow. *wrocena* is obscure; emendation to *wreccna* would give an etymology 'stump of the fugitives', *v.* wrecca.
18 'Mēoc's hill', *v.* dūn: the pers.n. may occur also in Mexborough YW **1** 77. The rise in the ground is very noticeable here.

19 'burial', v. byrgels; there is now no trace of this.

20 'the water channel at swine path's slough at the junction of ways', v. flōde, swīn[1], weg, slōh, (ge)lǣte and map. The reference is to the flat hollow S. of Lower Chance Fm, which would certainly have been muddy.

21 'landslip', v. eorðe, (ge)byrst. There is no sign of this, the area being a smooth hillside, partly used for racetracks.

22 Fox Barrow, Pt 2 503, v. map. This is a tumulus.

23 Grim's Ditch, Pt 1 6, v. map.

24 Ridge Way, Pt 1 5. The modern boundary does not touch the Ridgeway, v. map. The name may, as Grundy suggests, have been applied to a number of tracks, or the boundary may originally have come further S.

25 'red stone', v. rēad, hān.

26 'narrow way', v. smæl, weg.

27 'Totta's valley at the barrow'; for Tadcombe v. p. 756, n. 3. There is no barrow there now.

28 This should be here-pæð, the reference being to the Port Way, v. map.

29 'end of the linchet', v. 627.

30 'Ordstān's ditch', v. dīc; probably a drainage channel.

31 'ploughed land', v. 626.

32 'the stream which leads to tree-stump stream', v. lacu, stocc, w(i)ell and map.

33 'the ditch which the king's son marked', v. dīc, æðeling.

34 'the sheep-wash on Hacca's brook', v. scēap-wæsce, Pt 1 10–11 and map.

35 '*Hudd's island', v. īeg. It is uncertain what the name denotes, but Fulscot Fm (v. map) may occupy slightly raised ground, of the sort which would be called īeg.

36 v. 626.

37 'end of the little ditch', v. lȳtel, dīc; doubtless a drainage channel.

38 'the tall crucifix at Hadden', cf. n. 5. For Hadden v. Pt 2 518 and map.

39 'narrow path', v. smæl, pæð.

40 v. dīc; sticcea is probably the acc.pl. of *sticce, v. 907. Professor Löfvenberg points out that this n. is wrongly said to be a masc. noun dīcsticca in Campbell's Enlarged Addenda and Corrigenda to BTSuppl.

41 'horse-enclosure', v. stōd-fald.

42 'old ditch'; the western part of the 'old ditch' mentioned in the Brightwell survey, *infra*, n. 2 and map.

43 'Æðelstān's plantation', *v.* trēow, st(e)all.

44 'bend of the ditch', *v.* byge and map.

45 'Brightwell boundary', *v.* (ge)mǣre; the spelling of Brightwell (Pt 2 515–16) is corrupt.

46 'marsh', *v.* mōr.

47 'Mǣring's thorn-tree', *v.* þorn.

48 'plough-gate', *v.* sulh, geat, perhaps a gap giving access to plough-land.

49 *v.* 633; wyrtwala may here be the W. edge of Cholsey Hill.

50 'red-leafed maple-tree', *v.* mapuldor.

51 *v.* lacu.

52 Amwell, *v.* n. 1 *supra*, 'west stream' perhaps distinguishes it from the parallel watercourse about 400 yards E.

G V THE BOUNDS OF BRIGHTWELL AND SOTWELL: 945 (12TH) BCS 810

Ærest of þam more be westan þam tune[1] on þa ealdan dic[2] west and lang dic on þa hæþenan byrgyrlsas[3] þonne east and lang weges Of þam wege[4] on ænne littelne þorn[5] of þam þorne east and hwon suð on ge rihte to þam wege to gafer bice[6] þanon norð be þam and heafdon[7] oð þa lace[8] and lang lace ut on temese oð midne stream and lang ea of þa ealdan stret ford[9] and lang gea to holan wylle[10] of holan wylle on holan weg[11] Of holan wege on bric weg[12] of bric wege on ærnincg weg[13] Of ærninge wege on meosdene[14] of meosdene on meldanige eastewerdne[15] on sandlace[16] and lang sand lice to ceolesige[17] to þam hnottan stocce[18] Of þam stocce norð and lang gybhilde[19] to þære ealdan dic[2] þær we her on fengan. þonne ligcaþ be norðam þam porte xxxvi ækera yrþ landes and x æceras mæde and 1 myln and binnan porte fram east geate on norð healf strete on þæne broc and VII heorþas buton þam and þreo cyrican.

NOTES

1 'the marsh to the west of the tūn', *v.* mōr; tūn probably refers to Brightwell village.

2 'the old ditch'; there is a drainage ditch along this section of the boundary, *v.* map.

3 'heathen burial-places'.

4 'way', *v*. weg.

5 'a little thorn tree'.

6 *gafer bice* is the same boundary-mark as *caberes bec* (*caberes bæc*) in the Wittenham survey, p. 754, n. 3. Elements **1** 33–4 discusses *gafer bice* under bīc 'point', but it does not belong there, as was acknowledged in Journal I 12. The place is a col on the Sinodun Hills, and bæc 'back' (referring to the flat top of the pass) is a possible second el. The first may be tentatively connected with that of OE *cafertūn* 'vestibule', perhaps meaning 'entrance passage'. *v*. also p. 763, n. 6. Professor Löfvenberg regards this as very unlikely; he considers the second el. corrupt and the first el. obscure.

7 *v*. 626.

8 *lace* (*v*. lacu) refers to the *scillinges broc* of the Wittenham survey, p. 753, n. 2.

9 'old street ford', *v*. map. The street (*v*. strǣt) is the Roman road from Silchester (CALLEVA ATREBATUM) to Dorchester.

10 'hollow spring', *v*. hol², w(i)ell.

11 'hollow way', *v*. hol², weg.

12 'bridge way', *v*. brycg.

13 This may be a road-name of the same type as Tidgeon Way O 4, which was nearby on the other side of the Thames; if so, the els. are a pers.n. *Earn(a)*, -ing- and weg. Alternatively, Professor Löfvenberg suggests the first el. may be OE *ærning* 'running, riding, racing'. The three ways of 11, 12 and 13 may have run along the three short E.–W. stretches of the boundary after it leaves the Thames, *v*. map (the boundary is from O.S. 6″).

14 'marsh valley', *v*. mēos, denu.

15 'the eastern part of orach island', *v*. melde (a plant-name), īeg. Grundy has located a field called Millony (*v*. map), which may preserve the name *meldanige*. The plant is believed to have been grown for food in prehistoric and Anglo-Saxon times.

16 'sand stream', *v*. sand, lacu, and map.

17 This is the 'island' from which Cholsey is named, *v*. Pt **1** 162.

18 'bare tree-stump', *v*. hnott, stocc.

19 Kibble Ditch, *v*. Pt **1** 12 and map.

G VI THE BOUNDS OF BRIGHTWELL EXCLUDING MACKNEY:
947 (12TH) BCS 830

Ærest of þam more be westan þam tune¹ on þa dic² west and lang Dic
of þa hæþenan byrigelsas³ þonne east and lang þan an heafdan⁴ on
anne litelne þorn⁵ þonon east and hwon suð on ge rihte to þam wege
to gafær bæce⁶ þo nord be þam and heafdan⁴ of þa lace⁷ andlang lace
ut on temæse of midne stream andlang ea of ða ealda stræt⁸ and lang
stræte on þone ford⁹ of þam forde west and lang mores of þæt man
ær on feng.

NOTES

1, 2, 3 v. p. 761, n. 1, 2, 3.

4 v. 626.

5, 6 v. p. 762, nn. 5, 6. *gafær bæce* is *caberes bæc, gafer bice* in other
surveys.

7, 8 v. p. 762, nn. 8, 9.

9 This is the *Maccaniges ford* of the Sotwell survey, *infra*, n. 1,
v. map.

G VII THE BOUNDS OF SOTWELL: 957 (C. 1400) BCS 988

Ærest of Maccaniges forda¹ andlang stræte² ut on Temese oð midne
stream andlang streames to holan pylle³ þære gerit of holan pylle up
andlang dic to Brycgwege⁴ andlang Brycgweges an furlang of
Brycgwege to meosdene⁵ andlang meosdene wið easten Meldanige⁶
oð midne mor up andlang mores on Langanforda suðweardne⁷
andlang Langanforda oð Maccanige⁸ swa be Maccaniges wirðland
swa swa oxa went and swa on Maccaniges forda¹ suðweardne.

NOTES

1 'ford of Mackney', v. map.

2, 3 v. p. 762, nn. 9, 10.

4 v. p. 762, nn. 12, 13. The boundary does run for about a furlong
along the middle of the three ways mentioned in the Brightwell
and Sotwell survey.

5, 6 v. p. 762, nn. 14, 15.

7 'the south part of long ford', v. lang, ford. This was probably a
causeway.

8 Mackney, v. Pt 2 516.

G IX THE BOUNDS OF HARWELL: C. 960 (12TH) BCS 1183

of þa ellen stubbe[1] on ðane oðerne ellen stubbe[2] þanone on þa ealdan fyrh[3] þanone to smalan wege[4] on butan flegges garan[5] Ðonne and lang þæs smalan weges þæt hit sticað on humbracumb[6] þonne on icenilde weg[7] þæt eft on ellen stubb[8] þonne on þone herepað[9] on haran dune[10] þonne be herepaðe on cranwylle[11] þonne on hesleabroc[12] on hreodmede[13] þonne on þa ealdan cot stowe[14] þonne on smalan broc[15] þonne on þæt longe furlang[16] þonne on cylmes cumbe[17] on snelles garan[18].

Ðonne ys þis sio með þe þærto ge byreð and lang þæs ealdan broces[19] þæt hit sticad on syðtuninga lace[20] þonne on stocwylle broc[21] þonne on þane ealdan broc[22] þanone on wudubricge[23].

NOTES

1 'elder stump', *v.* elle(r)n, stubb.
2 'the other elder stump'.
3 'old furrows', *v.* 627.
4 'narrow way', *v.* smæl, weg.
5 *v.* 756, n. 7.
6 *v.* Pt 1 11 and map.
7 Icknield Way, *v.* Pt 1 5 and map.
8 'elder stump'.
9 *v.* here-pæð, referring to the road to Abingdon, *v.* map.
10 Horn Down, *v.* Pt 2 480–1 and map.
11 'crane stream', *v.* cran, w(i)ell and map.
12 This is *hæsel broc* in the Milton survey, p. 714, n. 6, 'hazel brook', *v.* hæsel, brōc, the spelling here may indicate that there was a 'hazel-wood', *v.* lēah.
13 'reed meadow', *v.* hrēod, mǣd.
14 'old cottage sites', *v.* (e)ald, cot-stōw.
15 'narrow brook', *v.* smæl, brōc.
16 'long furlong', *v.* 626.
17 'Cylm's valley', *v.* cumb. The boundary touches a valley at the S.E. corner of the parish.
18 'Snell's gore', *v.* 626.
19 'old brook', *v.* eald, brōc; this has not been identified.
20 'stream of the people of Sutton'; this is the stream which flows along the S. of Sutton Courtenay parish, *v.* map.
21 'tree-stump spring or stream', probably identical with *stoccæs*

wælle in the Hagbourne survey, p. 756, n. 10; *v.* map for probable position.

22 It is not certain whether this is the same stream as 19.

23 'wood bridge', *v.* wudu, brycg; this has not been identified.

GX THE BOUNDS OF HARWELL: 973 (12TH) BCS 1292

Ærest of þam ællan stubbe[1] on þone oðerenne elle stub[2] and swa on þa ealdan firh[3] þanon to smalan wege[4] and swa ymbutan flegges garan[5] þanon and lang þæs smalan weges utt on humbracumb[6] swa on ycenilde weg[7] a forh be wege eft on þone ellen stub[8] þa non on þone hærepað[9] on harandune[10] and swa on cranwylle[11] þa non on heslea broc[12] and swa on hreo mæde[13] þa non on þa ealdan cot stowa[14] and swa on smalan broc[15] þa non on þæt lange furlang[16] swa on cylmæscumb[17] on snelles garan[18].

Ðis syndon þæra mæda ge mæra Ærest and lang þæs ealdan broces[19] of suðtuniga lace[20] and swa on stocwylle broc[21] þa non on þone ealdan broc[22] and swa and wudubrigge[23].

NOTES

The notes on these bounds correspond to those on IX *supra*.

GXI THE BOUNDS OF HARWELL: 985 (12TH) KCD 648

Ærest of haran dune wege[1] þonne hit sticað on middelhæma ge mæra[2] on suttuninga lace[3] of suttuninga lace on leof siges ge mæra[4] on þa hnottan dic[5] of þære hnottan dic on brembel þorn[6] of brembel þorne on hengestes geat[7] of hencstes geate on ða ealdan dune[8] to bricthwoldes ge mæra[9] of brictwoldes ge mæra æft on harandune.

NOTES

1 'Horn Down way', *v.* p. 764, n. 10: this corresponds to the *herepæð* of the other two Harwell surveys.

2 'boundary of the people of Milton', *v.* Pt 2 416.

3 *v.* p. 764, n. 20; the meadow, which is separately described in the other two surveys, is apparently included in these bounds.

4 'Lēofsige's boundaries', *v.* (ge)mǣre; presumably the boundary of Didcot.

5 'bare ditch', *v.* hnott, dīc. There are drainage ditches on the E. boundary of Harwell.

6 'bramble-thorn', presumably a blackberry bush.

7 'Hengest's gate', or 'horse's gate', v. p. 693, n. 2; possibly identical with the 'wide gate' of the Hagbourne survey, p. 756, n. 8.

8 'old down', v. eald, dūn; the sense of the term is not obvious, but it may refer to Hagbourne Hill.

9 'Brihtwold's boundaries', v. (ge)mǣre. This can hardly, as Grundy suggests, refer to Bishop Beorhtwold, who was given Chilton in 1015 (XIII *infra*); the pers.n. is a common one.

G XII   THE BOUNDS OF ASTON UPTHORPE: 964 (c. 1240) BCS 1143

Ærest of hacce broce[1] on rugan dic[2] þonne andlang weges on þone fulan forda[3] of þan fulan ford on eanulfing þorn[4] of þan þorne on þone hwitan holan weg[5] of þan hwitan wege andlang langan dune[6] þæt eft on þone stanihtan weg[7] of þan wege on þone crundel[8] þonon on geritha on brochylle slæd[9] of ðan slade on hiccan ðorn[10] þonon ofer bleo byrig dune[11] on hæcceleas dic[12] þonne and lang þære dic þæt eft on hæcce broc[1].

NOTES

1 *v.* p. 756, n. 1.

2 'rough ditch', *v.* rūh, dīc; the boundary follows a crooked drainage ditch after leaving the brook.

3 'dirty ford', *v.* fūl, ford, a common p.n., here possibly referring to the stream-crossing in the centre of Aston village.

4 'thorn-tree connected with Ēanwulf', *v.* -ing-, þorn.

5 'white hollow way', *v.* hwīt, hol[2], weg and map. This is the same track as the 'stony way' *infra*, but the surface is white until it reaches the northern tip of Langdon Hill. It is a true hollow way near Icknield Street; further S., it has a bank on alternate sides.

6 Langdon Hill, *v.* Pt 2 510 and map.

7 'stony way', *v.* stāniht, weg; over Lowbury Hill this road is very stony, with a thick deposit of gravel and flints. This surface ends abruptly at the junction with The Fair Mile, where the road becomes an earth track.

8 *v.* crundel.

9 'brook hill valley', *v.* brōc, hyll, slæd; possibly the valley in which Sheepcot Fm is situated, *v.* map.

10 'Hicca's thorn-tree'; the pers.n. is probably related to *Hicel* in
   Hiceles wyrþe BCS 27.
11 Blewburton Hill, *v.* Pt **1** 152.
12 *v.* Pt **1** 10–11 and map.

G XIII THE BOUNDS OF CHILTON: 1015 (c. 1200)
KCD 1310

Ærest of waddune[1] andlang weges to þam gærstune[2] swa andlang ðæs
gærstunes dic[3] to þam wege on eastewyrdne þæne tun[4] swa andlang
weges to þære dice hyrnan[5] swa andlang dic innon þære æsc[6] of ðam
æsce innon ðæne ealdan mere[7] of þam ealdam mere innon þa bræce[8]
of þam bræce andlang beces[9] innon rod stybban[10] swa of rodstybban
to lodder þorne[11] swa of lodder þorne to flegestane[12] of flegestane to
ðam ferngaran[13] of ðam ferngaran eft on waddune to þam ealdan
bece[14].

[A]nd þis sind þære wudu bære land gemæru æt ðæt lege[15] þe
þærto hyrað Ærest of þam hæcce[16] to dudemeres hele[17] of dudemeres
hele to merc lege[18] of mærclege to stanlege[19] of stanlege to þere
dunlege[20] of ðære dun lege swa eft innon þænre hæcc.

NOTES

1 'woad hill', *v.* wād, dūn, probably Hagbourne Hill.
2 'paddock', *v.* gærs-tūn.
3 'ditch of the paddock', *v.* dīc.
4 'the way on the east on the tūn', i.e. Chilton, *v.* map.
5 'angle of the ditch', *v.* hyrne.
6 'ash-tree', *v.* æsc.
7 'old pool', *v.* eald, mere.
8 'land broken up for cultivation', *v.* brēc.
9 Grim's Ditch, *v.* Pt **1** 6. *andlang beces* (bæc 'back' used of the bank
   of the ditch) carries the survey along the whole southern boundary
   of Chilton.
10 Apparently 'clearing-stumps', *v.* rod[1], stybb.
11 'beggar thorn', *v.* loddere, þorn.
12 *ClaudiusBvi* has *flecge stane*, *v.* p. 756, n. 7.
13 'fern gore', *v.* p. 756, n. 7.
14 'old bank', *v.* eald, bæc; this is a large 'lynchet terrace' running
   along the boundary on the S.W. side of Hagbourne Hill, *v.* 627.
15 The bounds of the woodland pasture (*v.* bǣr[2]) are wrongly copied

in *ClaudiusBvi* as the bounds of Bessels Leigh, *v.* Pt **2** 442–3. *ClaudiusBvi* has *æt Ðæclege* for *æt ðæt lege* in *ClaudiusCix*. Probably *Bvi* is right, and the n. means 'wood where thatching material is obtained', *v.* þæc. For the probable location of this wood *v.* n. 19 *infra*.

16 'gate', *v.* hæc(c).

17 'Dudemǣr's nook', *v.* healh.

18 'boundary wood or clearing', *v.* mearc, lēah.

19 'stone wood or clearing', *v.* stān, lēah. It seems probable that this is identical with the *stanleage* mentioned in the bounds of Farnborough (*v.* p. 673, n. 26), which was near Ilsley, about 3 miles from Chilton.

20 'hill wood or clearing', *v.* dūn, lēah.

OLD ENGLISH WORDS IN THE
BOUNDARY-MARKS OF BERKSHIRE
CHARTERS

This index to the charter boundaries includes most of the terms used in boundary-marks, apart from personal names, which are listed on pp. 793–94. Well-established river-names (e.g. *alaburnan, cynetan* A (b) II 5, 19) are not included. When a boundary-mark occurs in two or more surveys, only one reference is given, as the others are listed in the notes which accompany the text of the boundaries. Prepositions such as *andlang, be, ofer, on* are not usually quoted in the index, but an exception is made under some items, such as dīc, furh, haga[1], where the manner in which the object is referred to may be important to the understanding of the nature of the boundary-mark.

As in the list of place-name els., p. 848, surviving archaeological features are marked †.

abbod 'abbot'. *abbedes dic* E VII 3
āc 'oak tree'. *acdene* B (b) I 2; *ænlypan ac* D II 4; *fulan æc* E VII 14; *seofan acon* A (b) V 10
æcer 'plot of arable land, measure of land'. *æcer under æcere* D V; *æcer dic* E VIII 33; *an æcer near þæm hlince* C III 19; *and lang fyrh ænnæ æcer* C I 7; *feower æcras be norðan lakincg* F I 5; *on þan gemanan lande – fif and sixti æccera* B (a) III 12; *fleax æcyres* A (b) III 9; *gar æcer, twam gar æceron* C III 9, 25, 36; *heafd æceres west furh* C IV 36; *heafod æcere* D IV 7; *heafod æcera, -æcer* D XIV 7, 18; *heafod æceras* D V 3; *healfan æcer* E IV 26; *sceaceling æcer* E III 9; *seouan æcera* E IV 23; *buton six æcerum* B (a) II 26; *xii æceres mede – xii æceres landes* C VI 21; *xii mæð æceras* A (a) I 13; *xxxvi ækara yrþ landes and x æceras mæde* G V
ærning 'running, riding, racing'. *? ærnincg weg* G V 13
æsc 'ash tree'. *æsc* B (b) III 26, G XIII 6; *æsc meres hammas* B (b) VII 4
æwylm 'source of a river'. *æwulm* C I 26; *æwylma* F VI 11
alor 'alder tree'. *ælrbed* C III 34
andhēafdu (pl.) 'headlands, ground at the end of the furrow where

the plough was turned'. *andheafda* B (a) II 25, B (b) VIII 3, C II
21, G IV 36; *andheafdum, anheafodum, on hæfde, an heafde* C III
11, 17, 26, 38; *andheafdan* D IV (two); *and heafdon* G V 7

ānlī(e)pig 'solitary'. *ænlypan ac, ænlipe ellyn* D II 4, 2; *anlipan
beorh* D XIII 5

apuldor 'apple tree'. *haran apoldre* B (a) II 6, 37; *haran apeldre*
B (b) II 11

bæc 'back'. †*bæce* B (a) II 19 (the bank of a linear earthwork);
†*drægeles bæce* G III (b) 5 (Grim's Ditch); †*andlang beces* G XIII 9
(the bank of Grim's Ditch); *caberes bec* G I 3 (?the flat top of a
col); †*ealdan bece* G XIII 14 (a linchet terrace); *gynan bæce* D XIII
7 (?a causeway)

bǣr² 'woodland feeding-ground for swine'. *wer bæra* A (b) IV 13;
wudu bære land gemæru G XIII 15

bēam 'tree, post'. *cristen mælbeam* A (b) III 4

bēan 'bean'. *bean broc* C X 7; *bean furlang* C VI 19

bece¹, 'stream, valley'. *beche* C VIII 24

bedd 'plot of ground where plants grow'. *ælrbed* C III 34; *riscbedde*
C IV 38; *riscbed* C VI 17; *wiðig bæd* E IV 27

bēo 'bee'. *beocumb* B (b) VIII 10

beofor 'beaver'. *befer ig* A (b) II 17

beorg 'tumulus, hill'. *ælfredes beorh* D V 6; *anlipan beorh* D XIII 5;
babban byorh F VII 16; †*beorg* C II 26; †*beorh – oþærne* C II 32;
†*beorh* E IV 42; *beorge* G IV 27; *borsenan beorge* B (b) I 9; *bradan
beorge* G IV 17; *brocenan beorg* B (b) VIII 13; *cat beorh* B (a) I 6;
dinra beorh C VII 17; †*eceles beorh* C IV 34; *elden berwe* C VIII
10; †*ennanbeorgum* E IV 39; *fearnbeorhge* B (b) VIII 1; †*foxes
beorge* G IV 22; *grenan beorh* B (b) III 33; †*heafd beorh* A (b) II 1;
imman beorge A (b) II 24; *laurocan beorghe* D XIV 4; *litel berwe*
C VIII 14; †*lytlan beorg* B (a) II 40; *loddere beorge* F VI 2;
Lortanberwe C VIII 30; *Mereberwe* C VIII 32; *mærbeorh* C X 11;
gemærbeorg F I 3; *miclan beorge* G IV 3; *ruwanbeorh* A (b) V 13;
stan beorh C X 14; *stanberwe* C VIII 13; †*twegen beorgas* B (a) II
28; †*ðrymbeorgum* F VII 4; *weardæs beorh* C II 5

bere 'barley'. *berege* E III 12 (later Berry)

biscop 'bishop'. *biscopes weg* B (a) IV 8

blæc 'black'. *blacan grafan* B (b) VII 18, *blacan graue* E IX 22 (mod.
Blagrove); *blacan hylle* F VII 17; *blachelace* C IV 3; *blacan mære*
G III (a) 9; *blacan mor* A (b) V 4; *blæc pytt* C VII 10

*blēo 'variegated'. †*bleo byrig dune* G XII 11 (mod. Blewburton)

bōcland 'land granted by charter'. *þurh bocland* D XIV 16 (mod. Buckland)

borsena ?*recte borstena* 'burst'. *borsenan beorge* B (b) I 9

brād 'broad'. *bradan beorge* G IV 17; †*bradan ford* B (a) II 30; *bradan ham* B (b) III 11; *bradan hærpaðæ* F II 8; *bradanlea* B (a) IV 4 (mod. Bradley); *bradan mere* E VII 16; *bradan meare* C V 8; *bradan mor* C IX 10; *bradan stanas* C VI 7; ?*brandan stane* B (b) I 6; *bradan þorn* C VII 7; *bradan weg* D XIV 6; – C V 11

bræc 'land broken up for cultivation'. *bræce* G XIII 8

brembel 'bramble'. *brembæl hyrnan* C I 22; *bræmbel þyfelan* C II 12; *brembel þorn* G XI 6; *brembel ðyrnan* E VIII 28

brōc 'brook'. *bacgan broc* E VII 32; *bean broc* C X 7; *broc* D II 8, D IX 8, E IV 33; *broce* E VII 7; *broces* C V 22, E VII, E IX 28, G IV 33; *þær þa brocas twisliað* C X 9; *brochylle slæd* G XII 9; *cocbroc* C X 3; *crawan broc* G I 6; *ealdan broc* F II 6; *ealdan broces* G IX 19; *andlang fearn broces* C IX 7; *Gæing broc* F VI 10 (mod. Ginge Brook); *haccebroce* G III (b) 1; *hæg hylles broces byge* C III 35; *hæsel broc* D XIII 6; *holan broc* D VII 8; *holan broces heafod* B (b) V 12; *lacing broc* F VI 9 (mod. Lockinge Brook); *landbroce* D I 7 (mod. Land Brook); *Lortanbrock'* C VIII 29; *lundscore broc* D II 1; *meosbroces ford* B (b) V 10; *Milanbrok'* C VIII 28; *mylen broc* C X 4; *risc broc* F VII 12; *scillinges broce* G I 2; *smalan broc* G IX 15; *stocwylle broc* G IX 21; *sunninga wylle broces* E IV 29; *swynbroc* C I 15; *wanontinge broc* F II 2; *wulfrices broc* E III 2

brocen 'broken'. *brocenan beorg* B (b) VIII 13

brōga 'prodigy, monster'. ?*brogan gete* E V 13

brōm 'broom'. *bromcumbes heafod* E VII 18 (mod. Brumcombe)

brycg 'bridge'. *bric weg* G V 12; *brycge* E IV 34; *byrcg* A (b) IV 8; *brycg ford* A (b) III 6; *pyppel bricge* E VII 13; *stan bricgge* D III 1; *stanbrycge* D I 3; *weala brucge* A (b) II 13; *wudubricge* G IX 23

brystæ (obscure). *brystæ del* C I 6. Tengstrand 107–8 suggests the gen. of a fem. noun *bryst 'landslip, chasm'.

bucca 'he-goat'. ?*buccan crundel* B (b) II 10

burna 'stream'. *burnan* B (a) II 26; *burn stowe* B (a) II 31; *Burnestowe* C VIII 4; *fisces burna* A (b) II 4; *grægsole burnan* A (b) VI 2; *Tealeburnan* F V 2

byge[1] 'corner, angle, bend of a river'. *byge* C III 28 (apparently a feature of the field-system); *dice byge* G IV 44; *hæg hylles broces byge* C III 35; *riscsledes byge* C III 3

byrgels 'burial-place'. *byrgelse* G IV 19; *byrgelsas* B (a) II 4; *bæah-hildæ byrigels* C I 16; *æþenan byrigelsæ* C I 24; *hæðenan byrgelsan* C X I; *hæðennan byriels* D II 9; *hæðenan byrgelse* D IV (two); *hæðenan byrgels* E IV 24; *hæðenum byrgelsum* G IV 15; *hæþenan byrgyrlsas* G V 3

byrig (dat. of *burh*) 'fort'. †*æscæsbyriges suðgeate* C IV 31; †*bleo byrig dune* G XII 11; *duddenbyrig* C IV 33; †*ealdan byrig* B (a) II 22; *friðelabyrig* E V 23; *hæðbyrg* G III (b) 13; †*hremnes byrig* C V 23 (mod. Rams Hill); *lauercebyrig* C IV 28; *paddebyrig* C IV 23; †*Rammesbury* C VIII 35; †*telles byrg* C III 7

byt (obscure). *on þone byt beneoðan Cyngestune* D V 9

bytme 'head of a valley'. ?*byttman dic* F VIII 4

catt 'cat'. *cat beorh* B (a) I 6; *catleage* E V 9

cāwel 'rape, cole, cabbage'. *cawel dene* A (a) I 9

***ceacga** 'broom, gorse, brushwood'. *ceaggan heale* A (a) I 2

cealc 'chalk'. *cealcford* D XI 4, *cealc seaþas* C V 7

ceald 'cold'. *cealdenwulle* E VII 4 (mod. Cholswell)

cealf 'calf'. *Cealues wylle* E IV 12

***ci(e)stel** 'heap of stones'. *stan cystlum* B (a) II 24

***cille** 'spring'. ?*cilla riþ* D X 3 (mod. Childrey)

***cilte** (obscure, *v.* Elements 1 88). *ciltewudes gemære* B (a) II 8

clǣne 'clean, free from weeds'. *Clænan crundel* B (b) V 4; *clene med* C IV 46

clāte 'burdock'. *clatford* B (b) VII 10

clif 'cliff, escarpment, river-bank'. *gateclife* G I 1; *readan clif* C III 39; *sciteres clif* E IV 14

***clodd** 'lump of earth'. *Clodhangran* B (b) IV 26

cocc[1] 'heap'. *weg cocce* A (a) I 4 (mod. Weycock Hill)

cocc[2] 'cock, wild bird'. *cocbroc* C X 3

***col-man** ?'charcoal burner'. *colmanora* E VII 39

cot 'cottage'. *ælsiges cotan* D IV 15; ?*cotan* E II 4; *Sceolles ealdcotan* B (b) X 2 (-*an* has been assumed to represent the dat.pl. ending -*um*)

cot-stōw 'collection of cottages'. *cuðulfes cotstowe* A (b) III 11; *ealdan cot stowe* G IX 14

cran 'crane, heron'. *cranwylle* G IX 11

crāwe 'crow'. *crawanbroc* G I 6

cristel-mǣl 'cross, crucifix'. *cristen mælbeam* A (b) III 4; *langan cyrstel mæle* G IV 5, 38

cristesmǣl 'cross, crucifix'. *cristes mæle* C IX 14

croh¹ 'saffron'. *croh hamme* A (b) II 10

crundel 'chalkpit, quarry, gully'. *buccan crundel* B (b) II 10; *clænan crundel* B (b) V 4; *crundel* B (b) III 25, C VIII 7, E IV 4, G XII 8; *crundle – oþrum crundle* B (a) II 11, 12; *crundelun* B (a) I 1; *haran crundol* B (a) III 10; *lillanhlæwes crundele* F VI 1; *mæres crundel* C VII 16; *rinda crundel* B (b) VII 19; *ruwan crundele* B (b) IV 25; *Ruancrundele* C VIII 3; *ruwan crundle* B (a) II 39; *stan crundele* B (b) I 11; *stancrundele* B (b) VIII 11; *þryscytan crundel* B (b) IV 24

crypel 'burrow'. *crypeles heale* C IX 6

cumb 'valley'. *beocumb* B (b) VIII 10; *bromcumbes heafod* E VII 18 (mod. Brumcombe); *andlang cumbes* E V 20; *cumbes heafod* E IX 18; *cylmes cumbe* G IX 17; *foxholacumb* E IX 21 (mod. Foxcombe); *furcumbe* B (b) VIII 20; *geatescumb* E VII 40 (mod. Yatscombe); *humbracumb* G IX 6; *leacumb* C VI 10; *Loppancomb'* C VIII 18; *mulescumbes* B (b) VIII 16; *smalan cumb* C II 6; *tiddamcumb* E V 17; *tottencumbe* G III (b) 3; *wendlescumb* E IX 13

cwene 'woman'. *quenan dene* B (a) III 6

*cylfe 'hill, eminence'. ?*cylf hongran* G III (a) 10

cyning 'king'. *cyninges dic* G III (b) 12; *Kinggesdych* C VIII 27; *cinges hagan* B (a) II 17; *cinges gemære* F II 1; *cincges scypene, þornas* C VI 16, 18; *Cyngestun* D V 7 (mod. Kingston)

cyrps 'curly'. ?*curspandic* B (b) I 1

cȳta 'kite'. *cytan igge* E V 3; *Cytan seohtresford* B (b) IV 18

cytel 'kettle'. *cytel flodan* B (b) VIII 15

dell 'pit, dell, valley'. *brystæ del* C I 6

denu 'valley'. *acdene* B (b) I 2; *cawel dene* A (a) I 9; *dene* B (b) III 2, B (b) VIII 21; *dene, dene pyt* B (b) II 15, 1; *dene mor* E VII 10; *deopan dene* F VI 15; *duddes dene* C VI 5; *fisceras dene* D XIV 8; *gyddan dene* B (b) II 13; *holan dene* E VII 34; *Hydene* B (b) X 4 (mod. Hidden); *ines dene* B (a) I 10; *lindene* B (b) VII 7; *meosdene* G V 14; *mules dene* B (b) IV 28; *quenan dene* B (a) III 6; *santan dene* B (a) IV 7; *stan dene* B (a) II 33; *weterdene* F VI 14; *ylfing dene* B (b) IV 15

dēop 'deep'. *deopan dene* F VI 15; *deopan furh* D IV 11; *diopan wei* G III (c) 5

dīc 'ditch'. *abbedes dic* E VII 3; *æcer dic* E VIII 33; *ælfðryþe dic* D VII 7; *bican dic* C VII 5; *bulen dic* C IV 6; *byttman dic* F VIII 4; *cyninges dic* G III (b) 12; *Kinggesdych* C VIII 27; *curspandic* B (b) I 1; *dic* A (b) III 2, A (b) IV 4, B (b) VII 17, B (b) VIII 5,

C I 20, C II 19, 29, E II 8, E II 10, E IV 9, E VI 2, E VIII 9, 29, E IX 23, F IV 3, F VII 8, 18, G II 4; *dic þære se æþeling mearcode* G IV 33; *andlang dice* D V 14; *endlangdiches* C VIII 11; *andlang dices* G III (c) 10; *dices wyllan* G II 7; *dic on doccan grafe – doccan dic* E I 2; *dice byge* G IV 44; *diceænde* E IV 40; *dice hyrnan* G XIII 5; *dic sticcea* G IV 40; *æaldan dic* C I 32; *ealdan dic* D IV 9, D VIII 5, D XI 9, E III 4, E VI 6, E VIII 32, F III 1, F VIII 2, G II 6, G III (c) 13, G V 2; *ealdun dic* G IV 15; *andlang ðæs gærstunes dic* G XIII 3; *hæcceleas dic* G XII 12; *hæseldic* E II 5, E IV 17; *hnottan dic* G XI 5; *holan dic* F VI 5; *langen dic* C IV 30; *lippan dic* E IV 22; *lytlan dice ende* G IV 37; *mæd dic* D I 8; *mærdic* B (b) V 2, D IV 15, F V 1, 4; *mær dic* D XI 5 (mod. Mere Dike); *Middildych* C VIII 16; *mylen dic* A (b) IV 7; *niwan dic* E IV 35; *norðlange dic* C IV 43; *occenes gerstun dic* E VII 37; *ordstanes dic* G IV 30; *readan dic* C VII 8, C IX 8; *rugan dic* G XII 2; *scortan dic* C II 30, D VII 6; *wæter slædes dic* G IV 2; *wulfstanes dic* E IV 18

d(i)erne, dyrne 'hidden, secret'. *dyrnan grafan* A (a) I 3; *dyrnan gelade* G II 1; *dyrne stan* C IV 39

dīnor 'coin'. *dinra beorh* C VII 17

docce 'dock'. *doccan grafe – doccan dic* E I 2; *doccena ford* A (b) VI 9.

*drægel ? 'ribbon'. *drægeles bæce* G III (b) 5

dūn 'hill'. *abbendune* E VII 19; †*bleo byrig dune* G XII 11 (mod. Blewburton); *betweonan mæde and dune* E IV 43; *dunlege* G XIII 20; *ealdan dune* G XI 8; *Earnesdune* F VI 4; *grenan dune* G III (c) 2; *hægdune* E II 10; *hæþ dune* G IV 38 (mod. Hadden); *heað dune* D II 10; *haran dune* G IX 10 (mod. Horn Down); *hean dunæ* C II 31; *hunes dune* B (a) I 20; *langan dune* G XII 6 (mod. Langdon); *meoces dune* G IV 18; *mordune* C IV 47; *mules dune* B (a) II 40; *rigedune* D VIII 10; *waddune* G XIII 1; *weardan dune* B (b) II 14

*dūni(g)e (obscure). *dunian mere* B (b) I 7 (mod. Dunmore)

dunn 'dark'. *dunnan hole* C IV 21

dȳð 'fuel, tinder'. *dyþmere* D XI 2

ēa 'river'. *ea* A (b) IV 5 (R. Kennet), E IV 38 (R. Thames), G V (R. Thames); *æa* D XIV 11 (R. Thames); *middel ea* A (b) II 16 (R. Kennet)

eald 'old'. †*ealdan bece* G XIII 14; *elden berwe* C VIII 10; †*ealdan byrig* B (a) II 22; *ealdan broc* F II 6, G IX 22; *ealdan broces* G IX 19; *ealdan cot stowe* G IX 14; *æaldan dic* C I 32; *ealdan dic*

D IV 9, D VIII 5, D XI 9, E III 4, E VI 6, E VIII 32, F III 1, F VIII 2, G II 6, G III (c) 13, G V 2; *ealdun dic* G IV 15; *ealdan dune* G XI 8; *ealdan fyrh* G IX 3; *ealdan garan* C VI 6, D V 5; *ealdan halh* G III (a) 3; *ealdan hege* D IX 10; *ealdan hege ræwe* B (b) III 8; *æaldan hole* C I 29; *ealdan hord wylles wæg* C I 13; *ealdan hyrne weg* B (a) I 18; *ealdan lace* G III (b) 2; *ealdan læghrycge* E VIII 12; *eald gemære* D V 12; *ealdan mere* G XIII 7; *ealdan stigele* B (a) I 16; *ealdan stret ford* G V 9; *ealdan wanatiting* F III 7; *ealdan wæg* C I 17; *ealdan weges* B (a) III 7; *ealdan wudu weg* C III 6; *ealdan wulfhaga* E II 13; *Sceolles ealdcotan* B (b) X 2

ealdormann 'chief officer of a shire'. *ealdormonnes gemere* F VII 11

earn 'eagle'. ?*Earnesdune* F VI 4

ecg 'edge'. *a bæ ecgæ* C II 25

eclēs 'Romano-British Christian church'. ?*eceles beorh* C IV 34

edisc 'enclosure, enclosed park'. *sundran edisce* E V 14

efisc ?'edge'. *efisc* A (b) II 8, E III 8

elebēam 'olive tree' (presumably used of some English tree). *elebeame* G IV 10; *Elebeam* B (b) IV 16 (corresponds to *elebeam styb* B (b) III 15)

ellen 'elder'. *ænlipe ellyn* D II 2; *ællen stub* C II 16; *ellen styb* E IV 21, E VIII 14; *ellen stubbe – oðerne ellen stubbe – eft on ellen stubb* G IX 1, 2, 8

ende[1] 'end'. *bulen dices ende* C V; *diceænde* E IV 40; *hagan end* A (b) I 4; *hagan ende* A (b) II 3; *linces ende* G IV 29; *lytlan dice ende* G IV 37; *andlang dic oþ þone suð ende* G IV

eoccen (?another R. Ock). *Eoccenford* B (b) IV 13

eorðburg 'earthwork'. *Ertheburgh'* C VIII 8

*eorð-gebyrst 'landslip'. *eorþ geberste* G IV 21

fearn 'fern'. *fearnbeorghe* B (b) VIII 1; *fearnbroces* C IX 7; *ferngaran* G XIII 13; *fearnhilles sled* C III 18

feld 'open land'. *ut on þone feld* B (b) VIII 31; *ut to felda* A (b) VI 6; *gamafeld* D XIV 2 (mod. Gainfield); *ut on heaþ felda* A (b) II 22; *ut to heaðfelda* A (b) VI 12; *ut on þone hæðfeld* B (b) VII 6; *utan þone lytlan hæþfeld* (B (a) II 20

fēower 'four'. *feower gemæra* E VI 7

fisc 'fish'. *fisces burna* A (b) II 4; *fisclace* C IX 5

fiscere 'fisher'. *fisceras dene* D XIV 8

fleax 'flax'. *fleax æcyres* A (b) III 9; *flexhammes* B (b) IV 21

flecg (obscure, Holthausen suggests 'piece of land'). *flecges garan* G III (b) 7; *flegestane* G XIII 12

flēot 'small stream'. *snoddan fleote* F II 7

flōde 'stream, intermittent spring or stream'. *cytel flodan* B (b) VIII 15; *flodan* G IV 20; *mær flodan* B (b) VIII 6

ford 'ford'. †*bradan ford* B (a) II 30; *brycg ford* A (b) III 6; *cealcford* D XI 4; *cerenforda* D I 6; *clatford* B (b) VII 10; *Cytan seohtresford* B (b) IV 18; *doccena ford* A (b) VI 9; *dunanford* E IV 28; *ealdan stret ford* G V 9; *eglafes forda* D XII 1; *eoccenforda* E VII 1; *Eoccen ford* B (b) IV 13; *forda* E IX 5; *fordwere* E VIII 2; *fulan forda* G XII 3; *Garaforda* D X 1 (mod. Garford); *Gunredesford* A (b) V 9; *gyrdford* A (b) V 7; *læcesforda* E II 15 (mod. Lashford); *Langanforda* G VII 7; *Maccaniges forda* G VII 1; *mægðæ ford* E V 1; *mearcforda* E VII 5; *meosbroces ford* B (b) V 10; *myþ ford* A (b) II 15; *runesforda* G III (c) 1 (mod. Runsford); *Sandforda* E II 1 (mod. Sandford); *scealdan ford* A (b) II 20 (mod. Shalford); *Stanford* E III 10; *stapolford* B (b) V 16; *tubba forda* D IX 5 (mod. Tubworth); *welingaforda* G III (c) 14 (mod. Wallingford); *wuda-ford* E IV 30

forierð ?'projecting piece of ploughland'. *forierð* C III 12, 30, 37

fox 'fox'. †*foxes beorge* G IV 22 (mod. Fox Barrow); *foxhola* C II 3; *foxholacumb* E IX 21 (mod. Foxcombe)

Frīgedæg 'Friday'. *frigedæges treow* F VI 13

fūl 'dirty'. *fulan æc* E VII 14 (perhaps a rotting as opposed to a 'fair' oak); *fulan forda* G XII 3; *fulan lace* E II 2; *fulan riþe* A (b) VI 8 (mod. Foudry); *fulan wege se hatte stific weg* B (b) VIII 30

furh 'the furrow between ridges of an open-field system'. *on þa deopan furh* D IV 11; *to þære gedrifonan fyrh andlang fyrh* C VII 22; *on þa ealdan fyrh* G IX 3; *on ða furh to furcumbe* B (b) VIII 19, 20; *andlanges þere furh* C III 10, 16; *on ane furh* C III 19, 22, G II 2; *andlanges anre fyrh – on ane fyrh* C III 27, 29; *andlang fyrh* C I 7, E IV 26; *be þes heafd æceres west furh dun ofer þa þwyrs furh* C IV 36, 37; *endlangfurth, endlangfurtz* C VIII 19, 31; *andlang furh* C X 14; *andlang furh – on ða furh* E VIII 20; *innan þa furh* F V 5; *andlang fura* F VI 7; *on þa niwan furh andlang þære furh* G I 5

furlang 'furlong, the length of a furrow'. (i) a unit of cultivation in the open-field system. *bean furlang* C VI 19; *þwures ofer an furlang* C III 33; *longe furlang* G IX 16. (ii) a linear measure. *norþ an furlang* B (a) II 27; *andlang Brycgweges an furlang* G VII; *andlang þære dic twa furlanc norðweard þanon east be hæfdan twa furlang andlang fura* F VI 6; *west twa furlang* F VII fyrd (meaning uncertain). *fyrd hammas* B (a) I 4

(ge)fyrhðe 'wood'. *accangefyrðæ* B (b) V 9

fyrs 'furze'. *fyrs ige* A (b) II 18

gærs-tūn 'paddock'. *gærstune – gærstunes dic* G XIII 2–3; *occenes gerstun dic* E VII 37

gāra 'land in the triangular remnant of a field after a rectangular pattern of furlongs has been laid out'. *bryxstanes garan* C VI 4; *ealdan garan* C VI 6, D V 5; *flecges garan* G III (b) 7 (corresponding to *ferngaran* G XIII 13); *garan* C I 1, 18, C III 8, 15; *gar æcer* C III 9, 25; *twam gar æceron* C III 36; ?*Garaforda* D X 1 (mod. Garford, here probably in a different sense, *v.* Pt 2 410); *snelles garan* G IX 18

gāt 'goat'. *gateclife* G I 1

*geafling ?'river-fork'. *geafling lace* E VII 36

*gear 'enclosure for catching fish'. *mulen ger* A (b) IV 6

geat 'gate, gap, pass'. *brogan gete* E V 13; ?*geatescumb* E VII 40 (mod. Yatscombe); *hengestes geat* G XI 7; *norþ geatt – suð geat* C II 27–8; *norðgeate – suðgeate* C IV 13, 15; *Rammesbury yate* C VIII 35; *screget* B (b) V 11; *stod lege get* D II 11; *sulgeate* G IV 48; *widan geat* G II 3; *wide geat* C VII 2

gōd² 'good'. ?*godan pearruce* A (a) I 5

gor 'mud'. *gorgræfas* E IV 1

græf 'pit'. *gorgræfas* E IV 1

grāf 'grove'. *blacan grafan* B (b) VII 18; *blacan graue* E IX 22 (mod. Blagrove); *cearna graf* D IV 3; *doccan grafe* E I 2; *guman grafe* E VII 12; *hærgraf* B (a) IV 2; *haran grafas* B (a) I 21; *hyrde grafe* C VI 21 (later *Hurgrove*); *suggan graf* E VIII 26

grafa¹ 'ditch'. *dyrnan grafan* A (a) I 3

grēat 'thick, bulky'. *greatan stoc* A (a) II 4; *greatan þorn* E V 15, E IX 20; *gretan ðornstyb* F VII 5; *greatan welig* E IV 36

grēne¹ 'green'. *grenan beorh* B (b) III 33; *grenan dune* G III (c) 2; *grenan hlince* F VI 3; *grene weig* C IV 48; *grenan weg* B (b) III 22, C VII 21; *grænan weges* C II 10; *grenen weig* E VII 6

Grīm (probably a byname for Woden). *grim gelege* G III (c) 7 (mod. Grim's Ditch)

gybhild (stream-name). *gybhilde* G V 19 (mod. Kibble Ditch)

gyna (obscure). *gynan bæte* D XIII 7

gyrd, gierd (i) 'twig, rod, spar'. *gyrdford* A (b) V 7; (ii) 'linear measure of 5½ yds'. *vi gyrda be westan yttinges hlawe* E I 9; *andlang hærpaðes. seofan and fiftig gyrda* C X 13

hæcc 'gate'. *to þam hæcce* B (a) II 10; *to þæm hæcce* E V 20; *of þam hæcce* G XIII 16

***hæcce** 'fence'. *on þa heccan andlang heccen, ondlang heccan* B (a) III 2, 9; *andlang hæccan* B (b) IV 33

hæcc-geat 'hatch-gate'. *hæcget* B (b) V 13.

(ge)hæg 'fence, enclosure'. *hægdune* E II 10; *hæg hylles broces byge* C III 35; *hæglea* E VII 15

-hǣma- 'of the inhabitants'. *byden hæma gemæres* B (a) II 5; *cing hæma gemære* D III 3; *middelhæma ge mæra* G XI 2; *orhæme gemære* B (a) II 7; *stifingc hæma gemære* F VII 9

***hǣr** 'rock'. *hærgraf* B (a) IV 2

hæsel 'hazel'. *hæsel broc* D XIII 6; *hæseldic* E II 5, E IV 17; *hæsl hylle* C VII 20; *hæsel lea* B (b) I 8, E I 3

hǣð 'a heath'. *hæðbyrg* G III (b) 13; *hæþ dune* G IV 38 (mod. Hadden); *heað dune* D II 10; *hæðfeld* B (b) VII 6; *heaþ felda* A (b) II 22; *heaðfelda* A (b) VI 12; *lytlan hæþfeld* B (a) II 20. The compound *hæðfeld* could probably be translated 'common', *v.* 633.

hǣðen 'heathen'. *v.* **byrgels**.

h(e)afoc 'hawk'. *heafoces hamme* D IX 4; *hafeces hlæwe* C IV 26; *heafoces oran* E VII 33; *hafuc þorne* G IV 5

haga¹ 'hedge, enclosure'. *hagan end þonne andlang hagan* A (b) I 5, A (b) II 3; *hagan – andlang hagan – a be hagan* A (b) III; *hagan andlang hagan – seo east mearc eal se haga scæt* A (b) IV; *andlang hagan* A (b) II 21, B (a) IV (twice), B (b) I 5, G III (a) 2; *cinges hagan – andlang hagan – andlang hagan* B (a) II 17–19; *ealdan wulfhaga* E II 13; *grægsole hagan andlang hagan to hagena gemyðum – on tichan stedes hagan andlang hagan – to beorhfeldinga gemære to þen hagan* A (b) VI; *gemær hagan* E VIII 43, E II 3; *of westleas hagan on ceawan hrycges hagan* A (b) V 15–16

hālig 'holy'. *halige stowe* C IV 8

hamm 'river-meadow, enclosure'. *on anne ham – on anne ham – bradan ham – rige hamme – cardan ham* B (b) III; *flexhammes – minthammas – weterhammas* B (b) IV; *æsc meres hammas* B (b) VII 4; *cnottinga hamme* A (b) I 5; *croh hamme* A (b) II 10; *fyrd hammas* B (a) I 4; *on butan þone ham* F V 8; *þa hammas þa þer midrihte to ge byriað* A (b) IV 15; *haniges hamme* D II 7; *heafoces hamme* D IX 4; *heorthamme* E IX 24; *hlippem ham* C IV 41; *preosthamme* C IX 11; *sceaphammes* B (a) II 35; *sprindlesham* D XIV 1; *stigel hammas* B (b) II 5; *wassan hamme* A (a) I 1; *wihtlufe hamme* F VIII 9 hāmstede 'homestead'. *mules hamstæde* G III (a) 7; ?*tichan stedes hagan* A (b) VI 5ₓ

hān 'stone'. *readan hane* B (b) II 4, B (b) V 5, G IV 25

*hangra 'wood on a steep hillside'. *ceobban hangran* E IX 6; *Clod-hangran* B (b) IV 26; *cylf hongran* G III (a) 10; *hangran* B (b) VIII 32; *higran hongran* G III (c) 3; *hodduces hancgran* D II 3; *perhangran* E VIII 46; *scilling hangran* B (b) III 10; *seal hangran* B (a) II 3; *wirhangran* G IV 7; *wopig hangran* B (b) III 9; *wroht-hangran* E IV 10

hār² probably 'boundary'. *haran apoldre* B (a) II 6, 37; *haran apeldre* B (b) II 11; *haran grafas* B (a) I 21; *haranstan* B (b) I 10; *haran stane* E II 12; *horeston* C VIII 34; *haran þornan* B (b) VIII 24; *haran þyrnan* B (a) III 3

hassuc 'clump of coarse grass'. *pricelles hæssecas* C X 2

*Hāra ?hill-name. *haran dune* G IX 10 (mod. Horn Down)

hēafod 'head'. This el. occurs in several senses:

(i) 'chief, most important'. †*theafd beorh* A (b) II 1; *heafodweg* E V 19

(ii) 'human head'. *heafod stoccas* B (a) IV 5, C VI 2; *heafud stoccun* D III 4; *heafod stoccan* F III 2

(iii) 'source, end'. *bromcumbes heafod* E VII 18; *cumbes heafod* E IX 18; *holan broces heafod* B (b) V 12; *lytlan mores heafde* D XIV 3; *mænan mores heafud* D VII 3; *meos broces heafod* B (b) VII 11

(iv) 'headland' (in an open-field system). *on anum heafde* C III 21; *on ða heafda* C I 9; *andlang þere heafde* C IV 9; *be þam heafde* C IV 12, 16; *on þa heafda* D IV 18, F III 9; *to þam heafdan* E VIII 21; *be hæfdan* F VI 6; *andlang heafda* F VII 3 (variants of this phrase recur several times in this survey). For instances of *hēafod-æcer* v. æcer, for instances of *hēafod-land* v. land. v. also andhēafdu.

hēah 'high'. *hean dunæ* C II 31; *hean hrycg* B (a) II 16

healf 'half'. *healfan æcer* E IV 26; *healfan streame* B (b) V 17

healh 'nook, valley, corner, projection of an administrative area'. *braccan heal* A (b) V 12 (mod. Bracknell); *ceaggan heale* A (a) I 2; *crypeles heale* C IX 6; *dudemeres hele* G XIII 17; *ealdan halh* G III (a) 3; *healhwere* D XIV 12; *heal wicum* A (a) I 11 (later Hollicks); *rige wurðe heal* E III 5; *swæfes heale* A (a) I 7; *totan healas* E V 16

hecge 'hedge'. *andlang hecgan* B (a) I 20

hēg, hīg 'hay'. *hig weg* D XIV 15, G I 7; *hig wege* E IV 15

hege 'hedge, fence'. *on ðone ealdan hege* D IX 10; *to þam rah hege* E III 6

hege-rǣw 'hedgerow'. *on þa ealdan hege rǣwe* B (b) III 8; *andlang þære hege rǣwe* E IV 37; *on þa hege rǣpe* B (b) VII 16; *andlang hegerewe* B (b) IV 6

hengest 'horse, stallion, gelding'. *?hengestes geat* G XI 7

heorot 'hart'. *heorthamme* E IX 24; *hiorotlege* G III (a) 8

here-pæð 'military road, highway'. *bradan hærpaðæ* F II 8 (corresponding to *smalan weg* F III 10); *herpaþe* A (b) II 7, 23; *hearpoþe* B (a) II 29; *heorpaþes* B (a) III 5; *herpaðes* B (b) VII 2, 13; *herpað* C X 12; *hearapod* D II 5; *hearpaþes* F VI 12; *here page* G IV 28; *herepað* G IX 9

hierde, hyrde 'herdsman'. *hyrde grafe* C VI 21 (later *Hurgrove*); *hyrdige* E III 14; *an hyrde wic* C VI 21

higera 'jay, magpie, woodpecker'. *higran hongran* G III (c) 3

hlāw, hlǣw 'tumulus'. *cardan hlæw* B (b) III 12; *ceawan hlewe* F IV 5 (mod. Challow); *hafeces hlæwe* C IV 26; *hildes hlæw* C VII 9 (later *Hildeslowe*); *hodes hlæwe* C IV 17; *hundeshlæwe* C IV 25; *hwittuces hlæwe* C VII 14; *lillanhlæwes crundele* F VI 1; *rupelemes hlau* F VII 2; *stanhlæwe* C IV 18; *wintres hlewe* D X 5; *yttinges hlawe* E I 10 (mod. Titlar)

*hlid¹ 'slope'. *?hild leage* A (a) I 6 (mod. Littlewick); *be þan hlide* C V 29 (the boundary runs along the 600' contour)

hlid² 'gate'. *?hild leage* A (a) I 6 (mod. Littlewick)

hlid-geat 'swing gate'. *lid geat* G III (a) 4

hlinc 'ridge, bank', probably used of 'strip linchets' or cultivation terraces. *on æþelmes hlinc on forwerde dune* C VII 3; *to grenan hlince* F VI 3; *on ðone hlinc – on oðærne hlinc* C III 19–20; *to þam hlincæ* C I 8; *andlang hlinces* B (b) III 30, C II 2; *on ða hlinc rewe* B (b) VIII 4; *to þæs linces ende* G IV 29; *to hord hlince ufeweardum* B (b) III 19; *on þone rugan hlinc niðæwearde* C VI 3; *on þone ruwan hlync andlang þæs rowan linces* G IV 14; *of snelles hlince* C VI 20; *on uuon hlinc. And lang hlincæs* C I 4

Hlȳde, stream-n. *hlydan* C IX 9 (mod. Lyde Copse)

hnæf (obscure, Professor Löfvenberg suggests a word cognate with ON *hnafa* 'to hew, cut'). *hnæfleage* B (a) II 18

hnott 'bare'. *hnottan dic* G XI 5; *hnottan mæræ* C I 19; *hnottan stocce* G V 18; *hnottan þorn* B (b) II 2

hol¹ 'hole, hollow'. *dunnan hole* C IV 21; *æaldan hola* C I 29; *foxhola*

C II 3; *foxholacumb* E IX 21 (mod. Foxcombe); *hwitan hole* C IV 19; *readan hole* C IV 20

hol² 'hollow, lying or running in a hollow'. *holan broc* D VII 8; *holan broces heafod* B (b) V 12; *holan dene* E VII 34; *holan dic* F VI 5; *holen weg* B (b) IV 3; *holan weg* G V 11; *hwitan holan weg* G XII 5; *holan wylle* G V 10

holt 'wood, thicket'. *bullanholt* G III (c) 4

hord 'treasure'. *hord hlince* B (b) III 19; *hordwyllæ* C I 12 (mod. Hardwell)

horu 'filth, dirt'. *horo pytte* E VIII 30

hræfn 'raven'. †*hremnes byrig* C V 23 (mod. Rams Hill); †*Rammesbury* C VIII 35; ?*rammes hrycg* B (a) I 17

hram(e)sa 'wild garlic'. *hrameslea* G IV 3

hrēod 'reed'. *hreodmede* G IX 13

hring 'circle'. *hrung putt* C I 28 (later The Manger)

hritm (obscure). *hritmes mere* A (b) V 3

hrycg 'ridge'. *ealdan læghrycge* E VIII 12; *hean hrycg* B (a) II 16; *hryc* B (b) V 7; *hric* B (a) III 11; *andlang hricgges* B (b) IV 19 (corresponds *to hord hlince* B (b) III 19); *andlang hrycges* E IV 31; *hrycgweg* B (a) II 41, E IX 11; *hricg weg* C IX 13; *rammes hrycg* B (a) I 17. A number of surveys refer to The Ridge Way.

Humbre, r.n. *humbracumb* G IX 6

hund 'hound'. *hundeshlæwe* C IV 25; *hunda leage* A (b) VI 1

hunn (obscure). *hunnes wylle* A (b) II 11

hwīt 'white'. *hwitan hole* C IV 19; *hwitan holan weg* G XII 5; *hwite more* D IX 3; *hwitan pearruc* A (a) II 3 (mod. Paddock Wd); *hwitan stane* A (b) I 8; *Whytestone* C VIII 12; *hwitan wege* B (b) VIII 23

hyll 'hill'. *blacan hylle* F VII 17; *brochylle slæd* G XII 9; *fearnhylles slæd* C III 18; *hæg hylles broces byge* C III 35; *hæsl hylle* C VII 20; *snoddes hylle* E II 11; *teonan hylle* G IV 13; *tetan hylle* E V 18; *wærnan hylle* D III 5; *wrangan hylle* G IV 8; *wrestleshylle* B (b) II 9

hyln (obscure). *hylneslea* A (b) V 11

hyrne 'angle, corner, projection of land'. *brembæl hyrnan* C I 22 (this may be a mistake for *þyrnan*, but as the compound makes reasonable sense there is no reason for emending it); *dice hyrnan* G XIII 5; *ealdan hyrne weg* B (a) I 18

hȳð 'landing-place on a river'. *Hydene* B (b) X 4 (mod. Hidden)

īeg 'island, dry ground in marsh, river-meadow'. *befer ige* A (b) II

17; *berege* E III 12 (later *Berry*); *bottanige* F VIII 6; *ceolesige* G V 17 (mod. Cholsey); *cyddesige* D VIII 9; *cytan igge* E V 3; *fyrs ige* A (b) II 18; *huddes igge* G IV 35; *hyrdige* E III 14; *yge* A (b) I 3; *maccan eige* G III (c) 12 (mod. Mackney); *meldanige* G V 15; *micclanige* E VII 29; *snitan ige* C IX 3; *swanesig* D V 4; *tun ege* A (b) IV 11

ig(g)oð 'small island'. *on norðhealfe þæs igeðes* C IX 3; *igoð* E III 11

imbe 'swarm of bees'. *imbelea* A (b) V 5

in-fyrde ?'entrance to a ford'. *in fyrde* E I 12; *infyrde* E VI 3

-ing-[4], connective particle. ?*ærnincg weg* G V 13; *Æðeleahing wudu* E VII 38; *eanulfing þorn* G XII 4; *lilling lea* B (b) VIII 7 (mod. Lilley); *pocging rode* B (a) I 13; ?*wopig hangran* B (b) III 9; *ylfing dene* B (b) IV 15

-inga-, gen.pl. of -ingas. *beorhfeldinga gemære* A (b) VI 13; *catmeringa gemære* B (b) VIII 30; *cearninga gemære* D III 8; *heantunninga gemære* D III 9; *kingtuninge gemære* D IV 14; *lamburninga mearce* B (b) X 5; *linfordinga gemere* D X 4; *sandfordinga gemære* (error for *stan-*) C IX 1; *stanmeringa gemere* B (b) VIII 28; *syðtuninga lace* G IX 20; *welingaforda* G III (c) 14 (mod. Wallingford); *winterburninga gemære* B (a) II 21

kasa (obscure). *kasan ðorne* D XIV 5

lacu 'stream'. *blachelace* C IV 3; *ealdan lace* G III (b) 2; *fisclace* C IX 5; *fulan lace* E II 2; *geafling lace* E VII 36; *lace* C IV 2, C X 9, D I (several), E VII 27, G II 1, G IV 32, 51, G V 8; *land lace* E V 4; *ge mærlace* D IV 2; *mærlace* B (b) V 15; *sandlace* G V 16; *syðtuninga lace* G IX 20; *tibbælde lace* G III (c) 11; *ðyreses lace* C V 13; *won lace* E IV 41

(ge)lād 'watercourse, passage over a river'. *dyrnan gelade* G II 1; *eanflæde gelade* E V 26; *hudes lade* D VII 5

læce 'bog'. ?*læcesforda* E II 15 (mod. Lashford); ?*læcesmere* C V 14; ?*læce mere* F VII 6

læce[2] 'leech'. Possible in ns. listed under læce.

læge 'fallow, unploughed'. *ealdan læghrycge* E VIII 12

lām 'loam'. *lam pyt* E IX 17; *lam pyttas* B (b) III 24, F VIII 3

land (i) 'strip in an open field'. *heafod lande* E I 8; *hæfod land* F VII (2 examples); *scorteland* E IV 25. (ii) 'cultivated land'. *an hid landes – xii æceras landes* C VI 21; *gemanan lande* B (a) III 12. (iii) 'estate', hence (as first el.) 'boundary'. *on easte wardum þam lande* G IV; *landbroce* D I 7 (mod. Land Brook); *land lace* E V 4 *land-scoru 'boundary'. *lund score broc* D II 1.

lang 'long, tall'. *langan cyrstel mæle* G IV 5, 38; *langen dic* C IV 30; *langan dune* G XII 6 (mod. Langdon); *Langanforda* G VII 7; *longe furlang* G IX 16; *langan treowe* B (b) I 12; *langan þorne* G IV 6

lāwerce 'lark'. *laurocan beorghe* D XIV 4; *lauercebyrig* C IV 28

lēah 'wood, clearing in a wood, meadow, pasture'. *bacgan leah* E VII 23 (mod. Bagley); *bradanlea* B (a) IV 4 (mod. Bradley); *catleage* E V 9; *dunlege* G XIII 20; *hæcceleas dic* G XII 12; *hæglea* E VII 15; *hæsel lea* B (b) I 8, E I 3; *hesleabroc* G IX 12; *hiortlege* G III (a) 8; *hild leage* A (a) I 6 (mod. Littlewick); *hnæfleage* B (a) II 18; *hrameslea* G IV 3; *hrocanleage* E II 9; *hunda leage* A (b) VI 1; *hylneslea* A (b) V 11; *imbelea* A (b) V 5; *lea* B (b) III 6, 32; *leag* B (b) VIII 25; *leacumb* C VI 10; *lilling lea* B (b) VIII 7 (mod. Lilley); *linleahe* B (a) III 8; *maduces lea* E IV 19; *merc lege* G XIII 18; *pippes leage* B (b) I 4; *plumleage* E V 22; *preosta leage* E V 8; *riscleahe* E IX 15; *ruwanleage* E V 12; *stanleage* B (b) VIII 26; *stod lege get* D II 11; *Đæclege* G XIII 15; *þornihtan leage* A (b) III 5; *wadleahe* E VI 5; *wealcottes leahe* B (a) IV 6; *wæst legæ* G III (a) 5; *westleas hagan* A (b) V 15; *wigferþis leage* B (b) I 3; *wulfa leage* A (a) I 8 (mod. Woolley); *ydyrleage* E V 24; *yfemæstan leage* E IV 13

*gelegu 'tract of land'. *grim gelege* G III (c) 7 (later Grim's Ditch)

licgende 'lying down'. *licgendanstoc* A (b) VI 11

lichanga (obscure, ? error for *lichaga*). *lic hangan* B (a) I 12

līn 'flax'. *lindene* B (b) VII 7; *linleahe* B (a) III 8

lippa 'lip'. ? *lippan dic* E IV 22

*lōcere 'shepherd'. *loceres weg* B (a) I 15

loddere 'beggar'. *loddere beorge* F VI 2; *loddæræs sæccinge* C I 5; *Loddera stræt* A (b) I 10; *lodder þorne* G XIII 11

lucring (? error for *lutring*), stream-n. *lucringes* E II 16

lȳtel 'little'. †*lytlan beorh* B (a) II 40; *litel berwe* C VIII 14; *lytlan dice ende* G IV 37; *lytlan hæþfeld* B (a) II 20; *lytlan mores heafde* D XIV 3; *littelne þorn* G V 5; *lytlan weges* G IV 11; *lytlan wil* F VI 8; *lytlan wyl* F VII 14

marge (obscure). *marge wei* G III (c) 6.

mæd 'meadow'. *bulan mædæ* C I 21; *clene med* C IV 46; *codan mæd* B (b) V 18; *hreodmede* G IX 13; *betweonan mæde and dune* E IV 43; *mæd* C II 13, D XIV 9; *seo mæd on tun ege – seo mead be*

norþan ea A (b) IV 11, 14; *xii æceras mede* C VI 21; *x æceras mæde*
G V; *mæd dic* D I 8; *sihtre mæde* B (b) III 20. Cf. also *xii mæð*
æceras A (a) I 13

mǣgen 'great'. *mægen stan* C I 3
mǣgðⁱ¹ 'maiden'. ?*mægðæ ford* E V 1
mǣgðe 'may-weed'. ?*mægðæ ford* E V 1
(ge)mǣne 'common'. *gemanan lande* B (a) III 12; *mæne mor* D IX 2;
  gemænan treowe A (b) V 1
(ge)mǣre 'boundary'. *ælfheages gemære* B (a) I 7; *ælflæde gemæra*
  A (b) IV 1; *ælfwiges gemære* B (b) X 6; *beorhfeldinga gemære* A (b)
  VI 13; *bricthwoldes ge mæra* G XI 9; *byden hæma gemæres* B (a) II
  5; *byrgwylle gemære* G IV 45; *catmeres gemære* B (a) II 42;
  catmeringa gemære B (b) VIII 30; *cearninga gemære* D III 8;
  ciltewudes gemære B (a) II 8; *cinges gemære* F II 1; *cing hæma*
  gemære D III 3; *kingtuninge gemære* D IV 14; *Eadgife gemære* B
  (b) X 3; *eadulfes mære* G III (b) 9; *eald gemæra* D V 12; *ealdor-*
  monnes gemere F VII 11; *feower gemæra* E VI 7; *heantunninga*
  gemære D III 9; *leofrices gemere* F VIII 7; *leofsiges ge mæra* G XI
  4; *linfordinga gemere* D X 4; *gemere* F VIII (twice); *gæmeres* B (b)
  IV 35; *gemæres* B (a) I (twice), D V (several), E II, E IX; *gemeres*
  B (a) IV; *meres* C VIII 15; *mære* E VI; *gemærbeorg* F I 3;
  mærbeorh C X 11; *Mereberwe* C VIII 32; *mæres crundel* C VII 16;
  mærdic B (b) V 2, D IV 15, F V 1, 4; *mær dic* D XI 5 (mod. Mere
  Dike); *mær flodan* B (b) VIII 6; *gemær hagan* E VIII 43, E II 3;
  mærlace B (b) V 15; *ge mærlace* D IV 2; *mærpol* C X 6; *mereþorn*
  D V 2; *mær weg* B (a) III 1; *mære weges* B (a) I 8; *gemærweg* E IV
  8 (two), E VIII 35; *gemær weige* G III (b) 6; *Merewelle* C VIII 20;
  middelhæma ge mæra G XI 2; *Ordulfes gemære* F IV 4; *orhæma*
  gemære B (a) II 7; *sandfordinga gemære* C IX 1; *stanmeringa*
  gemere B (b) VIII 28; *stifingc hæma gemære* F VII 9; *þrim ge-*
  mærum B (b) III 37; *þrio gemæru* E V 11; *winterburninga gemære*
  B (a) II 21; *wittan mære* G III (b) 11; *wulfrices gemære* B (b)
  III 18
mapuldor 'maple tree'. *read leafan mapuldre* G IV 50
mǣse 'tit-mouse'. *masan mere* A (b) III 10
mearc 'boundary'. *ægelwardes mearce* C IV 11 (corresponding to
  æþelferðes mearce C V 18); *east mearc* A (b) IV 12; *lamburninga*
  mearce B (b) X 5; *mearce* B (b) VII (several), D III (twice); *mearc-*
  forda E VII 5; *merc lege* G XIII 18; *mearc weg* B (b) III 35
melde 'orach'. *meldanige* G V 15

mēos 'moss, lichen', probably 'swamp'. *meosbroces ford* B (b) V 10; *meosdene* G V 14; *myos wyllan* C IX 12

mere 'pool'. *æsc meres hammas* B (b) VII 4; *blacan mære* G III (a) 9; *bradan mere* E VII 16; *bradan meare* C V 8; *Buckanmer'* C VIII 2; *bulemere* C IV 4; *dunian mere* B (b) I 7 (mod. Dunmore); *dyþmere* D XI 2; *ealdan mere* G XIII 7; *hnottan mæræ* C I 19; *hritmes mere* A (b) V 3; *læce mere* F VII 6; *læcesmere* C V 14; *masan mere* A (b) III 10; *mere* C VII 7, C X 8; *readan meare* F III 4; *scyldmere* B (b) VIII 18; *stan mæræ* C I 23; *þwyrsmere* C IV 1; *wintermere* B (a) IV 1

mersc 'marsh'. *mersc* B (b) VII 14

micel 'big'. *miclan beorge* G IV 3; *micclanige* E VII 29

middel 'middle'. *Middildych* C VIII 16

mint 'mint'. *minthammas* B (b) IV 22

mōr 'marshland, moor, barren upland'. *ælfsiges mor* D XIV 21; *baccan mor* C II 17; *blacan mor* A (b) V 4; *bradan mor* C IX 10; *dene mor* E VII 10; *hwite more* D IX 3; *lytlan mores heafde* D XIV 3; *mæne mor* D IX 2; *mor* C IV 49, D IV 17, D VIII 4, E IX 4, 27, G II 5, G IV 46, G VII; *more* A (b) VI 10, G V 1; *mores* D IX 6, G III (c) (twice), G VII; *mordune* C IV 47; *morsled* D IV 21; *pyrtanmore* D IX 11; *sceortan mor* D XIII 4; *torhtwoldes mor* E VIII 8; *westmor* E IV 32; *yrnendan mor* D XIV 20

muttic (obscure). *muttic* F IV 2

myln 'mill'. *mylne* C II 8; *Milanbrok'* C VIII 28; *mylen broc* C X 4; *mylen dic* A (b) IV 7; *mulen ger* A (b) IV 6; *mylen þaþes* B (b) III 28; *mylen stede* A (b) IV 9; *myle streame* C IV 42; *wulfmæres mylne* F II 5

(ge)mȳðe 'junction'. *hagena gemyðum* A (b) VI 4; *gemyðum* D I 5; *myþ ford* A (b) II 15; *wega gemyþan* B (b) VIII 22

næss 'headland'. *dunferðes hnesse* C IV 22

nīwe 'new'. *niwan dic* E IV 35; *niwan furh* G I 5

norðlang 'running north and south'. *norðlange dic* C IV 43

ōra[1] 'border, margin, bank, edge'. *colmanora* E VII 39; *heafoces oran* E VII 33; *scobban oran* E IV 9; *wulforan* B (a) I 9 (mod. Woolver's)

oxa 'ox'. *oxena wic* A (b) IV 10. Cf. also *be Maccaniges wirðland swa swa oxa went* G VII

padde 'toad'. *paddebyrig* C IV 23

pæð 'path'. *mylen þaþes* B (b) III 28; *paðe* D IV 16; *pæð* D IX 9; *paðe stocce* E V 21; *smalan þaþes* G IV 39

pearroc 'paddock'. *bogeles pearruc* A (b) V 2; *godan pearruce* A (a) I 5; *hwitan pearruc* A (a) II 3 (mod. Paddock Wd)

peru 'pear'. *perhangran* E VIII 46

plūme 'plum'. *plumleage* E V 22

pōl 'pool'. *mærpol* C X 6; *styrian pol* E II 7

port 'town, market-town, market'. *port strete* E VII 20; *port weg* E IX 19; *port wege* D IV 10

potten, pottel (obscure). *potteles treow* E VIII 13

prēost 'priest'. *preosthamme* C IX 11; *preosta leage* E V 8

pricel 'point'. *pricelles hæssecas* C X 2

***putta** 'kite'. *?puttan pyt* B (a) II 43

pyppel 'pebble'. *pyppel riðiges ut scyte – pyppel bricge* E VII 9, 13

pyrta (obscure). *pyrtanmore* D IX 11

pytt 'pit, hollow'. *blæc pytt* C VII 10; *dene pyt* B (b) II 1; *eadulfes pytte* D IV 5; *horo pytte* E VIII 30; *hrung putt* C I 28 (later The Manger); *lam pyt* E IX 17; *lam pyttas* B (b) III 24, F VIII 3; *puttan pyt* B (a) II 43; *pyt* E IV 20

rāha 'roe, roe-buck'. *rah hege* E III 6; *rah slede* G III (a) 6

ræw 'row'. *on ða hlinc rewe* B (b) VIII 4; *on þa ræwe* E I 11; *on ane stanræwe* C III 23; *to þære ðorn rewe* E IX 30; *andlanges þære westran risc ræwe* C VII 11

ramm 'ram'. *?rammes hrycg* B (a) I 17

rēad 'red'. *readan clif* C III 39; *readan dic* C VII 8, C IX 8; *readan hane* B (b) II 4, B (b) V 5, G IV 25; *readan hole* C IV 20; *readan meare* F III 4; *readan stane* F VI 16

rind 'bark'. *rinda crundel* B (b) VII 19

risc, rysc 'rush'. *riscbedde* C IV 38; *riscbed* C VI 17; *risc broc* F VII 12; *riscleahe* E IX 15; *risc ræwe* C VII 11; *risc slæd* E VIII 7; *riscslæd* C III 3; *hriscþyfele* C IV 40

rīð 'stream'. *cilla rið* D X 3 (mod. Childrey); *fulan riþe* A (b) VI 8 (mod. Foudry); *riþe* A (b) I 2; *riðæ* C I 15; *riðe* C VI 13, E IV 7

rīðig 'stream'. *pyppel riðiges ut scyte* E VII 9; *riðig* D VIII 7, E I 6, F V 6

***rod**[1], ***rodu** 'clearing'. *pocging rode* B (a) I 13; *andlang rode* B (b) IV 27; *on ða rode* B (b) V 14; *rod stybban* G XIII 10

rūh 'rough'. *ruwanbeorh* A (b) V 13; *Ruancrundele* C VIII 3; *ruwan crundele* B (b) IV 25; *ruwan crundle* B (a) II 39; *rugan dic* G XII 2; *rugan hlinc* C VI 3; *ruwan hlync* G IV 14; *ruwanleage* E V 12; *rugan weg* E IX 16

***run** 'stream'. *runesforda* G III (c) 1 (mod. Runsford)

rupelm (obscure). *rupelmes hlau* F VII 2

ryge 'rye'. *rigedune* D VIII 10; *rige hamme* B (b) III 23; *hrige weorðæ* E III 3

sæccing 'sacking, bed made of sacking'. *loddæres sæccinge* C I 5

sand 'sand'. *Sandforda* E II 1 (mod. Sandford); *sandlace* G V 16; *sand·ge wyrpe* G II 8

sandiht 'sandy'. ?*santan dene* B (a) IV 7

*sceaceling, *scæceling. ?derivative of **scacol* 'point of land'. *sceaceling æcer* E III 9 (corresponding to *scecyling æcer* E V 5, *scæceling æcer* E VII 24)

sceald 'shallow'. *scealdan ford* A (b) II 20 (mod. Shalford)

scēap 'sheep'. *sceaphammes* B (a) II 35

scēap-wæsce 'place for dipping sheep'. *sceap wæscan* G IV 34

scield 'shield'. *scyldmere* B (b) VIII 18

sc(e)ort 'short'. *scortan dic* C II 30, D VII 6; *scorteland* E IV 25; *sceortan mor* D XIII 4

scilling (obscure). *scillinges broc* G I 2; *scilling hangran* B (b) III 10

*scitere, stream-n. *sciteres clif* E IV 14

scypen 'cow-shed'. *cincges scypene* C VI 16

sealh 'willow'. *seal hangran* B (a) II 3

sēað 'pit'. *cealc seaþas* C V 7

seofan 'seven'. *seofan acon* A (b) V 10; *seouan æcera* E IV 23; *seofan þornum* D XIII 9

seohtre 'drain, ditch'. *Cytan seohtresford* B (b) IV 18; *sihtre mæd* B (b) III 20

sīc 'small stream'. *sic* E I 3, E VII 14

slæd 'valley, hollow'. *brochylle slæd* G XII 9; *fearnhilles sled* C III 18; *gorgrafes slede* E IX 1; *morsled* D IV 21; *rah slede* G III (a) 6; *riscslæd* C III 2; *risc slæd* E VIII 7; *slades* A (b) I 7, E IV 2; *slædes* E II 14; *sledes* D IV 6; *wæter slædes dic* G IV 2; *weterslæd* E IX 7

slōh 'slough'. *swin weges slo* G IV 20

smæl 'narrow'. *smalan broc* G IX 15; *smalan cumb* C II 6; *smalan paþes* G IV 39; *smala þornas* C IV 44; *smalan weg* B (b) VIII 12, 29, F I 2, F III 10; *smalan wege* D XIII 10, G IX 4; *smaleweyes* C VIII 6; *smalan weges* G IV 26

snād 'detached piece of woodland'. *herred snad* A (b) II 6

snīte 'snipe'. *snitan ige* C IX 3

sprindel 'bird-snare'. *sprindlesham* D XIV 1

stæð 'bank'. *temese stæde* E III 1

stān 'stone'. *ælfðryþe stan* D V 13; *bradan stanas* C VI 7; *brandan stane* B (b) I 6; *cenelmes stan* B (b) III 21; *ceobban stan* E IV 11; *dyrne stan* C IV 39; *æcgstanes stan* A (b) V 8; *flegestane* G XIII 12; *haranstan* B (b) I 10; *haran stane* E II 12; *horeston* C VIII 34; *Hordenestone* C VIII 9; *hwitan stane* A (b) I 8; *Whytestone* C VIII 12; *ibban stane* B (a) II 32; *mægen stan* C I 3; *readan stane* F VI 16; *stan* C X 1; *stane* B (a) II 9, C III 14, E V 25; *stone* C VIII 5, 23; *ston* C VIII 17; *stanum* B (b) VIII 2; *stan beorh* C X 14; *stanberwe* C VIII 13; *stan bricgge* D III 1; *stanbrycge* D I 3; *stan crundele* B (b) I 11; *stancrundele* B (b) VIII 11; *stan cystlum* B (a) II 24; *stan dene* B (a) II 33; *Stanford* E III 10; *stanhlæwe* C IV 18; *stanleage* B (b) VIII 26; *stan mæræ* C I 23; *stanræwe* C III 23; *stan wege* A (b) III 7; *stanwei* G III (c) 9; *stanweges* G IV 4; *tættucan stan* C I 31

*stande 'pond'. *standan* A (a) I 13, A (b) IV 3

stāniht 'stony'. *stanihtan weg* B (a) II 23, B (b) VIII 27, G XII 7

stapol 'post'. *ællanstapole* B (b) V 8; *stapolford* B (b) V 16; *winegares stapule* F VIII 8

stede 'place, site'. *mylen stede* A (b) IV 9

steort 'tail of land'. *buleferðes steorte* C IV 5; *steort* D XIV 19

sticca 'stick'. *Buckansticke* C VIII 1

*sticce ?'place where hurdles are erected'. *dic sticcea* G IV 40

stigel 'stile'. *ealdan stigele* B (a) I 16; *ecgeles stiele* A (a) II 2; *stiele* B (a) I 11; *stigel hammas* B (b) II 5

stocc 'tree-trunk, stump'. *greatan stoc* A (a) II 4; *heafod stoccan* F III 2; *heafod stoccas* B (a) IV 5, C VI 2; *heafud stoccun* D III 4; *hnottan stocce* G V 18; *licgendanstoc* A (b) VI 11; *paðe stocce* E V 21; *stoc welle* G IV 32; *stoccæs wælle* G III (b) 10; *won stocce* B (a) II 13

stōd 'stud, herd of horses'. *stod lege get* D II 11

stōdfald 'stud-fold'. *stodfalde* C IV 27, D XIII 8, G IV 41; *stodfaldon* B (b) VIII 5

stōw 'place, place of assembly, holy place'. *burn stowe* B (a) II 31; *Burnestowe* C VIII 4; *halige stowe* C IV 8

strǣt 'Roman road, paved road'. *ealdan stret ford* G V 9; *ikenilde streate* C IV 10; *Loddera stræt* A (b) I 10; *port strete* E VII 20; *stræt* A (b) I 9; *stræte* B (a) I 2, E I 7

strēam 'stream, current, flowing water'. *Cynetan strem* B (b) X 1; *myle streame* C IV 42; *temese streame* D VIII 6. The phrase *andlang streames* occurs in a number of surveys. *mid streame* '(with the flow', i.e. 'downstream') occurs in E V, E VII, and *ongean stream* 'upstream' in C IX. *midstream* 'midstream' occurs in *andlang midstreames* E IV, *up midstreame* A (b) III, *up mid stræme* D VII. Cf. also *midne stream(e)* E IV, G V, *healfan streame* B (b) V 17

stubb 'stub, tree-stump'. *ællen stub* C II 16; *ellen stubbe – oðerne ellen stubbe – eft on ellen stubb* G IX 1, 2, 8; *Lippanstubbe* C VIII 26

stybb 'stub, tree-stump'. *elebeam styb* B (b) III 15; *ellen styb* E IV 21, E VIII 14; *gretan ðornstyb* F VII 5; *rod stybban* G XIII 10; *þorn styb* C I 11; *þorn stybbe* C IV 7, D IV 14, 20; *wrocena stybbe* G IV 17

*styfic 'stump'. *stific weges* B (a) I 5

styria, a kind of fish. *styrian pol* E II 7

sulh 'plough, furrow, gully'. *sulgeate* G IV 48

swān² , 'herdsman, swine-herd, peasant'. *swan weg* E IX 14

swelgend 'deep place'. *wigmundes swelgende* B (b) V 6

swīn¹ 'swine, pig'. *swynbroc* C I 15; *swin weges slo* G IV 20

syrfe 'service tree'. *syrfan* A (a) I 10, B (a) II 15

tēona 'harm, trouble'. *teonan hylle* G IV 13

tibbælde (obscure). *tibbælde lace* G III (c) 11

ticce 'kid'. ? *tichan stedes hagan* A (b) VI 5

trēow 'tree'. *burgilde treowe* G III (b) 4; *cyneeahes treow* B (a) III 4; *deoran treowe* B (b) III 14; *ecgunes treow* B (b) III 34; *frigedæges treow* F VI 13; *gemænan treowe* A (b) V 1; *langan treowe* B (b) I 12; *potteles treow* E VIII 13; *teappan treow* A (b) V 14; *wines treowe* B (b) II 3

trēow-steall 'plantation'. *æþelstanes treow steal* G IV 43; *treow steall* G IV 16

tūn 'enclosure, farmstead, village, estate'. *æppeltune* D IX 7 (mod. Appleton); *Cyngestun* D V 7 (mod. Kingston); *tun* B (a) II 38; G XIII 4; *tune* B (b) VII 15, G V 1; *tun ege* A (b) IV 11 (mod. Towney); *tun wegas* B (a) II 36

twēgen 'two'. †*twegen beorgas* B (a) II 28

twisla 'fork of a river, junction of two streams'. *twislan* C X 10

þæc 'thatch'. *Ðæclege* G XIII 15

þorn 'thorn tree'. *aþelunes þorn* B (a) II 2; *aþulfes þorne* B (a) I 3; *bibban þorn* A (a) II 6; *bradan þorn* C VII 7; *brembel þorn* G XI 6; *cincges þornas* C VI 18; *eanulfing þorn* G XII 4; *greatan þorn* E V 15, E IX 20; *gretan ðornstyb* F VII 5; *hafuc þorne* G IV 5; *haran þornan* B (b) VIII 24; *hiccan ðorn* G XII 10; *hnottan þorn* B (b) II

2; *kasan ðorne* D XIV 5; *langan þorne* G IV 6; *littelne þorn* G V 5; *lodder þorne* G XIII 11; *mæringes þorne* G IV 47; *mereþorn* D V 2; *seofan þornum* D XIII 9; *smala þornas* C IV 44; *þorn* C II 14, 22, D II 6, D V 10, E IV 3; *þorne* D III 6; *ðorn rewe* E IX 30; *þorn styb* C I 11; *þorn stybbe* C IV 7, D IV 14, 20; *þriddan þorne̦ – feorþan þorne – fiftan þorne – þorne* G IV 7–12; *þrie þornas* B (b) III 29; *þrim þornon* B (b) VII 20; *weoccan ðorn* B (b) VII 8

þorniht 'thorny'. *þornihtan leage* A (b) III 5

þrēo 'three'. *ðrymbeorgum* F VII 4; *þrim gemærum* B (b) III 37; *þrio gemæru* E V 11; *þrie þornas* B (b) III 29; *þrim þornon* B (b) VII 20

þriscȳte 'triangular'. *þryscytan crundel* B (b) IV 24

þwyrs 'crosswise'. *þwyrsmere* C IV 1; *þwyrs furh* C IV 37

þȳfel 'bush, thicket'. *bræmbel þyfelan* C II 12; *hriscþyfele* C IV 40

þyres (obscure). *ðyreses lace* C V 13

þyrne 'thorn bush'. *brembel ðyrnan* E VIII 28; *haran þyrnan* B (a) III 3

ūtscȳte 'outfall'. *pyppel riðiges ut scyte* E VII 9

wād 'woad'. *waddune* G XIII 1; *wadleahe* E VI 5

wǣnweg 'cart way'. *wenweg* D IV 19

*wǣsse 'marsh'. *?wassan hamme* A (a) I 1

wæter 'water'. *weterdene* F VI 14; *weter hammas* B (b) IV 31; *weterslæd* E IX 7; *wæter slædes dic* G IV 2; *weter weg* B (b) IV 30

wealh 'foreigner, Welshman, serf'. *weala brucge* A (b) II 13

*wearde 'beacon'. *?weardan dune* B (b) II 14

weg 'way'. *ærnincg weg* G V 13; *beden weg* B (a) I 19; *biscopes weg* B (a) IV 8; *bradan weg* D XIV 6, C V 11; *bric weg* G V 12; *diopan wei* G III (c) 5; *ealdan hord wylles wæg* C I 13; *ealdan hyrne weg* B (a) I 18; *ealdan weges* B (a) III 7; *ealdan wæg* C I 17; *ealdan wudu weg* C III 6; *fulan wege se hatte stific weg* B (b) VIII 30; *grenan weg* B (b) III 22, C VII 21; *grænan weges* C II 10; *grenen weig* E VII 6; *grene weig* C IV 48; *haran dune wege* G XI 1; *heafodweg* E V 19; *hig weg* D XIV 15, G I 7; *hig wege* E IV 15; *holan weg* G V 11; *holen weg* B (b) IV 3; *hricg weg* C IX 13; *hrycgweg* B (a) II 41, E IX 11; *hwitan wege* B (b) VIII 23; *hwitan holan weg* G XII 5; *loceres weg* B (a) I 15; *lytlan weges* G IV 11; *gemærweg* E IV 8 (two), E VIII 35; *gemær weige* G III (b) 6; *mær weg* B (a) III 1; *mære weges* B (a) I 8; *marge wei* G III (c) 6; *mearc weg* B (b) III 35; *pættes wege* D VIII 11; *port weg* E IX 19; *port wege* D IV 10; *rugan weg* E IX 16; *smalan weg* B (b) VIII 12, 29,

F I 2, F III 10; *smalan wege* D XIII 10, G IX 4; *smaleweyes* C
VIII 6; *smalan weges* G IV 26; *stanihtan weg* B (a) II 23, B (b)
VIII 27, G XII 7; *stan wege* A (b) III 7; *stanwei* G III (c) 9; *stanweges* G IV 4; *stific weges* B (a) I 5; *suðeran weges* B (b) VIII 8;
swan weg E IX 14; *swin weges slo* G IV 20; *tun wegas* B (a) II 36;
weg B (b) III 3, B (b) VIII (two), D IV 20, E IV 12; *wege* B (b)
VIII 32, G VI 6, G XIII 4; *weg cocce* A (a) I 4 (mod. Weycock);
wege gemyþan B (b) VIII 22; *weter weg* B (b) IV 30. The phrase
andlang weges occurs in B (a) II, B (b) I, B (b) IV 2, B (b) VII 21,
C I 2, C II 15, C VIII, G V, G XII and G XIII. A number of
surveys refer to the Ridge Way and the Icknield Way.

weg-gelǣte 'road junction'. *wege gelæton* G IV 20
welig 'willow tree'. *greatan welig* E IV 36
wer 'weir'. *fordwere* E VIII 2; *healhwere* D XIV 12; *wer bæra* A (b)
IV 13; *west wær* G I 8; *wiredes wær* G III (a) 11
werð 'marsh'. *werð welle* F I 4
west 'west'. *westleas hagan* A (b) V 15; *wæst legæ* G III (a) 5;
westmor E IV 32; *west wær* G I 8; *west welle* G III (c) 10
westerra 'more westerly'. *westran wiðige* D XIV 13
wīc 'dwelling, farm, dairy farm'. *heal wicum* A (a) I 11 (later *Hollicks*);
an hyrde wic C VI 21; *oxena wic* A (b) IV 10
wīd 'wide'. *widan geat* G II 3; *wide geat* C VII 2
w(i)ell, wyll 'well, spring, stream, river-source'. *amman welle* G IV
1 (mod. Amwell); *cæccam wæl* G III (a) 1; *cealdenwulle* E VII
4 (mod. Cholswell); *Cealues wylle* E IV 12; *ceolbaldes wylle* B (b)
III 16; *ceollanwylle* A (b) I 1; *cranwylle* G IX 11; *dices wyllan* G
II 7; *hæddeswyl* B (b) V 3; *holan wylle* G V 10; *hordwyllæ* C I 12
(mod. Hardwell); *hunnes wylle* A (b) II 11; *kynnan wylle* D XIV
17; *lytlan wil* F VI 8; *lytlan wyl* F VII 14; *Merewelle* C VIII 20;
myos wyllan C IX 12; *occene wyllas* C II 7; *oðerne wil* F VII 15;
sceobbanoranwylle E IX 8; *sicanwylle* C III 32; *stoccæs wælle* G
III (b) 10; *stoc welle* G IV 32; *tidewaldes wille* E VII 35; *wernan
wille* A (b) V 6; *werð welle* F I 4; *west welle* G III (c) 10; *wifeles
wyll* A (a) II 8; *wylle* E IV 5
winter 'winter'. *wintermere* B (a) IV 1
wīr 'bog-myrtle'. *wirhangran* G IV 7
wiðig 'willow tree'. *wiðig bæd* E IV 27; *westran wiðige* D XIV 13
wōh 'crooked'. *uuon hlinc* C I 4; *won lace* E IV 41; *won stocce* B (a)
II 13
*****wōp** ?bird-name. *wopig hangran* B (b) III 9

wrang 'crooked'. *wrangan hylle* G IV 8

*wrǣna 'stallion' or **wrenna** 'wren'. *wærnan hylle* D III 5

*wræstel ?'twisted hill'. *wrestleshylle* B (b) II 9

wrenna 'wren'. *wernan wille* A (b) V 6

wrocena (obscure). *wrocena styb* G IV 17

wrōht 'accusation, crime, quarrel'. *wrohthangran* E IV 10

wudu 'wood'. *Æðeleahing wudu* E VII 38; *ciltewudes gemære* B (a) II 8; *ealdan wudu weg* C III 6; *wuda* B (a) II 14; *wudu bære land gemæru* G XIII 15; *wudubricge* G IX 23; *wudaford* E IV 30

wulf 'wolf'. *wulfhaga* E II 13; *wulfa leage* A (a) I 8 (mod. Woolley); *wulforan* B (a) I 9 (mod. Woolver's)

gewyrpe 'heap'. *sand ge wyrpe* G II 8

wyrtwala 'root'. ?'edge' (*v.* 633). *forþ be wyrtwalan* A (b) I 6; *on wyrt walan – eft on wyrt walan* A (b) II 2, 9; *a be weortwalan* A (b) III 8; *a be wyrtwalan* A (b) VI 7; *to þam wyrtwalan* B (a) II 34; *a be wyrt walan* E VII 17; *be wyrt walan* G IV 49

wyrð 'enclosure'. *baggan wurðe* E III 7; *dunan wyrþe* B (a) I 14; *ecgunes wyrðe* E VII 22; *hrige weorðæ* E III 3

wyrðig 'enclosure'. *sunemannes wyrðige* C VI 1

ydyr (obscure). *ydyrleage* E V 24

yfemǣst 'highest'. *yfemæstan leage* E IV 13

*yfer 'brow of a hill'. *yfre* A (b) II 12

ylf 'elf'. ?*ylfing dene* B (b) IV 15

yrnende 'flowing'. *yrnendan mor* D XIV 20

yrðland 'ploughed land'. *to þam yrðlande* D XIV 14; *wiþ norþan þæt yrþland* G IV 31; *þan stone whytoute þar Irwelond'* C VIII 23; *be Maccaniges wirðland swa swa oxa went* G VII; *xxxvi ækera yrþ landes* G V

PERSONAL NAMES IN THE BOUNDARY-MARKS
OF BERKSHIRE CHARTERS

Acca (*accangefyrðæ* B (b) V 9); *Ægelweard* (*ægelwardes mearce* C
IV 11); *Ælfhēah* (*ælfheages gemære* B (a) I 7); *Ælflǣd* fem.
(*ælflæde gemæra* A (b) IV 1); *Ælfrǣd* (*ælfredes beorh* D V 6); *Ælfsige*
(*ælfsiges mor* D XIV 21, *ælsiges cotan* D IV 15); *Ælfðrȳð* fem.
(*ælfðryþe dic* D VII 7, *ælfðryþe stan* D V 13); *Ælfwīg* (*ælfwiges
gemære* B (b) X 6); *Ælla* (*ællanstapole* B (b) V 8); *Æðelferð* (*æþel
ferðes mearce* C V 18); *Æðelhelm* (*æþelmes hlinc* C VII 3); *Æðelhūn*
(*aþelunes þorn* B (a) II 2); *Æðelstān* (*æþelstanes treow steal* G IV 43);
Aðulf (*aþulfes þorne* B (a) I 3)

Babba (*babban byorh* F VII 16;) *Bacga* (*bacgan broc* E VII 32,
baggan wurðe E III 7, the 2 boundary-marks probably refer to the
same man); *Bēaghild* fem. (*bæahhildæ byrigels* C I 16); **Bǣgel*
(*begeles pearruc* A (b) V 2); **Bibba* (*bibban þorn* A (a) II 6); *Bica*
(*bican dic* C VII 5); *Botta* (*bottanige* F VIII 6, also listed on p. 919);
Brihtwold (*bricthwoldes ge mæra* G XI 9); *Brihtstān* (*bryxstanes garan*
C VI 4); *Bucca* (*Buckanmer'* C VIII 2); *Bula* (*bulemere* C IV 4, *bulen
dic* C IV 6, the 2 boundary-marks probably refer to the same man);
Burghild fem. (*burgilde treowe* G III (b) 4)

*Carda (*cardan hlæw* B (b) III 12); *Cyn(e)helm* (*cenelmes stan* B
(b) III 21); *Ceobba* (*ceobban hangran* E IX 6, *ceobban stan* E IV 11,
the 2 boundary-marks probably refer to the same man); *Cēolbald*
(*ceolbaldes wylle* B (b) III 16); *Ceolla* (*ceollanwylle* A (b) I 1);
Cyddi (*cyddesige* D VIII 9); *Cylm* (*cylmes cumbe* G IX 17); *Cynehēah*
(*cyneeahes treow* B (a) III 4); *Cynna* (*kynnan wylle* D XIV 17)

Dēora (*deoran treowe* B (b) III 14); *Dudd* (*duddes dene* C VI 5);
Dudda (*dudden byrig* C IV 33); *Dudemǣr* (*dudemeres hele* G XIII 17);
Duna (*dunan wyrþe* B (a) I 14); *Dunferð* (*dunferðes hnesse* C IV 22);
Dunna (*dunnanforda* E VIII 17, also listed on p. 920)

Ēadgifu fem. (*Eadgife gemære* B (b) X 3); *Ēadwulf* (*eadulfes mære*
G III (b) 9, *eadulfes pytte* D IV 5); *Ēanflǣd* fem. (*eanflæde gelade* E
V 26); *Ēanwulf* (*eanulfing þorn* G XII 4); **Ecgel* (*ecgeles stiele* A (a) II
2); *Ecghūn* (*ecgunes treow* B (b) III 34, *ecgunes wyrðe* E VII 22);
Ecglāf (*eglafes forda* D XII 1); *Ecgstān* (*æcgstanes stan* A (b) V 8);
*Enna (*ennanbeorgum* E IV 39, also listed on p. 920)

*Friðela (friðelabyrig E V 23)

*Guma (guman grafe E VII 12); *Gunræd (Gunredesford A (b) V 9, also listed on p. 920); Gydda (gyddan dene B (b) II 13)

Hæddi (hæddeswyl B (b) V 3); Hengest (hengestes geat G XI 7); *Hicca (hiccan ðorn G XII 10); *Hod (hodes hlæwe C IV 17); *Hodduc (hodduces hancgran D II 3); *Hud (hudes lade D VII 5); *Hudd (huddes ig G IV 35); Hūn (hunes dune B (a) I 20); Hwittuc (hwittuces hlæwe C VII 14)

Ibba (ibban stan B (a) II 32); Imma (imman beorge A (b) II 24); Ine (ines dene B (a) I 10)

Lēofrīc (leofrices gemere F VIII 7); Lēofsige (leofsiges ge mæra G XI 4); Lilla (lillanhlæwes crundele F VI 1); *Lippa (Lippanstubbe C VIII 26); *Loppa (Loppancomb' C VIII 18); *Lorta (Lortanberwe C VIII 30)

Maduc (maduces lea E IV 19, this is the Welsh pers.n. Madog); *Mǣring (mæringes þorne G IV 47); *Mēoc (meoces dune G IV 18); Mūl (mulescumbes B (b) VIII 16, mules dene B (b) IV 28, mules dune B (a) II 40, mules hamstæde G III (a) 7)

*Ordstān (ordstanes dic G IV 30); Ordwulf (Ordulfes gemære F IV 4) *Pætti (pættes wege D VIII 11); *Pipp (pippes leage B (b) I 4); *Pocg(a) (pocging rode B (a) I 13)

*Sceobba (scobban oran E IV 9); *Sceolh (Sceolles ealdcotan B (b) X 2); *Sica (sicanwylle C III 32); Snell (snelles garan G IX 18, snelles hlince C VI 20); *Snodd (snoddes hylle E II 11); Sucga (suggan graf E VIII 26); *Sundra (sundran edisce E V 14); Suneman (sunemannes wyrðige C VI 1); *Swǣf (swæfes heale A (a) I 7)

*Tættuca (tættucan stan C I 31, also listed on p. 921); *Teappa (teappan treow A (b) V 14); *Tell (telles byrg C III 7); *Tidda (tiddamcumb E V 17); Tīdweald (tidewaldes wille E VII 35); Torhtweald (torthwoldes mor E VIII 8); Tōta (totan healas E V 16); Totta (tottencumbe G III (b) 3, also listed on p. 921); *Tȳta (tetan hylle E V 18)

*Weard (weardæs beorh C II 5); *Wendel (wendlescumb E IX 13); *Weocca (weoccan ðorn B (b) VII 8); *Wifel (wifeles wyll A (a) II 8); Wīgferð (wigferþis leage B (b) I 3); Wīgmund (wigmundes swelgende B (b) V 6); Wihtlufu fem. (wihtlufe hamme F VIII 9); Wine (wines treowe B (b) II 3); Winegār (winegares stapule F VIII 8); Winter (wintres hlewe D X 5); Witta (wittan mære G III (b) 11); Wulfmær (wulfmæres mylne F II 5); Wulfrīc (wulfrices broc E III 2, wulfrices gemære B (b) III 18); Wulfstān (wulfstanes dic E IV 18)

II INTRODUCTION AND ANALYSES OF MATERIAL FOR 'THE PLACE-NAMES OF BERKSHIRE'

NOTES ON THE PHONOLOGY OF BERKSHIRE PLACE-NAMES

1. OE æ̆ becomes Mod. *a*, except in Cresswells. The usual ME spelling is *a*. There are occasional ME *e* spellings for ns. in æppel and hæc(c), and for Thatcham and Watchfield. Ns. in æsc and (ge)wæsc have occasional ME spellings *Ei,- Ai-, Ay-, -ay-*. Ashampstead, Ashbury and *Ashden* also have a number of ME *E-* spellings.

2. OE ǣ normally appears as ME *a* when shortened in the first el. of a compound, as in Hadden (hæð), Manwood (gemæne), What-combe (wæt). Otherwise, in such els. as læs, mæd, it is usually represented by ME *e*. Ns. in hæma sometimes have ME *e*, but Charnham St has only *a* spellings. In Stratfield and Streatley the vowel of stræt has been treated differently. Stratfield has *a passim*, with only sporadic *e*, but Streatley has more *e* than *a* spellings. Ns. in bær² have mainly ME *e*, with occasional *i*.

3. OE ă before nasals shows very little trace of rounding to *-o-* in ns. containing cran, hamm, sand. There is no rounding in ns. from hangra, and not a great deal in ns. from lang, though it is common in f.ns. containing furlang. Ns. containing camp, however, have mostly *-o-* spellings, with the exception of *Campeden* in Newbury. Ns. in land frequently have *-lond(e)* in ME, and the few minor ns. and f.ns. from *stande, strand, strang, þwang all show rounding. There are occasional ME spellings with *-au-* for OE ă before a nasal, but this is not common. Speenhamland has 2 ME spellings with *-u-*, Eastmanton has one *-u-* spelling from 1542.

4. OE ă in other positions (e.g. bagga, cat(t), lacu, walu) either remains or is lengthened to ME *-ā-*. Shurlock is a 19th-cent. development from South Lake.

5. OE ā either develops to ME ō, which usually remains, or is shortened to ă. In ns. containing āc ME ō is sometimes shortened (Ockwells, Ogdown). In ns. containing brād and stān, shortening to ă is usual, though Broad- and Stone- are the mod. forms in

some instances. Ns. from stān have occasional ME spellings with *au*.

Where *ā* shows the normal development to *ō*, the *a* spellings continue in some instances to the end of the 13th cent. (Broadway, Grove).

6. OE *ĕ* normally remains, except where subject to normal lengthening (as in feld). There are sporadic *a* spellings from 1086 to l. 13th cent. There are few signs of raising to *i*, but this occurs in Hinksey, where the *i* spelling is first noted in 1535. Cf. also the f.n. *Milloney* from melde.

7. OE *ē* shows the normal development to the sound usually spelt *ee* in ModE. The usual ME spelling is *e*, but Speen has occasional *ie ey*. There is little sign of shortening or of raising to *i*, but *Spinhamland'* occurs in 1257 for Speenhamland, and the f.n. *Bin(s)* may be from bēn.

8. ME *er* does not always become *ar*, and when the change does occur it is rather late, compared, e.g. with Gl 4 67. There are some instances of *er* spellings persisting till the e. 17th cent. (Bulmershe has *er* 1607, *ar* 1658). In ns. containing bere the change seems likely to have occurred after 1500, and it may be up to a century later in some ns. from mersc. It is very late in Sparsholt, which has *Sperse-* 1517, *Spares-* 1761 (*Sparseholte* 1284 is probably an example of *a* for *ĕ*, cf. 6). The *ar* spelling is earlier in *Parsoneswode*, 1519 in Ashbury. In ns. containing ersc the change is rare; there are no *a* spellings for Beynhurst, Ryeish, Winnersh. Ryehurst, however, is *Rye Arsh* 1647.

9. OE *ĕa* usually gives a mixture of *a* and *e* spellings in ME, the one which predominates often being preserved in the mod. spelling. Berkshire has only occasional *a* spellings, Earley has *E- passim*, with very occasional *A-*. Padworth, Chaddleworth and Wallingford, on the other hand, have only or predominantly *a* spellings. In ns. containing fearn the spellings are about equally divided between *e* and *a*, but Fernham is the only one in which *e* survives. In f.ns. containing fleax and sceard *e* spellings are common. For *ĕa* before *l*+consonant *v.* 23.

10. OE *ēa*, when shortened, may become *a* (Aston, Radley), or *e* (Eddington, Leckhampstead, Henley, Reading). In the 2 instances of Aston it is possible that this form was substituted for *Eston* because it is the commonest form elsewhere; Aston in Remenham has only *E-* forms in ME, Aston Tirrold and Upthorpe have only *E-* till e. 14th cent. On the other hand, neither instance of Radley has any *e*

spellings. Leckhampstead (from lēac) has mostly e, but there are some signs of a long vowel (*Leyk-* 1286, *Leyc-* 1308) and one early and one mod. form with *a* (*Lack-* 13th, *Lack-* 1761). Reading has numerous forms with *e* and *a*, and one (1268) with *ey*. The 2 examples of *Hēantūne* have very similar spellings, predominantly *e* with occasional *ea* and *ey, ye, ee*. The raising of *e* to *i* appears to be earlier in Hinton in S. N. Hurst (*Hyn-* 1400); Hinton Waldrist is *Henton* 1591, *Hinton* 1676.

When not shortened, *ēa* develops like *ǣ* or *ē*, cf. Beenham, Eastbury, Easton, Eaton (2). Beenham has a 13th-cent. spelling *Bien-*. The forms for Beynhurst (also from bēan) are probably much corrupted, and so not relevant here.

11. OE *ĕo* is mostly represented by *e* and *u* in ME spellings, the *e* forms being generally more frequent. Binfield and Burghfield both have a single early spelling with *i* (*Bine-* 1224–5, *Bire-* 1393). Some ns. containing beorg (Burghfield, *Roeberg*) and ceorl (Charlton) have also occasional *or*. In some ns. where *e* predominates there are occasional early *a* spellings (*v.* 6).

12. OE *ēo* usually gives ME *e*, with occasional *eo, eu, u*. The rounded vowel survives into the modern period in Beckett (*Beckett als Bewcott* 1661), and gives the mod. form in Blewbury, in spite of early *i, y, ie* for the latter.

13. OE *ĭ* remains in a number of ns. with only ME *i(y)* spellings, e.g. Chilton, Finchampstead, Milton, Ripplesmere. Some ns. have *e* spellings, either frequently (as Childrey, Winkfield), or occasionally (as Chieveley, Frilsham). Ilsley and Winkfield have occasional *u*, and micel and mixen give *Muchele-* and *Muxen-* in some f.ns.

14. OE *ī* remains or is shortened to *ĭ* in a number of ns. with only ME *i(y)* spellings, e.g. Lyford and ns. from hwīt, wīd, wīl. In other ns. the *i* spellings are accompanied by some *e* forms, as in Fifield (*-hede* 1491), Shrivenham, Swinford. Hendred has only *e* in the second el. (rīð) in ME. Steventon has mostly *i*, but also some *e* spellings, from which the mod. form derives.

15. OE *ie* occurs in *Scīene*, first el. of Shinfield. ME spellings have mostly *e*, but *i* is frequent, and there are 4 *u* spellings (1155–8, 1224–5, 1284, 1310–11). cīeping occurs as a prefix to Faringdon and Lambourn, all ME forms having *e*. Shefford, probably from scīep, has mostly *i*, but some *e*.

16. OE *ŏ* remains or is lengthened to *ō* in many ns. Unrounding to *a* is only found in the 2 ns. from *clop(p), Clapcot and Clapton. In

Clapton, *a* is first noted in 1675, but in Clapcot it is seen early in *Clappecot'* 1241; cf. also *Adecote* 1235–6 for Hodcott (first el. *Hoda*). Hodcott has mostly *o*, but *Hud-* occurs 1235–6 and 1241. The *u* of Thrupp in Radley is first noted in 1608, that of Thrupp in Faringdon in 1749, and (Aston) Upthorpe is *Upthrup als Upthropp* 1754.

17. OE *ō* is sometimes shortened to *ŭ* as in Buckhold, Buckhurst and Buckland, the *u* spellings for these ns. being first noted in 1687, 1342 and 1412 respectively. In Bockhampton, shortening to *ŏ* seems to have occurred in e.ME, and the spellings, with occasional *a* and *u*, resemble those of some ns. discussed in 16. In Cookham, Crookham, Goosey, ns. from **mōr** and most ns. from **brōc**, *ō* develops as in standard English *cook, crook, goose, moor, brook*. In some ns. from **strōd**, such as Deepstrood, Gibstrude, Strood, the development is regular, but several instances of Stroud probably have a mod. spelling pronunciation, like Stroud Gl.

18. OE *ŭ*, when not subject to lengthening, is generally represented by *o* or *u* in ME, the two spellings alternating for many ns. In mod. forms both are well represented (e.g. Sonning, Compton, Donnington, Sotwell, and Sulham, Ufton, Uffington, Tubney). In most ns. from **wudu** the vowel has developed as in *wood*. In Didcot the change to *i* is noted 1657 (*Didcot or Dudcot*). Sotwell (from *Sutta*) has mostly *o*, but some *a* spellings (1220, 1742, 1761, 1830), and Compton B. has *Camp-* 1370; *v.* 16.

19. OE *ū* develops to the sound usually spelt *ou, ow* (as in Foudry, Rowney, and ns. in *-down*), except when shortened. If shortened, it is represented by ME, ModE *o* in ns. from **dūn** and **tūn**, otherwise mostly by ME, ModE *u* (but with occasional *o* spellings, as *Sottone* 1377 for Sutton Courtenay).

20. OE *ȳ* give ME spellings in *u, e, i(y)*, with *u* predominating in most instances, and remaining in some ns., e.g. Hurley, Culham, Rush Ct. Exceptions include Kennet, which has mostly ME *e* with one *a* spelling (*v.* 6), Beedon, which has more *e* than *u*, and Midgham and Dedworth, which have *i(y)*, exclusively for Midgham, most frequently for Dedworth. Ns. in **cyning** and **fyrhð** have only *i(y)* spellings. In ns. from **hrycg** and **hyll** the mod. forms are mostly *-ridge* and *-hill*, probably due to substitution of standard English forms. In some ns. which have mod. *i, i* and *u* alternate well into the modern period, e.g. Bisham is *Bisham als Bustleham* 1746, Hidden is *Huddon* 1517. In Dedworth, *e*, first noted in 1401, appears to be a late substitution for *i*.

21. Voicing of *F-* to *V-* is not very common. It occurs in all early spellings of Fobney and Vastern, in some forms for Farn Combe, Fawley and Furzewick, and in some f.ns. from **fenn**, **fīn** and **forð-ēg**. It is not found in Faringdon, Farley, Farnborough, Fernham, Fifield, Fyfield, Finchampstead, Fulscot. There is no instance of *Z-* for *S-*.

22. Norman French confusion of *l–n–r* is common, as in Basildon, Ganfield, Sandleford, Shellingford, Watchfield. Sometimes this interchange is modern, as in *Charleburye* 1591 for Cherbury, *Lorington* 1761, 1790 for Lollingdon. French influence has given *T-* for *Th-* in Tidmarsh, if this contains **þēod**, and *T-* occurs in early spellings for other ns. in *þ-*, such as Thatcham. *C-* for *Ch-* and *S-* for *Sh-* are found in early spellings (e.g. Charney, Shottesbrooke), but have not survived in modern forms.

23. Where there are distinct WSax and Anglian forms of els., Berks p.ns. probably derive from WSax forms, though this is not always apparent from ME spellings. Ns. containing **cealc**, **ceald**, **cealf** mostly have *Ch-*. The exceptions are Calcot and Caldecott, where *C-* is probably due to influence from the *c-* of **cot(e)**; the n. regularly appears in such forms as this in areas where *Ch-* might have been expected. There is little sign in ME forms of such spellings as *Eld-* for ns. from **(e)ald**, though WSax **eald** is regular in charter boundaries (*v.* 774–5). Aldworth is *Elleorde* 1086, Oldlands in Inkpen is *Le Heldelonde* 14th, Aldermaston is *Ældre-*, *Heldre-*, *Eldre-* 1086. The OE forms for Waltham have *Wealt-*, but there is only *a* in ME spellings. Similarly, the *-ea-* of WSax **wealh** only appears in OE spellings for Wallingford, and in an OE spelling for Wawcott. WSax **scīep** occurs in Shefford and possibly in Sheep Bridge.

No systematic attempt has been made to give modern pronunciations of Berks p.ns. This is to be regretted, but the editor of this Survey was not able to spend sufficient time in the county to collect the necessary information, and it seemed better not to cite pronunciations which could not be vouched for with absolute confidence.

INTRODUCTION TO
'THE PLACE-NAMES OF BERKSHIRE'

This is the first Introduction to a County Place-Name Survey to be written since 1965, when A. H. Smith prepared his *Introduction to the Place-Names of Westmorland*. The intervening nine years have been a period of rapid development in English place-name studies, particularly as regards the historical bearing of the material. Starting with Professor Kenneth Cameron's Inaugural Lecture, *Scandinavian Settlement in the Territory of the Five Boroughs* (1965), and John Dodgson's article 'The Significance of the Distribution of the English Place-Name in *-ingas*, *-inga-* in South-East England' (*Medieval Archaeology* x, 1966), there has been a series of papers discussing aspects of the chronology of place-name types, which have culminated in a radical change of attitude on the part of most workers in this field. In this Introduction an attempt will be made to examine the Berkshire material in the light of these new approaches. Even so, the subject is moving so rapidly at the moment that this discussion may seem to be out of date by the time it appears in print.

I. CONTACT BETWEEN BRITISH AND GERMANIC PEOPLES

If the place-names of Berkshire are to be considered in chronological layers, the first task is to isolate pre-English names, and those English names which refer to the inhabitants or the institutions of the pre-English countryside in such a way as to suggest contact between the descendants of the Romano-British population and Germanic peoples. An attempt has been made to present this portion of the material on Distribution Map II.† Distribution Map I, which should be studied with Map II, shows most of the archaeological evidence relating to Roman Britain and the pagan Anglo-Saxon period in this area.‡

† The Maps referred to in this Introduction were supplied with part II of *The Place-Names of Berkshire*, EPNS 50.

‡ As regards the Berkshire portion of Map I, I have had generous assistance from Mrs Jill Greenaway of Reading Museum and Mr David Brown of the Ashmolean Museum, dealing respectively with the Roman and A.S. material. For Berkshire, the map was probably reasonably up to date at Easter 1974. The material for the portions which are shown of the

Some of the place-name evidence shown on Map II belongs to the same categories as material shown on previous distribution maps of this type, some of it is of kinds not previously used in this way.

Names wholly or partly in the British language have, of course, always been recognised as evidence of verbal contact between English speakers and the people who were here before them. It must be admitted at the outset that Berkshire is a county in which these names are very scarce. The first element in the county-name is a wood-name *Barroc*; the location of the wood is not certain, but it has been tentatively placed on Map II in the light of other place-name evidence (*v.* 837). Some of the major river-names, Thames, Loddon, Kennet and Ock, have long been recognised as of pre-English origin. The place-name survey has been able to add to these some names of small streams; there is a new instance of the name Severn, and two instances of Humber, and it has been possible to locate the stream called *Cern* in charter boundaries. In the category of minor settlement-names, it is suggested for the first time in these volumes that Pinge near Reading may be a British name identical with Penge Sr, and that Altwood near Maidenhead may have a British first element; Cruchfield near Bray has long been recognised as a British–Old English hybrid.

Special interest attaches to the major settlement-name Speen, as this belongs to the rarest category of place-names in this country, those which were coined in the Latin language. Latin place-names are a minute proportion of the names (mostly British) which are recorded from Romano-British times, and only the merest handful (probably less than half a dozen) have survived to the present day. Speen cannot be directly derived from Latin *Spinae*, but there can be little doubt

surrounding counties was taken from the Ordnance Survey maps *Roman Britain* and *Britain in the Dark Ages*, and no systematic attempt was made to correct or supplement this. New discoveries of archæological sites are being made constantly, and no map should be considered definitive. Through the excellent conferences on the Anglo-Saxon period organised by Trevor Rowley for the Oxford University Department for External Studies I have been able to gain a general impression of the work in progress in the Thames Valley (and elsewhere). In the Oxford region this impression is that new discoveries mainly consist of more material in the areas where sites were previously known, so it is possible that although distribution maps are never likely to be complete for long the general pattern of known Roman and pagan A.S. material is not changing drastically. It is this general pattern which matters for the present discussion.

that the substitution of OE *Spene* was made by English-speaking people to whom the Latin name was familiar. This survival contrasts with the apparent loss of the British name *Calleva* for the Roman town on the Berks/Hants border which was later known in English as Silchester. DEPN suggests that Sil- may be from substitution of OE *sele* 'hall' or **siele* 'willow copse' for *Calleva*, and this is perhaps not out of the question, though it did not seem sufficiently convincing to justify the inclusion of the name Silchester on Map II. No other Romano-British town-names have survived in Berks. The first element of Dorchester, just over the boundary in O, may be British, but it is probably not the Romano-British name of the town, as that appears to be *Tamese* in the Ravenna cosmography. *Landini*, listed in Ravenna before *Tamese*, was probably in Berks. The survival of Speen is noteworthy in this context of non-survival.

Three other types of name have been plotted on Map II; these comprise the two examples of wīchām, the place- and field-names which contain camp, and the names which probably contain wealh, either as a noun or as a personal name.

The evidence concerning the first category was set out in an article published in 1967 (M. Gelling, 'English Place-Names derived from the Compound *wīchām*', *Medieval Archaeology* XI). This study had its origin in the observation that the two Berks examples were both situated on Roman roads, and that one of them like Wycomb Gl, was the name, not of a modern settlement, but of a modest Romano-British site (the Gl site has since been revealed as much larger). When all the examples of the place-name in the country were assembled, it was found that the situation on or not more than a mile from a major Roman road was a characteristic of all but four, and that over half of the thirty examples were close to Romano-British remains suggestive of habitation. It was therefore suggested that OE *wīchām* was a compound appellative in which wīc retained its original meaning of Roman *vicus*, and that places called *wīchām* were very early English settlements bearing a special relationship to some of the administrative units known in Roman Britain as *vici*. Most recorded instances of the place-name avoid the immediate vicinity of the grander sites of Roman Britain, so it is not surprising to find the two Berks examples well to the E. and W. of the town of Silchester. The western example is a few miles W. of Speen, and the existence of a settlement of the kind adumbrated might account for the survival of the name Speen. The wīchām may have coincided with an unlocated Roman site very

close to Wickham from which Roman pottery has been found, *v.* Pt
I 274.

On the distribution map published in *Medieval Archaeology* the two
Berks names appear as units in a line of seven names, stretching from
the E. coast of Kent to the single Wiltshire instance, which lies about
10 miles W. of the S.W. corner of Map II. There is a cluster of
wīchām names to the N., the most southerly of which is just too far N.
to be shown on the portion of Akeman Street which appears in the
N.W. corner of Map II. This O *wīchām* (one of three in that county)
is of special interest because of its proximity to the Roman and Anglo-
Saxon remains at Shakenoak Farm; there is a further discussion of the
name and its implications in an appendix to A. C. C. Brodribb, A. R.
Hands and D. R. Walker, *Excavations at Shakenoak Farm, near
Wilcote, Oxfordshire, Part III: Site F* (privately printed, 1972).

The inclusion of names in camp on Map II cannot be justified by
reference to a study of this element such as has been made of wīchām,
though preliminary investigations suggest that such a study would
produce similar results. For the moment it can only be stressed that
OE *camp* is a loan-word from Latin *campus* 'a field'. The word occurs
also in Frisian and Saxon, and by analogy with its use in those
languages it is sometimes translated 'an enclosed piece of land'; but
it is not recorded in OE except in place-names and charter boundary-
marks, so the translation is conjectural. The distribution suggested to
A. H. Smith that 'The element fell into disuse generally at an early
period'. The Anglo-Saxons were not short of words for fields or
enclosures, and it seems possible that their occasional use in the S.
and E. of Britain of this loan-word from Latin is due to a period
of co-existence with Latin speakers in which certain stretches of
country were called 'the *campus*'. The element occurs in one Berks
parish-name, Ruscombe (where it is combined with an OE personal
name, as in Addiscombe Sr, Epcombe and Sacombe Herts, Hans-
combe Bd), it occurs uncompounded in the field-names of Bray,
Earley and Hurley, and in Newbury field-names there is another
instance of the Gl name Campden. These occurrences have a limited
distribution pattern which is discussed *infra*. There is one ancient
name containing camp in O, Campsfield in Kidlington, which is
shown on the N. edge of Map II. Romano-British remains have
recently been discovered at Camp Corner, 4 miles S.W. of Thame O,
but it cannot be proved that Camp Corner is an ancient p.n.

Names containing OE *w(e)alas*, plural of w(e)alh, were plotted

(along with names containing *brettas* and *cumbran*) on A. H. Smith's
extremely interesting map *British Names*, which was one of those
supplied with Elements. In spite of this, Professor Smith appears in
the article on walh in Elements 2 242–4 to favour the translation 'serf'
rather than 'Welshman'. The OE use of w(e)alh was discussed by
J. R. R. Tolkien in the first of the O'Donnell lectures printed in
Angles and Britons (1963). Professor Tolkien concluded that in the
earlier part of the period the Anglo-Saxons used w(e)alh to denote a
person who spoke Latin or Celtic. It certainly meant 'slave' in the
later OE period, however, and this place-name element cannot be
regarded as a certain guide to the presence of British-speaking people
among the Anglo-Saxons; but it has seemed worth while to enter all
the names in which it occurs on Map II. It is possible that the
personal name *Wealh*, which is probably the first element of Wallingford, is more likely to be significant of racial origin than the use of the
genitive plural in the other names shown. Walcot and Wallingtons
can reasonably be explained as 'cottages and farm where there are a
number of serfs'; but when the term is used as a personal name
(perhaps a nickname) the sense 'serf' seems very unlikely. The names
shown on Map II by the symbol Wh are Wallingford, which lies on
the Thames S. of Dorchester, a lost *Walton* in the parish of Old
Windsor, Wallingtons and Wawcott in Kintbury, and the 'Welshmen's bridge' which occurs in the charter bounds of Brimpton. The
hill-fort of Walbury, on the Berks/Hants boundary, has been marked
with a query. As no instances of names in *weala-* have been noted in
the portions of the adjacent counties shown on the Distribution Maps,
even this meagre harvest may be a significant feature of the place-
names of Berks, and the position of three of the names (four if Walbury
is included) in the S.W. may be meaningful.

Maps I and II were compiled in the hope that the place-name
material on Map II would bear a meaningful relationship to the
Roman archaeology plotted on Map I. It probably does show such a
relationship, though the evidence is hardly strong enough to convince
anyone who is not looking for evidence of continuity between Roman
Britain and Anglo-Saxon England.

One of the difficulties about compiling a map of Roman remains in
Berks is the uncertainty as to the line of the Roman road which almost
certainly came from St Albans Herts and entered the county near
Cookham, probably crossing the Thames in the vicinity of *Shaftsey*
(*v.* the article by N. Brooks referred to under *Shaftsey* Pt **1** 81). The

line of Roman villas shown on Map I in N.E. Berks must be near a road, and the settlement at Reading would seem to be a possible point on its route to Silchester; but no definite trace has yet been found of this road, and Mrs Greenaway agrees with my decision that it is not a known physical reality in the same way as the other roads which are shown on Map II. Discussion of pre-English and very early English names in the county will, however, assume the presence of a Roman road in the N.E.

The two parts of the county in which there seems to be most evidence for some co-existence between British and Old English speakers are the E. and the S.W. In the S.W., it may be objected that only the inclusion of the elements camp and wealh gives an appearance of concentration, and this is a valid observation; but very special significance may be claimed for Speen and Wickham in Welford. The area adjacent to and S. of the Roman road which runs N.W. from Silchester is one in which traces of Romano-British habitation are well evidenced, and in which Anglo-Saxon remains have not yet come to light.

In E. Berks, the most impressive of the scraps of place-name evidence plotted on Map II is perhaps the survival of the name Severn for the tiny stream which flows into the Thames through Temple Park in Hurley. If the etymology suggested for Pinge (Pt 1 206) be accepted, this also is important as an instance of a compound British name of which both elements are preserved. The four instances of names in camp in this region may be regarded as a concentration of this rare element, and the second Berks instance of wīchām, which refers in this case explicitly and solely to a Romano-British village, lies beside the Roman road in the S. of this area. Attention has been drawn (S. Applebaum, *The Agrarian History of England and Wales* vol. 1 11, 260 n.) to some evidence for continuity of religious cults in this region from Roman to later times. Professor Applebaum instances the church dedication of Waltham St Lawrence, the tradition of Herne the Hunter in Windsor Forest, which is an echo of Celtic Cernunnos, and the hermit's chapel dedicated to St Leonard (Pt 1 20), who had attributes similar to those of Cernunnos. (*Herne* is presumably an English name coined in this country to describe the deity, and referring, like the Gaulish name *Cernunnos*, to his horns.) This is another area in which Roman archaeology heavily outweighs traces of Anglo-Saxon activity, though there are pagan burials along the Thames.

It is noteworthy that place-names in the parts of O and Berks adjacent to the small Roman town of Dorchester do not provide much evidence for the co-existence of British- and Germanic-speaking people, and that in the Ock valley to the W. of this the evidence is limited to river-names, though three of these (*Cern* and the two Humbers) are small streams, not larger rivers like the Ock itself.

The archaeological case for and against continuity at Dorchester has recently been examined, and the evidence seen to be against rather than for. There are several papers bearing on this subject in *Anglo-Saxon Settlement and Landscape*, ed. T. Rowley (British Archaeological Reports 6, 1974). In 'Early Settlements in Dorchester on Thames', Mr Rowley concludes that at present we have evidence of Saxon occupation within and around the Roman town none of which can be shown to be early enough to support a theory of continuity, and little of which seems to be related to the Roman street-plan. He concludes (p. 48): 'All this does not necessarily mean that there was not continuity at Dorchester, but that so far the vital archaeological evidence is missing. It may also mean that perhaps we should seek a term other than "continuity", which, however modified, implies survival. Whatever else may have happened Romano-British Dorchester did not survive into the sixth century.' The evidence available from Abingdon, a few miles up river from Dorchester, is considered by D. Miles in 'Abingdon and Region: Early Anglo-Saxon Settlement Evidence'. Mr Miles regards the association of Roman and Saxon settlements in and near the Roman settlement at Abingdon as closer than that suggested at Dorchester. This view has been stated more firmly by J. N. L. Myres in 'The Early History of Abingdon and its Abbey', *Medieval Archaeology* XII (1968). Dr Myres concludes (pp. 39–41) 'The upshot of this enquiry is, therefore, to show that the evidence of the pottery confirms the conclusion derived by its excavators from the metalwork and the prevalence of cremation. The Abingdon cemetery came into use unexpectedly early for a site so far from the east coast and so centrally placed in the southern midlands. It cannot in fact be doubted that Saxon folk were established here, in whatever capacity, within a generation or so of the breakdown of Roman rule in Britain and very possibly before the final extinction of Romano-British life on the site of the later abbey and in the centre of the present town.' In spite of this archaeological material, no evidence has been noted in the immediate vicinity of Abingdon to suggest that the Saxons took any note of the place-names used by

Romano-British people; there is not even the survival of a Celtic name for the town, such as appears to be the first element in Dorchester. It seems possible that a later and more gradual penetration is conducive to the slightly higher degree of linguistic survival seen in the E. and S.W. of the county.

Another type of evidence for continuity in the English countryside has recently been brought forward in an original and stimulating paper by D. J. Bonney, 'Early Boundaries in Wessex' in *Archaeology and the Landscape: Essays for L. V. Grinsell*, ed. P. J. Fowler (1972). This article demonstrates that in Wiltshire there are pre-Roman linear earthworks, particularly Grim's Dyke on the Grovely Ridge W. of Wilton, which are likely to have served as estate boundaries since they were built, in or before the Iron Age, whereas post-Roman earthworks, in particular the eastern part of Wansdyke, cut across parishes in a way which suggests that the parish units are earlier than the earthwork. Roman roads can be shown to be used as parish boundaries in areas where there is little or no sign of pre-Roman habitation, and where the Roman road was probably the first feature in the development of the landscape; but they are consistently ignored in areas where habitation can be shown to go back before Roman times. The Fosse Way, which is the exception, may fairly be supposed to have disrupted the existing pattern of estates along its line. This study takes the subject a good deal further than Mr Bonney's earlier paper, 'Pagan Saxon Burials and Boundaries in Wiltshire', *Wilts Arch. and Hist. Mag.* 61 (1966), which had established the probability that many parish boundaries were fixed before the end of the pagan Anglo-Saxon period, because of the high proportion of pagan burials which lay on or near them. These conclusions are highly relevant to some of the problems discussed here and in the *Introduction to the Charter Boundaries of Berkshire* on pp. 615–34; and it is clearly worthwhile attempting an evaluation of Mr Bonney's findings as they may be applied to the land-units of Berks.

The coincidence of a short stretch of the boundary (on 6″ map 20 N.E.) between E. and W. Lockinge and a right-angle bend in Grim's Ditch, the prehistoric linear earthwork which traverses the Berkshire Downs (Pt 1 6), was noted by O. G. S. Crawford in 1953 (Crawford, p. 114), and this might, at first sight, be thought to be a similar phenomenon to those noted by Bonney in Wiltshire; but the ancient estate boundaries in this area are difficult to recover (v. the discussion of a charter-survey of parts of Lockinge and Ardington, pp. 746–7), and the evidence is not clear enough to build on. Further east, the S. boundaries of Chilton and Blewbury run along Grim's Ditch for relatively short stretches (v. pp. 756, 760), but it cannot be said that this earthwork bears a very striking relationship to estate boundaries considering the evidence for the whole of its length. A much more consistent relationship has been demonstrated for some prehistoric linear earthworks in Wiltshire.

More striking is the extremely limited use which the modern parish and pre-Conquest estate boundaries make of the known Roman roads in the county. This can be studied by superimposing Distribution Map I on the Map showing Hundreds and Parishes.

The line of the road which traversed N.E. Berks is not known, but it is difficult to see how the parish boundaries between Maidenhead and Reading could be laid out along it. It is fortunate that we have Old English surveys for the area of White Waltham, Shottesbrooke and Waltham St Lawrence (v. pp. 636–9), as this enables us to be sure that the northern boundary of these parishes was in the 10th cent. much as it is now; it could only have the briefest coincidence with a Roman road. In the S.E. of the county, on the other hand, the Roman road called Devil's Highway (Pt 1 4) does form boundaries for some of its course E. of Silchester. It separates Stratfield Mortimer Berks from Stratfield Say Ha, perhaps indicating that the name Stratfield ('open land by the Roman road') was given by the English to a district not divided into estates. After a slight gap the county boundary again follows the Devil's Highway, separating Swallowfield Berks from Heckfield Ha. There is a belt of land S. of Reading in which all the ancient parish-names end in feld, and feld may have been used to denote unsettled land used for a time as common pasture, v. pp. 835–6. Continuing to the E., the boundaries of Finchampstead and Easthampstead pay no attention to the Roman road, but between these parishes is a stretch in which it forms the N. boundary of Crowthorne. Crowthorne is not an ancient land-unit (Pt 1 125), so this is really the boundary between Wokingham and Sandhurst. Sandhurst may, as postulated for the parishes with names in feld, be a land-unit carved at a relatively late date from heathland which had been common. Half of the S. boundary of Winkfield, the next parish to the E., lies along the road, but the parish of Sunningdale (Pt 1 87) is a modern creation which obscures the evidence for the S.E. corner of the county.

The relationship of the parish boundaries to the Devil's Highway

E. of Silchester could be interpreted as suggesting that Finchampstead, Wokingham and Easthampstead are based on pre-Roman land-units, whereas Stratfield, Swallowfield, Sandhurst and Winkfield took shape in Roman or post-Roman times. Much land in this area is still common and heath.

In the vicinity of Silchester, the county boundary is modern. On the 1st edition of the O.S. 1″ map, Mortimer West End, now in Ha, is shown as part of Berks, and the county boundary runs fairly closely round the N. edge of the Roman town. This is consistent with the local administrative landscape having evolved at a time when Silchester was no longer an important centre.

W. of Silchester, the use of the Roman road for boundaries ceases almost entirely. On the long stretch of road between the E. boundary of Aldermaston and the W. boundary of Lambourn, there is no coincidence that is more than a mere touch, and this is true also of the Roman road which branches off between Welford and Kintbury.

The road which runs N. from Silchester bears no significant relationship to parish boundaries until it comes up to the Thames, E. of Dorchester. Then it forms the boundary between Brightwell and Sotwell. This is interesting as confirmation of the general validity of this test for distinguishing between more ancient and less ancient land-units, since the charter material shows that Brightwell and Sotwell were parts of a single estate in A.D. 945, but were granted as separate units in 947 and 957 respectively (v. 751). The road is referred to as 'the old street' in the boundaries of these grants.

The remaining Roman road known in Berks is the one which crosses the River Ock at the ford from which Garford is named, at a spot where there is a remarkable superimposition of Saxon on Roman remains. The parish boundaries pay some attention to this road. It forms part of the E. boundaries of Frilford and Tubney, separating both units from Marcham; but again this only demonstrates that Roman roads were used as boundaries when estates were divided late in the Anglo-Saxon period, since Marcham, Frilford and Tubney were a single estate in A.D. 965 (v. 701).

If the lack of coincidence between Roman roads and parish boundaries be indeed a sign that the land-units may be of pre-Roman origin, then Berkshire must be allowed a high score for this type of continuity, except on the heathlands traversed by the Devil's Highway E. of Silchester. The evidence brought forward for Berks should, however, be viewed as a rather slight corroboration of Mr Bonney's findings for Wilts. The latter county is a more satisfactory field for this study, on account of the greater area traversed by dramatic earthworks and known Roman roads, and the reader is recommended to study the paper in *Archaeology and the Landscape* referred to on p. 807, rather than to judge the method by what is said here.

Yet another type of evidence bearing on this question is that tirelessly advocated since the early 1950s by Professor Glanville Jones. Professor Jones believes that some large estates survived from prehistoric times through the Roman period and the upheaval which followed it, so that in some cases they are recognisable in medieval or even modern administrative arrangements. The arguments by which this belief is supported in Professor Jones's writings will be drawn together in his forthcoming book *Celts, Saxons and Vikings: Studies in Settlement Continuity*; they do not lend themselves to summary. He has concerned himself mainly with estates in northern England and on the Welsh border, but there are in Berks some large pre-Conquest estates which, if his views be accepted, could be taken as examples, the best being perhaps Blewbury, which is named from the hill-fort on Blewburton Hill and which was in A.D. 944 an estate of 100 hides which included both Astons and both Moretons (*v.* 751). Another possibility is the Hundred of Lambourn, which consists of the exceptionally large parish of Lambourn and that of East Garston, which became a separate land-unit in the 11th century (Pt 2 330). The possibility that Great Faringdon was once the centre of a great estate lying on both sides of the Thames is discussed in Pt 2 366. A determined searcher could certainly find other instances in Berks, and the discussion of the charter boundaries, which brings out the process whereby areas known by such names as *Æscesbyrig* and Sparsholt were subdivided into estates with such names as Woolstone, Uffington and Kingston, should be a useful guide for this type of investigation. There seems to be no question in this county of such estates keeping their pre-English names, but it is desirable that the possibility that neighbouring settlements, which may now give their names to separate parishes, were once associated as parts of a much larger estate should be borne in mind when the chronological relationship between some types of English place-names is studied. This matter is discussed further in section III.

Another modern scholar whose researches led him to a belief in continuity from Romano-British to Anglo-Saxon times was the late H. P. R. Finberg. Two of the papers in *Lucerna* (1964) are specifically concerned with this. 'Continuity or Cataclysm', the O'Donnell lecture of 1957, is suggestive of possible fruitful lines of investigation, but most of these have not yet been worked out in detail. The second paper, 'Roman and Saxon Withington', is one of the best-known essays on this subject; but as Finberg presents it his case for continuity at Withington has not much relevance to our problem in Berkshire, as he pictures the first land-taking of the Anglo-Saxons in the Cotswolds as happening after the Battle of Dyrham in A.D. 577, by which time some of our north Berks Saxons had been in residence for nearly two hundred years. At the date of the Withington paper, Professor Finberg had no reason to attach any significance to the name Wycomb, derived from *wīchām*, which belongs to the site of the large Romano-British settlement near Andoversford, on the northern edge of the map of Withington parish on p. 26 of *Lucerna*. In later work, after the appearance of the paper on *wīchām* referred to above, he accepted the general significance proposed for the name, but without examining the difference it might have made to his reconstruction of the course of events at Withington. His thesis was that the Roman villa at Withington (and probably those in adjoining parishes) was the centre of an estate which was likely to continue as an entity, perhaps with an absentee landlord after it had become impossible to maintain the villa as a dwelling-place, and that this situation would continue till 577, when such estates would be shared out among the 'companions in arms' of Cuthwine and Ceawlin, who would become overlords to the British farmers working the land.

This view of the relationship of Anglo-Saxon to Briton in the countryside (which appears also in some of the writings of Professor Glanville Jones) seems incompatible with the linguistic evidence. Neither the Roman occupation of the 1st century A.D., which brought a Latin-speaking administrative class to Britain, nor the Norman Conquest of 1066, which brought a new French-speaking aristocracy, caused a major replacement of the pre-existing place-names by new place-names in the language of the conquerors. It seems likely that a replacement of the kind which happened after the end of the Roman period (and which can be compared with later place-name developments in Man, Orkney, the Hebrides and parts of the Danelaw) occurs only when the newcomers are farmers rather than, or as well as, overlords. In Berkshire, where there is archaeological evidence for English settlements much earlier than any recorded in historical sources (see section II), it may be possible to postulate an infiltration of the farming units by people who would work side by side with British farmers. If there was a manpower shortage such infiltration might not have been wholly unwelcome, and there may have been a period during which most people in the countryside were concerned, not with their ethnic identity or with the precise social gradings which fascinate the historian, but only with the need to keep the land in cultivation so that they might all continue to eat. In north Berkshire, unless we postulate a war of conquest which is not recorded in any chronicle, the English established themselves peacefully, partly by expansion from settlements begun under Roman authority, partly by fresh immigration from the north-east. The warlords who became rulers of Wessex are said in ASC to arrive at the end of the 5th century, long after the first contacts of Anglo-Saxons and Britons, and if estates were shared out among their companions in arms this was probably the start of the manorialisation which, it is argued in section III, gave rise to the type of place-name which has a personal name in the genitive as first element. The Saxon farmers of humble status who are here postulated as responsible for the introduction of English speech and English place-names might well respect existing boundaries, which had been proved by long experience to provide suitable divisions, and which formed an interlocking pattern which could hardly be changed by a piecemeal process.

No attempt has been made at a 'Withington-type' study in Berks, but the position of the known Roman villas is shown on Map I, and their relationship to parish-units can be studied by superimposing the parish-index map on this. The multiple estate studies seem more obviously to bear a possible relationship to estate patterns in Berkshire. The presence of a hill-fort as the postulated focal point of many of these estates suggests comparison with Berkshire units like Blewbury and *Æscesbyrig*, which are named from hill-forts. The two models are not, of course, mutually exclusive; advocates of the multiple estate as a continuing phenomenon often include a Roman villa as the seat of authority in succession to the hill-fort.

II. THE FIRST SAXONS

The evidence for the first English settlements in Berkshire is archaeo-logical, not historical. The written traditions of the foundation of Wessex are concerned with landings on the south coast at dates which are too late to have any relation to the first coming of Germanic settlers to north Berks. Discussing these annals in *Anglo-Saxon*

England Sir Frank Stenton comments (p. 21) 'If, for example, the compiler of the annals says nothing about the circumstances under which the West Saxons reached the Thames Valley, the reason may well be that these circumstances were as obscure to him as they are today.' Archaeological evidence shows that there were soldiers who are likely to have been of Germanic race, probably accompanied by German women, on the Oxfordshire side of the Thames in the late 4th century. The burials from the Dyke Hills, near Dorchester, of a mercenary soldier and a woman wearing a cruciform brooch, and the more recent finds of late Roman military equipment at Shakenoak near Witney, provide evidence for this. More important for the history of settlement is the 'ceramic evidence for barbarians settled before the end of the Roman occupation' set out by J. N. L. Myres in *Anglo-Saxon Pottery and the Settlement of England* (1969). This evidence includes pottery from both banks of the Thames, and Dr Myres specifies carinated bowls on pedestal feet, of early 5th-cent. date, from Dorchester O and Sutton Courtenay Berks (p. 77), late 4th-cent. pottery in cemeteries at Oxford and Abingdon (p. 81), and 'undecorated biconical accessories' from Frilford and Long Witten-ham (both in Berks), which can be dated c. 400 (p. 82). He also says (p. 85) that finds from some sites, many of them along the south bank of the Thames below Oxford, show continuous development from c. 400 to c. 500 in metalwork and ceramics. Cemeteries in which this has been observed were at Frilford, Abingdon, Long Wittenham, Wallingford, Reading, Aston in Remenham, and one Oxfordshire site, Lower Shiplake. Dr Myres suggests that the Anglo-Saxon commu-nities responsible for these cemeteries 'began as groups of soldier-settlers planted out among the existing villages on the riverside gravels and dependent perhaps in the first instance on the fortified bridge-head at Dorchester', and that they may have been related to a political frontier on the Berks bank of the Thames, being placed there to defend the northern frontiers of a sub-Roman power centred on Silchester. At Silchester itself there is a mass of very late Roman material coupled with an apparent absence of early Anglo-Saxon settlement in the immediate neighbourhood of the town. The sub-Roman rulers of this area perhaps employed friendly Germanic barbarians to defend their northern frontier in the Thames valley against the barbarian settlers whose cremation cemeteries are to be found to the north and east of this region.

E. T. Leeds suggested in 1925 (*History* x, 97 ff.) that some very early Saxon settlements in north Berks were the work of immigrants who came from the north-east along the Icknield Way, this opinion being based on the study of brooches from cemeteries. Dr Myres has found confirmation in the pottery for such a movement from the north-east, but he favours a route south-west up the Ouse and south down the Cherwell to the Thames, rather than the Icknield Way route postulated by Leeds. This incursion is to be regarded as a later phenomenon than the settlements of the late Roman period referred to above. There is a type of urn known as a *Buckelurn*, of which there are two main categories, one differing from the other in being mounted on a foot. The *Buckelurnen* with feet can be shown to spread from East Anglia south-westward through Middle Anglia to the upper Thames valley, reaching the Thames at an early stage; they are found at such Berks sites as Harwell and E. Shefford. These urns belong to the period after A.D. 450, and Dr Myres considers that the valley of the upper Thames, which had been partly under Saxon control at least since the early 5th century, received a fresh influx of Germans at this time. Some movement could have come up the Thames from places like Croydon and Shepperton Sr, but the archaeological evidence suggests that most of it came from Middle Anglia, and the p.n. evidence does not support early contact with E. Surrey, *v.* 820.

Another important feature of the archaeological evidence is that only the four earlier classes into which these *Buckelurnen* have been divided are evidenced in the valley of the upper Thames and those of its tributaries; Dr Myres's Group V *Buckelurnen* are not found there. This hiatus in the pottery development may be due to the isolation of the Germanic people of N. Berks after the British victory at the Battle of Mons Badonicus in c. 500. They may have been relatively isolated from that date until the expansion of Wessex in the second half of the 6th century.

We are fortunate to have an archaeological sequence as precise as this for north Berkshire, and the next task is to determine whether any of the English place-names in the county can be supposed to have arisen in this early period from c. 400 to c. 500. It has been noted above that the Oxford–Dorchester–Abingdon region, which lies at the heart of the area where the earliest material is found, is not marked by a high degree of Celtic linguistic survival, and that the place-names which may show cognisance of Romano-British institutions occur in other parts of the county.

This is the first introduction to a County Place-Name Survey to be written since the appearance of John Dodgson's article on place-names in -ingas and -inga- (v. 800), which challenged the long-established belief that such names denoted the settlements of the first English arrivals in an area. The Berks evidence does not clash uncompromisingly with the old belief, but neither could it be said to give strong support to it. There are three names in -ingas along the Berkshire/Oxfordshire stretch of the Thames; Reading and Sonning in Berks, which certainly have personal names as first elements, and Goring in O, which is probably in the same category. Reading is one of the very few instances in S.E. England in which this type of place-name coincides with a pagan burial-site of the 5th century, v. Audrey Meaney's appendix to John Dodgson's article (*Medieval Archaeology* x, p. 29). It is not certain, however, that Reading is the exact site of the first settlement of the *Rēadingas*; v. 933, where it is suggested that Reading and Sonning are respectively on the east and west boundaries of the provinces of the *Rēadingas* and the *Sunningas*. Some of the -inga- names of Berks, notably Sunningwell and Wokingham, refer to groups of people detached from the main area of such provinces as the *Sunningas* and *Woccingas*, and this use of -ingas to denote settlements on the boundary of provinces and of -inga- to denote groups of settlers from another province lessens the force of the argument which saw names of this type as indicating the centre of regions of early settlement. Nevertheless, these names are represented in the area of Berks which lies along the stretch of the Thames where the very early archaeological material has been found. They are all plotted on Map IV, and it is their relative scarcity rather than their exact position which seems inconsistent with the old belief that they are our best toponymical indication of very early settlement. The concentration of early Anglo-Saxon material between Frilford and Remenham is such that one might, in accordance with the old theory, have expected a real concentration of -ingas and -inga- here. The place-name survey has not added any new specimens, and two names, Wasing and Eling, which had formerly been considered to contain -ingas, have been shown to belong in another category. Both -ingas and -inga- are considerably more frequent in north-east Hampshire and west Surrey, and there is something more like a local concentration between Basing Ha and Godalming Sr, in a stretch of country where, in contrast to north Berks, the archaeological evidence for pagan Saxon settlement is negligible.

The only suggestion yet put forward for a large category of place-

names which might fill the gap left by the dethronement of the
-ingas and -inga- names is that of habitative place-names ending in
hām. This suggestion was made by Barrie Cox in 'The Significance
of the Distribution of English Place-Names in -hām in the Midlands
and East Anglia', *Journal* v (1973). In this article Dr Cox brings
together evidence relating to the physical situation, archaeological
context and early history of place-names containing hām in thirteen
counties. This evidence strongly suggests that in the region studied
by Dr Cox these names belong to very early Anglo-Saxon settlements,
bearing a fairly close relationship as a class to the Roman road system
and being in many instances on or near the site of Romano-British
settlements. It seems likely that in these areas the -*ingahām* names
arose at a later stage than the -*hām* names, and the -*ingas* names at a
later stage still.

In the light of this article it is necessary to look with special care at
the distribution of the ten names in Berks which certainly contain
hām. This total does not include the two examples of wīchām which
are discussed *supra*. All possible names in hām are plotted on Distribution Map IV, with a query beside some in which it is not possible to
decide between hām and hamm.

First, it is noteworthy that the peculiar circumstances of the
English settlement in the Oxford–Abingdon–Dorchester region (if
we accept the outline postulated by Dr Myres) are not exceptionally
conducive to the formation of English place-names in hām. Wytham
is very close to Oxford, but this is the only specimen in N.W. Berks,
and there is none on the Oxfordshire bank of the Thames above Dorchester. On the Oxfordshire side E. of Dorchester the only possible
relevant names are Stadhampton, earlier *Stodham* (classified as a hamm
name in O 154, but which appears on reflection more likely to be
identical with Studham BdHu 132), and the lost *Ingham* in Watlington
(O 96). Newnham and Nuneham (marked 'nh' on Map IV) should
probably be disregarded for the purpose of the present discussion, as
there is evidence to suggest that this name ('at the new village') continued to be used after hām had otherwise ceased to be a living place-
name element. The hām names lower down the Thames should be
considered with the names in E. Berks and Sr which are discussed *infra*.

This relative scarcity of names in hām in an area where Roman
occupation is known to be dense, and where fresh evidence of it is
now continually appearing, seems to be at variance with the findings
of Dr Cox in the thirteen counties he has studied. There is a little

evidence of a more positive nature in the S.W. of the county. In this area Orpenham, Ownham and Crookham lie on or close to the Roman roads. It must be noted, however, that these are minor settlements; the first two names are not recorded till the late 12th cent., and while Crookham is a DB estate it is only assessed at one hide. None of them is a parish. Two Wiltshire names in hām are plotted on Map IV: Tottenham in Bedwyn and Upham in Aldbourne. Tottenham lies directly on a Roman road. Upham is not on a Roman road, but is especially noteworthy, as Desmond Bonney's recent article in VCH Wilts 1 Pt 2 states (p. 484) that a substantial Romano-British settlement underlies the later hamlet of Upper Upham. Tottenham and Upham are minor settlements in the parishes of Great Bedwyn and Aldbourne, however, and one can only see them as ancient English administrative centres by assuming that the shift from the uplands to the river valleys happened after the English had first established themselves on upland sites. It would be in accordance with other evidence discussed *infra* to regard Bedwyn and Aldbourne as the primary English names in this area.

The evidence relating to names in hām in E. Berks is of a different character to that in the rest of the county. Frilsham, which lies in west central Berks beside the R. Pang, was omitted from the preceding paragraph as it seems better to regard it as a western outlier of the major names in hām which occur in E. Berks and W. Sr. All the other names in this group lie E. of Silchester. The Berks names plotted on Map IV which form part of this group are Frilsham, Sulham, Wokingham, Waltham and Cookham. All are parishes, and all except Wokingham are described in DB. These are very different from the tiny places which have names in hām in S.W. Berks and the adjacent portion of Wiltshire; and the group of major names in hām is continued into Sr by Windlesham and Chobham, both parishes, in the S.E. corner of Map IV, while on the O bank of the Thames lies Mapledurham, another parish-name. Some of the names in S.W. Buckinghamshire now ending in -ham are likely to be hām names; the most likely are the major names Amersham and Hitcham; the other Bk name which has been plotted without a query on Map IV is Hicknaham, a tiny settlement in Dorney for which the earliest form is 1199.

As regards the proportion of major to minor names, the hām names E. of the R. Pang present a very different picture from those to the W. They are also appreciably more numerous. It seems clear that some factor has operated to inhibit the use of hām for major names in N.W. Berks in spite of the early English arrival. In S.W. Berks, when hām does occur it may be said to bear a close relationship to Roman roads and Romano-British settlement. In the northern part of this area W. of Silchester there are occasional parish-names in hām, like Wytham Berks and Bloxham, Kingham, Rousham O. Further S., in S.W. Berks and E. Wiltshire, the element is used in the naming of much less important settlements. In S.W. Berks the position occupied elsewhere by hām in the hierarchy of habitative place-name terms may have been usurped by hāmstede. Details of names in hāmstede are given on pp. 929–30. The compound is un-usually frequent in S.W. Berks, and most of the examples are major place-names; but only three of the ten specimens plotted on Map IV can be said to bear a close relationship to the Roman road system.

One more observation should be made about hām. Mrs Rhona Huggins, in an article to be published in *Medieval Archaeology* XIX, suggests that **weald-hām* (*v.* Waltham St Lawrence Pt 1 112) was an appellative applied to estates which were the centres of areas reserved for royal hunting. She demonstrates that most of the Walthams lie beside Roman roads. The Berks example may fairly be supposed to lie near the lost Roman road which traversed the N.E. of the county, and it is suggested on p. 635 that the name Waltham applied originally to a large area now divided into three parishes.

The last two sections of the discussion, demonstrating that neither the -ingas and -inga- names nor those in hām are characteristic of the part of Berks where the archaeological evidence demonstrates Saxon occupation from the early 5th century, are sadly negative. A more fruitful approach is perhaps to look at the area in question and see which types of place-name are specially characteristic of it. An approach of this nature may be required for some other counties, as well as Berks. John Dodgson, who first made plain the fact that -ingas and -inga- were not the answer, has since assembled evidence for Kent, Surrey and Sussex which makes it clear that in these counties hām does not have the necessary close relationship with the areas where the pagan burials are best evidenced. In his article 'Place-names from *hām*, distinguished from *hamm* names, in relation to the settlement of Kent, Surrey and Sussex' (*Anglo-Saxon England* II, 1973), he expressed himself satisfied as to the general connection of *hām* names with the Romano-British settlement pattern, but saw them mainly as occurring on the edges of the Romano-British settlement areas, and in a distribution which extends out from it. He notes that *hām* names occur both in districts where there are Anglo-Saxon pagan burial-sites, and also in districts where there are none, and from this concludes that some *hām* names belong to the period of pagan burial, but the type continued to be formed after the burials became obsolete. He agrees with Dr Cox that the *hām* names are earlier than the -ingas and -inga- types. On studying the maps in this article one is struck by the number of areas in the three counties where the clusters of symbols showing the pagan burial-sites are hardly mixed with the symbols for the types of place-name discussed, even for those in hām. It seems time to look at the areas of the burials to see what the place-names are which actually coincide with them.

The answer in Berks seems to be that some categories of topographical settlement-names are especially characteristic of the N.W. portion of the county. The point does not emerge at a glance from Map V, on which all topographical settlement-names have been plotted, but some of the necessary details are set out on pp. 928, 931–2, in the discussion of the distribution and usage of the elements ford and īeg. Settlement-names containing these are marked 'f' and 'i' on Map V, and it can be seen that there is a marked concentration of them in the valley of the R. Ock and along the Thames from Chimney O to Moulsford. If it is noted that Basildon was *Bæstlæsford* in OE (Pt **2** 513), the line can be continued lower down the Thames. By superimposing Map V on the map showing hundreds and parishes it can be quickly seen that nearly all the Berks names belong to parishes. It is perhaps worth noting that the use of these terms in major names is particularly marked all along the great length of the R. Ouse, through Cambridgeshire, Huntingdonshire, Bedfordshire and Buckinghamshire. The parishes along the Ouse with names in ford and ēg can be identified easily from the maps showing hundreds and parishes supplied with C, BdHu and Bk. Obviously it would be a mistake to treat this as positive evidence for common place-name-forming traditions, as the names are not exclusive to these areas. Both ford and īeg are well evidenced in major names in Surrey, though not (perhaps for topographical reasons) in the region where most of the early burials lie. But when all allowance is made for these being elements which could become frequent in any area where patches of dry ground in marsh and ways across streams were particularly important, the concentration which occurs in N.W. Berks still appears striking.

It may be noted in passing that the place-names of the Croydon region in Surrey, where there is a similar concentration of pagan Anglo-Saxon burials, show a marked contrast with those of N.W. Berks. There, the characteristic names in areas immediately adjacent to those of the burials are those ending in hām and stede, the first of which is rare and the second not evidenced at all in N.W. Berks. When considering the distribution of the element stede it should be noted that there are two categories of names: those (like Hampstead) in which stede is part of an OE appellative, and those (like Banstead Sr) in which stede is used in the coining of names in which the first element is variable. It is the latter type which is specially well represented in areas of Sr adjacent to those where the pagan burials are thickest. Distribution Map I in Sandred shows that with very few exceptions this type of name is confined to a group of counties S. and E. of Berks, and it is absent from the group of counties to the N.E. of Berks which are traversed by the R. Ouse. If the stede names in Sr represent colonisation by the Saxons first evidenced in the pagan burials of the Croydon area, this type of place-name would probably have been evidenced in Berks if much early settlement had come from that direction.

Settlement-names of topographical meaning are relatively frequent in N.W. Berks, more so in the valley of the Ock than along the Thames. This is partly due to the concentration of names in īeg and ford, already noted, partly to the use of stream-names as settlement-names in this area. Balking, Childrey and Wantage are named from small streams draining into the Ock, and Lockinge, Ginge, Hagbourne and Hendred from streams draining into the Thames; all except Ginge are parish-names, and Ginge is in DB. Balking, Ginge, Lockinge and Wantage are stream-names of a special type, formed by the addition of ing[2] to the stem of a verb which describes the action of the stream. This use of small stream-names for settlements should probably be considered, along with the frequent use of ford and īeg, to show special concern with the drainage on the part of the earliest English settlers. There is every reason to believe that the names in these categories go back to a very early stage in the use of English place-names; they are not the types of parish-name (like Buckland, Fyfield, Kingston) which are likely to have replaced earlier English ones. The stream-names which became major settlement-names, the names in ford and īeg, and some of the other topographical names in N.W. Berks, like Coxwell, Brightwell, Harwell, Sotwell and the major

names in hamm – Shrivenham, Fernham, Marcham, Wittenham –
could be seen as forming a coherent group, coined by farmers whose
main concerns were water supply, water control, water crossings, and
dry sites for villages. It may be that such a concentration of homo-
geneous topographical settlement-names, showing concern with a
particular aspect of the terrain, is more typical of an area of exceptionally early English settlement than any of the other categories
(names in -ingas and -inga-, names in hām) which have been
suggested.

There are, of course, some habitative settlement-names in the
region of Berks where the early archaeological material occurs. The
area has a significantly high proportion of the major names in worð.
These are marked 'wð' on Map IV. Littleworth and Longworth were
both formerly *Worth*, and these and Denchworth are major settlements. Seacourt in Wytham, Bayworth in Sunningwell and Sugworth
in Radley have lost their importance now, but all three were DB
manors. Some of these names in worð may date from a very early
period. The names in þrop and wīc are probably of relatively late
origin, but a high proportion of the names in cot(e) are DB manors,
and Buscot has a high assessment there (*v.* 924–5). In N.W. Berks and
the adjacent portions of W and O cot(e) is not certain to be restricted
to settlements of late origin and humble status.

Before concluding this section, in which an attempt has been made
to identify types of place-names which may date from the first coming
of the English to Berkshire, mention should be made of two arguments bearing on this problem which were put forward by Sir Frank
Stenton. In 'The English Occupation of Southern Britain' (*TRHistS*
XXII, 1940, reprinted in *Preparatory to Anglo-Saxon England*, pp.
266–80), Sir Frank used the -ing[2] names of the Ock Valley as evidence
to confirm the ASC account of the founders of Wessex landing on the
south coast, on the grounds that another area in which there is a
concentration of these names is in S. Hampshire. Sir Frank's list of
these names in Berks included Pinge, which is here ascribed to a
different origin, and *Ætheleahing*, which is shown (Pt **2** 462) to be a
ghost name; but *Mydeling* (Pt **1** 14) has been added in N.W. Berks,
and Wasing (Pt **2** 271–2) in S.W. Berks, so the number is not dimin-
ished. The distribution of this type of name is more widespread than
was realised in 1940, and there are more than the 'few scattered
examples of the type between the Wash and the Thames' which
seemed to Sir Frank to rule out the possibility of this type of name-

giving reaching Berkshire by immigration from the N.E. The type is well evidenced in Cambridgeshire, and in C 333 Dr Reaney says that it is especially frequent in minor names in the Isle of Ely. I should prefer, however, to think of these names as going back to an earlier period of English settlement in Berks, earlier than any invasion implied by the ASC annals for 495–514, earlier even than the incursion from the N.E. after 450 evidenced in the archaeology. This type of place-name may have been part of the language of Germanic settlers who made their homes in the Oxford region before the end of Roman Britain, and who were possibly newcomers to Britain, not immigrants from settlements on the south coast or in the region round the Wash.

The development to -inge found in some of these names (Ginge, Lockinge, Wantage, some f.ns. from *Mydeling*) is most probably caused by a locative inflection -*i*. The most recent discussion of the type is by J. McN. Dodgson in *Beiträge zur Namenforschung* Band II (1967), Heft 3, pp. 237–45. Dodgson considers the locative -*ingi* to be the reason for palatalisation in some of the names, and he believes (p. 244) that the survival of forms derived from this ancient locative constitutes one of the reasons for considering the -ing[2] names to be among our most ancient English place-names.

Sir Frank Stenton's other suggestion for a category of significant early names in Berks was put forward in 1924 in IPN 188. Here he listed some personal names compounded in the place-names of Oxfordshire and Berkshire which belonged to characters in heroic literature, and which he thought indicated the use of a distinctive stock of archaic personal names in this area. This possibility was considered in some detail in the Introduction to my thesis *The Place-Names of West Berkshire* (1957), a copy of which can be consulted in the library of the EPNS at Nottingham University. It does not seem worth while to reproduce that discussion here, though more will be said on the topic in the next section of this Introduction which discusses the significance of the use of personal names as the first elements of place-names.

III. THE SIGNIFICANCE OF HABITATIVE PLACE-NAMES
AND OF PLACE-NAMES CONTAINING PERSONAL NAMES

Two assumptions underlying much of what was written up to 1965 about place-name chronology may fairly be questioned now. One is that habitative names (i.e. those containing words like hām, tūn, worð) are likely to be of greater antiquity than settlement-names of purely topographical meaning. The other is that some place-names with personal names as first element are likely to date from the earliest use of the English language in an area and can therefore be assumed to preserve the names of some of the earliest English settlers. Both assumptions can be traced in the introductions to the surveys of Gloucestershire and Westmorland, the last to be published before the present one. Cf. Westmorland 1 xxxviii 'The older English settlements are represented by some 30 or more habitative names of parishes and villages', and Gloucestershire 4 36 'The personal names *Becca* in Beckford, *Hagena* in Hampen and *Widia* in Withington also belong to heroic poetry and the place-names may therefore belong to an early stratum.' This last statement is less confident than those in earlier Introductions (e.g. Bk xiv–xv, which asserts that the occurrence of *Hygerēd* in Harlington Mx and of the short form *Hycga* in Hitcham, Hedgerley and Hughenden Bk provides 'a slight but definite piece of evidence in favour of an original connection between Middlesex and south Buckinghamshire'); but these quotations from A. H. Smith's last two Introductions, together with the general tenor of his writing, indicate that the two assumptions in question were still considered valid in 1965.

Insufficient attention has been paid to several sources of evidence bearing on the relative chronology of topographical and habitative place-names, and on the processes which gave rise to some at least of the '*x*'s tūn', '*x*'s byrig' type of place-name. These sources are:

1. The evidence of the major settlement-names which actually occur in the vicinity of some of the earliest Anglo-Saxon pagan burials.

2. The documentary evidence showing the process of formation of some habitative names of the '*x*'s tūn' type and the Kingston type.

3. The relationship of places with such 'geographically related' names as Aston, Sutton, Upton to estate-centres like Blewbury and Abingdon.

The first line of enquiry has already been followed in relation to N.W. Berks, and the results are set out above. The other two will be considered in this section.

In west Berkshire surviving documentary evidence enables us to observe the evolution of some major habitative place-names in the 10th and 11th centuries. At this late date estates were carved out of the three areas known as *Æscesbyrig*, Sparsholt and Lambourn. The

evidence relating to *Æscesbyrig* is set out in Pt **2** 379, 380, 383, and on
pp. 675–7 of the present volume. Estates later known as Uffington
and Woolstone formed part of the larger unit till the mid-10th cent.,
and both the habitative place-names arose after that. Uffington means
'Uffa's tūn'; Woolstone ('Wulfrīc's tūn') is named from a thegn who
appears in a number of records at this date, and whose property in
960 consisted of 8 villages in Berks, 5 in Sx and 2 in Ha. The connection of this Wulfric with Woolstone was not known to Sir Frank
Stenton in 1911, when he used Woolstone and Uffington to illustrate
his belief in the 'seignorial implication' of this type of place-name
(Stenton 25). The names are indeed seignorial, but not in the way that
Stenton adumbrated there and in later writings. When the bearing of
the charters is understood, it becomes impossible to 'see in the
original Uffington the house and farm steading of Uffa, standing with
the cottages of his labourers in the middle of his fields and pasture
lands', and it is clear that neither Uffa nor Wulfric has anything to
do with the history of settlement. The land-unit which was later
exploited as two estates by Uffa and Wulfric had probably been in
existence from the Iron Age or earlier. With the change to English
speech this land-unit became known as *Æscesbyrig* from the hill-fort
which lies on the boundary between the modern parishes, and this
topographical name was only superseded by the two habitative names
in the second half of the 10th cent. The field-systems in use at that
date were bisected by these late boundaries, *v.* 627.

Sparsholt is a topographical name which was used in DB of three
estates, corresponding to Sparsholt, Fawler and Kingston Lisle (Pt **2**
372). There is some reason to think that the name Kingston was in
occasional use before 1066, but it does not finally supersede Sparsholt
till the 13th cent. Here again the habitative name referring to manorial
tenure supersedes a topographical one. In the third example, Lambourn, the topographical name still covered Lambourn and East
Garston in 1086 (Pt **2** 330), though the 30 hides of East Garston had
been held TRE by the Esgar from whom the smaller unit was
eventually named.

The name Lambourn, transferred from the river to a settlement, is
probably more typical than *Æscesbyrig* or Sparsholt of the topographical names which were once applied to a number of villages in a
large area, and which were superseded by habitative names referring
to manorial owners, so that they either went out of use or remained
as the name of one of the original group of settlements. The process

has been demonstrated in E. Wiltshire by Desmond Bonney ('Two Tenth-Century Wiltshire Charters concerning Lands at Avon and Collingbourne', *Wilts. Arch. and Nat. Hist. Mag.* LXIV, 1969). In this paper Mr Bonney demonstrates that a grant probably to be dated 933 of land 'at Collingbourne' to the king's thegn Wulfgar can be firmly identified with the tithing of Aughton in Collingbourne Kingston. Wulfgar's will leaves this estate to his wife Æffe with reversion to the New Minster, and there can be no doubt that the name Aughton ('Æffe's tūn') arises from this lady's tenure. This example again shows the manorial habitative name superseding the topographical one which had referred to several settlements; and it is particularly important to note that an enduring name of the '*x*'s tūn' type can arise from a tenure which is only the length of a widowhood – though it is possible that Wulfgar's wife resided there for several decades while her husband was mainly at the king's court, so that the estate may have been hers in the eyes of the local people for much longer than her legal tenure, and possible that she lived there as a widow for many years.

It may be thought that the Berks and W names discussed above (and ns. in other counties which refer to 10th-cent. tenants) are late exceptions, which do not destroy the concept of the Hygered of Harlington Mx as founding father of the village at a much earlier date. But not all the place-names which refer to identified thegns are as late as the 10th cent.; the same process can be seen in operation in the part of Gloucestershire adjacent to Berks in the first half of the 8th cent. Bibury Gl, which probably contains byrig in the sense 'manor house', is named from Beage, the daughter of Leppa, to whom the estate is leased in a document of 718–45, for their two lives. The estate is not named in the lease, but is identified as 'by the river called Coln' (which may indicate that, as in the case of Lambourn and Collingbourne, the river-name was used as the name of several settlements; the parishes E. and W. of Bibury are Coln St Aldwyn and Coln St Denis). The name Bibury, first recorded in a charter of 899, may have come into use c. 750, when Beage, having inherited the lease, may have built a new manor house, referred to by the local people as *Bēagan byrig* (the evidence for the p.n. Bibury is set out in Gl **1** 26, but the earliest form quoted there is wrongly dated, as it is from a heading to the lease of 718–45, not from the document). About 25 miles N. of Bibury lies Tredington Wo 172, which may be named from the 'comes Tyrdda' said in a charter of 757 to be a former owner of the estate. If this example be accepted, it is important as being an -ingtūn formation which refers to a manorial owner of the type under discussion; but in the case of Tredington we have no evidence bearing on the earlier name of the estate. A marginally relevant name is Donnington Gl 1 217–18, which may have had its name remodelled from an earlier *Strǣttūn*, through *Dunnestreatun* (recorded in 779) to the eventual Donnington, on account of a temporary ownership by one Dunna whose name is compounded in some boundary-marks in an OE survey of this estate; but this example is not in the same category as the other names adduced here, since Dunna is not himself mentioned in a document, and this is an instance of a habitative name replacing an earlier name also in tūn not a topographical one.

Leaving aside, for the moment, the question of whether habitative names need necessarily be regarded as older than topographical ones, some further remarks may be offered on the question of the signifi-cance of personal names in place-names. Reasons have been given for regarding the pers.n. + tūn and the pers.n. + byrig ('manor house') type as arising from the type of overlordship enjoyed by a thegn or one of his female dependants in relation to an estate, and it has been shown that there are instances in which these names can be linked with people mentioned in land grants. Whether this type of origin can be postulated for names in hām which have a personal name as first element must be left an open question; it does not affect many Berks names – only Frilsham and Ownham are certain examples, though Caversham and Bisham may belong in this category – but it is, of course, very important for the study of areas where hām is more common. The 'manorial' explanation seems applicable to names in which cot(e), wīc and worð are compounded with personal names, though no evidence has been noted which has a direct bearing on these. The great outstanding problem about the personal names, however, is whether we should attach this 'manorial' significance to the large category of place-names in which they are compounded with a topographical term. Are the *Cēol* of Cholsey and the *Friðela* of Frilford to be regarded as temporary manorial overlords, or were these the leading settlers at the time of the coming of the English?

It is doubtful whether there is any method of investigation which would enable an objective answer to be given to this last question. Each investigator will probably incline to one answer rather than the other for subjective reasons, based ultimately on his own instinctive approach to the study of this period of history. In Berks, the use of personal names as first elements of major topographical settlement-names is best evidenced with feld (Watchfield, Winkfield, Wokefield), ford (Duxford, Frilford, Moulsford) and īeg (Cholsey, Hinksey, Mackney, Tubney). It is argued on pp. 923 ff. that these elements have a quasi-habitative significance in major place-names, and it might be suggested that an estate given to one Friðela at some un-known date was known as 'Friðela's ford' rather than 'Friðela's tūn' because of the popular recognition that the ford was the most impor-tant feature of the estate. This is not firm ground to build on; but the uncertainty as to the significance of personal names in this type of place-name should at least induce caution about the use of the personal names as evidence for the course of the English settlement. The only personal names which can be fairly certainly regarded as dating from a relatively early period are those compounded with -ingas or -inga-, which in Berks are *Herela* (Arlington), *Pǣga* (Pang-bourne), *Rēad(a)* (Reading), *Scīene* (Shinfield), *Sunna* (Sonning), *Wealh* (Wallingford), *Gēat* or *Ēata* (Yattendon). As explained *supra*, we no longer regard these -ingas, -inga- names as representing the earliest English settlements, but the type of formation implies that *Herela*, *Pǣga*, etc. lived in the area as leaders of a family or tribal group, and this exempts them from the suspicion of being king's thegns with a temporary manorial overlordship, which attaches to the other eponymous men (and women) mentioned in the major settle-ment-names of Berks.

If Sir Frank Stenton's writings on the subject of personal names in place-names are studied, it can be seen that his awareness of the late origin of many '*x*'s tūn' names increased between 1911 and 1942, the date of his address to the Royal Historical Society on 'The Place of Women in Anglo-Saxon Society'; but that he still maintained a belief that some of the personal names in place-names were those of men and women who had founded new settlements or cleared wasteland on the borders of earlier settlements. This last belief appears in the address of 1942 (reprinted in *Preparatory to Anglo-Saxon England*, the relevant passage being on pp. 321-2). Here he argued that the occurrence of feminine names in the boundary-marks of charters showed that 'the part which women had taken in the occupation of new lands for settlement had been by no means inconsiderable'. This use of personal names in the charter boundary-marks has some bearing on the significance of personal names in settlement-names, and the systematic examination of a body of charter evidence in the present volume provides an opportunity to consider the function of the personal names, both masculine and feminine, which occur in Berks boundary-marks. All the boundary-marks containing personal names are listed on pp. 793–4.

If the boundary-marks are studied as a whole, and the use of personal names considered together with the use of terms like *biscopes-*, *cinges-*, *ealdormonnes-*, it appears probable that such compounds as *ælfheages gemære*, *ælfsiges mor*, *ælfðryþe dic*, *cyneeahes treow* are shorthand for 'boundary of the estate now or recently in the possession of a thegn called Ælfhēah', 'ditch on the boundary of the lady Ælfðrȳð's estate', etc. This must be so in the case of the boundary-marks containing *cyning* 'king'. In the two examples in the bounds of part of Kingston Lisle, *cincges scypene* and *cinges þornas*, it is only sensible to translate 'cow-shed and thorn-bushes on the boundary of the royal estate'. There is no likelihood of royal participation in the erection of sheds or planting of thorns, and similarly there is no reason to suppose that the men and women whose names occur in similar boundary-marks were responsible for any settling or clearing. From the list printed on pp. 793 f. and 919 ff. it can be seen that the frequency of personal names in charter boundary-marks is high compared to that in the place-names of the county. This is probably because the boundary surveys date from a period when the type of manorialisation discussed here was widespread; but this type of boundary-mark also occurs in earlier charters than most of the Berks examples. The boundaries of the Bibury lease of 718–45, discussed above, mention *Leppan crundlas*, 'Leppa's chalkpits', Leppa being the name of the grantee.

One class of place-names in which personal names may have a special significance is the type in which a personal name is compounded with hlāw, hlǣw 'tumulus'. A well-known example elsewhere is Taplow Bk, 'Tæppa's tumulus', which may reasonably be held to incorporate the name of the 7th-cent. prince whose rich grave-goods were found in a barrow in the old churchyard; and it is very probable that a number of the Db names in which hlāw is compounded with a personal name refer to the man buried in the tumulus (Db xxv). In Berks this category comprises Challow, *Hildeslowe* and Titlar among names which survived, and *cardan hlæw, hodes hlæwe, hwittuces hlæwe, lillanhlæwes crundele, wintres hlewe* in charter bounds. Scutchamer Knob was OE *Cwicelmeshlæwe*, but has been omitted from this list because archaeologists say that it is not a burial mound, and *hundeshlæwe* and *hafoces hlæwe* have been omitted because it seems unlikely that two Saxons called 'Hound' and 'Hawk' should be buried in neighbouring Bronze Age barrows. Some of the boundary-marks listed under **beorg** on p. 770 may belong with the *wintres hlewe* type, but **beorg**-names can frequently be identified with Bronze Age tumuli (*hundeshlæwe* and *hafoces hlæwe* are *beorh – oþærne* in another account of the same boundary), and while a Bronze Age barrow might have been used for an Anglo-Saxon 'secondary' burial, it seems safer to regard boundary-marks like *Ælfredes beorh* as elliptical for 'tumulus on the boundary of Ælfrēd's estate'. If, on the other hand, it is assumed that some of the men whose names are compounded with hlāw or hlǣw were buried in the tumuli referred to in the place-names, this provides a sort of contact with Saxons of the pagan period, but probably only of the end of that period, since Anglo-Saxon barrow burials seem to be predominantly 7th-century in date. Challow became a major settlement-name, but it may have replaced an earlier place-name, as it is hardly likely that there was no settlement at Challow till after the burial of Ceawa in a tumulus. This was not a common type of Anglo-Saxon burial, and it is easy to imagine such a tumulus becoming an object of note to the people of the region, especially if it came at the end of the practice of pagan burial.

The last five paragraphs have constituted a lengthy digression on the general significance of personal names in settlement-names and charter boundaries. It is necessary now to take up the thread of the discussion about the relative chronology of habitative and topo-graphical settlement-names. Two sources of information bearing on this have been explored, these being the character of the place-names in the part of Berkshire where the archaeological evidence for early Anglo-Saxon occupation (or at any rate burial) is thickest, and the documentary evidence which shows the late coining of some habitative names which replaced topographical ones. The third source (which has already been tapped in connection with the '*x*'s tūn' names, but which should now be examined as a whole) consists of the names of land-units which charter and other evidence shows to have had an ancient association with each other, though they are now separate parishes.

The charter numbered G IV in this volume records a grant in

A.D. 944 of 100 hides at Blewbury to Bishop Ælfric. In HistAb 46, Sir Frank Stenton stated that this was probably a gift of Blewbury Hundred as it existed in the 10th cent. The bounds describe the modern parishes of Blewbury, Aston Tirrold, Aston Upthorpe, North Moreton and South Moreton, and the size of the area can be gauged from the map showing hundreds and parishes, though it is not marked as a Hundred there. The area is roughly comparable to that of the Hundred of Lambourn, but is perhaps a bit smaller. What is important for the present discussion is that this great estate was called Blewbury, which was the name of the hill-fort on Blewburton Hill, now on the boundary between the parishes of Blewbury and Aston Upthorpe. The large village of Blewbury lies a mile to the W. of this, and there seems little doubt that this is the primary Old English name. Aston is so called because of its position in relation to Blewbury. Moreton is not a geographically related name, but it would surely be perverse to think it earlier than Blewbury because it is a habitative name. The naming of a large estate from an Iron Age hill-fort is closely paralleled by *Æscesbyrig*, the evidence relating to which is set out above. There also the division into smaller units resulted in the hill-fort being on a parish boundary, though it must originally have been fairly central to the estate. The development differs in that *Æscesbyrig*, unlike Blewbury, did not become the name of a village.

Lambourn Hundred is a territorial unit of some similarity to the 10th-cent. Hundred of Blewbury. The hundredal organisation survived in this instance, and Lambourn Hundred still consists only of the very large parish of Lambourn, and the smaller one of East Garston, earlier *Esgareston* from the 11th-cent. tenant Esgar. The whole unit may represent the royal estate of Lambourn bequeathed to his wife by King Alfred, for which no hidage is known. By 1086 there are a number of estates here: a royal estate of 20 hides, a holding of 30 hides TRE which had belonged to Esgar, King Edward's staller, and two estates of 8 hides TRE and 4 hides which had been held in alod of King Edward. In addition to these, which are all described under the name Lambourn, there is Bockhampton, surveyed under its own name, which was an estate of 8 hides TRE, held by three freemen in alod of King Edward. From this it appears that King Edward had at his disposal 70 hides in Lambourn and East Garston, a figure which does not preclude an earlier assessment of 100 hides, as Blewbury, assessed at 100 hides in 944, had enjoyed a substantial hidage reduction by the time of King Edward (*v*. 753). What is important for the present investigation is that the two main settlements of Lambourn and Upper Lambourn have a topographical name, taken from the river at the source of which they lie, and that the habitative settlement-names in the Hundred are clearly of later origin. If hāmtūn in Bockhampton could be understood as 'farm dependent on a great manor', this would seem appropriate to what may be supposed to be its early relationship to Lambourn. Eastbury, which is referred to by that name c. 1090, probably means 'manor to the east of Bockhampton', and East Garston is, of course, a manorial tūn name of late origin.

Adjoining Lambourn to the N.W. is the land-unit of Ashbury, which is a different name from *Æscesbyrig* and probably refers to the Iron Age hill-fort now called Alfred's Castle (*v.* Pt 2 345). This is the subject of two royal charters of 840 and 947, in which the name of the estate is given as *Asshedoune, Aysshedun*. The habitative names in the estate, Idstone, Kingstone and Odstone, may fairly be supposed to be of later origin, though the documentary evidence is not so clear in this case as in those already cited. Immediately N. of Ashbury is Shrivenham, which was until 1863 a much larger parish, including Bourton, Longcot and Fernham. Shrivenham is a name in -hamm, and Bourton and Longcot, which are certainly of subsidiary status, are habitative names.

A particularly clear example of an estate-centre with a topographical name is Great Faringdon. The evidence for regarding this as the administrative centre of a large territorial unit extending on both sides of the Thames is set out in Pt 2 366. Not so many of the units connected with Faringdon have habitative names as in some of the instances already cited, but it is important that the name of the chief manor is a purely topographical statement meaning 'fern-covered down'.

This account of topographical place-names which refer to the centres of large composite estates is not exhaustive, and interested readers will be able to find other possible examples in the material presented in these three volumes. It is necessary now to consider whether any Berks names containing the habitative terms hām, byrig 'manor house', tūn and worð seem likely to have been applied to such important centres.

There is a clear possibility that hām is used in somewhat this way in Waltham. It is suggested on p. 635 that the 30-hide estates of BCS 762 comprised both Walthams and Shottesbrooke, which lies between them. These three parishes constitute a much smaller area than that of Lambourn or the old Blewbury Hundred, but the use of the same name for two settlements 1½ miles apart, with another settlement between them, suggests that the name was that of a district, not just of a village. Mrs Huggins has suggested that Waltham was an appellative used of an estate which was a royal hunting centre, and this seems appropriate to the Berks example. If Thatcham (Pt 1 188) could be considered a name in hām, this would be an important addition to the examples in which hām denotes an ancient administrative centre, as Thatcham was the centre of a hundred in 1086 (Pt 1 231), and Brian Kemp ('The Mother Church of Thatcham', ArchJ LXIII, 1967–8) has shown that it had a minster church serving a large area. Unfortunately it is impossible to decide whether hām or hamm is the second element of this name. On the whole, hamm seems a little more probable, in which case this example belongs with the topographical names of administrative centres. It is the wide jurisdiction of the church at Thatcham, as reconstructed by Mr Kemp, which makes it seem particularly likely to be an ancient centre of authority. Mr Kemp suggests (p. 19) that the Domesday Hundred of Thatcham, which he considers coterminous with the ancient *parochia*, is a unit much older than the hundred system, dating back at least to the time when Thatcham's church was first established, which may have been in the 7th cent.

The term byrig is sometimes of habitative significance, and the five Berks names in which this sense occurs are listed on p. 923. Kintbury, with the name of the R. Kennet as first element, is the only one of the five which seems likely to have been of special importance in the early Anglo-Saxon period. There was a Hundred of Kintbury in 1086 (Pt 2 280), and the large parish contains a number of hamlets which were separate estates in DB. Bucklebury was also a Hundred in 1086, but does not contain lesser settlements. It is doubtful whether this significance can be attached to any Berks places with names in worð, though Littleworth (Pt 2 367) may have served for a time as the administrative centre of the Faringdon estate. As regards tūn, the names in which this element occurs are fully analysed on pp. 939–42. Most of the names in tūn and -ingtūn seem likely to belong to a relatively late stratum in the toponymy of the county. Some of the places to which they belong, such as the adjacent group of Steventon, Milton and Sutton in the Hundred of Ock, were important estates in 1086; but Sutton is named from its position in relation to Abingdon, and Milton from its position between Sutton and Steventon, and this must raise a suspicion that these names have replaced others of a different type. Compton and Moreton became centres of hundreds, but there is no reason to suppose that either was a very early centre of administration; Moreton was part of Blewbury in 944.

As further illustration of the importance of topographical settlement-names in Berks, the relative frequency of topographical and habitative names which have come to refer to modern parishes might be adduced. Omitting recent creations like Beech Hill, Crowthorne and Sunningdale, the topographical parish-names in this county outnumber the habitative ones by almost 2:1. It is not advisable to be too precise about these statistics, as difficulties of classification cause slightly different scores every time a count is taken; but the figures are something like 56 habitative parish-names to 103 topographical ones. If a similar analysis is made of the names in DB, where places of very varying size and status are recorded, the habitative category is larger, about 76, but still smaller than that of manors with topographical names, which number about 104. The higher proportion of habitative manors in DB is explained by the disappearance of some places like *Ortone* in Ripplesmere Hundred, the re-naming of others such as *Elentone* later Maidenhead, and most of all by the status of a number of the DB manors, like Leverton, Odstone, Avington, as subordinate settlements in large parishes. Not all names of modern parishes or DB manors can be placed in these two categories, and some major names, like Clewer, Reading and Sonning, and Buckland and Fyfield, stand outside this classification.

IV. SUMMARY OF SECTIONS I–III

Nearly all the names discussed hitherto have been those of land-units which I would consider to have been organised and farmed before the coming of the English. The settlements from which the land was worked may not have been in exactly the same places in the pre-historic, Roman and pagan Anglo-Saxon periods; but settlement-sites can move or disappear without a radical alteration in the pattern of administrative units, and without a total break in the process of wresting a living from the soil. The desertion of numerous villages in the late Middle Ages has not caused the parishes named from them to vanish from the modern map. It is not fashionable now to view the Anglo-Saxon settlement as involving the assarting of vast areas of land not previously exploited, or lying desolate after a period of chaos.

Whatever the situation as regards the mixture of people (and that is
the obscurest question in English history), there was probably a high
degree of continuity in the outlines of land-units, and the names
hitherto discussed are mostly assumed to refer to land-units which
bore a direct relationship to the earlier history of the region. Some
expansion of cultivated land must, however, be allowed for during the
long period from c. 400 to 1086. If we accept the current interpretation of the evidence of the Danish place-names in eastern England,
there was room in the Danelaw for a considerable amount of colonisation of less attractive areas after A.D. 865. If this was so, there is every
reason to suppose that there was still ample room for expansion from
existing settlements outside the Danelaw as late as the 10th century.

Some Berkshire place-names may be expected to refer to new
English settlements, in land not used for farming in Romano-British
times, and the next section of this Introduction will consider some
likely categories of names. Before embarking on this, however, it
seems advisable to try to summarise the conclusions arrived at by the
tortuous arguments of sections I–III.

First, it appears that even in an area such as Berks, where there is
very little linguistic continuity from Romano-British to Anglo-Saxon
times, there may be some evidence for continuity of estate boundaries.
Secondly, Berkshire is an area where none of the categories of names
previously considered to be signs of early Anglo-Saxon settlement
appears in sufficient strength to correspond to the archaeological
evidence for an early Anglo-Saxon presence. It is suggested here that
the topographical parish-names of N.W. Berks, particularly those in
ford and īeg and those referring to small streams, constitute the
necessary material. Some of the parish-names of the region, such as
Buckland, Fyfield, Kingston, refer to manorial ownership, legal
tenure or tax assessment, and names like these are likely to have
replaced earlier ones; but there is no other class of place-name which
seems to suggest the loss of an earlier English one, so names in ford
and īeg and names referring to small streams together with Faringdon
and the major names in hamm and wiell(a) may reasonably be
accepted as the primary Old English place-names of N.W. Berks.
There is no way of knowing whether they bear any relationship to
earlier British names. They can hardly be adaptations (like Eoforwic,
later York, from Evorōg), or they would not make such consistent
sense. The possibility of translation can never be ruled out, but there
is no evidence for it. Scientific opinion might be able to help with the

question of whether the Ock valley was cultivated in Roman times, or whether it is likely to have been brought into cultivation by Anglo-Saxons starting from scratch. The general tenor of the English p.ns. suggests that the Anglo-Saxons were much aware of the importance of the drainage arrangements, whether these were their own or those of previous cultivators. The earliest Saxons of north Berks, who were there at the end of the Roman period, needed cultivable land to maintain themselves. It is a question for the geographer whether in the Thames and Ock valleys land previously uncultivated or neglected during a period of chaos could have been rendered productive quickly enough to support the people of the early cemeteries at Frilford and Abingdon.

Thirdly, here and elsewhere in the county we have evidence for large estates subsequently split into smaller units, and there is no doubt that the larger units had topographical names more frequently than they had habitative ones. The documentary evidence shows that names in tūn were sometimes coined as a result of the late division of large estates. It is certain that some habitative names in which the first element is a personal name arose as the result of small land-units being allotted to king's thegns, and that a permanent name could be coined from the last lay holder when it was known that reversion was to a religious house. The difficult question of the significance of place-names in which a personal name is combined with a topographical term remains unsolved, and no evidence has been noted which throws light on the circumstances of their coining.

V. NEW SETTLEMENTS?

It has already been noted (808 f.) that the only part of Berks in which the land-units are laid out with respect to a Roman road is the S.E., where the Devil's Highway, traversing the heathland on the Berks/Sr/ Ha border, forms stretches of the boundaries of Stratfield, Swallow-field, Sandhurst (including Crowthorne) and Winkfield. Three of these parishes have names in feld, and it is possible that in Berks this el. is characteristic of regions which were first divided into land-units after the coming of the English. The names in feld are plotted on Distribution Map III, and some aspects of the use and distribution of the element are discussed on pp. 926–7. In E. Berks feld is used mainly in major names, and it is noteworthy that several parishes with names in feld (Binfield, Shinfield, Swallowfield and Winkfield) contain places with names in lēah, suggesting that if both types of name occur in the same vicinity feld refers to the more important settlement. In the charter boundaries the term hǣð-feld appears to mean 'common' (v. 633), and it is possible that the belt of country W. and S. of Reading where eight contiguous ancient parishes have names in feld was once a belt of land used for common pasture. Two of these eight names, Englefield and Shinfield, have folk-names as first elements. A high proportion of all Berks names in feld has a noun or descriptive term as first element (e.g. Binfield, Bradfield, Burghfield, Sheffield, Stratfield), but the term is compounded with personal names in Watchfield (in the N.W.), Winkfield and Wokefield. All three places are the subject of charters, showing that this type of estate was suitable for a thegn's holding, and it may be that the personal names *Wæcel*, *Wineca* and *Weohha* became attached to them as a result of earlier grants of this type; but we have no direct evidence bearing on this.

The connection of feld with woodland, outlined on pp. 926–7, has not always been stressed in EPNS volumes. The suggestion in Gl 4 193 that feld will be most common in counties with least woodland is misleading, and the statement that 'feld ... is rare in major p.ns., there being only 10 parish names, all of which occur in DB' plays down the proportion of all pre-Conquest names in feld which refer to major settlements. It is noteworthy, however, that feld is not found in major ns. in Berks in the two wooded areas west of Windsor Forest, namely Hormer Hundred and the district round Chieveley. The occurrence in the boundaries of Farnborough of the phrase *ut on þone feld* (p. 671) shows that in the 10th cent. the typical use of feld to mean 'open land on the edge of woodland' was known in S.W. Berks, but the element is not used in settlement-names there or in the woodland area N. of Abingdon. If, as is tentatively suggested here, there was a connection between feld and land used for common pasture, then the absence of names in feld in these two regions could be due to there being no large area of such land which was subsequently broken in for farming. There is heathland in Hormer Hundred, particularly on the slopes of Boar's Hill, and there are commons and heaths S. of Chieveley; but these are relatively small patches of land which today are not settled or farmed.

Some settlements with names ending in lēah may be the result of woodland clearing in Anglo-Saxon times. The main area in which lēah clusters is the part of S.W. Berks which contains the parish-names Chieveley, Fawley and Ilsley. The Hundred of Eagle (Pt 2 289), which has a name in lēah, included Fawley and the parishes N. and S. of it. This area has been assumed to be the heart of the wood of *Barroc* from which the county is named. It is the only part of the county in which manors held outlying woodland at the time of the charters (*v.* 619). There is a smaller cluster of names in lēah on the W. side of Hormer Hundred, where *Earmundesleah* was the name of a district in the 10th cent. (*v.* Pt 2 443). In E. Berks lēah is well evidenced, but the examples are more widely spread.

All names in lēah are marked on Map III. This brings out the general connection of the element with the wooded areas of the county, but no attempt is made to distinguish between the different senses, which range from 'wood' through 'glade or clearing' to 'pasture, meadowland'. It is noteworthy that areas in which the sense 'meadowland' is clearly evidenced are not far from woodland; this sense is certainly found in Lea, Whistley and Woodley on the W. boundary of Windsor Forest, and it may be evidenced in Radley on the E. side of Hormer Hundred. Only 14 out of the 54 names in lēah are major settlement-names, and only 10, a small proportion of the whole, are parish-names. The Berks names in lēah are analysed in some detail on pp. 935–6. Care must be taken to distinguish as far as possible between the senses 'wood' (well evidenced in Berks), 'clearing', and 'meadow', but this is not difficult in most cases, and it seems reasonable to see settlement-names in which the last two senses are clearly present as referring to new settlements of the Anglo-Saxon period. This is likely in the case of 'clearing' names because of the meaning, and in the case of 'meadow' names because lēah developed that sense relatively late in the OE period. A similar argument may be applied to Snelsmore and Southmoor, which contain mōr in the late sense 'barren upland'.

There are three parish-names in E. Berks containing hyrst. Sandhurst and Tilehurst may be late Anglo-Saxon or early post-Conquest settlements. St Nicholas Hurst seems to be the 10-hide land-unit granted under the name Whistley to a king's thegn in A.D. 968, and described under that name in DB. It has already been suggested that Whistley is a name of late OE origin, and assarting may have begun here in the early 10th cent. and continued till after the Conquest. Newland is obviously a late settlement, and Winnersh, the parish between Newland and St Nicholas Hurst may be another, though ersc is an ancient element in the vocabulary of E. Berks (*v. infra*).

Bray is a parish-name of French origin, but although the name is late, and the village may be a post-Conquest foundation, the large royal estate which DB describes here must have been an ancient unit, probably with scattered centres of habitation. The sparse French p.ns. listed on p. 945 show a marked concentration in Bray, Clewer and Winkfield.

VI. THE FORMATION OF THE SHIRE; EARLY ADMINISTRATIVE UNITS

Little has been said in this Introduction about the recorded history of Wessex in the 5th and 6th centuries, because the records do not throw light on the transformation of Berkshire into an English-speaking area with English place-names. The people of Berkshire presumably played some part in the expansion of Wessex in the second half of the 6th cent., but their own settlements were established long before this, and the victories and defeats of the period from A.D. 552 to 593 are not likely to have affected the pattern of settlement in Berks. It has been suggested by A. and C. Fox ('Wansdyke Reconsidered', *The Archaeological Journal* cxv, 1958) that after the defeat of 584 the West Saxon rulers withdrew to a position defended by the Wansdyke. This would leave Berkshire outside Wessex; but the theory has not gained general acceptance, and in any case such a withdrawal by the rulers of Wessex would be unlikely to involve a mass evacuation of peasants from their lands. The probability is that the farmers of Berkshire, probably English-speaking but perhaps of mixed Germanic and Celtic stock, stayed where they were throughout these troubled centuries and paid taxes to whatever authority was in a position to collect them.

The political history of the Upper Thames in the 7th and 8th cents. is of more concern to the place-name survey, as the survey is carried out on a county basis, and it is due to the events of this period that Berkshire became a shire. The course of events in this region from c. 650 to c. 850 was established by Sir Frank Stenton in HistAb 19–29. The key factor was the rivalry between Wessex and Mercia which made the areas later known as Oxfordshire and Berkshire debatable land between the two kingdoms. The district to the north of the river had passed to Mercian overlordship by 672–4, when BCS 34 was confirmed by King Wulfhere of Mercia, who was holding his court at Thame O. The district to the south of the river, however, was subject to Ine of Wessex in the late 7th and early 8th cents., and the monastery of Abingdon is a West Saxon foundation of this date. After Ine's resignation in 726 there is evidence that Æthelbald of

Mercia exercised direct authority south of the Thames. He gave the monastery of Cookham to the Archbishop of Canterbury (as mentioned in BCS 291), and the monks of Abingdon regarded him as their protector. After Æthelbald's murder in 757, the Mercian supremacy had to be re-established by Offa, and the Berkshire district was under the rule of Cynewulf of Wessex until 779, when Offa defeated him at Benson O and re-occupied the debatable land. Cenwulf, who became King of Mercia in 796, also ruled this territory, and even after the victory of Wessex at *Ellendun* in 825, which was followed by the permanent attachment of Kent, Surrey and Sussex to the West Saxon monarchy, the Berkshire region seems to have remained Mercian. A Mercian ealdorman named Æthelwulf was governing it under Beornwulf of Mercia in 844 (BCS 443), and he continued to do so when the land at last became West Saxon. The birth of the future King Alfred at the royal vill of Wantage in 849 is considered by Stenton (*Anglo-Saxon England*, p. 242, n. 4) to show that Berkshire had again become part of Wessex, and after that it was permanently a West Saxon shire.

The phonology of the place-names of Berkshire clearly suggests that the position of the region as a border district between Wessex and Mercia, and its periods of subjection to Mercian rule, did not affect the composition of its population. The place-names contain none of the Anglian features noted in O xix, and the Mercian dominion may be assumed to have been a political circumstance unaccompanied by any substantial incursion of Anglian settlers. The Angles of Englefield (Pt I 211) would not have been mentioned in a place-name if they had not been exceptional.

The main effect of the political vicissitudes of this period was the emergence of Berkshire as an administrative unit. There is no hint in records or place-names that the people of the wooded area of E. Berks (whose connection with the people of Sr is discussed *infra*) and the people of the Downs and the White Horse Vale regarded themselves as a coherent group, or that they were organised round a royal estate, as the people of Hampshire were round Southampton in the late 8th cent. During the period when the other West Saxon shires were coming into being in this way, and the ancient units of Mercia such as the *Tomsæte* were being administered by their own ealdormen, Berkshire may have been regarded mainly as the part of Mercia south of the Thames. There are two specific references to places annexed to Mercia as a result of King Offa's war with Cynewulf of Wessex. One of these is the statement in the Abingdon Chronicle (1, 14) that Offa added to his rule all the country between the Icknield Way and the Thames, from Wallingford to Ashbury, and the other is the statement in BCS 291 that Offa took away the monastery of Cookham and very many other towns from King Cynewulf, and added them to the Mercian kingdom. Ashbury is on the W. boundary of Berks, and Cookham on the E. boundary, and these two statements are suggestive of the way in which the two halves of the county became united.

It is after the return of the area to Wessex in the middle of the 9th cent. that the shire is first mentioned by its modern name. In ASC under the year 860 it is recorded that the ealdormen of *Hamtunscir* and *Bearrucscir* fought together against Danish raiders. *Bearrucscir* is anomalous among the shire-names of Wessex. It is neither formed from a settlement-name, like Hampshire, Dorset and Wiltshire, nor is it the name of a group of people, like Devon. Moreover, the wood called *Bearruc* was in the S.W. of the county, and while Berkshire is perhaps a natural enough name for the west of the area, there is something arbitrary about the inclusion in it of E. Berks, the country of the *Sunningas*.

It was perhaps in the reign of Edward the Elder that some of the south Midland shires, such as Oxfordshire and Warwickshire, were organised round and named from a town which was fortified against the Danes. Had the Mercian dominion south of the Thames lasted until after the accession of King Alfred, it is possible that Berkshire would have been named in a similar fashion, probably from the town of Wallingford, or that it would have been included in the region dependent on Oxford. If the area had been permanently part of Wessex, there might have been a shire named from one of the royal estates, perhaps Wantage, but it is not likely that its area would have resembled that of the modern county.

Some of the elements in the place-name-forming vocabulary of the people of E. Berks which link the region with Surrey are discussed on pp. 925–39 under the headings ersc, scēat, strōd. The more frequent use of hām for major settlements is discussed *supra*. The people from whom Wokingham is named are almost certainly the group referred to in the Surrey name Woking. Negative evidence for a connection between E. Berks and Sr is to be found in the absence of names in -hǣma- and -ing[2], and the rarity of names in tūn. The use of a similar vocabulary continues into ME with minor names like The Throat, The Hockett, Burchetts Green, and field-names like *Le Lymost* in

Windsor (*v.* Sr 356) and those in *rȳde, *ryde (*v.* 901 and Sr 364–5).

It is possible that the territory of the *Sunningas*, and even that of the *Rēadingas* of Reading, once formed part of a Middle Saxon kingdom which, though now represented only by the tiny shire of Middlesex, has been considered to include Surrey (Sr xiv–xv) and the part of Buckinghamshire between the Chilterns and the Thames (Bk xiv), which is adjacent to this part of Berks. The belt of names in feld, which may be an area of unsettled land used for common pasture in the early Anglo-Saxon period, separates this region from the rest of Berkshire.

The overlordship of Surrey belonged to Mercia in 672–4, when Frithuwold, sub-king of Surrey under Wulfhere of Mercia, granted 200 hides to the monastery of Chertsey (BCS 34). The bounds of this grant go along the Thames 'as far as the boundary of the next province which is called Sonning'. This manner of referring to the *Sunningas* does not suggest that their province is part of another kingdom. Frithuwold's under-kingship of Surrey is paralleled by the position of Cissa, who gave land for the foundation of Abingdon. Sir Frank Stenton (HistAb 18) regarded Cissa as an under-king of Wessex, though the gift of land for Abingdon happened at a time, between the death of Cenwalh in 672 and the rise to power of Cædwalla in 685, when the under-kings of Wessex had no overlord. The boundary between territory subject to Frithuwold and that subject to Cissa could have lain S.W. of Reading. When Cædwalla came to power in Wessex he extended his rule over at least part of Surrey, as is shown by the Farnham foundation charter (BCS 72); but Farnham is well to the south of Chertsey and Sonning, and this charter does not prove that Cædwalla had power on the Berks/Sr stretch of the Thames. His successor Ine was certainly king in Surrey, however, as he speaks of the Bishop of London as 'my bishop' in the prologue to his laws; and after this Surrey was in Wessex till the mid-8th cent. So far there is no indication of a kingdom-boundary corresponding to the modern one between Berks and Sr. Offa of Mercia is credited with taking Cookham from King Cynewulf of Wessex, but as Offa also ruled Surrey in the second half of the 8th cent. this event did not necessarily create the modern boundary. The break may have been as late as 825, when, after the victory of Wessex at the Battle of *Ellendun*, the men of Surrey submitted to Egbert of Wessex together with those of Kent, Sussex and Essex. It may be argued that the

failure of the *Sunningas* and **Rēadingas* to revert to Wessex at that
date suggests that they were never part of Surrey, but it seems equally
possible that their territory formed part of an arbitrary area which the
kings of Mercia felt able to retain. In any case, the east boundary of
Berks is probably the boundary of the *Sunningas*. If it was demarcated
as a kingdom-boundary after *Ellendun* it is perhaps a tidier version of
the ancient folk-boundary. It contains more straight stretches than
other parts of the county boundary, *v.* 844.

It may be noted in passing that Ekwall, PN -ing 27, has a misleading entry about this province. He questions the connection with
Sonning on the grounds that it is too far from Chertsey, and suggests
an association with Sunbury Mx on the grounds that the charter says
the province was N. of the Thames. BCS 34 (which is translated by
Professor Whitelock in *English Historical Documents* I, pp. 440–1)
does not say that the province called *Sunninges* was N. of the Thames;
and the list of places included in the grant contains Egham and
Chobham which lie immediately E. of the Berks/Sr boundary. The
actual settlement of Sonning lies on the N.W. boundary of the ancient
province, that of Sunninghill on its S.E. boundary. It is not certain,
however, that it included E. Berks north of a line from Sonning to
Windsor. Clewer, 'dwellers on the river-bank', is a folk-name, which
may indicate that there was another province in this angle of the
Thames, though there is no hint of this in surviving records.

Sir Frank Stenton (*Anglo-Saxon England*, p. 291) stated that the
Sunningas were the only West Saxon example of a primitive *regio* for
which there is documentary evidence. (A distinction must, of course,
be observed between the *Sunningas*, specifically called a province in
BCS 34, and the *Rēadingas*, whose corporate existence is an inference
from the place-name Reading and the size of the ancient manor.) If it
were accepted that this part of Berks was once part of Surrey, and
perhaps originally of a Middle Saxon kingdom, this would mean that
we have no record of ancient *regiones* or *provinciae* in Wessex, in spite
of the great wealth of charter material for some of the West Saxon
shires. Wessex, apart from the anomalous area of Berkshire, was
apparently divided into shires before the end of the 8th cent., and it
may be that the early date of the change to a system of shires subdivided into hundreds prevented more ancient administrative units
being mentioned in land-grants. On the other hand, there may have
been in parts of Wessex some traces of an even earlier type of unit,
perhaps based on pre-English arrangements. This would be the

'multiple estate' recognised by Professor Glanville Jones mainly in the North of England. It seems possible that the Blewbury estate of A.D. 944, the Hundred of Lambourn, and the *parochia* of the minster church at Thatcham represent such units, and another, based on Faringdon, may have extended on both sides of the Thames. The administrative system of Wessex before the creation of shires and hundreds was perhaps a mixture of 'tribal' units, represented in W. Berks by the sporadic -inga- names discussed on pp. 932–3, and these great estates, which in spite of their English names may have been based on pre-English units.

Since the political history of the shire was so unstable, it is not surprising that no permanent bishopric was centred within its boundaries. The first West Saxon see had its centre in Dorchester, only just across the Thames, and it is probable that the conversion of Berkshire, or at least the elimination of centres of pagan worship, was achieved from Dorchester in the years following the establishment of Birinus's see in 634. It seems clear that there are no place-names of heathen significance in Berks, and this has been considered (M. Gelling, 'Place-Names and Anglo-Saxon Paganism', *Univ. of Birmingham Hist. Journ.* VIII, 1961, and 'Further Thoughts on Pagan Place-Names', *Otium et Negotium*, Stockholm 1973) to be a characteristic of areas where pagan shrines were destroyed or converted to churches at an early stage of the conversion. The see of Dorchester was held by a second West Saxon bishop, the Frank Agilbert, but he abandoned it after 660, when the King of Wessex set up another bishop in Winchester. Between 675 and 685 and again in 737 Mercian bishoprics were briefly established at Dorchester, but for most of the time during which Berkshire was part of Mercia it came under the ecclesiastical authority of the Bishops of Leicester. In BCS 443 (*v.* 839) it is a Bishop of Leicester who gives Pangbourne to Beorhtwulf of Mercia, who then gives it to the Mercian ealdorman of Berkshire. The seat of the Bishops of Leicester was transferred to Dorchester after 877, but this did not affect Berkshire, as it was by then a West Saxon shire, and within the province of the Bishop of Winchester. When Edward the Elder subdivided the two West Saxon sees of Winchester and Sherborne he gave Wiltshire and Berkshire to a bishop whose seat in the late 10th century became fixed at Ramsbury W, near the border between the two shires. This bishop's manors included Sonning in Berks, and Bishop Osulf is referred to as 'of Sonning' in 964 (*v.* Pt I 133). The status of Cynesige, called 'Bishop of Berkshire' c. 931 in BCS 687, is uncertain. The see of Ramsbury was united with that of Sherborne before the death of Edward the Confessor, and the see of Sherborne became the see of Salisbury in 1075. Berkshire remained in the see of Salisbury till 1836, when it was transferred to the diocese of Oxford.

Some remarks on the outline of the county and the hundredal divisions may be of interest. In the main, the area of Berkshire was determined by the Mercian conquests south of the Thames in the 8th cent., and the portion of these Mercia retained after 825. In detail, the boundaries have been subject to some adjustments in recent times (leaving out of consideration the most recent alteration, which has removed the whole N.W.). In considering the outline presented on the map showing hundreds and parishes allowance must be made for a combination of ancient and recent boundary demarcations.

The N.W. boundary follows the Thames except for the line between Oxford and the Berks parishes of Wytham and N. and S. Hinksey; the charter bounds of Wytham (731) suggest that the line of the boundary here may have been the main course of the Thames in the 10th cent. The N.E. boundary follows the Thames, with some minor deviations along rivulets which may once have been the main course, but there is a major deviation in the vicinity of Reading; this is modern, resulting from the addition of part of Caversham (formerly in O) to the borough of Reading in 1911.

The boundary between Old Windsor and Egham Sr, which is the E. boundary of Berks, follows a rivulet for the first stretch after leaving the Thames, then is laid out in several straight stretches, the first two running S.W. from the source of the rivulet, the third running almost due S. The modern line is identical with that on the 1st ed. O.S. map, and this may be an arbitrary boundary laid out by the Mercian kings when they retained part of their province south of the Thames after the defeat at *Ellendun* in 825 (*v.* 841). The S.E. corner of the county, now occupied by the modern parish of Sunningdale, has been the subject of 19th-century adjustments, and the boundary line is not quite the same on the 1st ed. O.S. map as on the modern ones.

The south boundary of Berkshire is presumably the limit of Mercian rule in the 8th and 9th centuries, though none of the places mentioned in authentic records as being in Mercian hands at that period is in the S. of the county. A spurious charter of King Cenwulf of Mercia, BCS 366, gives a list of properties confirmed to Abingdon which includes places in the S.W. of Berks, the most southerly being Speen. This charter is a fabrication, however, and the main reason for assigning the boundary between Berkshire and Hampshire to this period is the difficulty of finding a better context. As described on p. 808, the portion of the boundary E. of Silchester makes some use of the Roman road called the Devil's Highway. It also makes use of the stream in Wishmoor Bottom and the R. Blackwater. The detour round Silchester is due to the transfer of Mortimer West End to Ha in the late 19th cent.; the old boundary respected the actual outline of the Roman town, which lay against the north boundary of Silchester parish, but there was only a slight indentation of Ha into Berks. Immediately west of Silchester the county boundary follows no ancient feature, but, like the E. boundary, it gives the impression of being laid out in straight sections, which is in marked contrast to the W. boundary of the county, and probably indicates that the land being divided was uncultivated heath. After this, the boundary meets the R. Enborne, conveniently flowing due E., and it follows that for a stretch. On leaving the Enborne, the boundary runs between E. and W. Woodhay, leaving the former in Ha, which is comparable to the divide between Stratfield Mortimer Berks and Stratfield Saye Ha in the S.E. The parish of Combe, which is now a projection of Berks, was only transferred from Ha in 1895; it has not been treated in these volumes, as the minor ns. and f.ns. of the parish may be closely linked with the material for the adjacent Ha parishes, which is not yet available.

The S.W. boundary, between Berkshire and Wiltshire, is late and artificial as a county boundary, but the irregular outlines of both the 1086 county and the modern one are following estate boundaries of the type discussed on pp. 626–7. These estate boundaries probably result from the splitting of larger estates in the Old English period, and some of the irregular outlines are probably due to the bisection of field-systems. Parts of the W. boundaries of Inkpen and Hungerford parishes can be seen on large-scale maps to have the 'step' outline which is often found in parish boundaries where charter surveys refer to furlongs and headlands (v. 626 f.). The parishes of Shalbourne W, Hungerford Berks and Chilton Foliat W were divided between Berkshire and Wiltshire at the time of DB. Adjustments made in the 19th cent. resulted in the present outline, but the DB county, shown on the map in VCH 1 after p. 321, has an outline of similar irregularity in the S.W. corner. The units of cultivation here are older than all the administrative systems of which we have record, and all boundaries have been obliged to respect the details of ancient arable arrangements, by contrast with the relatively straight lines which could be drawn in the heathlands of the E. and S.E. of the county. Even when one moves north from the extreme irregularity of the S.W. corner to the smoother outline of the W. boundaries of Lambourn and Ashbury, there are still traces of a 'step' pattern, which may indicate cultivation systems which were in use before the Mercian conquests of the 8th cent.; it must be noted that the charter bounds of Ashbury (694) only mention two cultivation features here, and some rectangular projections on this boundary could relate to pre-English fields, which influenced the estate boundaries before being replaced by different systems of cultivation, v. 627. The border parishes N. of Ashbury have the R. Cole as their W. boundary, which brings the county boundary back to the Thames. There are traces in historical records of an association of estates in Wiltshire, Berkshire and Oxfordshire which may be older than this boundary along the Cole and the Thames, v. Pt 2 366.

The hundredal divisions within which the material has been arranged in Pts 1 and 2 are those described in Professor O. S. Anderson's (now Arngart's) invaluable work, *The English Hundred-Names: The South-Western Counties* (Lund, 1939), which have been operative since the 13th cent. This conforms to the methods of most EPNS surveys of southern counties, though a slightly different system was followed in the Gloucestershire vols., where Professor Smith used a rationalised hundred pattern, treating detached portions of hundreds with the other parishes in their geographical area. The 13th cent. pattern used for Berks has marked disadvantages, the most noticeable arising from the artificial nature of the late Hundred of Reading, which is composed of eight scattered portions formerly belonging to the Abbey of Reading. This has caused the parishes of Blewbury, Cholsey, Bucklebury and Thatcham to be included in Pt 1 although they are geographically situated in the part of the county treated in Pt 2. If hundreds are to be used at all for this purpose, however, it seems advisable to accept the inconveniences under which the system operated in the Middle Ages. The scattered portions of Reading Hundred probably do not preserve, by their association in this late hundred, any pre-Conquest arrangements, but some other anomalies may be more significant. The attachment of Goosey to the Hundred of Ock, and that of Sparsholt to the Hundred of Wantage, may have their origin in apportionments of outlying meadow and woodland for which we have no other evidence. The Hundred of Cookham was only formed in the 12th cent. from the Hundred of Beynhurst, but although it is not ancient as a hundred, the fact that it consists of the scattered units of Cookham, Binfield and Sunninghill is significant, as these are the ancient components of the royal manor of Cookham. The Domesday hundreds, of which details are given in Anderson, might have been more useful units for the historian looking for significant pre-Conquest patterns, but the boundaries between them are not always ascertainable, and they are too far from the realities of the post-Conquest period to be a suitable framework for the place-name survey.

The location of hundred meeting-places is one respect in which the place-name survey has been disappointing. Mrs Lambrick's note on the meeting-place of Hormer Hundred (Pt 2 431–2) is conclusive, but this is not based on place-name evidence. Other hundred-names, such as Ripplesmere, Beynhurst, Charlton, Eagle, *Wifold*, *Nachededorn*, *Slotesford*, have not appeared as minor ns. or f.ns. in contexts which would have enabled them to be precisely located.

THE ELEMENTS IN BERKSHIRE PLACE-NAMES
(APART FROM PERSONAL NAMES)

The division of names into categories, practised in the corresponding lists in recent EPNS surveys, has not been followed here. The names quoted under each entry are arranged in alphabetical order, with no distinction between compounds and simplex names. Names which survive on maps are listed first, followed by a summary of the use of the el. in field-names. Names in which an element is compounded with a personal name are marked '(pers.n.)'. Elements marked * are not independently recorded in the form cited, or are hypothetical reconstructions from place-name evidence. Names marked † refer to surviving ancient monuments. Many terms are included which are not in Elements, but it has not been felt necessary to distinguish these. The list is cross-referenced to the list of *Old English Words in the Boundary-Marks of Berkshire Charters* on pp. 769–92.

āc OE, 'oak tree'. Broadoak, Nancry Coppice, Oakley (2), Ockwells, Ogdown. Occasionally in f.ns., e.g. *La Brodeok, Okdon* (Hurley), *Bissopesok, La Crikeledeock* (Windsor), *La Fayr(h)ok* (Bray), *La Pleyok* (Swallowfield). Also in charter bounds, 769.

*ācet OE, 'oak wood'. The Hockett, Hockett Wd; f.ns. in Burghfield and Tilehurst.

ād OE, 'beacon'. Noads Copse, Olding Hill; possibly Oad Ground (f.n. Wytham). For a detailed discussion of ād *v.* R. Forsberg, NoB 58 (1970), pp. 20–82.

æcer OE, 'plot of cultivated land, measure of land'. *Freq.* in f.ns., often with a numeral, e.g. *Le Fifacres* (Sotwell), *Lez Hundred Acr'*, *Twelfacres* (Reading). Occasionally with a pers.n., e.g. *Brungiveaker* (Wallingford), *Levegares-acre* (Earley), or a surname, e.g. *Reyneres-acre* (Kintbury). References to crops are rare, but cf. *Benacre* (Brightwalton). Other compounds include *Brodaker* (Bray), *La Burchacre* (Burghfield), *Le Free Acr* (Blewbury), *Long Aker* (Earley etc.), *Le Portaker* (Lambourn), *Le Ridacre* (Kintbury), *Shepacrs* (Earley), *Thuuelheker* (Waltham S.L.); *v.* gāra, smoke. Also in charters, 769.

æcer-mann OE, 'farmer'. *Acremanstrete* (lost street-n. Faringdon),

Akermanslande (f.n. Cumnor). The el. may be a surname, *v.* Reaney 1.

*ǣling OE, 'eel fishery'. Eling; Ealing Furlong (f.n. Steventon). G. Fellows Jensen, *Notes and Queries* March 1973, p. 118, suggests that this is the first el. of *Elington.*

æppel OE, 'apple'. Appleford. Occasionally in f.ns., e.g. *Aple Close* (Sandhurst).

æppel-tūn OE, 'orchard'. Appleton.

æsc OE, 'ash tree'. Ashampstead, Ashbury, *Ashdown,* Ashdown Pk, Ashridge. Occasionally in f.ns., e.g. *Aysshecroft* (Chieveley), *Assherugge* (Bray), *Asschforlong* (Cookham), *Asshurst* (Reading), *Naysshemede* (Aston T), *Nasshes* (Reading). Also in charters, 769.

æscen OE, 'growing with ash trees'. *Ashden.* Occasionally in f.ns., e.g. *Le Ayssengarden* (Moreton), *Ashen Moore* (Woodley).

æspe, æpse OE, 'aspen tree'. *Aps Mead* (f.n. Cookham).

æt OE, 'at'. Titlar.

ǣwiell OE, 'source of a stream'. The Evils (f.n. Sotwell).

*alt PrWelsh, 'hill'. Altwood.

alor OE, 'alder tree'. *Auborn* (R., later Enborne). One instance in charters, 769.

*alren OE, 'growing with alders'. *Aldern Wood* (f.n. Radley).

amore OE, bird-name. *Amberlond* (f.n. Windsor).

ancra OE, 'hermit'. *Ankerhawe* (f.n. W. Waltham).

angle ME from Old French, 'angle, corner, nook, outlying spot'. Angeldown, Anger Cottage.

apuldor, apuldre OE, 'apple tree'. *Brodappeldure* (f.n. Hurley), *Appull Dores* (f.n. Reading). Two instances in charters, 770.

āst OE, 'oast, kiln'. *Le Lymost* (f.n. Windsor).

āte OE, 'oats'. Occasionally in f.ns., e.g. *Otearshe* (Shottesbrooke), *Ote Close* (Hamstead Marshall), *Otecroft* (Speen, Sunningwell), *Otelandes* (Harwell), The Oatlands (Moreton).

atten, atter ME, 'at the'. Nancry Coppice, Noads Copse, Nuptown, Ray Ct, Rivar. Occasionally in f.ns., e.g. *Nasshes* (Reading), Nokes (W. Waltham), The Nyatt (Buckland), Nyatt (Radley), *Raymede* (Clewer), *La Rye* (Abingdon), *The Reves* (W. Hagbourne).

bæc OE, 'back'. *drægeles bæce* (later Grim's Ditch), and other instances in charters, 770.

bǣr² OE, 'woodland feeding ground for swine'. Bare Leys, Bear Grove, Bear Wd, Bere Ct, Billingbear; *Bere, Wodebere* (f.ns. Windsor). Two instances in charters, 770.

bærned, *berned OE, 'burnt'. *Brend Lane*. Occasionally in f.ns., e.g. *Brendebrigge*, *Barndestone* (Windsor), *Brendemulle*, *Brendelewe* (Bray), *Burnedhoke* (Winnersh).

bærnet OE, 'piece of land cleared by burning'. Barnets Mead (f.n. Reading), *Barnett Copse* (f.n. Cumnor).

bæð OE, 'bath, pool'. Balking; *The Bathe* (f.n. Finchampstead).

*bagga OE, probably 'badger'. Bagnor.

bake, beak ModE, 'land reclaimed for ploughing by clearing it with a mattock and burning the rubbish'. Occasionally in f.ns., e.g. Bake Ground and Pightle (Thatcham). *v.* burnbake.

balk ModE, 'strip of ground left unploughed between adjacent strips of the common field'. Occasionally in f.ns., e.g. Hanging and Mear Balk (Moulsford).

banke ME, 'bank'. Occasionally in f.ns., e.g. *Le Banke* (Swallowfield), *The Olde Bancke* (Sonning).

bār² OE, 'boar'. Boars Hill.

barge ME from Old French, 'barge'. *Milne Barge* (f.n. Reading), ?*Le Barge*, *Westbargeways* (f.ns. Wallingford). Modern ns., e.g. Barge Lane, Barge Piece (f.n. Bray). The Bargeway in Chilton leads up the Downs, and Mr F. J. Denzey informs us that *barge* has been heard locally as a term for a farm waggon.

barre ME from Old French, 'rod used as a gate-fastening, barrier closing an entrance, esp. to a city'. Occasionally in f.ns., e.g. *Le Barredich* (Windsor), *Le Barres* (Moreton), *Le Est Barre* (Newbury).

*barrōg PrWelsh, 'hilly'. Berkshire.

*beall OE, 'ball, rounded hill'. ?Ball's Hill, ?Cakeball. Occasionally in f.ns., e.g. *Ballelands* (Hungerford), Bigg Ball (Aston T), *Sawalla Balle* (Inkpen).

bēan OE, 'bean'. Beenham, Beynhurst. Fairly freq. in f.ns., e.g. *Benewell'* (Sulhampstead), *Benacre* (Brightwalton), *Bandon'* (Balking), *Benehull'*, *Beneland* (Coleshill), *Bene Lands* (Wargrave). The Balance (Bray) may be a corruption of the fairly common f.n. Bean Land(s). Two instances in charters, 770.

bearu OE, 'wood, grove'. Coombesbury. Occasionally in f.ns., e.g. Bear Hill (Cumnor), *Ernesber'* (Appleton), *The Beare* (Reading).

beau lieu, French p.n., 'beautiful place'. ?Beaulieu Ct Fm; *Bewley Lane*, *Beawlewstile* (f.ns. Clewer).

beau mes, French p.n., 'beautiful dwelling'. Beamy's Castle.

beau repaire, French p.n., 'beautiful retreat'. *Beaurepir* (f.n. Clewer).

bēce² OE, 'beech tree'. ?Beches, Beech Hill. Occasionally in f.ns., e.g. *Beche* (Harwell, Wallingford), *Bechamtone* (Hurley).

bedd OE, 'plot of ground where plants grow'. Occasionally in f.ns., e.g. *Netelbedde* (Uffington), *Trostelbedde* (Abingdon). *v.* also wīðig.

bel ester, French p.n., 'beautiful sojourn', or **bel estre** 'beautiful place'. *Belestre* (later Foliejon).

bēn OE, 'boon', possibly used in f.ns. with reference to manorial custom (*v.* Pt **2** 419). The Bins (Remenham), The Been (Steventon), Bin Mdw (Aston U.), *Bynemede* (Hagbourne).

beneoðan OE, 'beneath'. *Benethedowne* (f.n. Streatley).

bēo OE, 'bee'. Beckett. One instance in charters, 770.

beonet OE, 'bent grass'. Binfield.

beorc OE, 'birch tree'. Barkham. Occasionally in f.ns., e.g. *Berkele* (Windsor), *Berkemore* (Burghfield).

beorg OE, 'hill, mound, tumulus'. †Barrow Fm, †-Hill, †-Hills, †*Barrowe Streete*, †Brightwell Barrow, Burghfield, Farnborough, †Fox Barrow, *Roeberg*. Fairly freq. in f.ns., several instances referring to tumuli. *v.* brocen, lang, rūh, sinder. Also in charters, 770.

beorht OE, 'bright'. Brightwell.

bere OE, 'barley'. Barcote, ?Barwell Fm, *Berry*. Occasionally in f.ns., e.g., *Berlegh'* (Tilehurst), *Bereshortland* (Steventon).

bere-ærn OE, 'barn'. Great Barn. Occasionally in f.ns., e.g. *Le Bernhawe* (Windsor), *Berneye*, *Le Heybern* (Earley), *Berneacres* (Goosey).

beretūn, bærtūn OE, 'corn farm, outlying grange'. Barton Ct, Barton. Occasionally in f.ns., e.g. *Bertoncroft*, *Bartonemede* (Boxford), *Schepusberton* (Speen), *Le Barton* (Faringdon, Long Wittenham).

*bete² ME, beat ModE dial., 'rough sods hacked off for burning in preparing land for cultivation'. The Bates (f.n. Thatcham).

betwēonan OE, 'between'. Occasionally in f.ns., e.g. *Bytwenestret'* (Bray), *Bytweene Townes*, *Bytwynewayes* (Ashbury), Tweenbrooks (Bourton), *Twenedich* (Abingdon), *La Tweneheghe* (Uffington), *Tweentown Piece* (Marcham), *Tweenway Furlong* (Shrivenham).

*bic(a) OE, 'beak-like projection'. *Bikemere* (f.n. Hurley).

bile OE, 'bill-like projection'. *Bilefeld* (f.n. Hungerford), Sparrow Bill Piece (f.n. Kintbury).

*billere OE, a water-plant. *Bilderwell* (f.n. Bray).

binnan OE, 'within'. *Byn Milles*, Norbin's Wd. Occasionally in f.ns., e.g. *Byndyche* (Steventon), *Byn Mershe* (Boxford).

birce OE, 'birch tree'. Birch Fm, *Burchehurst*.

bircen² OE, 'growing with birches'. Birchen Inhams. Occasionally in f.ns., e.g. *Le Birchyn Close* (Hamstead M), *Burchencrofte* (Reading).

*bi(e)rcet OE, 'birch copse'. Burchetts Green. *Le Birchet* (f.n. Arborfield), *Burchat Coppis* (f.n. Finchampstead).

biscop OE, 'bishop'. *Bishops Beare* (later Bear Wd); *Byshoprich* (f.n. Englefield), *Bissopesok* (f.n. Windsor). One instance in charters, 770.

blæc OE, 'black'. Black Ditch, Blacklands, Blackmoor Stream, Blackwater, Blagrave, Blagrove, *Blakesole* (later Sole Fm). Fairly *freq.* in f.ns. The compound with land occurs in Ashbury, Brightwell, Childrey, Hagbourne, Moreton, Sotwell, Winkfield, that with mōr in Moreton, that with dīc in Shaw. *Blakewelle* occurs in Abingdon and Kintbury. Also in charters, 770.

*blæc-þorn, *blæc-þyrne OE, 'black-thorn, sloe'. *Blakeyern* (f.n. Lambourn), *Le Blakeyurn* (f.n. E. Shefford).

blēat OE, 'wretched, bare'. *La Blete More* (f.n. Englefield).

*blēo OE, 'variegated'. Blewbury.

blind OE, 'blind, hidden by vegetation, having no outlet'. Blind Lane; *Blyndelake* (f.n. Ashbury), *Le Blynd Pyttes* (f.n. Coleshill), *Blinde Posterne* (Winkfield).

bōc¹ OE, 'beech tree'. Bockhampton, Buckhold, Buckhurst; *Bukhurst* (f.n. Sandhurst).

bōc-land OE, 'land granted by charter'. Buckland, Bucklands; *Buckland* (f.n. Bucklebury), *Bokeland* (f.n. Cookham).

boga OE, 'bow, arch'. Bow; *Bofurl, Bowlonds* (f.ns. Ashbury), *Bowe Bridge* (f.n. Bucklebury), *Bowecrofte* (f.n. Winterbourne).

bolla OE, 'bowl'. *Bollewellethorne* (f.n. Longworth).

bordland ME, 'land held in bordage tenure', occurs as a f.n. in Appleford, Arborfield, E. Hendred.

bōt OE, 'help, remedy'. ?Botley.

botm OE, 'valley bottom'. Bothampstead. Occasionally in f.ns., e.g. *Le Botomes* (Stratfield M.), *La Bottoin* (Ashbury), The Bottoms (Buscot), *Bottne* (Hagbourne), *Bottondene* (Reading).

box OE, 'box tree'. Boxford, Boxhill Walk; *Le Boxes* (f.n. Aldermaston).

brād OE, 'broad'. Bradfield (2), *Bradley*, Bradley (2), Bradleywood, Broadoak, Broad St (Abingdon), Broadway, Broadway Copse. *Freq.* in f.ns.: the compound with feld occurs in Thatcham, with lēah in Hamstead M, Shinfield and Shottesbrooke, āc in Hurley, strǣt in Longworth, weg in Earley, Challow and E. Hendred. Broadmoor is common in minor ns. and f.ns. Cf. also *Brodeford* (Windsor), *Brademer'* (Bray), *Brodemed* (Swallowfield). Also in charters, 771.

brǣc[1] OE, 'brake, brushwood, thicket'. Brake occurs in minor ns. and f.ns., e.g. The Brake, Pine Brake, Rivey Brake. There are no early spellings.

brǣc[2], brēc, OE, 'land broken up for cultivation'. Breach Ho, Breaches Copse, and other minor ns. with mod. spellings. *Freq.* in f.ns., usually as a simplex n. with def.art., but occasionally with an adj. or surname prefixed. Cf. *Oldbrech'* (Steventon), *Woodbrech* (Cumnor). One instance in charters, 771.

brǣdu OE, 'breadth, broad strip of land'. Occasionally in f.ns., e.g. Bread Croft, (Shottesbrooke, Warfield), The Braids (Shaw).

brǣr, brēr OE, 'briars'. *Le Brerefurlonge* (f.n. Abingdon). Cf. also *The Bryerye Groue* (Welford).

braken ME, 'bracken'. *Brakenhalecroft* (f.n. Ashampstead).

brand OE, 'flame, place where burning has occurred'. *?Brands Bridge*.

bray(e) Old French, 'mud'. (not previously noted in English p.ns.) Bray.

brēmel, brembel OE, 'bramble'. Occasionally in f.ns., e.g. *Brembeltheye* (Warfield), *Brymylbuysh* (Ashbury), *Brembelcroft, Brembellond'* (Steventon). Also in charters, 771.

brēow-ærn OE, 'brew-house'. *Bruernhayes* (f.n. Abingdon).

briff. Obscure el. noted in Briff Copse, Briff's Copse and The Briffs (f.n. Brimpton), Brief (f.n. Compton B). Great Briff occurs in *TA* for Ashmansworth Ha.

brōc OE, 'brook'. Brock Hill, *Dudbroke* (pers.n.), Hakka's Brook (pers.n.), Holy Brook, Land Brook, Lulle Brook (pers.n.), Nor Brook, Radbrook Common, Shottesbrooke (?pers.n.), Westbrook (2), White Brook, Winterbrook. Fairly *freq.* in f.ns., e.g. *Brokehill* (Hamstead M), *Brookslad* (Moreton), *Le Smale Broke* (Hagbourne). In *Portmanebroc* (Reading) the el. has the meaning 'meadow'. *v.* myln. Also in charters, 771.

brocc OE, 'badger'. *?Brocwod* (f.n. Windsor).

brocen OE, 'broken'. *Brokenboroughe* (f.n. Reading), Broken Berry f.n. Farnborough). This compound may refer to a tumulus (beorg) with a robber's trench in the top.

brōm OE, 'broom'. Broomhall, Brumcombe. *Freq.* in f.ns., several times with -croft and -hyll. Occurs as simplex n. in *Le Brome* (Clewer), and as second el. in *Spillemannesbrome* (Earley). Broom Close is a common mod. minor n. and f.n.

brūn OE, 'brown'. Possibly used as hill-name in *Bruningemere*. Occasionally in f.ns., e.g. *Brouncroft* (Bucklebury).

brycg OE, 'bridge'. *Brands Bridge*, Burghfield Bridge, Coleshill Bridge, Gad Bridge, King's Bridge, Loddon Bridge, *Lytelbrygstrete*. Fairly *freq.* in f.ns., e.g. *Briggebroc* ,(Wytham), *Briggheit* (Burghfield), *Bradenbrugg* (Bray), *Horsbrugg* (Steventon), *Newebrugge* (Sunninghill), *Stanbrige* (Bucklebury). Occasionally in the metathesised form *burge*, e.g. *Burge Close* (Winnersh), *Foxburge* (Bucklebury). Also in charters, 771.

*brȳde OE, 'gushing stream, welling spring'. *Broad Ford*.

bucca OE, 'he-goat'. ?*Buckenhull* (f.n. Hurley). One instance in charters, 771.

bufan OE, 'above'. ?Bill Hill, Bowden, Bowdown Ho. The compound with dūn occurs also in *Bovedowne* (f.n. Reading), cf. *Abovedoune* (Streatley).

*bula OE, 'bull'. Bulmershe; *Bolecrofte* (f.n. Kintbury), *Bulherne*, *Bullheyse* (f.ns. Reading).

bulluc OE, 'bullock'. *Bulkefeld* (f.n. Coleshill).

bune OE, 'reed'. *Bunhulle* (f.n. Coxwell).

bunting OE, bird-name. ?*Buntingbury*.

būr¹ OE, 'cottage, dwelling'. *Boure* (f.n. Thatcham). Possibly in mod. ns. The Bower, Bower Brook Copse, Bower Land (f.n. Ashampstead).

burh, gen. and dat. **byrig**, OE, 'fortified place'. †*Æscesbyrig* (?pers.n.). †Badbury (?pers.n.), Berry Croft, Berry's Stile, †Blewbury, Borough Fm, Bucklebury (pers.n.), Buntingbury (?pers.n. + ing), Burford Bridge, *La Bury*, Burycourt, †Cherbury, Eastbury, †Grimsbury, Kintbury, †Lowbury, Narborough, Newbury, Northbury, †Perborough, †Ramsbury, †*Ramsbury*, †Rams Hill, Sowberry, Southbury, Youlbury. Fairly *freq.* in f.ns., where there are several instances of *Oldbury* (Ashbury, Chieveley, Maidenhead, Sunningwell), some of which refer to hill-forts, and several compounds (e.g. *Burycroft* in Brightwell, Speen, Steventon, Sunningwell) which have byrig as first el. in the sense 'manor'. For the various senses of the el. *v.* 923. The compound *burh-ēg (Borough Fm) possibly occurs again in *Byrweye* (Wytham); *Burgham* (Earley) is comparable. Also in charters, 772.

burhtūn OE, probably 'enclosed manor-house'. Bourton.

burna OE, 'spring, stream'. *Auborn*, Borne Copse, The Bourne, Bourne Ditch, Cranbourne, Enborne, Hagbourne (pers.n.), Lambourn, Pangbourne, Winterbourne. Occasionally in f.ns., e.g. *Le Bournehacche* (Hurley), *The Lysborne* (Bucklebury), *La Bournemed* (Reading), *Le Burne Landes* (Peasemore). Also in charters, 771.

burnbake ModE, identical in meaning with **bake**. Fairly *freq.* in f.ns., e.g. Burn Bake (Didcot, Farnborough, Ilsley), Burn Beak (Steventon), Burnbake (Chaddleworth, Draycott Moor, Kintbury), Burn Bake Piece (Lockinge), -Ground (W. Hendred).

*busc OE, 'bush'. Occasionally in f.ns., e.g. *The Busshe* (Reading), *Wynnebusshe* (Finchampstead). Bushy Leaze is a common minor n. and f.n., cf. also *Busshie Hamme* (f.n. W. Hanney), Bush Ham (f.n. Remenham).

*buscuc OE, 'clump of bushes', (not previously noted in p.ns.). ?Bussock. (The regular development would have been **Bushock*).

butt ME, 'archery butt'. ?Butts Rd; *Archery Butts* (f.n. Cookham).

butte ME, 'strip of land abutting on a boundary, short strip at right angles to others, short strip ploughed in the angle where two furlongs meet'. Fairly *freq.* in f.ns., usually uncompounded (*Butt(e)s, The Butts, Lez Butt(e)s* etc.), but cf. Black Butts (Cookham), *The Broad Butts* (Steventon), *Botteland* (Shinfield), *Sortebuttes* (Windsor).

buttuc OE, 'buttock, rounded slope'. Occasionally in f.ns., e.g. *Bottokes* (Ashbury), *The Buttokes* (Denchworth), Buttocks (Shellingford), Buttock Furlong (Long Wittenham). Cf. *Mother Dunche's buttocks*, alternative n. for Sinodun Hills.

bydel OE, 'beadle'. Occasionally in f.ns., e.g. *Bedellond* (Easthampstead), *Bedeland* (Blewbury), *Budelham* (Upton), *Bedellys More* (Finchampstead). The *e*-forms may be from Old French *bedel*.

byden OE, 'vessel, tub, steep-sided valley'. Beedon; ?*Budemore* (f.n. Ashbury), ?*Bedemede* (f.n. Bray), *Budewell* (W. Waltham).

byge[1] OE, 'corner, angle, bend of a river'. *Buye* (f.n. Compton B). Also in charters, 771.

*(ge)bysce OE, 'copse of bushes'. Occasionally in f.ns., e.g. *Bysshepytforlong* (Steventon), and several ns. in *-buysh* in Ashbury.

bytme, byðme OE, 'head of a valley', ?'hollow'. *Le Butme* (f.n. Windsor), *Betime* (f.n. Bray). One instance in charters, 772.

cǣg OE, 'key'. *Keiclose* (f.n. Welford), *Key Close* (f.n. Windsor). Journal **1** 14 quotes Professor Löfvenberg's suggestion that the ns.

cited *s.v.* in Elements contain a formally identical word of different meaning; **cǣg** 'key' would be particularly appropriate in this f.n., however.

cærse OE, 'cress'. Carswell, *Carswell*, Castlewell, Cresswells.

calu OE, 'bald, bare'. Occasionally in f.ns., e.g. *Caleweshullesend* (Windsor), *Le Calwefeld* (Hurley), Callow Fd (Ashampstead).

camp OE, 'field, enclosed piece of ground', possibly referring to Romano-British agriculture. Ruscombe. F.ns. in Bray, Earley, Hurley, Newbury.

*cang OE, ?'bend'. *Cange* (f.n. Kingston B.), *Congeham* (f.n. Kintbury).

canne OE, 'cup, deep valley'. *Candene* (f.n. Abingdon).

canoun ME from Norman French, 'canon, member of a community of clerks or of a cathedral chapter'. Cannon Hill.

castel ME from Old French, 'castle'. Castle St (2); occasionally in f.ns., e.g. *Le Castel* (Hurley), *Castelmede* (Speen), *Le Castell Close* (Stratfield M).

catt OE, 'cat'. Catmore, Cat St. Two instances in charters, 772.

cat(t)el ME from Norman French, 'cattle'. *Catelryding* (f.n. Windsor).

*cattes-braȝen ME, 'cat's brain', applied to mottled soil. Occasionally in f.ns., e.g. *Catsbraine* (Harwell), Catbrain Piece (Moreton).

cauce, cause ME from Norman French, 'causeway'. Causeway. Occasionally in f.ns., e.g. *Le Cawsey Ende* (Windsor), *Causeway Pond* (Sunninghill).

cāwel, cāl OE, 'rape, cole, cabbage'. Calden (f.n. W. Waltham).

*ceacge OE, 'broom, gorse, brushwood'. *Chaggynham* (f.n. W. Waltham).

cealc OE, 'chalk, limestone', perhaps used also of soil treated with lime. Occasionally in f.ns., e.g. *Chalkeford* (Steventon), *Chalcrofte* (Wytham), *Chalke Pytt* (Cholsey). Two instances in charters, 772.

ceald OE, 'cold'. Calcot, ?*Caldcot*, Caldecott, Cholswell. Occasionally in f.ns.; the compound with cot(e) occurs in Welford and that with w(i)ella in Ashbury, Coxwell, Moreton, Sandhurst. Cf. also *Chaldefeld* (Kintbury). *v.* also **here-beorg**.

cealf OE, 'calf'. Chalmore, Chawley. Occasionally in f.ns., e.g. *Chalvecrofte* (Lambourn), *Calvecroft* (Ardington), *Calueham* (Appleford), *Calves Leaze* (Reading), *Chaleueye* (Wytham). One instance in charters, 772.

cēap OE, 'trade, merchandise, a market'. Cheap St, *Chepestrete* (there is interchange with cīeping in both ns.); *Westchepe* (f.n. Bucklebury). In *Chep(e)acre* and *Chepland* (f.ns. Ashbury, Lambourn) the sense may be 'obtained by bargaining', or 'of low rental'; the last is suggested Gl **1** 249 for *the Cheepe acres*.

*cearr(e) OE, 'turn, bend'. ?Charvil; ?The Chear (f.n. Ardington).

ceart OE, 'rough ground'. ?Charvil.

ceaster OE, 'city, old fortification'. ?Adchester; *Chastrewey* (f.n. Coxwell). M. Cotton, ArchJ LIX (1961), p. 19, says that no dating evidence is available from the rectangular enclosure Adchester.

*cēd PrWelsh, 'wood'. ?Pingewood.

ceorl OE, 'peasant'. Charlton, Charlton Hundred, Charnham St. Occasionally in f.ns., e.g. *Cherleford* (Inkpen), *Cherleia* (Bray), *Charlewood* (Reading).

Cern PrWelsh, r.n. (derivative of *carn, 'cairn, rock'). Charney, Cherbury.

chapel(e) ME from Old French, 'chapel'. Chapelwick; occasionally in mod. f.ns., e.g. *Chappelfeild* (Englefield).

cheker ME from Norman French, 'ground of chequered appearance'. Occasionally in f.ns., e.g. *Chequer Acre* (Cookham), *Chakerland* (Reading), The Chequers (Sulhampstead), Checker Mdw (Sandhurst).

cīeping OE, 'market'. *Chipping Lamborne, Chepyngfaryngdon. v.* also cēap.

cild OE, 'child, young nobleman'. Chilton; *Chyldesthorne* (f.n. Steventon).

*cille OE, ?'spring'. G. Kristensson, *Namn och Bygd* LXI (1973), pp. 49–54, gives evidence from surnames and p.ns. for a ME *chille*, which in one instance is the name of a *fons*, and which he considers to mean 'spring'. The term is related to ceole 'throat, gully'. This is a possible first el. of Childrey, though the present-day topography provides no special support for it.

cirice OE, 'church'. Church Speen. Occasionally as first el. in f.ns., e.g. *Chyrchbrokemed* (Easthampstead), *Chircheweye* (Kintbury), *Le Chirchefold* (Basildon). *Churchestude* (Lambourn) may have been the site of a church, *v.* stede, styde.

clǣfre OE, 'clover'. Occasionally in f.ns., e.g. *Clauerhull'* (Compton B), *Claverdon* (Childrey).

clǣg OE, 'clay, clayey soil'. Clayground. Occasionally in f.ns., e.g. *Le Cleye* (Cumnor), *Le Cley* (Shinfield), *Cleyhull* (Abingdon),

Cleymed (Steventon), *Cleypitts* (Clewer), *Cleyputtes* (Hungerford), *Cleypyttys* (Newbury). Clay Hill is a freq. modern minor n.

clǣne OE, 'clean, free from weeds'. Occasionally in f.ns., e.g. *Clan-hull'* (Steventon), *Clenhurst* (Bray). Two instances in charters, 772.

clām OE, 'mud, clay'. Occasionally in mod. f.ns., e.g. Great and Little Clam (Hurley), Clam Close (Easthampstead). *v.* Ch 3 47. Professor Löfvenberg comments that it is difficult to see why the vowel should have been shortened in these f.ns.

clapper ME, 'rough bridge or stream-crossing'. The Clappers; *The Claper* (f.n. Welford).

clapper ModE dial., 'rabbit burrow'. Occasionally in mod. minor ns. and f.ns., e.g. Clapper Border, Clapper's Green, Clapper Close (f.n. East Garston).

clerc OE, 'cleric', ME, 'scholar, secretary'. Occasionally in f.ns., e.g. *Clerkslond* (Englefield), *Clerkenwell* (Coleshill and Reading).

clif OE, 'cliff, escarpment, river-bank'. Cleeve Hill, Clewer, (Kingstone) Winslow. Occasionally in f.ns., e.g. *Baylesclyve* (Leckhampstead), *Le Cleve* (Kintbury), *Le Clyve* (Little Wittenham), *The Cleve* (Harwell), *Clifland'* (Sparsholt). Also in charters, 772.

clod ModE dial., 'lump of earth'. Clod Acres (f.n. Hampstead M), cf. *Clodhangran* 772.

*clopp, cloppa OE, 'lump, hill'. Clapcot, Clapton.

clos(e) ME from Old French, 'enclosure'. *Freq.* in f.ns., with forms from 16th cent. or later. Cf., e.g., *Le Lane Close, Le Mydleclose, Le Moteclose, Le Netherclose, Rowe Close, Le Shepehouse Close, Le Upperclose, Le Westeclose* (all 1547, Thatcham).

cnæpp OE, 'hill-top, hillock'. Occasionally in f.ns., e.g. *Le Knappe* (Lambourn, Windsor).

cniht OE, 'youth, servant, soldier, retainer'. Knighton.

cnoll OE, 'hill-top, knoll'. Knowl Hill, Knollend. Occasionally in f.ns., e.g. *Le Knolle* (W. Waltham), *Knolle* (Coleshill), *Knonhill* (Steventon).

cnotta OE, 'knot, hillock'. *Les Knotts* (f.n. Ashbury).

*cobb(e) OE, 'round lump'. *Cobbewellfurl'* (f.n. Ashbury).

cōc OE, 'cook' (not previously noted in p.ns.). Cookham.

*cocc[1] OE, 'heap, hillock'. Weycock.

*cocc[1] or cocc[2] (OE, 'cock, wild bird'). *Cockden*, Cock Marsh. One instance of cocc[2] in charters, 772.

coccel OE, 'tares'. Cockney Hill; *Cockleforlong* (f.n. Wallingford), Cockle Croft (f.n. Welford).

*cocc-geset OE, 'place where woodcock are found'. Cox Setters (f.n. Hurley). Professor Löfvenberg comments that the second el. may be sæt 'ambush' or gesæte 'snare, ambush'.

*cocc-scyte OE, 'cock-shoot, glade where nets were stretched to catch woodcock'. Occasionally in f.ns., e.g. *Cockshet* (W. Waltham), Cockshot (Reading), Cockshots (Burghfield), Cockshut (Chieveley).

col¹ OE, 'charcoal'. ?*Calcot*, Coldridge, Coleridge, Coley; *Cole Readings* (f.n. Winnersh), *Coleweye* (f.n. Kintbury). *v.* also *colman.

cōl² OE, 'cool'. ?Coombesbury.

*coll OE, 'hill'. ?Coleshill.

*Coll, PrWelsh r.n., ?Coleshill.

*col-man OE, 'charcoal burner'. ?*Colmanora*.

conduit ModE from Old French. *Conductheads, Le Conduit Houses* (f.ns. Winkfield).

coni, con(n)ing ME from Old French, 'rabbit'. Occasionally in f.ns., e.g. *Conyhill* (Enborne), *Conyfeild* (Bray).

coninger, coningre ME, 'rabbit-warren'. Occasionally in f.ns., e.g. *Ye Conygree*, Cunnygaw Hill (Welford), *Conagecrofte*, Conegar (Hungerford), Coneygore (Kintbury), *Le Conyngre, The Coninger* (Newbury), *Conigre* (Speen).

coning-erth ME, 'rabbit-warren'. Occasionally in f.ns., e.g. *Conyngherthes* (Hurley, *Conyngre* also occurs in this parish), *Le Connyngerth* (Wallingford).

cony-burrow obs. ModE, 'rabbit-warren'. Occasionally in f.ns., e.g. Coneyberry (Moulsford), Conny bury (Woodley).

copis ME from Old French, 'coppice'. Freq. in mod. minor ns. and f.ns. Coppice Close is a common f.n.

copp OE, 'top of a hill'. *Copwayte* (f.n. Ashbury).

coppede OE, 'having a peak or top'. Cobbetycroft, Coppid Hill. *v.* also heall.

*(ge)coppod OE, 'pollarded, having the top removed'. Coppidbeech Lane. Occasionally in f.ns., where there are several instances of the common compound with þorn, e.g. Copy Thorn (Shrivenham), *Le Coppedeþorne* (Brightwalton).

corn² OE, 'crane'. ?*Cornes Mede* (f.n. Bray).

cot(e) OE, 'cottage, hut, shelter, den'. Ascot, Barcote, Beckett, Buscot (pers.n.), Calcot, *Calcot, Caldcot*, Caldecott, Circourt, Clapcott, Coscote (pers.n.), Didcot (pers.n.), Draycott, Elcot (pers.n.), Fulscot (pers.n.), Hodcott (pers.n.), Longcot (earlier

Cote(s))), Maidencourt, Norcot, Northcourt, Southcote, Wawcott, Westcot, Woodcote. Occasionally in f.ns., where there are further instances with ēast and west (W. Hagbourne), and norð (Goosey). Cf. also *Alcot* (Bray), *Aldecote* (Coleshill), *Cotehous* (Ashbury). *v.* court. Also in charters, 772.

*cot-setl OE, probably 'cottage-holding or the land belonging to it'. In f.ns. *Cossettell* (Garford), *Cossicle* (Marcham), *Cossical* (Longworth). Cf. also *Cotsetelesyde* (Little Wittenham), *Cotsettlemed'* (W. Hagbourne), *Cotsetelcroft* (Abingdon), *Cossettell Meade* (Blewbury, Buckland). *cot-setle* is recorded in ME with the meanings 'cotter' (*v.* cot-setla *infra*) and 'cottage holding or the land belonging to it', and the Latinised forms *cotsetla* and *cotsetlum* are recorded meaning 'cottage'. Professor Löfvenberg considers this explanation better for the simplex f.ns. than his earlier one quoted Pt 2 394. The compound f.ns. could contain this el. or cot-setla.

cot-setla OE, 'cottager'. *v.* *cot-setl *supra*. This el. has influenced the hundred-name *Cotsetlesfeld'* (earlier *Gossetefeld*).

cot-stōw OE, 'collection of cottages'. Fairly *freq.* in f.ns., e.g. *Le Costouwe* (Bray), *Cotstowe* (Lambourn), *Costow* (Shottesbrooke), *Wlurone Cothstoe* (Burghfield). Mod. forms include Casters (Shinfield), Causters, Costers (Wokingham), Costards (Burghfield). Probably in mod. minor ns. Costard's Copse, -Fm. Professor Löfvenberg observes that the word is used in the plural in the OE instances recorded. Two instances in charters, 772.

co(u)pman ME, 'merchant'. *Copmaneford'* (f.n. Buscot).

court ME from Old French, 'space enclosed by walls or houses, large house, manor'. Amner's Fm (earlier *Amenerscourte*), *Le Dounecourt*, Sparsholt Ct. Fairly *freq.* in f.ns., usually as first el., e.g. *Le Courtefeld* (Buckland), *Courtfeld* (Steventon), Court Fd (Milton), *Courte Close* (Abingdon), Court Close (Appleton). Cf. also *Fennicourte* (Faringdon), *Venn Courte Knapp* (Hinton W), *Lach Courte* (Abingdon), and several ns. in Buscot with owners' ns. as first els. In some of these f.ns. court may have been substituted for cot(e), but *Courtefeld* etc. could equally well denote land adjacent to a manor house, or where the manorial court met. For the sense 'place where a court meets' cf. Courtoak.

covent AN, ME, 'company of religious persons'. *Le Covent Garden* (f.n. Bisham).

cran OE, 'crane, heron'. Cranbourne, Cranemoor. Occasionally in f.ns., e.g. *Cranford* (Englefield), *Cranmore* (Fyfield), *Cronwelle* (Lambourn). One instance in charters, 772.

crate, crout ModE dial., variants of croft. Occasionally in f.ns., e.g. The Crate (Lambourn), Five Crates (S. N. Hurst), Crouts (Sandhurst), Ash Crate (earlier *Asshe Crofte* Sandhurst), East Croft (earlier *East Crat* Bucklebury).

cräwe OE, 'crow'. Crowthorne. Occasionally in f.ns., e.g. *Crawley* (Clewer), *Croweye* (Steventon), *Crowescroft* (Enborne), *Crawemed* (Inkpen), *Croweputtes* (Hanney). One instance in charters, 772.

crest ME from Old French, 'summit of a hill'. *Le Crestes* (f.n. Lambourn).

*crikeled ME, ?'bent'. *La Crikeledeock* (f.n. Windsor).

Crist OE, 'Christ'. Crissels Star.

*cröc OE, 'crook'. Crookham.

*croccere OE, 'potter'. *Crockeresrowe* (f.n. Hurley), *Crokkerescroft*, *Crockereshaw* (f.ns. Windsor, possibly a surname).

croft OE, 'small, enclosed field'. Berry Croft, Grasscroft, Kine Croft, North Croft, Peascod St. Skillcroft, Stonecroft, Woodcraft Wd, Woodcroft. *Passim* in f.ns., cf., e.g. *Barrowe Crofte*, *Castle Crofte* (Buckland), *Lokyngecroft* (Arborfield), *Le Whetecrofte*, *Le Woode Crofte* (Thatcham), *v.* also crate.

crois ME from Old French, 'cross, the Cross'. Occasionally alternates with other els. (cros, crüc³), e.g. *Croyslan* (later Crouch Lane), *La Croiz* (f.n. Basildon).

cros OE, 'cross, the Cross'. Arborfield Cross, Faircross. Occasionally in f.ns., e.g. *Whytecrosse* (Ashbury), *Crosherne* (Easthampstead), *Crosforlong'* (Steventon, here used as an adj. 'lying across').

crüc³ OE, 'cross, the Cross'. Arborfield Cross (earlier *Alpheldecrouche*), Crouch Lane. Occasionally in f.ns., e.g. *Sottewelle Crouche* (Wallingford), *Crouchstrete*, *Cruchefeld* (Hurley), *Crucheputtes* (Windsor), *Le Crouchfer* (Bray).

*crüg PrWelsh, 'hill, tumulus'. Cruchfield; ?Crouch Hill (f.n. Winterbourne).

crundel OE, 'chalkpit, quarry, gully'. ?Grumble Barn. Occasionally in f.ns., e.g. *Le Crundle* (Bray), *Crundul* (Earley), *Crondle* (Enborne), *La Rowecrondele* (East Garston). Also in charters, 773.

cü OE, 'cow'. Coworth Pk. *Freq.* in f.ns., e.g. *Cowbriggeforde* (Bray), *Cueffold*, *La Couwyk* (Reading), *Kowyke* (Thatcham), *Cunemede* (Burghfield), *Le Cowpit*, *Coweweye*, *Cowdyche* (Steventon). Cow Lease, -Leaze is a very freq. mod. minor n. and f.n.

culfer, culfre OE, 'dove'. Culver Lane. Occasionally in f.ns., e.g. *Culver Close* (Cookham), *Culvercrofte* (Binfield), *Le Culver Garden* (Wokefield), *Culuerham* (Hinton W).

*culferhūs OE, 'dove-cot'. Occasionally in f.ns., e.g. *Culverhouse Piece* (Newbury), *The Culver House* (Hungerford).

cumb OE, 'valley'. Britchcombe, Brumcombe, The Coombe, Coombe Fm (2), Coombe Grange, Compton, Compton Beauchamp, Farn Combe, Foxcombe, Hutchcomb's Fm (?pers.n.), Letcombe (?pers.n.), Titcomb, Whatcombe, Whit Coombe, Yatscombe (?pers.n.). Fairly *freq.* in f.ns., e.g. *Combeforlong*, *Combeweye* (Inkpen), *Scortescumbe* (East Garston), *Holecomb'* (Lambourn). Also in charters, 773.

Cunētīū, British r.n. Kennet. The proximate source of Kennet is PrWelsh **Cænēd*.

cut ModE, 'piece of land, possibly one assigned by lot' (O 438). Occasionally in f.ns., e.g. Broad Cut, Stone Cuts (Thatcham), Wood Cutts (Kintbury), Long Cut Piece (East Garston).

*cuttel ME, 'artificial water-channel'. *Cuttellond* (f.n. Steventon).

*cwabba OE, 'marsh'. Quab Hill; ?Squabbs (f.n. Thatcham).

cwēn OE, 'queen'. Queen's Arbour; *Quenegrave* (f.n. Windsor).

cweorn OE, 'quern'. ?*Cornhullemor* (f.n. Wytham).

cwice OE, 'couch-grass'. Occasionally in f.ns., e.g. *Quychemede* (Newbury), *Squich Close* (Wootton), Scutch Close (Radley).

*cwielm OE, 'well, spring'. Quelm Lane.

cycene OE, 'kitchen', alluding to land where kitchen produce is grown. Kitchen Piece. Occasionally in f.ns., usually with **close**, e.g. Kitchen Close (Bucklebury, Warfield etc.), *Le Kechyn Close* (Speen), *Kechyn Close* (Clewer), *Kytchine Close* (Welford), *Kechyn Grove* (Winterbourne), *Kitchinfeild* (Binfield).

cyl(e)n OE, 'kiln'. Culham.

cyning OE, 'king'. *Kingescumbe*, King's Bridge, King's Meadow, Kingston Bagpuize, -Lisle, Kingstone Winslow, Kingwood Ho. Occasionally in f.ns., e.g. *Kingesfrid* (Windsor), *Kingesgrof*, *Kyngesdon'*, *Le Kynggesokes* (Bray), *Kingesmede*, *Kingeswood'*, *Kynges More* (Blewbury). Also in charters, 773.

cȳta OE, 'kite'. Kiddington. Two instances in charters, 773.

dæl¹ OE, 'pit, hollow, valley'. ?Daldridge; *Delfurlong* (f.n. Maidenhead), *Depindale* (f.n. Windsor), *Dimmings Dale* (f.n. Swallowfield).

dāl OE, 'share, portion, dole', used to denote divisions of communally farmed land. Fairly *freq.* in f.ns., e.g. *La Shortdole* (Uffington), *Longedole* (Sonning), *Le Langedole* (Ardington), *Sharedoles* (Shrivenham), *Midelmestedole* (Sulhampstead), *Le Northeredole*, *Le Sutheredole* (Streatley); there are several examples of *Dole Mead*, *Dolmed(e)*.

dēad OE, 'dead'. Fairly *freq.* in f.ns., sometimes referring to infertility – e.g. *Dederuding'* (Thatcham), *Dede Close* (Boxford), *Dedemersch* (Hungerford), *Dedemore* (Faringdon); sometimes to the discovery of dead people – e.g. *Dedecherll'* (Denchworth), *Dedemanne* (Kintbury), *Dedeman's Lane* (Cookham), *Dead Woman's Bush* (Wootton). Cf. also *Dedwater* (Swallowfield), *Le Dead Water* (Speen).

dēaw OE, 'dew', probably 'moist, damp, wet', v. Löfvenberg 53–4. *Deuaker* (f.n. Sutton C), *Le Dewlonds* (Bray).

(ge)delf OE, 'digging, quarry'. *The Delves* (f.n. Appleford). v. stān-(ge)delf.

denu OE, 'valley'. Arlington, *Ashden*, Basildon (pers.n.), Cookham Dean, The Dean, Dean Ct, Dean Place Fm, Dean Wd, Denford, Hidden, Kiddington, Yattendon. *Freq.* in f.ns., e.g. *Dene* (Childrey, Reading), *Denefelde* (Earley), *Campedene* (Newbury), *Candene* (Abingdon), *Horsfoldesdene* (Inkpen), *Monekedene*, *Stonedene* (Wallingford), *Pyddene* (Hungerford). Also in charters, 773.

dēop OE, 'deep'. Deepstrood. Occasionally in f.ns., e.g. *Depford'* (Wytham), *Dephames* (Childrey), *Depindale* (Windsor), *Depemede* (Sandhurst). Also in charters, 773.

dey ME, 'dairy'. Occasionally in f.ns., e.g. *Daylese* (Windsor), *Dayleaze* (Denchworth), Day Mead (Shaw cum D), *Daye Pidell* (Woodley). deierie ME, 'dairy', occurs in *Deyremede*, *Darye Lease* (f.ns. Moreton, Buckland), and the synonymous deyhus in *Daye House* (f.n. Bisham).

dial ME, 'dial, sun-dial'. Dial Close. Occasionally in f.ns., e.g. Dial Close (Bradfield, W. Waltham), Dial Fd (Wokingham), Dial Row (Kintbury). John Field in a personal communication expresses doubt whether the suggestion about sun-dials carved in turf (made by W. W. Gill in *Notes and Queries* in 1943, adopted in Cu 469) is satisfactory, especially for southern p.ns. Possibly these ns. belong to the category which denotes land dedicated to the upkeep of part of the church fabric, and refer either to sun-dials on the church, or to the dials of early church clocks.

dīc OE, 'ditch'. Black Ditch, †Grim's Ditch, Mere Dike, Moor

Ditch. *Freq.* in f.ns., in most instances referring to drainage and boundary ditches, rather than to linear earthworks. Cf. *Blakdiche* (Shaw), *Diche Mede* (Enborne), *Dysshemede* (Reading), *Hakedic* (Chieveley), *Hethendiche* (Lambourn), *Merkedich* (Hurley), *Newedik'* (Bucklebury), *Rededich* (Cookham, Sunninghill), *Le Roughe Deche* (Reading), *Sarndich* (Brightwell), *Thorsdiche* (Sparsholt), *Le Updyche* (Uffington), *Waldich* (Wallingford), *Weydic* (Abingdon). Cf. *Le Dykedemede* (Bucklebury). Also in charters, 773–4.

dicor OE, 'ten'. ?*Dickerleaze* (f.n. Cookham).

dierne, dyrne OE, 'hidden, secret'. ?The Durnals. Occasionally in f.ns., e.g. *Derneford* (Coleshill, Newbury), *Durneford* (Binfield), *Durnegate* (Inkpen), *Durnepitte* (Lambourn). Also in charters, 774.

Dieu l'acresse, French p.n., 'may God increase it'. *Deulacresse* (f.n. Clewer).

dimming ME, 'the action of growing dim'. *Dimmings Dale* (f.n. Swallowfield).

dove-house ME, ModE. *Le Douehouse* (f.n. Faringdon). Cf. culferhūs *supra*.

dræg OE, 'drag, portage, slip-way, dray'. Draycott, Drayton. Both settlements overlook marshy ground, and a meaning 'sledge' would be appropriate for dræg.

drægel OE, ?'ribbon'. *drægeles bæce* (later Grim's Ditch).

drāf OE, 'herd, drove, road on which cattle are driven'. Cow Drove, Drove Fm, Drove Lane, Drove Way. Fairly *freq.* in f.ns., e.g. *Le Drove* (Aston T), *Le Drouelane* (Reading), *Droveend*, *Drovehegge* (Ashbury), *Bochamdroue* (Lambourn), *Oxedrove* (Ashbury).

drift ModE, 'road on which cattle are driven'. Occasionally in mod. minor ns. and f.ns., e.g. Drift Fm and Hill, Drift Rd, The Driftway.

drit OE, 'dirt'. *Dirthangelles* (f.n. Harwell).

dūn OE, 'hill, expanse of open hill-country'. *Æbbendun* (pers.n.), *Ashdown*, Ashdown, Bowden, Bowdown, Charlton Hundred, Coppington (pers.n.), Down Fm (2), Downfield, Down Hill, Downs Ho, Evendon's Fm, Faringdon, Hadden, Harrowdown (pers.n. + ing), Horn Down, Langdon Hill, Lollingdon (pers.n. + ing), Ogdown, Ryedown, Sanden, Snow Hill (earlier *Snowdon Hill*), Standen, West Down Lane, Winterdown. Very *freq.* in f.ns., sometimes as a simplex n. (e.g. *La Dune* Burghfield, E. Shefford), usually as second el. There is another *Langedone* (Uffington) and two more instances of *Snowdo(w)n* (Basildon, W. Hagbourne). Cf.

also *Aldedune* (Compton), *Bandon* (Balking), *Claverdon* (Childrey), *Godedune* (Hungerford), *Haidune* (Lambourn), *Holedone* (E. Shefford), *Moredowne* (Uffington), *Ridon* (Watchfield), *Thornidon'* (Kintbury), *Thornydowne* (Didcot). Also in charters, 774.

dūne l.OE adverb, 'down, below'. *Dunledcome* (later Letcombe Regis).

(?)*dūni(g)e OE. Dunmore Pond. The same el. appears to be found as a simplex n. in Dunny Grove Sr 386 and Denny Lo in Beaulieu Ha, for which J. E. B. Gover sends the following forms: *Dunie* c. 1300, *La Dunye* 1331, *Le Dony* 1490.

dūst OE, 'dust'. Occasionally in f.ns., e.g. *Dusteshull'* (Kintbury), *Doustforw* (Steventon).

ēa OE, 'river'. Eaton (2), Egrove, Irish Hill. Also in charters, 774.

eahta OE, 'eight'. *Acteacris* (f.n. Moreton).

eald OE, 'old'. Aldfield Fm, (?) Aldworth, Oldfield, Oldfield Fm (2), Old Hayes's Barn, Oldland Copse, Oldlands Copse. *Freq.* in f.ns., where there are several more instances with feld and land; 'old land' may be arable land later left unused, but 'old field' is more likely to be the oldest arable still in cultivation, *v.* Pt 2 480. *Aldeduna* (Compton) and *Oldemershe* (Ashbury) may refer in a similar way to land known to have been brought into agricultural use at a very early date. In *Aldestrete* (E. Shefford) and *Aldebury* (Maidenhead, etc.) the el. refers to ancient monuments. In *Aldecote* (Coleshill) it may be the pers.n. *Ealda*. Cf. also *La Eldedene* (Hurley), *Heldeham* (Woolstone), *Le Oldegrove* (Cumnor). In *Olde Broc* (Abingdon) the reference may be to a former river-course, as in *ealdan lacing*, *ealdan wæneting* Pt 1 13, 17–18. Also in charters, 774–5.

ealdormann OE, 'nobleman of the highest rank, chief officer of a shire'. Aldermaston. One instance in charters, 775.

earn OE, 'eagle'. Earley. One instance in charters, 775.

ēast OE, 'east'. Ascot, Ashridge, Aston (2), Eastbury, East Fields, Eastley, Eastmanton, Easton. Fairly *freq.* in f.ns., e.g. *Le Estefeld* (Shinfield), *East Lands* (Wargrave), *Estend* (Bucklebury), *Estemore* (Pangbourne).

ēasterra OE, 'more eastern'. This el. and westerra occur several times in the f.ns. of Reading.

ecg OE, 'edge'. ?Edgehill. Occasionally in f.ns., e.g. *Eggeclose* (Enborne), *Edgemede* (Radley, this may contain edisc). One instance in charters, 775.

edisc OE, 'enclosure, enclosed park'. Occasionally in f.ns., e.g. *Edishe*

Mead (Winnersh), *Edishe Close* (Stratfield M). One instance in charters, 775.

efen OE, 'even, level'. ?Evendon's Fm, ?Hemdean; *Evenhame* (f.n. Stratfield M).

efes OE, 'edge, border'. ? *The Reves* (f.n. W. Hagbourne).

ēgeð OE, *v.* īegeð.

elle(r)n OE, 'elder tree'. Occasionally in f.ns., e.g. *Eldernestubbe* (Bray), *Elderstibbe* (Hungerford), *Ellenestubbe* (Inkpen, Lambourn), *Ellostubbe* (E. Shefford), *Ellestubbe* (Compton), *Ellestube* (Wallingford), *Elrefurlong* (Cholsey), *Elleforlang'* (Wallingford). Also in charters, 775.

elm OE, 'elm tree'. Occasionally in f.ns., e.g. *Le Elme, Elmestubbe* (Steventon), *The Elme Acre* (Wallingford).

enche ME, 'manorial servant or workman'. Inchland (f.n. Steventon), *Le Henchlond* (f.n. Moreton).

ende[1] OE, 'end, edge of an estate, district or quarter of a village or town'. Churchend, Hillend, Hookend, Knollend, Mile End, Moorend, Slade End, Southend. Fairly *freq.* in f.ns. The sense 'end of something' (as in Mile End) occurs in *Le Cawsey Ende* (Windsor), *Le Dycheend* (Steventon), *Merelanende* (W. Waltham), *Le Tounesende* (Brightwalton, etc.). The sense 'district' occurs in *Caleweshullesend* (Windsor), *Hilleende* (W. Waltham), *Parkende*, *Southend* (Moreton), *Le Sharpende* (Cookham), West End (Longworth). In such ns. as *Tounesende, Southend*, West End the two senses are not clearly differentiated. Also in charters, 775.

ened OE, 'duck'. Enborne.

Engle OE, 'Angles'. Englefield, ?Englemere.

eofer OE, 'wild boar'. *Eversole* (f.n. Brightwalton).

eorl OE, 'nobleman'. *La Erlespath* (f.n. Lambourn).

eorðburg OE, 'earthwork'.? Arborfield. One instance in charters, 775.

eowu OE, 'ewe'. Occasionally in f.ns., e.g. *Ewendowne* (Uffington), *Ewe Lease* (Aston T), *Ewelez* (W. Hagbourne).

erber, herber ME from Old French, 'grass-covered piece of ground, garden, orchard'. Queen's Arbour.

ermitage ME from Old French, 'hermitage'. Hermitage, The Hermitage; *Le Hermitage* (f.n. Reading).

ersc OE, 'ploughed field'. Beynhurst Hundred, Ryehurst, Ryeish, Winnersh and following f.ns.: *Oteershe* (Shottesbrooke), Oat Harish (Grazeley), *Ruyhersch, Whetersshe* (Clewer), *Whetershe* (Winnersh), *Westhersshe* (Shottesbrooke), *Wydnershe* (Sandhurst).

*esāco- British, 'salmon'. R. Ock. The proximate source of Ock is PrWelsh **ehǭg*. Another R. Ock occurs in charters, 775.

-et(t) OE, -et(e), ett(e) ME, noun suffix denoting 'place characterised by what is named', esp. referring to a clump of trees. *v.* ***ācet, *bi(e)rcet.**

fæger OE, 'fair'. Faircross Hundred; *Fayrefurres* (f.n. Clewer), *La Fayr(h)ok* (f.n. Bray), *Fair-Oak* (f.n. W. Waltham).

*fæst-ærn OE, 'fortified house'. Vastern Rd.

fal(o)d OE, 'fold, small enclosure for animals'. Wyfield, *Wyfold* Hundred, Wyvols Ct. Occasionally in f.ns., e.g. *Foldyate* (Cumnor), *Le Chirchefold* (Basildon), *Horsfoldesdene* (Inkpen), *Wdefold* (Welford). *v.* also stōd-fal(o)d.

fealh OE, 'ploughed land'. *Falghulle* (f.n. Enborne).

fealu OE, 'fallow, pale brown or reddish yellow', perhaps used as a noun meaning 'fallow-coloured animal' (i.e. deer) or 'fallow-coloured wood'. Fawley.

fearn OE, 'fern'. Faringdon, Farley, Farley Moor, Farnborough, Farn Combe, Fernham. Occasionally in f.ns., e.g. *Fernehill* (Clewer), *Farenhulle* (Appleton), *Le Veronhill* (Reading), *Le Fernedoune* (Woolstone), *Fernfurlang* (Harwell). *Verne Peece* (Wallingford), *Farnesmor* (Newbury). Also in charters, 775.

fearnig OE, 'growing with ferns'. Occasionally in f.ns., e.g. *Fernyhull* (Hungerford), *Vernylond* (Inkpen).

feld OE, 'open country, unit of arable land' (*v. infra* for discussion of various senses). Aldfield, Arborfield, Binfield, Bradfield (2), Burghfield, Cruchfield, East Fields, Englefield, Ganfield, *Gossetefeld* Hundred, Littlefield, *Losfield*, Mousefield, Old field, Pitfield, Sheffield, Shinfield, Stratfield, Swallowfield, Warfield, Watchfield (pers.n.), West Fields, Wickfield, Winkfield (pers.n.), Wokefield (pers.n.). *Freq.* in f.ns., probably in most instances with the sense 'common arable field'. There are further instances of 'old field' (*v.* **eald** *supra*) and 'broad field'. 'East', 'west', 'north', 'south' and 'middle field' occur in several parishes. Cf. also *Burchefeldingefeld* (Burghfield), *Le Burgfeld* (Windsor), *Le Calwefeld* (Hurley), *Chaldefeld* (Kintbury), *Le Courtefeld* (Buckland), *La Felde, La Feldhous* (Windsor), *Mulesfeld* (Thatcham, pers.n.), *Rutherfeld* (Shellingford). A few instances with a surname (e.g. *Gentilcorsfeld* Bray) may have the late sense 'enclosed plot'. Also in charters, 775.

fenn OE, 'fen, marsh'. Occasionally in f.ns., e.g. *Venne* (Bray),

Wyntefen (Windsor), *Venn Courte Knapp* (Hinton W), *Fanne Mead* (Finchampstead). Mod. minor ns., e.g. The Fens, Venn Mill.

fennig OE, 'marshy'. *Fennicourte* (f.n. Faringdon).

fēorðung OE, 'fourth part, quarter'. Occasionally in f.ns., e.g. The Farthings (E. Hendred, Thatcham), *Ferthynges* (Steventon), *Farthinges* (Harwell). The meaning of this f.n. has not been established.

fīf OE, 'five'. Fifield, Fyfield; *Fifacre, Le Fifacres* (f.ns. Thatcham, Sotwell).

fīn OE, 'heap, especially of wood'. *Vynheye* (f.n. Burghfield), probably an enclosure for heaping firewood; the compound has been noted in K and Wo.

finc OE, 'finch'. Finchampstead.

fisc-pōl OE, 'fish-pool'. *Le Fyshpollondes* (f.n. Sotwell).

*flage OE, 'flagstone'. Fawler.

fleax OE, 'flax'. Occasionally in f.ns., e.g. *Flaxhawe* (Cookham), *Flexlonde* (Ashbury), *Le Flex Land* (Coleshill), *Flexlands* (Shrivenham), Flax Lands (Milton), Flexlands (Lockinge), *Le Flexlond* (Wallingford), *Flexfurlong'* (Moreton). Two instances in charters, 775.

flēot OE, 'estuary, small stream'. Fleet Copse. Occasionally in f.ns., e.g. *Enverd Flete* (Buckland), *Flete Brige* (Stratfield M), The Fleet (Milton), *Alflete, Snogeflete* (Steventon). One instance in charters, 776.

flint OE, 'flint'. *Flynt(e)furl'* (f.n. Ashbury).

flōde OE, 'stream, channel, intermittent spring or stream'. Floodcross, Inglewood. Also in charters, 776.

*flōd-gang OE, ? 'mill-race' (not previously noted in p.ns.). *Flotgong, Le Flodgonge* (f.n. Clewer). In view of the -*t*- of the earliest spellings Professor Löfvenberg prefers flot[1] 'deep water' as first el.

flōr OE, 'floor, pavement'. Fawler.

folie ME from Old French, 'folly, extravagant or (later) bogus building'. Foliejohn Pk, Folly Ct, some instances of Folly Fm.

folly ModE dial., 'clump of trees on the top of a hill or on open ground'. *Freq.* in mod. minor ns. (e.g. Folly Hill, several instances of The Folly, Ashbury and Cumnor Folly) and f.ns. The relationship of this el. to folie *supra* is not certain. It has been suggested that *folly* in this sense derives from Old French *feuillie* 'leafy bower or shelter'. It seems possible, however, that it is a transferred use of folie, due to a fancied resemblance between a small, isolated clump of trees and a folly built on top of a rise in a landscaped park. Folly Trees in Steventon, e.g., is a clump of three trees on a mound.

fōr OE, 'hog, pig'. ?*La Formore* (f.n. Sulhamstead).

ford OE, 'ford'. Appleford, Burford, Denford, Duxford (pers.n.), Frilford (pers.n.), Garford, Hatford, Hungerford, Lashford, Lyford, Moulsford (pers.n.), Northford, *Ockford* Hundred, Runsford, *Russieford'*, Sandford (2), Sandleford, Shalford, Shelling-ford, *Shortford, Slotesford* Hundred, Smitham Bridge, Stanford (3), Swinford, Tubworth (pers.n.), Wallingford (pers.n. + -inga-), Welford. *Freq.* in f.ns., e.g. *Athelardesford* (Shinfield, pers.n.), *Brodeford* (Windsor), *Cherleford* (Inkpen), *Depford'* (Wytham), *Durneford* (Binfield, Coleshill), *Langford* (Clewer), *Langeford* (Faringdon), *Maydeneford'* (Garford), *Somerford* (Cumnor), *Stomford* (Longworth), *Wodeford* (Abingdon). Also in charters, 776.

fore OE, 'in front of'. The Forehead. Occasionally in f.ns. (e.g. *Forland* Cookham, *Forlesemed* Maidenhead, *Forlese* Swallowfield, *Le Formede* Burghfield, *The Foredowne* Steventon) and in mod. minor ns. (e.g. Forbury, Fore Down). In some of these the meaning is 'part (of the hill, etc.) which juts forward'.

fore-burg OE, 'outwork', also 'forecourt'. The Forbury; *Forbury* (f.n. East Garston), Forbury (f.n. Garford). The Garford f.n. only occurs in a mod. spelling, and could be a compound of **fore** and **beorg** 'hill', as suggested for Forbury in Kintbury.

*fore-shetere ME, 'projecting piece of land' (probably arable land). *Forshceter, Foreshooter, Forsshetase* (f.ns. Englefield, E. Hendred, Wallingford). The corresponding ***forth-shetere** (which is the more common of the two in O) has not been noted in Berks.

forge, ME from Old French. Occasionally in f.ns., e.g. *The Forge* (Coleshill), *Le Forge* (Moreton, Peasemore), *Le Forge Pidell* (Reading), *Le Forgehouse* (Stratfield M).

*forst-hyll OE, 'ridge-like hill'. *Forsthull'* (f.n. Brightwell).

*forð-ēg OE, 'island in marshland'. The Forty. Occasionally in f.ns., e.g. *La Vortye* (Hurley), *La Vortie* (Cholsey), *Fortheye* (Reading).

fox OE, 'fox'. †Fox Barrow, Foxhill (Earley), Foxley Covert. Occasionally in f.ns., e.g. *Fox Earthe Hill* (Windsor), *Foxheye* (Faringdon), *Foxhull* (Swallowfield), *Le Foxhills, Foxle* (Reading), *Foxhullehegge* (Cookham). Foxbury (mod. minor n.) and *Foxboro'* (f.n. Radley) may be 'fox burrow'.

fox-hol OE, 'fox's earth'. Foxcombe, Foxhold. One more instance in charters, 776.

frēo OE, 'free from service or charge'. Occasionally in f.ns., e.g. Freeland Orchard (Burghfield), *Frelond* (Sotwell), *Frilond* (Sandhurst), Freelands (Sulhampstead), Freelands Copse (Stanford D), Free Ground (Arborfield), *Le Free Acr* (Blewbury).

frogga OE, 'frog'. Frogmore (2), Frogmoor. Occasionally in f.ns., e.g. *Froggelane* (Lambourn, Speen, cf. Frog Lane mod. minor n.), *Frogmarsh* (Reading), *Frogg Pitt* (Cholsey); the compound with mōr occurs in several parishes.

fuglung OE, 'fowling, bird-catching'. *Fowlyngehill* (f.n. W. Waltham).

fūl OE, 'foul, dirty'. Foudry Brook. Occasionally in f.ns., e.g. *Fulwey* (Lambourn), *Fullyfare* (Clewer), *Fulpolmed* (Maidenhead). Also in charters, 776.

furh (dat. **fyrh**, *****fȳr**) OE, 'furrow'. Fairly *freq.* in f.ns., mostly in the E. of the county, e.g. *Le Fyre* (Clewer), *Langifur* (Bray), *Longefere* (Clewer), *Medulfur*, *Le Merefur* (Bray), *Brokefere* (Maidenhead), *Le Groffur'* (W. Waltham), *Parke Feere* (Sonning), *Wydeforowe* (Steventon), *Holeforgh* (Ashbury). Also, in a more technical sense, in charters, 776.

furlang OE, 'a piece of land the length of a furrow', later 'a division of the common field cultivated as a unit'. *Freq.* in f.ns., e.g. *Brocfurlong* (Burghfield), *Denefurlonge*, *Woghforlong* (Earley), *Langeforlong* (Sulhampstead), *Langfourlong*, *La Medforlong*, *Ochortfurlong* (Englefield), *Musfurlong'* (Newbury), *Stoniforlong* (Enborne). Particularly *freq.* in the f.ns. of Abingdon, Ashbury, Steventon. Many of the 'field-names' in ME sources are furlongnames. Also in charters, 776.

fyrhð, **(ge)fyrhðe** OE, 'wood'. Great Thrift, Thrift Wds, Bigfrith (pers.n.). Fifth Rd in Newbury should probably be connected with *Le Frithe* in Newbury f.ns. Fairly *freq.* in f.ns., usually as a simplex n. (*Le Frith(e)*, *Frithe*, *Fryth*, *Frif*, *Le Friht*, etc.) or first el. (e.g. *Frithland* Wokingham, *Frythlane* Winkfield, *Frithmore* Burghfield). Cf. also *Cuppynggesfryth* (Stratfield M, pers.n.), *Kingesfrid* (Windsor). One instance in charters, 777.

fyrs OE, 'furze'. Occasionally in mod. minor ns. (e.g. Furze Lane) and f.ns. (e.g. Furze Cover Swallowfield, Furze Common Ruscombe, *Fursecrofte* Boxford). Furze(y) Close, Furzen Close are fairly common mod. f.ns., *v.* *****fyrsen** *infra*. One instance in charters, 777.

*fyrsen OE, 'growing with furze'. Occasionally in f.ns., e.g. *Firson* (Shinfield), *Le Fryssen* (Sandhurst), *Le Furson* (Binfield), *Le Fussenfelde* (Chieveley). In the first 3 instances the adj. may be used as a noun, or alternatively these may be dat.pl. of fyrs.

gærs OE, 'grass'. Grasscroft. Occasionally in f.ns., e.g. *Grasacra* (Brightwalton), *Gressecumb* (Ashbury), *Le Graslond* (Steventon), *Grascroft* (Moreton), *Le Grasse Close* (Radley), *v.* gærs-tūn.

*gærsing OE, 'grazing, pasture'. *?Gressyng Cop'* (f.n. Radley).

gærs-tūn OE, 'grass enclosure, paddock'. Garson's Lane, Garston Lane (Wantage street-n.), Garston's Copse, and mod, minor ns., e.g. Rowgarson. Fairly *freq.* in f.ns., usually as a simplex n., but cf. *Ebbengegarstone* (W. Waltham), *Noue Garstone* (Reading), *Love-daysgarston'*, *La Newgarston'* (Burghfield). Two instances in charters, 777.

g(e)alga OE, 'gallows'. *?*Galley Hill; Galliford (f.n. Lyford).

galla OE, 'sore, wet spot in a field'. Mod. minor ns., e.g. Gormoor, Spring Galls Fm. Occasionally in f.ns., e.g. *Galmore* (Sonning), *Gallcrofte* (Welford).

gamen OE, 'game, sport'. Gainfield; *Gamon Grene* (f.n. Finchampstead).

gāra OE, 'gore, point of land', in f.ns. 'land in the triangular remnant of the field after a rectangular pattern of furlongs has been drawn up'. *?*Garford, Gore Fm, Gore Hill. *v.* Pt 2 387, 410, 505 for topographical details. Fairly *freq.* in f.ns., usually as a simplex n., e.g. *La Gare, Le Gores, Gore, Le Gore.* Cf. also Gore Acre (Purley), *Gore Acr'* (Inkpen), Gore Furlong (Moulsford), Old Gore (Abingdon). *v.* gorebrode *infra.* Also in charters, 777.

gardin ME from Norman French, 'garden, enlosed plot used for the cultivation of vegetables, fruit, etc.'. *Freq.* in f.ns. in the compound Hop Garden, *v.* hoppe *infra.* Cf. also *Garden Eyet* (Sonning), *Le Ayssengarden* (Moreton), *Haselgarden* (Wallingford), *Hemp Garden* (Wargrave), *Le Hall Garden, Le Highe Garden* (Clewer), *The Saffern Garden* (Moreton).

gāt OE, 'goat'. Gad Bridge. Occasionally in f.ns., e.g. *Gotelade* (Warfield). One instance in charters, 777.

geard OE, 'fence, enclosure, yard'. Occasionally in f.ns., e.g. *Horsyard*, Hoveyards (Steventon), *The Yardes, Yerden* (Welford), *Le Yerdole* (Bray). *v.* also hoppe.

geat OE, 'gate, gap, pass'. Easthampstead, *?*Yatscombe. Fairly *freq.* in f.ns., sometimes as a simplex n., e.g. *Yate, La Yate, Le Yete.*

Compounds include *Durnegate* (Inkpen), *Flapp Yate* (Reading), *The Fludgates* (Newbury), *Foldyate* (Cumnor), *Hokeyat* (Shaw), *Medeyate* (Ashbury), *Mor Yatte Close* (Moreton), *Le Pondfoldyate* (Steventon), *Smaleyatesweye* (Buckland), *Le Streate Yate* (Coxwell), *La Whyteyat* (Earley), *Wyteȝate* (Hungerford), *Woode Yates* (Hamstead M). *v.* *wind-geat. Also in charters, 777.

geolu OE, 'yellow'. Youlbury.

(ge)gilda OE, 'member of a guild'. ?*Gildon Strete* (lost street-n. Faringdon).

gild-heall OE, 'guild-hall'. Yield Hall Lane; *Yieldhall Green* (f.n. Wokingham).

*glæd³ OE, 'glade'. ?*Le Glede* (f.n. Clewer).

*glæs² OE, 'clear, bright, shining'. ?*Glasemore* (f.n. Clewer).

gōd² OE, 'good'. *Godingeflod*. Possibly in a few f.ns., e.g. *Godedune* (Hungerford), *Godestisele* (W. Waltham). One instance in charters, 777.

*gogge ME, 'bog'. Gogs (mod. minor n.), The Gogs (f.n. Wootton).

golde OE, 'marigold'. Gold Hill, Goldwell. Occasionally in f.ns., e.g. *Goldhegge* (Enborne), *Goldwell* (East Garston).

gold-hord OE, 'gold-hoard'. *Goldhorde* (f.n. Wytham), ?*Goldewurthefurlonge* (f.n. Abingdon). *Goldhordeslond* (Streatley) is from Walter *Goldhord*.

gor OE, 'dirt, dung'. *Gorford* (f.n. Newbury). One instance in charters, 777.

gorebrode ME f.n., 'broad strip in the gore of an open field'. *Gorbrode*, *Garbrodeland* (f.ns. Sotwell, Childrey).

*gorsiht OE, 'growing with gorse'. *Gossetefeld*.

gōs OE, 'goose'. Goose Acre Copse, Goosey, Goswell. Occasionally in f.ns., e.g. *Le Goosacres* (Cookham), *Gosebroke* (Burghfield), *Goosehame* (Hanney), *Gosemore* (Long Wittenham), *Gospath* (E. Hendred).

goule, gole ME, 'ditch, stream'. *Goleheys* (f.n. Aston T).

goulet Old French, **golet** ME, 'gully, water-channel, ravine'. Long Gully. Occasionally in f.ns., e.g. *Le Gullet* (Greenham). The ModE variant *gully* (with substitution of -y for -et) occurs in mod. minor ns., e.g. The Gully, and f.ns., e.g. *Le Golly* (Chieveley), *Abbotts Golly* (Greenham).

græf OE, 'pit, trench'. ?Wargrave. One instance in charters, 777.

græfe OE, 'grove'. ?Wargrave.

*græg² OE, 'badger'. Grazeley.

grāf OE, 'grove, copse'. Blagrave, Blagrove, Egrove, Grove, Grove Fm, The Grove (Cookham, Faringdon), *Hurgrove*, Katesgrove Lane (pers.n.), Pinsgrove (pers.n.), Slow Grove, ?Wargrave. Fairly *freq.* in f.ns., sometimes as a simplex n. Compounds include *Chalfgrove* (Stratfield M), *La Heghegrove* (Hurley), *Le Heygrof* (Tilehurst), *Heygrof* (Hampstead M), *Kingesgrof* (Bray), *Northgrof* (Easthampstead), *Quenegrave* (Windsor), *Roughgrove* (Binfield). *Esegaresgrave* (Marcham) and *Gunnoresgrave* (Farnborough) have pers.ns. as first el. Also in charters, 777.

graffadge ModE dial., a kind of fence (*v.* Pt I 115). Graphage Ground, Graffadge Grounds (f.ns. Barkham, Waltham S.L.). Graffage occurs in *TA* for Pamber Ha.

grange ME from Old French, 'grange, outlying farm belonging to a religious house or to a feudal lord, where crops were stored'. Grange Fm; *The Grange* (f.n. Cookham).

grēne¹ OE (adj.) 'green'. Greenham. Fairly *freq.* in f.ns., e.g. *Grenebarowe* (Ashbury), *Le Grene Dyche* (Steventon), *Le Grene-linch* (Kintbury), *Grenelane, Greneweys* (Appleford), *La Grenewaye* (Compton), *La Greneway* (Cookham), but it is seldom possible to be certain that a n. contains the adj. rather than grēne² used as a first el. Also in charters, 777.

grēne² OE, 'grassy spot, village green'. Brightwalton Green, Clewer Green, The Green (Steventon), ?Green Way, and minor ns. for which no early forms are available. Occasionally in f.ns., e.g. *La Grene* (Cookham), *Le Greene End* (Steventon), *Heyriggesgrene* (Kintbury). *v.* also grēne¹.

grēot OE, 'gravel'. Occasionally in f.ns., e.g. *Gretecroft* (Easthampstead), *Grets, Greats* (Pangbourne), *Gretes* (Speen).

***Grīm** OE, originally a by-name of Woden, later perhaps 'devil, demon'. †Grim's Bank, †Grimsbury Castle, †Grim's Ditch (2), *Grimeshole* (f.n. Reading), *Grymesdych* (f.n. Bray).

grub(s), grubbed, grubbing ModE, probably referring to land which has been cleared of trees or weeds. In f.ns., *v.* Pt I 281. grubbed is the commonest of the three terms, and there are several instances of Grubbed Coppice and Grubbed Ground.

grynde OE, 'abyss'. *Grendewyll, Gryndwyll* (f.n. Ashbury).

***grytte** OE, 'sandy, stony soil or land'. *La Grutte, Grutte* (f.ns. Chieveley, Ashbury).

gydig OE, 'mad, insane, giddy'. Giddy Bridge; *Gidihale* (f.n. Bucklebury).

haca OE, 'hook'. *Hakedic* (f.n. Chieveley).

hæcc OE, 'hatch, grating, half-gate, gate'. The Hatch (Bray), Hatch Fm (Burghfield), Hatch Ho (W. Woodhay), Hatch Lane, Hinton-hatch, Maidenhatch. Also in minor ns. for which no early spellings are available. Fairly *freq.* in f.ns., sometimes as a simplex n., e.g. *Hatch* (W. Waltham), but cf. *Le Ballehacche* (Bray), *Le Bourne-hacche*, *La Denehacche*, *Suthhache* (Hurley), *La Denehache* (Aldworth), *Morhacche* (Burghfield). *v.* **hæcc-geat**. Where the topography can be checked, the evidence suggests that hæc(c) is more likely to be used of a barrier on a stream or river, hæcc-geat of a woodland feature, but the distinction is not absolute. Also in charters, *v.* 778.

hæcc-geat OE, 'hatch-gate, wicket'. In minor ns. and f.ns. for which only late spellings are available. *v.* Hatchet-, Hatchgate- in Index, and cf. The Hatchet, The Hatchett Ground, Hatchet Lane (f.ns. E. Ilsley, Enborne, Cumnor). *v.* hæc(c). One instance in charters, 778.

(ge)hæg OE, 'fence, enclosure', **hay** ME, 'part of a forest fenced off for hunting'. ?Hailey, Hayward, Heywood, Mapleash, Old Hayes's Barn, W. Woodhay. *Freq.* in f.ns., often in the pl., with a considerable variety of first els., suggesting varied types of enclosure. Cf. e.g. *Le Acrehey* (Ashampstead), *Aldheghes* (Easthampstead), *Bruernhayes* (Abingdon), *Cotheyse* (Hagbourne), *Chircheheye* (Balking), *Marlehay* (Ashbury), *Oxhaye* (Hurley), *Le Racke Heys* (Newbury), *Rotherhey* (Cumnor), *Somerheyse* (Windsor), *Tanheye* (Wantage), *Tymber Heis* (Reading), *Vynheye* (Burghfield), *Water-heysse* (Hagbourne), *Wodehaye* (Newbury). There are two more instances of the compound with wīd (*q.v.*), found in Woodhay. In two f.ns. in Stonor the el. is used of the sites of manor houses. Cf. also *The Heye* (Childrey), *Le Heygrof* (Tilehurst), *Heygrof* (Hampstead N). Also in charters, 778.

-hæma- OE (gen.), 'of the inhabitants'. Charnham Street, *Drayhem-wyke* (later *Drayton Wyke*), *Goshamwyke* (later Gooseywick), ?Sanham Green, Speenhamland, and the following f.ns.: *Bocham-droue* (Lambourn), *Chyldhemewe* (Harwell), *Cokhemesweye* (Coxwell), *Dreyamlond* (Steventon), Fulham Way (Moreton), *Lyham Weye* (Cumnor). Cf. also *byrihæme tune*, *vp hæme toune*, two settlements at Lambourn mentioned *c.* 1090 (Pt 2 334). All these are in the W. half of the county. Also in charters, 778.

hænep OE, 'hemp'. Occasionally in f.ns., e.g. *Hempeclose* (Winterbourne), *Hempefelde* (Midgham), *Hemp Garden* (Wargrave), *Hempsey* (Moreton).

hæpse OE, 'hasp, hinge'. *?Hopswell, Hapswell* (f.n. Harwell).

hæsel OE, 'hazel'. *Haslewick,* Hazelhanger. Occasionally in f.ns., e.g. *Haslebroke* (Harwell), *Haselgarden* (Wallingford), *Haselmere* (Reading), *Hasell Park, Haselwood* (Sonning). Also in charters, 778.

hætt OE, 'hat'. †Stancombe Hatts.

hǣð OE, 'heath, heather'. Hadden, The Heath (Hungerford), Heath Pond, North Heath, and minor ns. for which no early spellings are available. Fairly *freq.* in f.ns., usually as a simplex n. (*Le Hethe, La Hethe*) or first el. (e.g. *Heathfelde* Sunninghill, *Le Hethefelde* Leckhampstead, *Hethhill* Fyfield, *Le Hethynnyngs* W. Waltham, *Hethelandes* Thatcham, *Hethplot* Sandhurst). Also in charters, 778.

hǣðen OE, 'growing with heather'. *Hethendiche, Le Hetenestrete* (f.ns. Lambourn, Kintbury).

hafoc OE, 'hawk'. Hawkridge. Occasionally in f.ns., e.g. *Hawkcome* (Wokefield), *Haukhill* (Hungerford), *Hawkehill* (Cookham), *Hawkehilles* (Finchampstead), *Haukeslade* (Winnersh), *Hawkslade* (Theale). Also in charters, 778.

hafocere OE, 'hawker, falconer'. *Hauekeresforde* (f.n. Sulhampstead).

haga¹ OE, 'hedge, enclosure'. Haw Fm. Occasionally in f.ns., e.g. *Le Bernhawe, Le Oldhawes, Wodehawe* (Windsor), *Flaxhawe* (Cookham), *Aldhawes, Lokehawe* (Bray), *Philpeshawe* (Clewer), *La Hawe* (Finchampstead), *Haghecrofta* (Brightwalton). The distribution suggests that the term may have denoted an enclosure in woodland. Also in charters, 778.

*hagga OE, 'haw (the fruit of the hawthorn)'. *Haggebussh* (f.n. Clewer), *?Haggemor* (f.n. Balking). Cf. Hag Thorn (minor n. Easthampstead).

hālig OE, 'holy'. *Holy Water Lane.* One instance in charters, 778.

hām OE, 'village, homestead'. Beenham, ?Bisham (pers.n.), ?Caversham (pers.n.), Cookham, Crookham, ?Culham, Frilsham (pers.n.), Orpenham, Ownham (pers.n.), ?Remenham, ?Sindlesham, Sulham, Waltham, Wokingham, Wytham. Cf. also *Newenham* (f.n. Compton B.).

hamel ME from Old French, 'hamlet' (*v.* O 39). *Hammell', The Hamell Closes* (f.ns. Newbury, Sunningwell).

hamm OE, 'land in a river-bend, promontory, river-meadow, enclosed plot'. Barkham, Benham (pers.n.), ?Bisham (pers.n.), Bungum Lane, ?Caversham (pers.n.), ?Culham, Culham Shaw,

Diddenham (pers.n.), Fernham, Greenham, Ham Bridge, Ham Copses, Ham Fields, Ham Ho, Hugman's Wd (pers.n.), Lendham (pers.n.), Marcham, Midgham, ? Remenham, Shrivenham, ? Sindlesham, Thatcham, Wane Bridge, Warnham (pers.n.), Wicklesham (pers.n.), Witnam's Barn, Wittenham (pers.n.), and minor ns. for which no early spellings are available. Very *freq.* in f.ns., sometimes as a simplex n., more often as a second el., e.g. *Blakeham* (Eaton H), *Bradenham, Busshie Hamme, Gooseham, Langenham* (Hanney), *Burham* (Earley), *Calueham* (Appleford), *Horseham* (Fyfield), *Le Medeham* (Coleshill), *Milham, Thorneham* (Goosey), *Peishame* (Reading), *Rixhamme* (Thatcham), *Sandham* (Tilehurst), *Schortham* (Wytham), *Sidenham* (Cookham), *Stodham, Stonham, Wetham, Wideham* (Sulhampstead). There are several instances with pers.ns. as first el. Also in charters, 778.

hām-steall OE, 'homestead', possibly 'the enclosure of a homestead'. *Hamstall'* (f.n. Inkpen).

hām-stede OE, 'homestead'. Ashampstead, Bothampstead, Easthampstead, Finchampstead, Hampstead Norris, Hamstead Marshall, Leckhampstead, Sulhamstead. Two instances in charters, 779.

hām-tūn OE, precise meaning unknown. Bockhampton; *Bechamtone* (f.n. Hurley).

hān OE, 'hone, stone'. Occasionally in f.ns., e.g. Hone, *Redhone* (Sandhurst, Welford). Two more instances with rēad in charters, *v.* 779.

hana OE, 'cock'. Hanney.

*hangel OE, 'slope'. *Dirthangells* (f.n. Harwell).

hangende OE pres. part., hanginde, hanginge ME, 'hanging', used of places on a hillside. Fairly *freq.* in mod. minor ns. and in f.ns. Modern *Hanging* may sometimes be substituted for an earlier form from hangende (as in *Hangindelond* c. 1255, *Hanging Lands* 1717 in Moreton), but the *-ing* form is sometimes instanced early (as in *Hangingelonde* c. 1220–30 in Uffington, *Le Hangingegrave* 1318 in Hurley). Other instances include Hanging Downs (Tilehurst), The Hanging Park (Ashampstead). ME hanging, verbal noun, occurs as a simplex n., cf. Hanging of the Hill (Appleton), *v.* The Hanging(s) in Index.

hangra OE 'wood on a steep hillside'. Channy Grove (pers.n.), Hangers Copse, Hazelhanger, Oakhanger, Old Hangers, Shoppenhangers (pers.n.). Occasionally in f.ns., e.g. *Hazelhanger* (Brightwalton), *Oakehanger* (Cholsey), *Puthangre* (Compton), *Smalhangre-dene* (Hurley), *Sydehanger* (Lambourn), *Thornhanger*, *Hangre* (Boxford). *v.* *scȳt(e)hangra. Also in charters, 779.

hār² OE, 'hoar, grey', in p.ns. probably also 'boundary'. ?Harcombe Wd, Hawthorn Hill, ?Hoarecroft Shaw. Possibly in a few f.ns., e.g. *Harelegia*, *Harewell'* (Kintbury), Harestone (Shrivenham). Also in charters, 779.

hara OE, 'hare'. Possibly in a few f.ns., e.g. *Harehurst*, *Harewelle* (Reading), *Harecroft* (Moreton). Impossible to distinguish from hār².

*Hāre, *Hāra OE hill-name, 'the grey one'. ?Harwell and Horn Down.

*hasse OE, 'coarse grass'. *Le Hasse* (f.n. Brightwell).

hassuc OE, 'clump of coarse grass', hassock Berks dial., 'wood usually of Scotch firs with much coarse rank grass'. The Hassock (2), Hassock Copse (2). Occasionally in f.ns., e.g. *The Hassacke* (Tilehurst), *Le Hassock* (Stratfield M). One instance in charters, 779.

hēafod OE, 'head', used in various senses in p.ns. Hatford (*v.* Pt 2 391 for topographical discussion). Occasionally in f.ns., usually in the sense 'headland' (*v.* hēafod-land), as in Hades (Appleton), *The Marshe Hades* (Fyfield), *Grenhaud* (Steventon); but cf. *Swineshead* (Cookham).

hēafod-land OE, 'head of a strip of land left for turning the plough'. Occasionally in f.ns., e.g. *The Havedlond* (Tilehurst), *Hedlond* (Ashbury), *The Headlands* (Wytham). *Hauedacr'* occurs in Brightwell, as well as *Le Hauedlond*. Also in charters, 779.

hēah¹ OE, 'high, important'. Henley, ?*Hennor Mill*, High St (several), Hinton, Hinton Waldrist. Occasionally in f.ns., e.g. *La Heghegrove* (Hurley), *Henlawe* (Compton B), High Mead (Steventon), *Highe Feld* (Clewer), *Hyfeld* (Windsor), *La Hyewode* (Inkpen). Two instances in charters, 779.

healf OE, 'half', in p.ns. sometimes 'half-acre'. Occasionally in f.ns., e.g. *Sunenhelve* (Wallingford), *Webbehalve* (Inkpen). Two instances in charters, 779.

healh OE, 'nook, valley, corner of land, projection (of a parish or county)'. Bracknell, Broomhall, Cockney Hill, Hale Fm, *Hollicks*, ?Rushall. *Freq.* in f.ns., where there are a number of instances of *Hale*, *Le Hale*, *La Hale*, *Hayles*, *Les Helys*, etc. Cf. also *Brakenhale-croft* (Ashampstead), *Dernefordeshale* (Newbury), *Tayloreshale*

(Clewer). The sense 'land in a projection of an administrative area' is well evidenced in Berks, and is probably the usual one in this county. The sense 'river-meadow' has not been noticed with certainty, but cf. Hale Meadow (f.n. Aldermaston). Also in charters, 779.

heall OE, 'hall'. Hallcourt, Hall Place, ?Rushall. Occasionally in f.ns., usually in the compound Copped Hall, 'peaked hall' (v. coppede), which occurs as a mod. minor n. in Warfield and in f.ns. in Buscot, Clewer, Faringdon, Finchampstead, Hurley, Pangbourne, with forms from the 16th cent. or later. There are several further examples of *Halleplace*. Cf. also *Hallehyde* (Steventon), *Hallemed* (Cumnor), *La Mothalle* (Wallingford), *Mote-hall* (Tilehurst), *Schollehall, The Tyled Hall* (Faringdon), *Tylehall* (Clewer).

heall OE, 'rock'. ?The Hall.

heals OE, 'neck of land'. Haweshill.

hēap OE, 'heap'. *Le Shitehap* (f.n. Wallingford).

heard OE, 'hard'. *Harde Mede* (Boxford), *The Hardweye* (f.n. Coxwell).

*hearpa OE, 'harper'. ?Orpenham.

hearpe OE, 'harp', also used in p.ns. of a harp-shaped piece of ground. Harpwood, ?Orpenham; *The Harpe* (f.n. Binfield).

*hēcing OE, 'part of a field sown while the rest lies fallow'. This is the correct form of the word given as heccing in Elements. *Freq.* in f.ns., as a simplex n. or with -feld, usually with the def. art., sometimes in the pl., e.g. *La Hechynge* (Brightwalton), *Le Hechyn* (Chieveley), *Hechynges* (Englefield), *The Hichins* (Boxford), *The Hitchyng* (Welford), *Hechingfeld* (Moreton), *Le Hychynfelde* (Pangbourne), *Hitchin Fields* (Wantage). Cf. also *Inhechyng* (Childrey).

hecg(e) OE, 'hedge'. Occasionally in f.ns., e.g. *La Hegge* (Hungerford), *Hegg* (W. Waltham), *Heggecrofte* (Burghfield), *Heggeend* (Ashbury), *Goldhegge* (Enborne), *Milkhegge* (Cookham), *Sheetehegge, Spytelhegge* (Earley), *Smalhegge* (Inkpen). One instance in charters, 779.

hēg, hīg OE, 'hay'. Occasionally in f.ns., e.g. *Haidune* (Lambourn), *Hayecrofte* (Stratfield M), *Heycrofte(s)* (Bucklebury), *Heimeda* (Arborfield), *Haywaye* (East Garston). Three instances with weg in charters, 780.

hege OE, 'hedge, fence'. *La Tweneheghe* (f.n. Uffington). Two instances in charters, 780.

helm OE, ?'cattle-shed'. *Helm.*

heme ME. *v.* Hemley and f.ns. *Hemeueld* (Burghfield), *Hemelond* (Brightwell), *Hememede* (Wallingford). Professor Löfvenberg agrees with Ekwall's suggestion (O liii) that *heme-* in ME f.ns. is from hǣme 'inhabitants', and thinks that *Hemelond*, etc. may denote land held in common on the outskirts of a parish.

hemm OE, 'boundary'. Possibly in f.ns., e.g. *Le Hem Close* (Longworth), *Hemcrofte* (East Garston), Hemleaze (Bourton), *The Hemmede* (Childrey), *Hemparock, Hem Downe* (Welford); but Professor Löfvenberg would ascribe these to the same source as ns. listed under **heme**.

hengest OE, 'horse, stallion, gelding'. Hinksey (the el. may be a pers.n.). One instance in charters, 780.

henn OE, 'water-hen'. Hendred. Cf. also *Hen(ne)-Mede, He(n)nemeed* (f.ns. Ashbury, Steventon).

heorot OE, 'hart'. Hartley, Hartridge. Occasionally in f.ns., e.g. *Le Hertestrete* (Bray), *Hertham* (Sunningwell). Two instances in charters, 780.

here-beorg OE, 'shelter'. In the minor n. and f.n. Coldharbour, *v.* Pt 1 283, Pt 2 540.

hiche ME, 'enclosure of hurdles for penning sheep'. This may be the source of Hitch Copse, and of f.ns. The Hitch (Bucklebury, Compton, Stanford D, Thatcham, Woolhampton), *Hechecroft* (Speen), Hitchfield (Basildon), The Hitches, Hitch Fd (Streatley). These ns. may, however, contain a shortened form of *Hitching*, *v.* **hēcing supra.*

hīd OE, 'hide of land, an amount of land for the support of one free family and its dependants'. This was the unit of taxation in DB. Fifield, Fyfield, Hyde End, Hyde Fm (2), Nunhide. Hyde Fm also occurs as a minor n. for which no early spellings are available. Occasionally in f.ns., e.g. The Hyde (Bucklebury, Thatcham), *Le Hyde* (Reading), *La Hide* (Frilsham, Hungerford), *Hallehyde* (Steventon).

hielde OE, 'slope'. ?Yeldhall Manor. Occasionally in f.ns., e.g. *Hyld* (Steventon), *Tigheleheld* (W. Waltham). The compound with **tigel** occurs also in Sr 126, cf. *Tylerhelde* PN K 498.

hierde, hyrde, heorde OE, 'herdsman'. *Hurgrove.* Occasionally in f.ns., e.g. *Hurde Welle* (Welford), Herd Eyott (Radley).

higera, OE bird-name. Professor Löfvenberg points out that this is a more likely first el. in *Hiremere* Pt 1 38 than the suggestion made there. The forms for Heathfield WRY 5 215, which certainly contains *higera*, should be compared. There is one instance of *higera* in charters, 780.

hīwan, hīgan OE, 'household, religious community'. Henwick, Hen Wood: *La Hinecrofte* (f.n. Kintbury).

hlǣfdige OE, 'lady, Our Lady'. Ladye Place, Lady Ferry. *v.* Index for other minor ns. for which only l. forms are available. Occasionally in f.ns., an early instance being *Leuedifurlong* (mod. Lady Furlong) in Moreton. The reference is usually to land connected with a church, chapel or altar dedicated to the Virgin. Cf. also *Seynte Marieclose* (Lambourn).

hlāw, hlǣw OE, 'mound, tumulus'. Challow (pers.n.), *Hildeslow* Hundred (pers.n.), †Scutchamer Knob (pers.n.), Titlar (pers.n.). Occasionally in f.ns., e.g. *Brendelewe* (Bray), *Henlawe* (Compton), *Sidlowe* (Clewer), *Wynslowe* (Cookham). hlǣw is less well evidenced than hlāw, but is in the OE forms for Challow, *Hildeslow* and Scutchamer. Also in charters, 780.

*hlid¹ OE, 'slope'. ?Littlewick. One instance in charters, 780.

hlid² OE, 'gate'. ?Littlewick.

hlīep-geat, hlȳp-geat OE, 'opening in a fence over which deer can leap'. *Lippattisfelde* (f.n. Chieveley).

hlinc OE, 'ridge, bank'. ?Bill Hill, Linch Fm, Lynch Wd, Olding Hill. Minor ns. such as The Lynch, Lynch Way, for which no early forms are available. Fairly freq. in f.ns., often as a simplex n., sg. or pl., with the def. art., but cf. *Langelinche* (Uffington), *Pydelynch* (Coleshill), *Roulynche* (Inkpen), *Stanlynche* (Cookham, Sunningwell), *Totlynche* (Steventon). Also in charters, 780.

hlōse OE, 'pig-sty'. *Losfield*; *Loose* (f.n. Didcot). Possibly also in f.ns. *Losden* (Lambourn), *Loselond* (Didcot), *Loslondes* (Sotwell), *Louseacr'* (Inkpen), *Losfurlong* (Moreton, mod. Louse Furlong). Some of these may contain lūs, *q.v.*

hlot OE, 'lot, share, allotment'. Occasionally in minor ns., such as Lotmead Lane, Peaked Lot, for which no early forms are available. *Freq.* in f.ns., usually as a simplex n. Lot, The Lot(s), or with mǣd, as in *Lotemede* (Earley), *Lotmede* (Englefield, etc.), Lot Mdw (Shellingford, etc.). Cf. also *Le Lotte Acre* (Sandhurst), Lot Moor (Tilehurst), Four Mans Lot (Draycott M).

Hlȳde, OE stream name, 'the loud one'. Lydbrook, Lydebank, Lyde Copse: *Lude* (f.n. Maidenhead).

hnutu OE, 'nut'. Nutters Lane: *Nuthurst* (f.n. Windsor).

hōc OE, 'hook, angle, bend in a river, hill-spur'. Hookend Fm, Ninnock's Border, ?Pennyhooks Brook. Fairly *freq.* in f.ns., e.g. *Hoke* (Inkpen), *Le Hoke* (Bucklebury, Hagbourne, Winterbourne), The Hook (Cumnor, Didcot, E. Hendred, Speen, Woolstone), *Blakewellehoc* (Abingdon), *Brodehoke* (Longworth), *Pinneshok* (Windsor), *Le Reuehoke* (Harwell). *Hokeyat* (Shaw) may refer to a fastening on a gate.

hocc OE, 'mallow'. *Hockmore* (f.n. Coxwell).

hōcede OE, 'hooked, curved'. *Hoked More* (f.n. Sonning).

hōfe, OE plant-name, *Hoveyards* (f.n. Steventon).

hogg OE, 'hog'. Occasionally in f.ns., e.g. *Hogheys, Hoggehous* (Wallingford), *Hogemore* (Reading), *Hogstie Grove* (Woodley). Hogmoor occurs several times as a minor n., but no early spellings are available.

hōh OE, 'heel, spur of land'. Very occasionally in f.ns., e.g. *La Ho* (Cookham, the only well-evidenced example in the county), *Le Westhowe* (Sparsholt). Some instances of *How-*, e.g. *How(e)croft* (Pangbourne), *Howmeade* (Radley), are perhaps more likely to be from hol, *q.v.*

hol¹ OE, 'hole, hollow'. Hoe Benham. Occasionally in f.ns., e.g. *Hole* (Hinksey), *Bunshole* (Hagbourne), *Grimeshole* (Reading), *Poghole* (Welford). *Holedone* (Shefford) is perhaps 'hill with a hollow'. Also in charters, 780–1.

hol² OE adj., 'hollow, lying or running in a hollow'. How Lane. Occasionally in f.ns., e.g. *Holecomb'* (Lambourn), *Holecroft* (Tilehurst, Windsor), *La Holecrofte* (Inkpen), *Le Hole Crofte* (Kintbury), *Holmed* (Easthampstead). Also in charters, 781.

holegn OE, 'holly'. ?Hollingsworth Cottage. Very occasionally in f.ns., e.g. *Holyndene* (Bray). Two instances of *Holm* (Basildon, Brightwalton) could be from holegn or holme, *q.v. Holly* is fairly *freq.* in modern minor ns. and f.ns.

holme ME, 'river-meadow'. *Swylyngholme* (f.n. Earley).

holt OE, 'wood, thicket'. Brightwalton Holt, Buckhold, The Holt (2), Kintbury Holt, Ockwells, Sparsholt, Unhill Wd. Also minor ns., such as The Holt, Holt Copse, for which no early forms are available. Occasionally in f.ns., e.g. *Holte* (Letcombe R), *La Holte* (G. Shefford), *Wikenholt* (East Garston). One instance in charters, 781.

home ME, used adjectivally to denote land near the manor or farmstead. Home Fm (Earley), Homefield Copse (Bucklebury), and numerous minor ns. for which only late forms are available, *v.*

Index. Occasionally in f.ns., e.g. *Le Homeclose* (Woolstone), *Home-close* (Hagbourne), *Homcroft'* (Bray), *Le Homcroft* (Hurley), *The Homefelde* etc. (Reading), *Homeleez* (Coleshill), *The Homelease* (Buckland).

hoppe ME, 'the hop plant'. Very *freq.* in f.ns. and minor ns. in the compound Hop Garden, the earliest form noted being *Le Hope Garden* c. 1605 in Woodley. Hop Yard, probably an equivalent term, occurs some six times, and is also recorded in the first half of the 17th cent. Cf. also (The) Hop Ground (Radley, Sulham), Hop Platt (Compton).

hord OE, 'treasure'. Hardwell. *v.* **gold-hord**. One more instance in charters, 781.

horig OE, 'filthy, squalid'. Holyport.

horn OE, 'horn, projecting hill, projection of land'. Hormer Hundred, Hornhill, Horn's Copse (2). Occasionally in f.ns., e.g. *Le Horncroft* (Thatcham), *The Horncroft* (Beedon), *Pykehornescrofte* (Newbury), *Le Hornemede* (Enborne), *Hornewaye* (Winnersh). **hornede**, 'horned', occurs in *Hornedwere* (Windsor).

hors OE, 'horse'. Occasionally in f.ns., e.g. *Horsbrugg'*, *Horsyarde* (Steventon), *Horseyelake* (Wytham), *Horsfoldesdene* (Inkpen), *Horsehill, Horselade* (Ashbury), *Horspole* (Abingdon, Newbury).

horu OE 'filth, dirt'. Worley's Fm. Occasionally in f.ns., e.g. *Le Horemede* (Moreton), *Horeput* (Tubney). One more instance with pytt in charters, 781.

hosa, hose OE, 'stocking'. applied to a stream or lane. Hose Hill; *La Hose* (f.n. Hurley).

hrace OE, 'throat, pass'. *Rakeweyoslonde* (f.n. Earley).

hræfn OE, 'raven'. †Ramsbury, †*Ramsbury*, †Rams Hill, ?Ramslands, ?Ramsworth; ?Ramridge (f.n. Beedon).

hrēod OE, 'reed'. ?Radbrook Common. Occasionally in f.ns., e.g. *Redelak* (Sandhurst), *Rodeie, Redeie* (Pusey). One instance in charters, 781.

hrēof OE, 'rough'. *Reuemorwelle* (f.n. Hinksey).

hring OE, 'circle'. *hringpyt* (later The Manger).

hrīs OE, 'shrubs, brushwood'. Riseley; *Rispole* (f.n. Wytham).

hrīðer, hrȳðer OE, 'ox, cattle'. *Rotherhey, Rutherfeld* (f.ns. Cumnor, Shellingford).

hrōc OE, 'rook'. Rookmoor Mead (f.n. Ufton N, *Rockmore* 16th) is the only possible early example. Minor ns., such as Rook's Copse, Rook's Nest, The Rookery appear to be modern.

hrycg OE, 'ridge'. Ashridge, Ashridgewood, Chawridge (pers.n.), Coldridge, Coleridge, Curridge (pers.n.), Daldridge, Hartridge, Hawkridge, Irish Hill, May Ridge, Sheep Bridge, Westridge. Occasionally in f.ns., e.g. *La Rigge* (G. Shefford), *La Rugge* (East Garston), *Rudge* (Draycott M), *The Rudges* (Faringdon), *Le Ruggele* (Lambourn), *Ruggelond* (Ashbury), *Mapeldorerugge* (Windsor), *Ramridge* (Beedon), *Stanrugg'* (Warfield). Also in charters, 781.

hrycg-weg OE, 'ridgeway'. Ridge Way; *Ruggeweye* (f.n. Reading) *Rugweye* (f.n. Sunningwell).

Humbre ? pre-English r.n. Humber (2).

humele OE, 'hop-plant'. *Humeleg'* (f.n. Englefield).

hund OE, 'hound'. *Hundestret* (lost street-n. Wallingford), ? Hutchcomb's Fm. Occasionally in f.ns., e.g. *Hundeshille* (Bucklebury), *Hundegrave* (Peasemore), *Hundstichene* (Ashbury). Two instances in charters, 781.

hūne OE, 'hoarhound'. ? Unhill Wd.

hungor OE, 'hunger'. Hungerford. F.ns. contain several examples of 'hunger hill', persumably a derogatory n., e.g. *Hungerhull* 1370 Bray, *Hungerhulle* 1208–9 Brightwell.

hunig OE, 'honey'. Honeybunch Corner. Fairly *freq.* in modern f.ns., probably referring to sticky soil, *v.* Pt **1** 284 and cf. Honey Pot (W. Hendred).

hūs OE 'house'. Chamberhouse, Pyt Ho. Fairly *freq.* in f.ns. in compounds such as **culferhūs, dovehouse, malthouse, scēaphūs** (*q.v.*). Cf. also *Bakehous* (Newbury), *Cotehous* (Ashbury), *Fishouse* (Marcham), *Hoggehous* (Wallingford), *Millehous* (Pusey), *The Slathowse* (Coleshill), *Le Stonhous* (Hurley), *Tilehowse* (Bray), *Tylehouse* (Aldworth), *Westhus* (Compton B).

hwǣte OE, 'wheat'. Occasionally in f.ns., e.g. *Whetcroft* (Hurley), *Le Whetecroft* (Midgham), *Whethill* (Radley), *Whethull* (Childrey), *Whetlond* (Arborfield). *v.* also **ersc**.

hwīt OE, 'white'. Whitelands (2), Whitley (2), White Waltham, White Shoot, White Shute, Whiteshute Row, *Witeparroch* (later Paddock Wd), Witman's Barn. Occasionally in f.ns., where there are further instances with **land** (Ashbury), **lēah** (Cookham) and **scīete** (Inkpen, Uffington). Other compounds which recur are *Whitefeld* (Swallowfield), *Whitefield* (Wantage), *La Whitecrofte* (Brightwalton), *Wytecroft* (Peasemore), *La Witecroffte* (Kintbury), *La Whyteyat* (Earley), *Wytezate* (Hungerford). Also in charters, 781.

hyll OE, 'hill'. Ashbury Hill, Beech Hill, Boar's Hill, Boxhill Walk, Brock Hill, Coleshill (?pers.n.), Crissels Star, Gold Hill, Haweshill, Hillend Fm, Hill Fm (Appleford), *Hull*, Merryhill, Rood Hill, ?Sandleford, South Hill Pk, Speen Hill, Steventon Hill, Sugnell (pers.n.), Sunninghill, *Swineshill*, Thorn Hill (Lambourn), Wood-hill. *Freq.* in f.ns., where there are further instances with **brōc** (Windsor), **myrge** (*q.v.*) and **wudu** (Earley). Cf. also *Hulle* (Cook-ham, etc.), *Hilleende* (W. Waltham), *Le Hillond* (Bray), *Benehull'* (Coleshill), *Blakenhylle*, *Clanhull'* (Steventon), *Bromhulle* (Sand-hurst, etc.), *Caleweshullesend*, *Muchelehull*, *La Rowehull*, *Stanhill'* (Windsor), *Chalffhull* (B. Leigh), *Cleyhull* (Abingdon), *Fernyhull'*, *Haukhulle*, *Ryhulle* (Hungerford), *Hodeshull'* (Tilehurst, pers.n.), *Nethulle* (Earley), *Pilhulle* (Theale), *Pushull* (Hinton W), *Puthulle*, *Radenhulle* (Uffington), *Thornhulle* (Enborne), *La Wlfhull'* (Sul-hampstead). *v.* **fox**, **hungor**, ***ing-hyll**. Also in charters, 781.

***hylloc** OE, 'hillock'. *Hulloc* (f.n. Kintbury, 1267).

hyrne OE, 'angle, corner, recess in hills, projection of land'. Galley-herns Fm, Hernehill Down, Hurley. Occasionally in f.ns., usually as a simplex n. (*Herne*, *(Le) Hurne*, *Le Heron*), but cf. *Bulherne* (Reading), *La Giggehurne* (Binfield), *Osannehurne* (Bray, ME pers.n.), *Threhurn* (Swallowfield). Also in charters, 781.

hyrst OE, 'wood, wooded hill'. Buckhurst, *Burchehurst*, Hurst Fm, Hurst Hill, Nutter's Lane, *Pailehirst*, St Nicholas Hurst, Sand-hurst, Tilehurst, Tittenhurst (pers.n.). Occasionally in f.ns. There is another instance of *Nuthurst* in Windsor, cf. also *Le Hurst* (Burghfield, etc.), *Asshurst* (Reading), *Bargherst*, *Redhurst* (Bin-field), *Clenhurst*, *Iwhurst* (Bray), *Langenhurst* (Barkham), *Spelt-hurst* (Windsor). All instances except Hurst Fm in Lambourn are in the E. of the county or in Hormer H.

hȳð OE, 'landing-place on a river'. Hidden, Maidenhead.

īdel OE, 'empty, useless'. ?Idlebush Barrow; *Idellstartes* (f.n. Sonning).

īeg OE, 'island, land partly surrounded by water, dry ground in marsh, well-watered land'. *Berry*, Borough Fm, Charney, Cholsey (pers.n.), Eney (pers.n.), Fobney (pers.n.), Goosey, Hanney, Hinksey (?pers.n.), Levery, Mackney (pers.n.), Odney (pers.n.), Pusey, Ray Ct, Rowney, Shaftsey (?pers.n.), Tidney (pers.n.), Towney, Tubney (pers.n.). Occasionally in f.ns., e.g. *La Rye* (Abingdon), *Raymede* (Clewer), *Berneye* (Earley), *Hucleseye* (Hampstead N, pers.n.), *Langeneia* (Reading), *Rugheneie* (Burghfield), *Turveye* (Kennington), *Wadeiam, Witeneie* (Sutton C). *v.* forð-ēg. Also in charters, 782.

īegeð OE, 'small island'. Professor Löfvenberg considers *īeget the correct form). Fairly *freq.* in f.ns., e.g. *Niet* (Buckland), *Le Eight* (Fyfield, etc.), *Eyte* (Remenham, etc.), *Briggheit* (Burghfield), *Theofait* (Hungerford). *v.* also rod.

igil, īl OE, 'leech'. ? Illwills Border; *Ilemore* (f.n. Speen), *Illemeregrof* (f.n. Streatley).

impa OE, 'young shoot, sapling'. *Impiforlong* (f.n. Balking).

in OE, 'in', used of land near the principal residence of an estate (cf. home) or of land taken into an estate by enclosure or clearing. Occasionally in minor ns., e.g. Inleaze, Inwood, for which only l. forms are available, and in f.ns., e.g. *Incrofte* (Hinton W), *Indune* (Blewbury), *Inffeilde* (Winkfield), *Infurlong* (Shrivenham), *In-hechyng* (Childrey), *Inmede* (Welford), *Inmoor* (Draycott M), *Inwode* (Maidenhead). *v.* also inland. Only one instance has been noted of the elliptical use to denote position in an estate, *Uppinton'* (Abingdon).

*ing OE, 'hill, peak'. Inkpen. *v.* also *ing-hyll.

-ing², OE p.n. forming suffix. Balking, Ginge, Lockinge, *lucring, mydeling*, Wantage, Wasing. *v.* also *æling.

-ing-⁴, OE connective particle. *Æþeleahingwudu*, ?*Buntingbury*, Farley Moor, *Farlingmore*, Harrowdown, Lilley, Lollingdon; *Doddinglegh* (f.n. W. Waltham), *v.* -ingtūn. Also in charters, 782.

-inga- OE, gen. pl. of ingas. ? Ardington, Arlington, Billingbear, *Bruningemere*, Hormer, Pangbourne, Shellingford, Shinfield, Sunninghill, Sunningwell, Wallingford, Wokingham, Yattendon; *Burchefeldingefeld* (f.n. Burghfield). Also in charters, 782.

-ingas OE, suffix added to a pers.n. or p.n. to denote a group of people. Reading, Sonning (both pers.ns.).

*ing-hyll OE, 'hill, peak'. Inglewood, Inkpen.

-ingtūn OE, added to a pers.n. to denote an estate associated with that person. ? Ardington, Avington, Betterton, Brightwalton, Brimpton, Donnington, ? Elton, Everington, Kennington, Steventon, ? *Ulvritone*, Willington's Fm, Woolhampton.

inhōke ME, 'land temporarily enclosed from fallow land for cultivation' (cf. *hēcing). *Inhok* (f.n. Kintbury), *Innocks* (f.n. Hamstead M), ? *Ennox* (f.n. Finchampstead).

*īnïs PrWelsh, 'island, riverside meadow'. ? The Ince (f.n. Cookham.)

inland ME, 'land near a residence, land cultivated for the owner's use and not let to a tenant'. Occasionally in f.ns., e.g. *Inlands* (Reading, etc.), *Le Inlands* (Chieveley, etc.), *Inlonde* (Coxwell), *Le Inlonde* (Hagbourne, etc.).

*innām OE, 'piece of land taken in or enclosed'. Professor Löfven-berg points out that the correct OE form of this el. is *innōm. Occasionally in minor ns., e.g. Inholmes, Birchen Inhams, for which no early spellings are available, and in f.ns., e.g. Inhams (Barkham, etc.), *Inholmes* (Shinfield, etc.), *Eliotes Innome* (Earley, 1309), possibly *Newname* (Winkfield). Most examples are in the E. of the county, but instances occur in Lambourn and Shaw.

*inning OE, 'piece of land taken in or enclosed'. Occasionally in f.ns., e.g. *La Innynge* (Hurley, Ed. 1), Innings (Binfield, etc.), Black Innings (Woodley), *Green Inning* (Wargrave), *Le Hethynnynges* (W. Waltham), *Lytylynnynge* (Easthampstead), *New Innings* (S. N. Hurst), *Terresynnyng* (Shottesbrooke), *Upp Inninge* (Wokingham). All instances are in the E. of the county.

īw OE, 'yew'. *Iwhurst* (f.n. Bray).

lacu OE, 'stream'. Shurlock Row. Occasionally in f.ns., e.g. *La Lake* (Wargrave), *Lakefurlonge* (Hagbourne), *Beterlake* (Windsor), *Horseyelake, Schiplake, Stanelak'* (Wytham), *Pudlake* (Buckland), *Redelak* (Sandhurst), *Shirlak'* (Tilehurst). Also in charters, 782.

(ge)lād OE, 'watercourse, passage over a river'. *Gotelade* (f.n. War-field), *Le Hodlode* (f.n. Garford), *Milleslhade* (f.n. Wallingford). Also in charters, 782.

*læc(c), *læce OE, 'stream, bog'. Lashford Lane. Occasionally in f.ns., e.g. *Lacche* (Hinksey), *Lach Courte* (Abingdon), *Lechemore* (Earley).

*lǣd OE, 'drain, watercourse'. *Le Lede, La Ledde, Les Leede(s)* (f.n. Ashbury).

lǣfer OE, 'rush, reed, yellow iris'. Levery; *Le Lauermore* (f.n. Maidenhead).

*lǣge OE, 'fallow, unploughed'. Occasionally in minor ns., e.g. Layland's Green, Lay Fields, for which no early spellings are available, and in f.ns., e.g. *The Leyclose* (Winterbourne), *Leycrofte* (Hamstead M), *The Lelandes* (Wootton).

lǣs OE, 'pasture, meadow-land'. In minor ns., e.g. Broadleaze, Coppice Leaze, Courtleaze, Cowleaze, for which only l. forms are available. *Passim* in f.ns., e.g. *Calves Leaze* (Boxford, etc.), *Cowelese* (Shottesbrooke, etc.), *Forlese* (Swallowfield), *Horselees* (Coleshill, etc.), *Newe Lease* (Buckland), *Oxlese* (Cumnor, etc.). Forms from the dat., lǣswe, lǣswum, are rare, but cf. *Lysowes* (Sunningwell), *Lasum* (Wytham). *v.* also *busc, dey, morgen, sumor.

*lagge OE, 'marsh'. Occasionally in f.ns., e.g. *Laggelee* (Swallowfield, c. 1270), The Lagg (Windsor), Lags (S. N. Hurst, etc.). The Laggett, possibly a derivative, occurs in Fernham.

lām OE, 'loam'. ?Lambourn, Lambwoodhill; *Lomewood* (f.n. Wargrave), *Lutloomerssh, Micheloomerssh* (f.n. Ashampstead). Three instances with pytt in charters, 782.

lamb OE, 'lamb'. ?Lambourn.

lammas ModE, *v.* Pt 1 281. To the f.ns. quoted there add Lammas Close (Sunningwell), -Down (Compton), -Hole and Shaw (Cumnor), -Leaze (Hungerford).

land OE, 'land' (*v.* 935 for discussion of the various senses). Blacklands, Eblands, Land Brooke, Longlands, Newland, Oldland Copse, Oldlands Copse, Speenhamland, Whitelands (2). *Passim* in f.ns., often in the sense 'strip in a furlong in an open field', which is particularly well evidenced in Steventon. Cf. *Beneland* (Coleshill, etc.), *Le Brodeland* (Cumnor), Broad Lands (Steventon), *Th Eleauen Lands* (Wallingford), Eleven Lands Furlong (Appleton), *Hangindeland* (Compton), Irregular Lands (Cholsey), *Lytullonde* (Denchworth), *Otelandes* (Harwell), *Popielonde* (Uffington), *La Putlonde, La Stonylonde, Wetlond* (Brightwell), *The Rowelond* (Childrey), *Shortlandes* (Steventon, etc.), *Stronglond* (Sotwell). *v.* blæc, eald, fleax, frēo, lang, nīwe, sūr, wǣt, wōh. Also in charters, 782.

lane OE, 'lane, narrow road'. Crouch Lane, *Halseslane*, How Lane, Marsh Lane, and lost street-ns. in Abingdon, Newbury, Reading and Windsor. Occasionally in f.ns., e.g. *Buddeslane, Wadeslane* (Bray), *Frythlaan* (Winkfield), *Godewykelane* (Wokingham), *Le Lanefurlonge* (Inkpen), *Merelanende* (W. Waltham), *Stonylane* (Bucklebury), *Strecchelane* (Burghfield), *Wyllesteveneslane* (Steventon). *v.* also frogge.

lang OE, 'long'. Langdon Hill, Langley (2), Longlands. As ME affix in Longcot, Longworth. Very *freq.* in f.ns., especially in the compound with land, usually referring to the shape of the strips in a furlong. Cf. also *Langeborh', Longebereue* (Inkpen, Lambourn, 'long barrow'), *Langclose* (Hamstead M), *Langcroft* (Hurley, Newbury, etc.), *Langeford* (Faringdon), *Langeforlong* (Sulhampstead, etc.), *Langeneia, Longemarshe, Le Longe Piddell* (Reading), *Langenhurst* (Barkham), *Longacre* (Tilehurst, etc.), *Le Longe Breche*

(Coleshill), *Longedole* (Sonning), *Longemed* (Cumnor), *The Longe More* (Wytham), *Longestrete* (Tilehurst). Also in charters, 783.

lanket ModE, *v.* Pt **1** 281. The Lanket. Langett (f.n. Coxwell, Faringdon) may be a variant of this, rather than an instance of OE **langet.

launde ME from Old French, 'open space in woodland, forest glade, woodland pasture'. Fairly *freq.* in minor ns., e.g. The Lawn, Lawn Hill, for which only l. forms are available, and in f.ns., usually as a simplex n. with the def. art., e.g. *Lez Launds* (Sonning), The Lawn (Hungerford). The earliest instance is *Lez Litill Launds* (Chieveley 1550).

lāwerce OE, 'lark'. *Lauerkemere* (f.n. Hurley). Two instances in charters, 783.

lēac OE, 'leek, garlic'. Leckhampstead, *Lekestrete* (lost street-n. Wallingford).

lēac-tūn OE, 'leek enclosure, herb garden', later 'kitchen garden'. Occasionally in f.ns., e.g. *Larks Leyton* (Bucklebury), *Leytoneacre* (Wallingford), *Moldesleythton'* (Englefield), *Le Nethere Leyghton* (Arborfield), *Pitleighton* (Boxford).

lēah OE, 'wood, glade or clearing in a wood', later 'meadow, pasture' (*v.* 935–6 for discussion of the various senses). Bagley (pers.n.), Botley (?pers.n.), *Bradley*, Bradley (2), Bradleywood, Chawley, Chieveley (pers.n.), Coley, Eagle Hundred (pers.n.), Earley, Eastley, Farley, Farley Moor, Fawley, *Foxele* (later Foxhill in Earley), Foxley, Gidley (pers.n.), Hadley (pers.n.), Hailey Copse, Hartley, Henley, Hurley, Ilsley (pers.n.), Langley (2), Lea Fm, Lee Fm (2), (Bessels) Leigh, Lilley (pers.n. + ing), Littlewick, Lye Fm, Oakley (2), Paley Street (pers.n.), Poughley (2), Purley, Purley Fm, Radley (2), Riseley, Rockley (pers.n.), Streatley, Surly, Swinley, *Trindley*, *Tywele* (later Tileplace), Wadley (?pers.n.), Whistley, Whitley (2), Woodley, Woolley (2), Worley's Fm. Fairly *freq.* in f.ns., often as a simplex n., e.g. *Lee* (Reading), *La Lee* (Shottesbrooke), *Le Lye* (Thatcham). Cf. also *Berlegh'* (Tilehurst), *Cherleia* (Bray), *Estlegh* (Midgham), *Graue Leghe* (Englefield), *Radleye* (Steventon), *Le Ruggele* (Lambourn), *Suthlye* (Peasemore), *Westleye* (Inkpen). *v.* brād, **lagge*. Also in charters, 783.

lēoht OE, 'light'. *Lichtwud*, *Lichtlond* (f.ns. Cookham).

leyne, lain ME, 'layer, tract of arable land'. Lain's Barn. Occasionally in f.ns., usually as a simplex n. in the pl., e.g. *Lez Laynes* (Long Wittenham), The Lains (Challow), Layings (Fernham), The Lines

(S. N. Hurst), Lyons (Shinfield), occasionally in sing., e.g. Lion Mead (Cookham, Remenham), Lion Piece (Compton). The earliest instances are 1548 (Pangbourne, Long Wittenham), 1550 (Longworth).

lilie OE, 'lily'. Lilyhill Fm.

līn OE, 'flax'. Leonard's Plantation, Lyford; Linlands (f.n. W. Waltham). One more instance in charters, 783.

loc OE, 'lock, fold, river-barrier'. Occasionally in f.ns., e.g. *Braylok*, *Lokehawe* (Bray), *Le Lock* (Streatley), *Lockelond* (Ashbury).

*lōcere OE, 'shepherd'. *Locreslegh'* (f.n. Kintbury). One instance in charters, 783.

log(g)e ME from Old French, 'hut, small house', later 'house in a forest for temporary use, house at the entrance to a park'. Fairly *freq.* in l. minor ns. (*v.* Index). Occasionally in f.ns., e.g. *Logge* (Windsor), *The Lodge, The Olde Lodge* (Hungerford).

*lort(e) OE, 'dirt, mud, muddy place, swamp'. ? Lertwell, *Lortemere Lane*.

lufu OE, 'love'. Love Lane.

lūs OE, 'louse'. Possibly in Lousehill Copse, Louse Copse (f.n. S. N. Hurst), and some f.ns. listed under hlōse. E. A. Pocock, 'The First Fields in an Oxfordshire Parish', *The Agricultural History Review* XVI, pt II (1968), pp. 97–8, says that if cattle are wintered in a field in Clanfield O earlier called *Louse Furlong* their necks become covered with lice.

lūs-þorn OE, 'spindle tree'. *Lusethorn'* (f.n. Kintbury).

lȳtel OE, 'little'. Littlefield, *Lytelbrygstrete* (later Bury St). As ME affix in Little Wittenham, Littleworth. Occasionally in f.ns., e.g. *Litelaker, Lyteldon'* (Thatcham), *Lutlebroc* (Sutton C), *Le Lyttell Downe* (Coleshill), *Lytelforlang'* (Steventon), *Litlefeld* (Abingdon), *Lytullonde* (Denchworth), *Litelmed* (Compton), *Litulmour* (Maidenhead). Also in charters, 783.

mǣd OE, 'meadow'. Bray Mead, King's Mead, Northmead Lane, West Meadow, Widemead, Widmead. *Passim* in f.ns., often with ēast, norð, sūð, west. Sometimes as a simplex n. or first el. (e.g. *Medgate* Ashbury, *Le Medeham* Coleshill), but usually as a second el., e.g. *La Bournemed, Landemede* (Reading), *Brodemede, Le Hornemede* (Enborne), *Chaluemede* (Burghfield), *Crawemed* (Inkpen), *Le Dykedemede* (Bucklebury), *Haymede* (Swallowfield), *The Hemmede* (Childrey), *Longemed* (Cumnor), *Mulnemed* (Hungerford), *Le Newmede, Oldemede* (Sotwell), *Suremed* (Abingdon),

Townmannemede (Denchworth), *Le Whytemede* (Sparsholt). *v.* dāl, hlot, (ge)mǣne, smæl, smēðe, stǣnen, wĭd. Meadow, from dat. mǣdwe, is common in mod. f.ns. Also in charters, 783–4.

mæddre, mædere OE, 'madder'. *Maderlond* (f.n. Newbury).

mægden OE, 'maiden'. Maidencourt, Maidenhead. Occasionally in f.ns., e.g. *Maydewell* (Bray), *Maydeneford'* (Garford), *Maydecroft* (Sutton C).

(ge)mǣne OE adj., 'common'. ?Kilman Knoll Down, Manwood. Occasionally in f.ns., e.g. *Mene Crofte* (Earley), *Menecroft, Meane Land* (Ashampstead), *Meane Meade* (Clewer), *Menemede* (Coleshill), *Mon Mede* (Long Wittenham), Mean Mead (Longcot, etc.), *The Manmore* (Reading), Minmoor (Fyfield). Also in charters, 784.

(ge)mǣre OE, 'boundary'. May Ridge, Mere Dike, ?Meashill. Occasionally in f.ns., e.g. *La Meredich'* (Greenham), *Merfurlong* (Steventon), *Merewey* (Leckhampstead), *Marwellfurl'* (Ashbury). In *The Common Meare* (Steventon) the el. means 'balk of a ploughland'. Also in charters, 784.

mæst OE, 'mast of a ship', possibly used of a pole stuck in the ground. ?*Mastforlong* (f.n. Steventon).

*malpas, Old French appellative, 'difficult passage'. Malpas. The Co example referred to Pt **1** 222 is 1½ miles S.E. of Truro.

malthouse ModE, fairly *freq.* in minor ns. (*v.* Index) and f.ns., e.g. Malthouse Corner (Windsor), -Close (Pangbourne), -Ground (Thatcham, etc.). Forms are 16th cent. or later.

mann, monn OE, 'man'. Eastmanton; *Le Monneswathe* (f.n. Faringdon). Cf. No Man's Land, etc., *v.* Pt **1** 284.

mantle ME from Old French, 'mantle'. ?*Mantel* (f.n. Windsor).

*mapel OE, 'maple tree'. Mapleash Copse.

mapuldor OE, 'maple tree'. *Mapeldorerugge* (f.n. Windsor). One instance in charters, 784.

mareis ME from Old French, 'marsh'. Occasionally in f.ns., e.g. *Ye Mares* (Faringdon), Marreys (Sparsholt), *Mareysdune* (Hurley).

marle ME from Old French, 'marl'. *Marlehay* (f.n. Ashbury), *v.* also pytt.

marled ME, 'fertilised with marl'. *Newemarledride* (f.n. Winkfield).

marling ME, 'marl pit'. *v.* pytt.

*mealm OE, 'sand, sandy or chalky soil, soft stone'. Occasionally in f.ns., e.g. Malm Close (Bucklebury), Malm Mdw (Thatcham), *Le Malme* (Newbury), *Malme Pitts* (Wallingford).

mearc OE, 'boundary'. *Merkedich* (f.n. Hurley). Also in charters, 784.

melde OE, a plant used for food (cf. *Anglo-Saxon Settlement and Landscape* ed. T. Rowley, Oxford 1974, p. 85). Millony (f.n. Brightwell).

meoluc, meolc, milc OE, 'milk', used of good pasture. Occasionally in f.ns., e.g. *Mylke Close* (Reading), *Milkhegge* (Cookham), *Milkehill* (Shaw).

mēos OE, 'moss, lichen', probably also 'swamp'. *Mesbroke* (f.n. Speen). Two more instances in charters, 785.

mere¹ OE, 'pool'. *Bruningmere*, Catmore, Coomsbury, Cranemoor, Dunmore, Frogmore, Hiremere, Hormer Hundred, *Lortemere Lane*, Peasemore, *Puckmere*, Ripplesmere Hundred, Stanmore. Fairly *freq.* in f.ns., e.g. *Asshemer'* (Boxford), *Bailliesmere, Brademer'* (Bray), *Dunmere* (Hurley), *Illemeregrof* (Streatley), *Oselakemere* (Reading, pers.n.), *Whytemerecrofte* (Kintbury), *Wichmere* (Winkfield), *Wodemer* (Brightwalton). There is another *Stanmere* in Woolstone. As a first el. (e.g. ?*Mereworth* Cookham) mere cannot formally be distinguished in ME spellings from **(ge)mǣre**, *q.v.* Also in charters, 785.

merece OE, 'smallage'. Marcham.

mersc OE, 'marsh'. Broadmarsh, Bulmershe, Challowmarsh, Marsh Lane (Newbury), Marsh Mill, Pinmarsh, Smallmarsh, Tidmarsh. Occasionally in f.ns., as a simplex n. with early forms (e.g. *La Mersche, Le Mershe, Mersshe, The Mersh*) in Childrey, Coleshill, Cookham, Reading, Steventon, Sulhampstead, Welford, Windsor. Cf. also *Dedemersch* (Hungerford), *La Northmersshe* (Sparsholt), *Oldmershe* (Ashbury), *Wydemersh* (Hungerford). One instance in charters, 785.

mes Old French, 'dwelling'. Beamy's Castle: ?*Shepartesmeez* (f.n. Steventon).

micel OE, 'big'. Occasionally in f.ns., e.g. *Mucheleham* (Abingdon), *Muchelehull* (Windsor), *Micheloomerssh* (Ashampstead), Mickle Riggs (S. N. Hurst). Two instances in charters, 785.

middel OE adj. 'middle'. Middle Leaze Fm, Milton. Occasionally in f.ns., most *freq.* with furlang. Cf. also *Middlecroft* (Englefield), Middle Fd (Beenham, etc.), *Middleham* (Sulhampstead), *Middelhulle* (Fernham), *Middelmede* (Hurley, etc.), *Middilmore* (Sandhurst), *Myddellrydings* (Clewer). One instance in charters, 785.

midmest OE, 'midmost'. *Mide(l)mestedole* (f.ns. Sulhampstead), *Midemest Furlong, Le Midemuste Dole* (f.ns. Moreton). The

Sulhampstead n. shows association with **middel**, but is probably too early to contain *middlemost*.

mīl OE, 'mile'. Mile End.

mix, meox, OE, 'dung'. *Lullemixhull* (f.n. Sutton C).

mixen OE, 'dunghill'. *Mixtenham* (f.n. W. Waltham), *Muxenbroke* (f.n. Reading).

mont ME from Old French, 'mount, hill'. *Freq.* in minor ns. for which only 16th-cent. or later spellings are available, *v.* Mount in Index and cf. Mount Pleasant Pt 1 283, Pt 2 540.

mōr OE, 'marshland, moor, barren upland'. (*v.* 937 for discussion of various senses). Bagmore Brook, Blackmoor Stream, Chalmore, Dunmore Fm (pers.n.), Farley Moor, Frogmoor, Gormoor, The Moor (Cookham), Moor Ditch, Moorend, Moor Fm, Moor Mill, The Moors (2), Moreton, Old Moor Cottages, Snelsmore (pers.n.), Southmoor, Wigmore, Wildmoor Brook, *Wydemor* (later Malpas). *Freq.* in f.ns., as a simplex n. with early forms (e.g. *La More, Mora, The More, Le Mores*) in Abingdon, Ashbury, Brightwalton, Bucklebury, Clewer, Finchampstead, Newbury, Sandhurst, Swallowfield, Woolstone. Cf. also *Dedemore* (Faringdon), *La Formore* (Sulhampstead), *Haggemor* (Balking), *Lechemore* (Earley), Long Moor, Short Moor (Sunningwell), *Moredowne* (Uffington), *Morhacche* (Burghfield), *Oxemore* (Reading), *Rademore* (Midgham), *Segemore* (Stratfield M), *Whitemore* (Sandhurst). *v.* **blæc, blēat, brād, (ge)mǣne, pēte, pudd, *wigga**. Also in charters, 785.

morgen OE, 'morning'. Three times in f.ns. with **lǣs**: *Innere-, Utteremornesleswe* (Kintbury), *Morowleez* (Uffington), *Morowe Lease* (Fyfield). Similar ns. have been explained as compounds of *morgen-gifu*, with loss of middle el. (*v.* Ess 276, Wa 224), but it seems advisable to allow for the possibility of *morgen* being a p.n. el.

morgen-gifu OE, 'piece of land or the like given by a man to his bride on the morning after their marriage'. *Le Moriȝene Gardyn* (f.n. Reading).

mote ME from Old French, 'moat, protective ditch filled with water around a building'. Occasionally in f.ns., e.g. *Le Mote* (Aston T, Hagbourne, Windsor). *La Mothalle* (Wallingford), *Motehall* (Tilehurst) are probably 'hall with a moat' rather than 'moot-hall'.

munuc OE, 'monk'. Occasionally in f.ns., e.g. *Monkcroft* (Abingdon), *Monekedene* (Wallingford), *Munekeye* (Cumnor), *Monekemulle* (Faringdon).

mūs OE, 'mouse'. Mousefield Fm. Occasionally in f.ns., e.g. *Mus-furlong*' (Newbury), Mouse Furlong (Abingdon), Mouse Hill (Stratfield M), *La Musewik*' (Garford).

mycg OE, 'midge'. Midgham.

Mydeling, OE stream-n. *Mydeling*. Early spellings for Midlington in Droxford Ha suggest that the first el. may be another instance (*ex inf.* Mr Gover).

myln OE, 'mill'. Bray Mill, Friarsmill, Hagbourne Mill, Letcombe Mill, Marcham Mill, Mill Bridge and Fm, Mill Lane (Reading), Uffington Mill, Woolstone Mill. Fairly *freq.* in f.ns., usually as first el. (e.g. *Mulnaker* Burghfield, *Millbrooke* Harwell, etc., *Milham* Eaton H, etc., *Mulnemede* Hungerford, *Mulwey* Brightwell, etc.). Cf. also *Berendemulle* (Cookham), *Nethyrmylle*, *Overmylle* (Moreton), *North Mill* (Wallingford). *v.* plæsc. Also in charters, 785.

mynecen OE, 'nun'. *Munchenelesse* (f.n. Cookham).

mynster OE, 'monastery, church serving several villages'. Minster St; *Mynster Myll* (f.n. Reading).

myrge OE 'pleasant'. Merryhill. The compound with hyll occurs in f.ns. (Binfield, Bucklebury, Reading), and as a lost street-n. in Newbury.

nacod OE, 'naked, bare'. *Nachededorne* Hundred.

nattok ME, meaning unknown. *Nattocks* (f.n. Aston T).

nǣp, nēp OE, 'turnip'. Occasionally in f.ns., e.g. *Nephull*' (Sulhampstead B), *Nepelonde* (Sandhurst), *Neplands* (Sonning).

nēat OE, 'cattle'. *Nethulle* (f.n. Earley).

neoðerra OE, 'lower'. Netherton. Fairly *freq.* in f.ns., e.g. *Netherecroft* (Hurley), *Le Netherdowne*, *Netherorchard* (Coleshill).

netel(e) OE, 'nettle'. *Netelbedde* (f.n. Uffington). *Net(t)elyhull*' 1359 Winkfield appears to contain a ME instance of the adj. *nettly*.

nīed OE, 'need, poverty'. *Nedacra* (f.n. Brightwalton).

nīwe, nēowe OE, 'new'. Newbury, Newland, Newton. Fairly common in mod. f.ns., occasionally in early f.ns. There are 8 more instances with land. New Broke occurs in Harwell, Lambourn, Steventon, Wantage. Cf. also *Newebrugge* (Sunninghill), *Newedik*' (Bucklebury), *Newgarston*' (Burghfield), *Neweweye* (Earley). Two instances in charters, 785.

norð OE, 'north'. Narborough, Norbin's Wd, Nor Brook, Norcot, Northcourt, North Croft, Northford, Northmead Lane, North Street, North Town. *Freq.* in f.ns., e.g. *Norden*' (Hungerford),

Northdene (Sotwell), *Northulle* (Hanney), *La Northmersshe* (Sparsholt), *Northmore* (Fyfield), *Northwode* (Reading, etc.). The comparative occurs in *Le Northeredole* (Streatley).

norðan OE, 'lying north of'. Northbrook St, Northbrook Wd; probably *Northbrok'* (f.n. Blewbury, Grove).

nunne OE, 'nun'. Nunhide.

ōfer¹ OE, 'bank, river-bank'. This el. interchanges with ōra in early spellings for *Hennor Mill* and Windsor. Cf. also *Overton* (f.n. Windsor).

ofer², ufer OE, 'slope, hill, ridge'. *Uverescumbe, Overescumbe* (f.n. Streatley).

ōra¹ OE, 'border, margin, bank, edge' (*v.* 938 for discussion of various senses). Bagnor, Boxford, *Colmanora*, Cumnor (pers.n.), *Hennor Mill*, Oare, *Ortone* (in Ripplesmere Hundred), *Underore*, *Upnor*, Windsor, Woolver's Barn. Occasionally in f.ns., e.g. *Kenesore, Ulkesore* (Lambourn), *Longnore* (Uffington). Two more instances in charters, 785.

orceard, ort-geard OE, 'garden, orchard'. *Freq.* in mod. f.ns., occasionally in early f.ns., e.g. *Orecharde* (Hurley), *Ochortfurlong* (Englefield), *Juardesorchard* (Coleshill).

ort Old French, 'garden'. Orts Rd.

oxa OE, 'ox'. In minor ns. for which only late spellings are available, *v.* Index. Occasionally in f.ns., usually with lǣs (e.g. *Oxenlese* Eaton H, *Oxlease* Steventon). Cf. also *Oxedrove* (Ashbury), *Oxenedoune* (Inkpen), *Oxhaye* (Hurley), *Oxemormed* (Reading). One instance in charters, 785.

pæð OE, 'path, track'. Occasionally in f.ns., e.g. *Cockespathe* (Inkpen), *La Erlespath* (Lambourn), *Gospath* (E. Hendred), *Le Pathe* (Wallingford). Also in charters, 785.

panne OE, 'pan'. *Brodepann, Froggepanne* (f.ns. Ashbury).

park ME from Old French, 'an enclosed tract of land for beasts of the chase'. Little Park, Parkside, Radley Park. *Freq.* in mod. minor ns. Occasionally in f.ns., e.g. *La Pilparc* (Earley), *Parke Feere* (Sonning), *Parkfeld, Parkemead* (Speen).

parting ModE, possibly referring to land which can be divided (*v.* O 460). Parting Ham (f.n. Buscot).

*peac OE, 'knoll, hill, peak'. *Le Peke* (f.n. Upton).

pearroc OE, 'ground enclosed with a fence, small enclosure, paddock'. Paddock Wd. Occasionally in f.ns., usually as a simplex n. (e.g. *Parrok, Le Parrok, The Parocke*, The Paddock). Cf. also *Cowe Perok*

(Pangbourne), *Hemparock, Russheparrock* (Welford), *Suthparroc* (Easthampstead). Two more instances in charters, 786.

pece ME from Old French, 'piece of land'. Fairly *freq.* as second el. in f.ns., with some forms from 16th cent., but mostly 19th cent. Cf. e.g. *The Mill Peece* (Shottesbrooke), Pit Piece, Pond- (Compton B), Sand Piece (Kingston L).

peddere ME, 'pedlar'. *Pedderesham* (f.n. Wytham).

pēl ME from Old French, 'stake, palisade, palisaded enclosure'. *Peal Mead, Peel Hill* (f.ns. Hungerford, Englefield).

pendant ME from Old French, 'slope of a hill'. *Le Pendant* (f.n. Lambourn).

pening, pending OE, 'penny', used of land paying a penny rent. Mod. minor ns. (*v.* Index). Occasionally in f.ns., e.g. *Pennymershe* (Binfield), *Penyham* (Hagbourne), *Peny Grene* (Sotwell). Cf. Sixpenny Patch (Balking) and Halfpenny (Pt 2 543).

*penn PrWelsh, 'end, height, hill'. ?Inkpen, ?Pingewood.

penn² OE, 'small, enclosure, fold', later 'enclosure for animals'. ?Inkpen, Pen Barn and Lane, Penclose Fm. Occasionally in f.ns., e.g. *Le Pen* (Longworth).

*penning OE or ME, a derivative of penn² or of ME verb *pennen* (not formerly noted in p.ns.) may be the source of f.ns. *La Pennynggestret* (Hurley), *Pening(e)croft, Little Penninge* (Fyfield). Gl 4 160 lists some f.ns. under penning ModE dial. 'cattle enclosure', but the Hurley example is from 1333.

*pennuc OE, penok, pinnok ME, 'small pen'. *Pynnokes*, Pinnock Furlong (f.ns. Childrey, Bourton).

persone ME from Old French, 'beneficed cleric'. *Personeshamme* (f.n. Steventon), *Parsoneswode* (f.n. Ashbury). These ns. may contain a surname.

peru OE, 'pear', used of the pear tree p. 1400, *Pereclose, Peremede* (f.ns. Winterbourne 1550.). One instance in charters, 786.

pete ME, 'peat'. Mod. minor ns., e.g. Peatmoor Copse, Peat Moor Lane; *Petemore* (f.n. Wallingford).

pīc¹ OE, 'point'. Pike Shaw. Fairly *freq.* in f.ns., usually as a simplex n., e.g. *Le Pyke* (Basildon), *The Pikes* (Hungerford), The Picks (E. Hendred), Pix (Moreton). Cf. also *Pykehornescrofte* (Newbury), Pike Mdw (Swallowfield).

*pīcede OE, 'pointed, having sharp corners'. Picked Point, and mod. minor ns. in Peaked-, Picked-. Fairly *freq.* in f.ns., e.g. *Pikidclose* (Hungerford), *Pykedcroft* (Cumnor), *Pykedehalue* (Inkpen),

Pykydlond (Moreton), Picked Mead (Faringdon), Peaked Piece (Radley).

piddle e. ModE, apparently a variant of pightel, 'small enclosure, croft'. *Freq.* in mod. f.ns., e.g. Piddle (Barkham), Piddle Mdw (Inkpen). Occasionally in earlier f.ns., e.g. *Le Well Piddell* (Shinfield 1550). Interchange between piddle and pightel is found in f.ns. in Binfield, Bucklebury, Chieveley, Enborne, Leckhampstead, Swallowfield, and in minor ns., e.g. Tinker's Pightle Copse is *Tinkers Piddle* in *TA*. In Binfield and Enborne *piddle* alternates with *pud(d)le* in 16th- and 17th-cent. forms, and in Reading occurs the series *Pydelles* 1544, *Pyddell, La Pedelle* 1551–2, *Le Puddells* Ed 6. This suggests that earlier f.ns. in *-pud(d)el* may belong here, e.g. *La Russipuddel* 13th, *Kelerespuddel* 14th Burghfield, *pudel* called *Waremundespudel* 1373 Newland, *Botulphus Puddellez* 1433 Shinfield, *Northpudell, Litelpudell* 1462 Tilehurst, *Puddlehey* 1519 Ashbury. If all these ns. belong together, the source may be a derivative *pyddel of pudd 'ditch, furrow', referring to a ditched enclosure; Professor Löfvenberg does not agree with this suggestion, however. Some of the early ns. may contain *puddel 'puddle' (certainly a derivative of pudd), but this el. is not well evidenced in early p.ns. and is not appropriate to the three Berks ns. in which the first el. is a surname, or to the use of *pudel* as a noun in the Newland reference. As regards *La Russipuddel*, it is noteworthy that Rushey Piddle occurs in Stratfield M. In other counties occasional f.ns. in *Puddel*, Piddle have been explained as 'pond, puddle', *v.* Sr 384, O 47; but the fuller material for Berks makes it clear that there is another term with about the same meaning as pightel *infra*.

pightel ME, **pightle** ModE dial., 'small enclosure, croft'. *Passim* in mod. f.ns., occasionally in mod. minor ns., e.g. Church Pightle, Little Pightle. The variant form *pickle* occurs occasionally, e.g. Pickles (Binfield), Farm Pickle (Bourton), Pig Hill (Chaddleworth). There are no certain ME instances in Berks (such as were noted Sx 561, O 29), but *Smertis Pytyll* (Remenham 1484) may belong here. The relationship between this el. and piddle *supra* is unexplained. It seems possible that two words of different origin but similar meaning have been associated. The origin of pightel is obscure.

*pidu, *pide OE, 'marsh, fen'. *Pyddene* (f.n. Hungerford), *Pydelynch* (f.n. Coleshill).

pīl OE, 'spike, shaft'. Pile Hill, Piling Hill. Occasionally in f.ns., e.g.

Pil(e)hulle (Theale), *La Pilparc* (Earley), *Pilefelds* (Reading), *Le Pyle* (Chieveley).

*pinca OE, 'finch, chaffinch'. Pinmarsh.

pinn OE, 'pin, peg'. ?*Pyn* (f.n. W. Hanney).

pirige OE, 'pear tree'. Perry's Bridge, Purley. Occasionally in f.ns., e.g. *Pyristob* (Bray), *Perrycroft* (Clewer), *Pericroft* (Earley), *Puriham* (Reading).

pise, peosu OE, 'pease'. Peascod St, Peasemore, Pusey. Occasionally in f.ns., e.g. *Pusecroft* (Burghfield), *Pusfurlong'* (Moreton), *Pushull* (Hinton W).

place ME from Old French, 'residence'. Hall Place (Hurley, etc.). Occasionally in f.ns., e.g. *Goldenesplace, Saundresplace* (Englefield).

*plæsc OE, 'pool'. *Milleplaschea, Le Water Plashe* (f.ns. Moreton), *Mylplasshes* (f.n. Wallingford).

plain ME from Old French, 'open ground adjoining woodland, flat meadowland'. Holliday's Plain, Plain Plantation, Winkfield Plain. Occasionally in f.ns., either as a simplex n. (Plain, The Plain) or with a village n. prefixed (*Ascot Playne*, Easthampstead Plain, *Snowswick* Plain, Chilton Plain).

plat² ME, 'plot, small piece of ground'. In minor ns. for which only mod. forms are available, e.g. Furzeplatt, Mead Platt, Platt Lane. Fairly *freq.* in f.ns. with forms from 16th cent. or later, usually as a simplex n. (*Platt, The Platt*, The Plat). Cf. also Hop Platt (Compton), *Marsseplat* (Radley), Mead Platt (Hagbourne), *Russhe Platte* (Reading).

plega OE, 'play, sport'. *La Pleyok* (f.n. Swallowfield).

pleg-stōw OE, 'sport-place'. Plaistowgreen; ?*Plaisters* (f.n. Cookham).

plek ME, 'small plot of ground'. Occasionally in f.ns., e.g. *The Pleck* (Windsor), Pleck (Lambourn), *Plecks* (Appleford). In Radley f.ns. there is interchange with plat² – *Marsseplat, Le Marshe Placke* 1547, *Masseplecke* e. 17th, Mass Plat *TA* (the 1547 form contains the variant *plack, v.* Löfvenberg 154).

plot l. OE, ME, 'small piece of ground'. Occasionally in f.ns., e.g. *Le Wooplote* (Sandhurst), *Hedsplot* (Kintbury), *Plotteaker* (Ashbury). In Buscot *Common Plott* 1744 is Common Plat in *TA, v.* plat².

pohha OE, 'pouch, bag'. Poughley.

point ME from Old French, 'sharp end'. Picked Point; *Le Poynt* (f.n. Reading).

pōl OE, 'pool'. Ruddles Pool (?pers.n.). Occasionally in f.ns., e.g.

Le Pole (Steventon), *Fulpolmed* (Maidenhead), *Le Were Pole* (Faringdon), *Widmerpole* (Hurley), *Wynegodespol* (Bray, pers.n.). *v.* hors. Two instances in charters, 786.

popel OE, 'pebble'. Popple Mede (f.n. Blewbury). An adj. in -ig³ may be the first el. of *Popleyclose, Pop(p)ley Crofte* (Shaw), *Poppley Yate* (Winterbourne).

popig OE, 'poppy'. *Popielonde* (f.n. Uffington).

port² OE, 'town, market-town, market'. Holyport, Hungerford Port Down, Port. Occasionally as first el. in f.ns., e.g. *Portebrugge* (Bray), *Le Portaker* (Lambourn), *Portfurlong'* (Sotwell). In charters with stræt and weg.

portmann OE, 'townsman'. Occasionally in f.ns., e.g. *Portmannesfeld, Portmannemore* (Wallingford), *Portmanlese* (Windsor), *Portmanebroc* (Reading).

port-weg OE, 'road leading to a town'. Portway. In f.ns. in Appleford, Balking, Steventon.

pre ME from Old French, 'meadow'. ?Pry Lane; *Prese Barne, The Preyes Lynche* (f.ns. Hungerford).

prēost OE, 'priest'. Occasionally in f.ns., e.g. *Prestacre* (Uffington), *Preste Crofte* (Winkfield), *Prestesforlang* (Cholsey), *Prestesmede* (Sonning), *Priest Meade* (Cookham). Two instances in charters, 786.

prior 1. OE from Latin, 'prior of a religious house'. Prior's Copse. Occasionally in f.ns., e.g. *Priors Leze* (Cookham), *Prioruscort* (Buscot), *Pryors Crofte* (Reading), *Prior's Grove* (Shaw). *Prioriees-mede* (cited under Prior's Copse) probably contains ME *priory*. *v.* Index for late-recorded ns. containing both words.

pūca OE, 'goblin, puck'. Puckmere. Occasionally in f.ns., e.g. *Powkecrofte* (Hamstead M), *Pokesden'* (Steventon), *Pukelane, Pokepirye* (Windsor), *Pookepidell* (Binfield). No instance has been found of the compound with pytt, noted in O and W and common in Gl.

pūcel OE, 'goblin'. *Pokelmede, Pokelande* (f.ns. Shaw).

pudd OE, 'ditch, furrow'. *Puddemore* (f.n. Abingdon), *Podmore, Pudmore* (f.n. Cholsey). Podmore St, Podimore So have been explained as from ME pode 'toad' (Elements, DEPN), but the *-u-* of the Berks ns. suggest pudd. *v.* also piddle.

*pud(d)el ME, ?'enclosure'. *v.* piddle.

*pund OE, 'pound, enclosure into which straying animals are put'. *The Pounde* (f.n. Welford). Three 16th-cent. ns. in Hungerford

(*Dun Mill Pound, Edynton Pound(e), Charleford Pounde*) probably contain this el. rather than a dial. form of *pond*. Pound is fairly common in mod. f.ns. The Wallingford f.n. *La Punde* 1327, *Le Pende* 1334, *Le Puynde* 1335 is from OE pynd, an i-mutated variant of pund.

pund-fald OE, 'pinfold, pound'. *Le Pondfoldyate* (f.n. Steventon). F.ns. in Englefield and Newbury have some spellings (*Pynfold(e)*) which indicate either substitution of ModE *pinfold* or part-derivation from *pynd-fald.

pūr OE, 'snipe, bittern'. Purley.

pyll OE, 'tidal creek, pool in a river, small stream'. Billingbear, Pill Ditch. Occasionally in f.ns., e.g. *Pylle* (Windsor), *Le Pylryche* (Arborfield), *The Pills* (Thatcham), *Pylle Mede* (Boxford), *Pillmead* (Sonning), *Parke Ende Pyll* (Moreton).

pynd OE, *v*. *pund.

***pyp(p)el** OE, 'pebble'. *Pyp(p)elakefurl'* (f.n. Ashbury). One instance in charters, 786.

pytt OE, 'pit, natural hollow, excavated hole'. hringpyt (later The Manger), Pitfield, Pitlands, Pyt Ho, Sandpit Gate, Stallpits. *Freq.* in f.ns., sometimes as a simplex n. or first el. (e.g. *Le Pytaker* Maidenhead, *Putcroft* Sulhampstead, *La Putlonde* Brightwell). Cf. also *Le Blynd Pyttes* (Coleshill), *Chalke Pytt* (Cholsey), *Le Cowpit, Russhepyt* (Steventon), *Croweputtes* (Hanney), *Le Gravell-pitts* (Clewer), *Horeput* (Tubney), *Marlyngpittes* (Windsor), *Marlepite, Merlin Pitts, Stonepitts* (W. Waltham), *La Rede Putte* (Brightwalton), Sand Pits (Hungerford), *Skynnesput* (Hurley). *v*. clæg, dierne, mealm, scitere, stān-pytt. The mysterious term Witch Pit, Wych Pit occurs in Chieveley and Hampstead N, *v*. Pt ɪ 253. *TA*s for Highclere and Ashmansworth Ha contain f.ns. Witch Pits, Whitch Pits. The first el. may be OE *wicce* 'witch', the compound being comparable to that with pūca, *q.v.* Also in charters, 786.

quarre ME from Old French, 'quarry'. *Le Quarre* (f.n. Ashbury).

rād OE, 'act of riding', used of a road suitable for riding. *Rodeweye* (E. Shefford 1247–8).

rainbow ModE (*v*. Pt ɪ 281). F.ns. in Basildon, Burghfield, Sandhurst.

rakke ME, 'rack, framework of bars'. Fairly *freq.* in f.ns., e.g. *Le Racks* (Faringdon), *Le Racke Heys* (Newbury, etc.), *Le Racke Close* (Stratfield M, etc.). The variant form *rekke* is found in the earliest spellings for the Newbury n.

ramm OE, 'ram'. ? Ramslands Shaw; *Rammesmede* (f.n. Inkpen).

rand OE, 'edge, border, shore'. *The Randes* (f.n. Harwell), ? *Randesweie* (f.n. Lambourn).

ratoun ME from Old French, 'rat'. Rotten Row, *Rotton Row* (lost street-n. Reading). Rottendown Hill may contain this el., but may be from *rotten* referring to soft land.

rāw, rǣw OE, 'row'. Occasionally in street-ns., e.g. *Le Bocher Row, Chese Rewe, Fish Row* (Reading), *Crockeresrowe* (Hurley). In mod. minor ns., e.g. The Row, Paddlehill Row, the meaning is sometimes 'strip of woodland'. Occasionally in f.ns., e.g. *New Rewe* (Bray), *Le Rewen* (Shinfield, poss. dat. pl.), Dial Row (Kintbury), *Stanrewemede* (Sandhurst). Also in charters, 786.

rēad OE, 'red'. Radley (2). Occasionally in f.ns., e.g. *Redecumbe* (Coxwell), *Rededich, Le Redhacche* (Sunninghill), *Radenhulle* (Uffington), *Redhurst* (Binfield), *Reddelonde* (Stratfield M, etc.), *Redemede* (Stratfield M). The compound with lēah occurs again in Steventon. The el. is not likely to refer to soil colour in either instance of Radley in major ns. v. hān. Also in charters, 786.

(ge)rēfa OE, 'reeve, bailiff'. Occasionally in f.ns., e.g. *Revehams* (Eaton H), ? *Repham* (Kintbury), *Le Reuehoke* (Harwell).

reille ME from Old French, 'fence, railing'. v. Pt **1** 281 for examples, to which add Pond Rail (f.n. W. Woodhay).

*rend OE, 'edge, border'. *La Rendiche* (f.n. Chieveley).

reoma OE, 'border'. ? Remenham.

rēoma OE, 'ligament'. ? Remenham.

ride, riding ModE, possibly used of a division of a royal forest in the charge of a particular forester, ? 15th-cent. f. ns. in Windsor, v. Pt **1** 34.

rima OE, 'border'. Possibly in Rhyme's Cottages, Rimes Fm, for which only mod. forms are available.

*rip(p) OE, 'strip, edge, shore'. *The Ripene* (f.n. Childrey).

*ripel OE, 'strip of land'. Ripplesmere Hundred.

risc, rysc OE, 'rush'. Rushall. Occasionally in f.ns., e.g. *Rixhamme* (Thatcham), *Russheparrock* (Welford), *Russhepyt* (Steventon). Also in charters, 786.

rīð OE, 'stream'. Childrey Brook (? pers.n.), Foudry Brook, Hendred, Nancry Coppice, Woodcray. Occasionally in f.ns., e.g. *Le Rythe* (Bray, Earley), *Pylryth* (Arborfield). Also in charters, 786.

rīðig OE, 'small stream'. ? Rivey Brake. Also in charters, 786.

*rod¹, *rodu OE, 'clearing'. *Estrode, Westrode* (f.ns. Bradfield). Also in charters, 786.

rōd² OE, 'crucifix, gallows'. Rood Hill.

rod ModE, 'osier' (v. O 463). Occasionally in f.ns., e.g. Rod Eyott (Moulsford), Rod Pits (Shinfield), Roy Eyot and Pits (Winnersh), Rodd Piece (Swallowfield).

rond ME from Old French, 'round'. Roundeforlonge (f.n. Steventon).

*roðu OE, 'clearing'. The Rothe (f.n. Englefield).

roundabout ModE (v. Pt 1 281). Some examples in Pt 2, e.g. Great Moorhens Roundabout, Northfield-, are at a junction of paths. The Roundabout in Pusey is surrounded by paths, – in Ardington is a clump of trees.

rouning ME, 'whispering, muttering'. ?Rownyngfurlong (f.n. Steventon), ?Rouning Ground (f.n. Brimpton).

rūh OE, 'rough'. Rowbury, Rowney, ?Rowstock. Occasionally in f.ns., e.g. Rughcroft (Hampstead N), La Rowecrundele (East Garston), Rugheneie (Burghfield), Rowgrove (Clewer), Roughgrove (Binfield), La Rowehull (Windsor), The Rowelond (Childrey). The compound with beorg found in Rowbury occurs again in Childrey, Inkpen and Sunningwell. Also in charters, 786.

*run OE, 'stream' (not previously noted in p.ns.). ?Runsford Hole.

(ge)ryd(d) OE, past part. used as adj., 'cleared'. Occasionally in f.ns., e.g. Le Ridacre (Kintbury), Rydelond' (Coleshill).

*rȳde, *ryde OE, 'clearing'. Occasionally in f.ns. in E. Berks, e.g. Feld Rede (Sandhurst), Marserude, Le Knaprude, La Rude (Windsor), Newmarlederyde (Winkfield), Le Ryde (Pangbourne).

*ryden OE 'clearing'. Woodridden (f.n. East Garston).

*ryding OE, 'clearing'. Ridings, Wildridings. Fairly freq. in f.ns. in E. of county, occasionally in W. Sometimes as a simplex n. (Le Rudingge, The Rudinge, La Rydynges, Rydinges); cf. also Brystetherudyngge (Easthampstead, pers.n.), Cole Readings (Winnersh), Dederuding' (Thatcham), Olderuding (Windsor).

ryge OE, 'rye'. Ryedown, Ryehurst, Ryeish. Occasionally in f.ns., e.g. Le Rie Close (Hamstead M), Ruycroft (Hurley), Le Ryecroft (Reading), Ridon (Watchfield), La Ryforlong (Brightwell), Ryefurlong' (Moreton), Ryhulle (Hungerford), Riwurde (Shrivenham). Also in charters, 787.

*rysce OE, 'rush-bed'. Rush Ct; Le Resshe, Le Ruyssh (f.n. Steventon), La Russe (f.n. Sutton C).

*ryscig OE, 'rushy' (not previously noted in p.ns.). Russiford (on site of Tyle Mill); La Russipuddel (f.n. Burghfield).

rȳt OE, 'rubbish for burning'. ?Rutewelle (f.n. Harwell).

sainfoin ModE (*v.* Pt **1** 282). Better represented in f.ns. in the W. of the county than in the E., cf. e.g. Saintfoin Piece (Milton, etc.), Sainfoin Ground (Faringdon), St Foin Ground (Shrivenham), Sainfoin Moor (Hatford), Saint Foin Close (E. Hendred).

sand OE, 'sand'. Sanden, Sandford (2), Sandhurst, Sandpit Gate. Occasionally in f.ns., e.g. *Le Sandes, Sanpitt Forlonge* (Coxwell), *Sonda* (Cumnor), *Sandfeld* (Bucklebury), *Sandhill* (Radley). Two more instances in charters, 787.

sandig OE, 'sandy'. *Sondilond* (f.n. Hungerford).

scēad OE, 'separation', used in stream-ns. to mean 'boundary'. Shadwell, *Shadwell* (f.ns. Cumnor, Pangbourne).

sc(e)aga OE, 'small wood, copse'. Shaw, Shaw Fm.

*sc(e)ald OE, 'shallow'. Shalford.

sc(e)amol OE, 'bench, stall for displaying goods'. *Fysshameles* (lost street-n. Wallingford).

scēap, *scī(e)p OE, 'sheep'. Shefford, Sheep Bridge. Occasionally in f.ns., e.g. *Shepacrs, Shepcroft* (Earley), *Shepacres* (Abingdon), *Schepgrove* (Windsor), *Shepeleez Close* (Woolstone), *Schiplake* (Wytham). One instance in charters, 787.

*scēap-cot OE, 'shelter for sheep'. Sheepcote Lane. Occasionally in f.ns., e.g. *Shepecote Croft* (Bray), *Shepecotefelde* (Reading).

*scēap-hūs OE, 'sheep-house'. Sheephouse is common in mod. minor ns. (*v.* Index) and f.ns. The earliest forms noted are *Schephousforlong* (Speen 1340), *Shepehous* (Hungerford 1429).

scear OE, 'plough-share'. ?Shellingford.

sceard OE, 'cleft, gap'. Occasionally in f.ns., perhaps referring to a gap in a fence. Cf. *Sherde* (Letcomb R), *Le Scherde, Cowe Sherdys, Lutonsherd'* (Steventon), *Hales Sherde, Stanpitts Sherde* (Clewer), *Medesherd, Roggerscherd* (Hagbourne), *Windesherde* (Hamstead M), *Wynterscerde* (Abingdon).

scearn OE, 'dung'. *Sarndich* (f.n. Brightwell).

scearp OE, 'sharp, pointed', perhaps 'steep'. Occasionally in f.ns., e.g. *Sarpacra* (Burghfield), *Sharpe Croft* (Kintbury), *Le Sharpende* (Cookham), *Serpenhil* (Abingdon).

scēat(a) OE, 'corner, angle, projection of land'. Bigshotte (pers.n.); *Wardshott* (f.n. Clewer). *v.* *sciete.

*scēo OE, 'shelter'. Sheffield.

sc(e)ort OE, 'short'. Shortford. Occasionally in f.ns., e.g. *Shortynden* (Maidenhead), *Short Doll* (Cookham), *La Shortdole* (Uffington), *Schortham* (Wytham), *Shortlond* (Steventon, etc.), *Shortefurlong*

(Hagbourne, etc.), *Shortmede* (Steventon). Also in charters, 787.

sc(e)ota OE, 'trout'. ?Shottesbrooke.

*scēotere, *scȳtere OE, 'archer'. Shooter's Hill.

scielf, scylf OE, 'ledge'. Rockshill (f.n. Marcham), Shelves (f.n. Brightwalton).

*scīete, *scȳte OE, 'land which shoots out'. Sheet St, White Shoot, White Shute, Whiteshute Row. In f.ns. there are two more examples of the compound with hwīt, *q.v.*; this refers to trackways on chalk hills, *v.* Pt **1** 153. This el. may be the source of the f.ns. *Shete* W. Hanney, *La Schete* Stratfield M, Sheets Tilehurst, *Sheetehegge* Earley. When there are only forms with -*e*-, -*ee*- it is impossible to say whether they are from scēat(a) or *scīete; but the simplex ns. like Sheet have a different distribution from those in which scēat(a) is a second el. (*v.* 938), and they may be from the variant form.

scīr[1] OE, 'shire', also used in p.ns. to mean 'county boundary'. Berkshire, Sheerlands; *The Sheare Streame* (f.n. Finchampstead).

scīr[2] OE, 'bright'. *Shirlak'* (f.n. Tilehurst).

scīr-gerēfa OE, 'sheriff'. *Schireveslane* (later Lombard St).

scite OE, 'dung'. *Le Shitehap* (f.n. Wallingford).

*scitere OE ?'sewer'. *Shyterespytte* (f.n. Steventon). One instance in charters, 787.

*scofl-brǣdu OE, 'narrow strip'. ?*Shelbred Hills* (f.n. Easthampstead).

scot ME, 'tax, payment'. Scotland(s) occurs several times in mod. minor ns. and f.ns. This may be the opposite of Freeland (*v.* frēo).

(ge)scrifen OE, past participle of *scrīfan*, 'decree, allot, pass sentence on, impose penance'. Shrivenham.

*scrubb OE, 'shrub, brushwood'. The Scrubbs; The Scrubs (f.n. Kintbury).

*scydd OE, 'shed'. *Schedday*, *Schuddaye* (f.n. Wytham).

scypen, scipen OE, 'cow-shed'. Shippon. Occasionally in f.ns., e.g. *Le Shippen* (Hamstead M), *Shepene* (Letcombe R). One instance in charters, 787.

*scyt(e)hangra OE. Löfvenberg 187 defines this compound as 'wood on the side of a steep slope'. It may, however, contain *scīete, *scȳte (*q.v.*), indicating that the wood juts out. *Shitehangercroftes* (f.n. Shottesbrooke), *Shutehangr'* (f.n. Kintbury).

sealh OE, 'willow'. Possibly in f.ns., e.g. Sale Mead (Hungerford).

This is, however, to be connected with Ric. *de la Sale*, a surname which occurs also in Cumnor, Midgham, Woolstone. sealh is only one possible source of this surname, *v.* Reaney 281. One instance in charters, 787.

sele[1] OE, 'house, hall'. ?*Le Sele* (f.n. Hamstead M).

seofon OE, 'seven'. Occasionally in f.ns., e.g. *Sevenacres* (Childrey). This compound occurs several times in mod. minor ns., *v.* Index. Also in charters, once with æcer, 787.

seten OE, 'occupied land'. *Setene* (f.n. Farnborough).

several ModE (Pt 1 282). Several Down, The Severalls. Occasionally in f.ns. usually as a simplex n., but cf. *The Seuerall Grounde* (Hampstead N), *Severall' Mede* (Coleshill).

Severn, r.n., PrWelsh *Saβren*, British *Sabrinā* (perhaps pre-Celtic). *Severn*.

*****shylving-stole** ME, 'ducking stool' (*v.* O 23). *Le Shylvyngstole* (f.n. Steventon).

*****shiteburgh** ME, 'privy'. *Schytebournelane* (lost street-n. Abingdon). *Shydbornstrete* Gl 4 108 is probably another instance, though listed under burna.

sīc OE, 'small stream'. Occasionally in f.ns., e.g. *Le Siche* (Hagbourne), *Sicchemersche* (Harwell), *Le Sitcheside* (Newbury). Two instances in charters, 787.

sīd OE, 'large, spacious, extensive, long'. Occasionally in f.ns., e.g. *Sydenham* (Cookham), *Sidlowe* (Clewer), *Sydweye* (Welford).

sīde OE, 'side'. *Kilmanside* (later Kilman Knoll Down). Occasionally in f.ns., e.g. *Cotsetelesyde* (Little Wittenham), *Le Esteside*, *Le Westeside* (Buckland), *Le Sitcheside* (Newbury).

sideland ModE (*v.* Pt 1 282). Occasionally in f.ns., e.g. Sideland Ground (Kintbury), Syde Land Piece (Cumnor), Great and Little Sideland (E. Ilsley).

*****sīdling** OE, 'strip of land lying alongside a stream (or some other feature)'. Sideling (f.n. East Garston). The mod. variant *sidelong* (O 465) occurs in Sotwell.

sinder OE, 'cinder, slag'. *La Synderbergh'* (f.n. Barkham). The same n. occurs Gl 1 181.

siuyere ME, 'sieve-maker'. ?Silver St.

skil ME, scyl l. OE, 'boundary' or 'separate'. Skillcroft.

slæd OE, 'valley, hollow'. Minor ns. for which only l. forms are available, *v.* Index. Occasionally in f.ns., sometimes as a simplex n. (*Slade, Le Slade, The Slade*) or first el. (*Sledbrugge* Bray). Cf. also

Brock Slade (Moreton), *Haukeslade* (Winnersh), *Wirslade* (Lambourn), *Waterslade* (Abingdon, E. Hendred, Hungerford, Hurley, Moreton, Steventon). *Hunytsled* (Windsor, incorrectly printed **Hunysled* Pt 1 35) has an obscure first el. Also in charters, 787.

slæget, *sleget OE, 'sheep pasture'. Thornslait Plantation; The Sheep Slait (f.n. Faringdon).

slǣp OE, 'slippery muddy place'. *Tadeslep* (f.n. Thatcham).

slāh OE, 'sloe'. ? Slow Grove.

*slege OE, 'sheep pasture'. Occasionally in f.ns., cf. The Slays (Lambourn). *The Sheep Slay* (Draycott M), Sheep Slays (Steventon), *Sleyfeld* (Windsor 1346), *Button Sleyes* (Blewbury). A word meaning 'sheep pasture' seems more likely for *Sleyfeld* than slege, 'slaying, slaughter', and should perhaps be considered for Slayhills K quoted under slege in Elements.

*slēot OE, 'bar'. *Slotisford* Hundred.

*slīete OE, 'mud'. ? *Slit Weie* (f.n. Wytham).

sling ModE (*v.* Pt 1 282). Slings Firs. Occasionally in f.ns., e.g. Sling (Bradfield, etc.), The Sling (East Garston), The Slings (Enborne), Sling Mdw (Appleton).

slipe, slippe ME, 'slip, narrow strip of land'. Occasionally in mod. f.ns., e.g. The Slip (Cumnor), Slipe (Cookham), The Slipe (Challow), *Long Slip* (Bray).

slōh OE, 'mud'. ? Slow Grove. One instance in charters, 787.

smæl OE, 'narrow'. *Le Smalebrugge* (lost bridge-n. Reading), Smallmarsh. Fairly *freq.* in f.ns., e.g. *Smalle Broke* (Faringdon, etc.), *Smelcombe* (Lambourn), *Smalhegge* (Inkpen), *Smaleland* (Fyfield), Small Mead (Steventon, etc.), *La Smalestret* (Hurley), Small Way (W. Hendred, etc.), *Smaleyatesweye* (Buckland). Also in charters, 787.

smēðe¹ OE, 'smooth, level'. ? Smitham Bridge. Occasionally in f.ns., e.g. *Smithevelde* (Warfield), Smethe Furlong (Bourton), *Smethemede* (Ashbury, Coleshill), *Smethe Meads* (Shrivenham).

smið OE, 'smith'. Occasionally in f.ns., e.g. *Smyth Crofte* (Winnersh), *Smitheshey* (Burghfield), *Smytheslond* (Steventon), *La Smytheslonde* (Cholsey).

smiððe OE, 'smithy'. Wayland Smith's Cave.

smoke ME (*v.* Pt 1 282). Occasionally in f.ns., usually with æcer (*Smokacre, Smoke Acres*, etc.), cf. also Smoke Furlong (Cholsey), Smoke Piece (Buscot).

snaca OE, 'snake'. *Snakemead* (f.n. Winnersh).

snāw OE, 'snow'. There are three instances of the compound with dūn, *q.v.*

sol¹ OE, 'mud, slough, wallowing place'. Black's Hole, Grazeley, Sole Fm (earlier *Blakesole*); *Eversole* (f.n. Brightwalton).

speld OE, ?'chip, splinter'. *Spelthurst* (f.n. Windsor).

*spēne OE, ?'place where wood-chips are found'. Speen.

spere OE, 'spear, spear-shaft'. ?Sparsholt.

spinney ME from Old French, 'copse, small plantation'. Spinney Copse.

spīr OE, spire ModE dial., 'reeds, rushes'. Spire Mdw, Spires (mod. f.ns. Theale, Tubney).

spitel ME from Old French, 'hospital'. Spital; *Spytelhegge* (f.n. Earley), *Spyttlefields* (f.n. Reading).

spoute ME, 'spout, gutter'. Spout Ditch.

*sprǣg OE, 'brushwood, twigs'. Spray Wd.

spring OE, ME, ModE. The ME sense 'copse' may occur in some instances of Spring Copse, Spring Wd (*v.* Index), but some of these have springs nearby, so the mod. sense is probably the usual one. The meaning 'copse' is, however, likely in *Lez Springs* (f.n. Leckhampstead 1547), as these are stated to be woods.

staca OE, 'stake'. *Stakpolemede* (f.n. Binfield).

stænen OE, 'stony'. *Steynemede, Steynemeade* (f.ns. Faringdon, Woolstone).

*stamp OE, 'tree-stump'. *Le Stompe* (f.n. Bray), *La Stompe, La Stamphulle* (f.ns. Hurley).

stān OE, 'stone'. Standen, Stanford (3), Stanmore, Stonecroft Copse. *Freq.* in f.ns., usually as a first el., e.g. *Stonacr'* (Inkpen), *Stambrygge* (Ashbury), *Stonedene* (Wallingford), *Stonham* (Sulhampstead), *Stonelake* (Wytham), *Stanlynche* (Sunningwell), *Stanrewemede* (Sandhurst), *Stanrugg'* (Warfield). The compound with dūn (as in Standen) occurs again in Hurley, that with ford in Bucklebury and Longworth, that with mere (as in Stanmore) in Woolstone. Cf. also *Barndestone* (Windsor), *Hopstone, Southstone* (Cumnor), *La Wayeyngstone* (Coleshill). *v.* stān-(ge)delf, stān-pytt. Also in charters, 788.

*stand OE, 'hunter's stand'. *The Stande* (f.n. Winkfield).

*stande OE, 'pond'. *Le Stonde* (f.n. Cookham). One more instance in charters, 788.

standing ME, 'hunter's stand from which to shoot game'. Kingstanding Hill; *Quenestanding Hill* (f.n. Easthampstead), Standing Hill (f.n. Bisham, Winkfield).

stān-(ge)delf OE, 'stone quarry'. *The Standelf, Stanidelf, Standale, Standelf' Standill* (f.ns. Childrey, Wallingford, Moreton, Steventon, Shrivenham).

stānig OE, 'stony'. Occasionally in f.ns., e.g. *Stony Close, Stoniforlong* (Enborne), *Le Stonicroft* (Earley), *Stony Bottom, Stoneycrofte, La Stonyfeld'* (Reading), *Stoniford* (Burghfield), *Stonylane* (Bucklebury), *Stonylond* (Brightwell), *Stonystretelese* (Moreton).

stank ME, 'pond, pool'. *Le Stanke* (f.n. Stratfield M).

*stān-pytt OE, 'stone pit'. *Stanpitts, Le Stanputtes, Stonpitts, Stanputcroft* (f.ns. Clewer, Windsor, Bray, Bucklebury).

stapol OE, 'post, pillar'. ? Stallpits. Three instances in charters, 788.

steall OE, 'site of a building, cattle-stall, fishing pool'. *Le Stalls* (f.n. Newbury).

stede, styde OE, 'place, site'. *Churchestude* (f.n. Lambourn), *Damagesestede* (f.n. Cumnor), *Le Weorthstede* (f.n. Steventon). One instance in charters, 788.

*steorce OE, 'heifer'. *Sterkeneye* (f.n. Coleshill).

steort OE, 'tail of land'. Stert Plantation, Stert St, Stirt Copse. Occasionally in f.ns., e.g. *Stert* (W. Waltham), *Le Sterte* (Brightwell, Enborne), Green Stirt (Uffington). Two instances in charters, 788.

stewe ME from Old French, 'pond for keeping fish till needed for the table'. *Le Stewe* (f.n. Hungerford, Welford).

*sticce[1] OE. The Stich (f.n. Cookham), *Le Stitche* (f.n. Welford), *Chynnyngstiche* (f.n. Kintbury). *v.* W 447, O 467 for examples in adjacent counties. Mr R. T. Honeybone informed us with reference to the O ns. that c. 1910 a *Stiche* or *Stitch* was an arrangement made with hurdles for the carefully controlled folding of sheep on root crops. He considered that *Nine Styches* O 467 would be a field wide enough to take nine foldings. It is not certain that a temporary structure would give rise to simplex f.ns., but a meaning 'place where hurdles are erected' might be considered for *sticce. This might be a formation with -e[1] (iii) from sticca 'stick'. Professor Löfvenberg prefers a meaning 'hurdle', taking *sticce to be a formation with -e[1] (v) from sticca. One instance in charters, 788.

*sticcen OE, meaning unknown. Stitchens Green; *Hundstichene* (f.n. Ashbury), *Lez Stycchones* (f.n. Steventon). This may be a diminutive of *sticce *supra*.

*stiell, still OE, 'enclosure, place for catching fish'. *Irish Still* (f.n. Hungerford).

stigel, -ol OE, 'stile'. Occasionally in f.ns., e.g. *Stihelhalfaker* (Windsor), *Le Medstighele, Stokingstyle* (Reading), *Totehill Style* (Cookham). Also in charters, 788.

stocc OE, 'tree-trunk, stump'. ? Rowstock; *Stockeyelake* (f.n. Radley). Also in charters,788.

stoccen OE, 'made of logs'. *Stoken Bridge* (f.n. Burghfield). In *Stockenestrete* (f.n. Hungerford) the el. may mean 'among tree-stumps'.

*stoccing OE, 'ground cleared of tree-stumps'. *Stokinge* (f.n. Reading).

stōd OE, 'stud, herd of horses'. *Stodham* (f.n. Sulhampstead). One instance in charters, 788.

stōdfal(o)d OE, 'stud-fold, horse enclosure'. *Statfold, Stodfoldis-hemd', Stutfalls* (f.ns. Uffington, Balking, Sonning). Also in charters, 788.

storc OE, 'stork'. *Storkesham* (f.n. Burghfield).

stōw OE, 'place, place of assembly, holy place'. *Helenestou* (later St Helen Without), Stow Bridge; *Dunstowe* (f.n. Denchworth), *Shipstowe* (f.n. Sutton C). Three instances in charters, 788.

*straca OE, 'strip of land'. *Le Strake*, Streaks (f.ns. Reading, Purley).

strǣt OE, 'Roman road, paved road, street in a town' later (in dial.) 'a straggling village'. Cat Street, Charnham Street, Stratfield, Streatley. Also in early ns. (*Longestret, Stonistrete*) for Devil's Highway, and in street ns. in Newbury, Reading, Wallingford. The sense 'a straggling village' is found in North Street, Leckhampstead Street, Winkfield Street, and mod. minor ns. Fairly *freq.* in f.ns., sometimes as a first el. (e.g. *Le Stretclose* Basildon, *Stretend'* Brightwalton, *Streetemore* Woodley), more often as a second el., e.g. *Aldestrete* (E. Shefford), *Burhstrete* (Sulhampstead B), *Le Hertestrete* (Bray), *Le Heyestret, Melnestrete, La Smalestret* (Hurley), *Kingestrete* (Boxford), *Longestrete, Yeldestrete* (Tilehurst), *La Morstret* (Cookham), *Stonystretelese* (Moreton). *v.* **brād, hǣðen, stoccen.** Also in charters, 788.

strand OE, 'land at the edge of a piece of water'. Strand Water.

strang OE, 'strong', used of firm soil. *Stronglond* (f.n. Sotwell).

strēam OE, 'stream'. Occasionally in f.ns., e.g. *Streeam Dyche* (Padworth), *The Brode Streame* (Hungerford). Also in charters, 788–9.

*strecca OE, 'stretch of land'. *Strecchelane* (f.n. Burghfield), *Wylkestrecche* (f.n. W. Waltham).

string(s) ModE (*v.* Pt I 282). Fairly *freq.* in mod. f.ns.

*strīp OE, 'narrow tract of land'. The Stripe (f.n. Tilehurst).

strōd OE, 'marshy land overgrown with brushwood'. Deepstrood, Gibstrude, Strood, Stroud, Stroud Copse, Stroud Green. Occasionally in f.ns., usually as a simplex n. or first el., e.g. *Strode* (Hurley, Wargrave), *Stroode* (W. Waltham), *Strowde* (Hamstead M), *Strodemede* (Binfield), *Strowde Grene* (Shaw). Cf. also *Aylmerestrode, Le Busshystrode, Wydestrode* (Windsor).

stubb, *stobb OE, 'stub, tree-stump'. Stubwood. Occasionally in f.ns., usually with elle(r)n, *q.v.* Cf. also *Elmestubbe* (Steventon), *Pyristob* (Bray), *Stubbecrofte* (Abingdon), *Stubbethorn, Les Stubbs* (*Ashbury*), Stubs (Beedon), Stubbs (Kintbury). Also in charters, 789.

*stubbing OE, 'place where trees have been stubbed, clearing'. Dean Stubbing Copse, Stubbings. Stubbings occurs occasionally as a mod. f.n.

styria OE, a kind of fish. *Sterepole* (f.n. Cumnor).

sulh, gen. sylh, OE, 'plough, furrow, gully'. Sulham, Sulhamstead. One instance in charters, 789.

sumor OE, 'summer'. *Somerdon'* (*v.* Winterdown). Occasionally in f.ns., e.g. Summerford (Cumnor), *Somerheyse* (Windsor), *Somerlez* (Shaw), *Sumerlese* (Uffington), Summer Leaze (Cookham, Hamstead M, Moreton), Summers Leas (Pusey).

sūr OE, 'sour'. Sower Hill Fm. Occasionally in f.ns., usually with land (*Le Sourlond, La Surlond, Sowerlands*, Sour Lands). Cf. also Sour Close (Kennington), Sour Ground (Hamstead M), Sour Leys Pightle (Wokingham), *Suermedowe* (Reading), *Suremed* (Abingdon).

sūtere OE, 'shoe-maker'. *Souteresgrof'* (f.n. W. Waltham), possibly a surname.

sūð OE, 'south'. Circourt, Southcote, Southend, South Hill Pk, Southmoor, Southridge, Sowberry Ct, Surly, Sutton Lo, Sutton Courtenay. *Freq.* in f.ns., e.g. *Soddone* (Hurley), *Southdoune* (Welford), *Southeye* (Wokingham), *Suthfeld* (Hanney, etc.), *Suthale* (Binfield), *Suthlye* (Peasemore), *Suthwyk'* (Buscot), *Suthwode* (W. Waltham). The comparative occurs in *Le Sutheredole* (Streatley).

sūðan OE adv. 'south, southerly'. Shurlock.

swæð OE, 'track', swathe ME, 'strip of grassland'. Occasionally in f.ns., usually as a simplex n. (e.g. *Lez Swathes* Abingdon, *Le Swathe*

Hamstead M). Cf. also *Le Monn(e)swathe* (Faringdon), The Bellman's Swath (Grove), Mill Swathes (Sutton C).

swan¹ OE, 'swan'. ? Swansea (f.n. Draycott M).

swān² OE, 'herdsman, peasant'. *Swancroft* (f.n. Lambourn), ? Swansea (*v.* swan¹). One instance in charters, 789.

Swealwe², OE r.n., *Swale*.

swēte OE, 'sweet'. *Swete Crofte* (f.n. Clewer).

*swielg, *swylg OE, 'gulf, pit, whirlpool', ModE dial. swilly, 'eddy, whirlpool, gutter washed out of the soil'. Swilly Copse. Occasionally in f.ns., e.g. The Swilly (Bisham), Swilly Ground (Bucklebury), Swilly Hole (Bradfield), Swilly Pits (Hampstead N). *Swylyngholme* (Earley), *Swilling Piece* (Bucklebury) may be partly from swylgend, of similar meaning to *swylg.

swīn¹ OE, 'swine, pig'. ? *Swineshill*, Swinford, Swinley; *Swineshead* (f.n. Cookham). Two instances in charters, 789.

*swin² OE 'creek, channel'. ? *Swineshill*.

tāde OE, 'toad'. *Tadeslep* (f.n. Thatcham).

tægl OE, 'tail, projection'. Occasionally in f.ns., e.g. Pond Tail Mead (Stratfield M), Old Pond Tail (Sulhamstead), *Twotayles* (Bray).

tān OE, 'twig, sprout, shoot', probably also 'stake'. *Tanheye, Tanlock* (f.ns. Wantage, Reading).

tarr ? ModE dial., apparently used of islands in R. Thames. F.ns. in Bray and Cookham (*v.* Pt **1** 85), cf. also Old Tar (Balking).

tēag OE, 'small enclosure'. ? *Brembeltheye* (f.n. Warfield).

tempel OE, temple ME, 'temple', referring in p.ns. to the properties of the Knights Templars. Templeton.

tēn, tīn, tȳn, tīen OE, 'ten'. Occasionally in f.ns., e.g. Teen Acres (Moreton), The 10 Acres (Bray), Ten Lands (Steventon).

tigel(e), -ule OE, 'tile', usually referring in p.ns. to places where tiles were made. Tilehurst, Tileplace Cottages. Occsaionally in f.ns., e.g. *Tigheleheld* (W. Waltham), *Tigheldfeld* (Inkpen). In *Tylehall* (Clewer) it probably refers to roofing material. *Tylehouse* (*v.* hūs) may refer to a building with a tiled roof or to one where tiles were stored; *Tyllehouse* and *Tylecroft* occur in Reading. *v.* also hielde.

*tita, *tite OE. An el. of this form is required for Titcomb, apparently identical with Tidcombe W, *v.* Pt **2** 317. Cf. also Titcomb Hill (mod. f.n. Hinksey) and Titcombe Gl **2** 243 (*Tetecumbe* c. 1250).

*tōt, *tōte OE, 'look-out place'. *Totlynche* (f.n. Steventon).

*tōtærn-dūn OE, 'hill with a look-out building (i.e. a hill-fort)'. Totterdown (3). F.ns. in Bucklebury and Sulhamstead.

*tōt-hyll OE, 'look-out hill'. *Totehull'* (later part of Minster St). F.ns. in Bray, Burghfield, Cookham, Lambourn, Pangbourne.

*trawe OE, meaning unknown (not previously noted in p.ns.). *Trawe.*

trendel, trindel, tryndel OE, 'circle, ring'. Trindledown; *Trendelham, Tryndle Acre*, Trundle Hill (f.ns. Hungerford, Cookham, Newbury).

trēow OE, 'tree'. Occasionally in f.ns., e.g. *Adelystre, Hachtrewe* (Bray), *Bihildestr'* (Hungerford). Also in charters, 789.

*trind OE, 'stake for fencing'. ? *Trindley.*

tuffe, tufte ME, 'tuft, cluster of trees or bushes'. *Le Marschalestuft* (f.n. Wytham). ? *Woodgates Toft* (f.n. Cumnor).

tūn OE, 'enclosure, farmstead, village, estate' (*v.* 939 ff. for discussion of the various senses). Aldermaston, Aston, Aston Tirrold and Upthorpe, Balsdon, *Bray Town*, *Charlton*, Charlton, Chilton, Clapton, Compton, Compton Beauchamp, Drayton, East Garston (pers.n.), Eastmanton, Easton, Eaton, Eaton Hastings, Eddington (pers.n.), *Elington*, ? Elton (pers.n.), Hinton, Hinton Waldrist, Idstone (pers.n.), Kingston Bagpuize, Kingston Lisle, Kingstone Winslow, Knighton, Leverton (pers.n.), Marlston, Milton, Moreton, Netherton, Newton, North Town, Nuptown, Odstone (pers.n.), Sutton Lo, Sutton Courtenay, Templeton, The Town, Towney, Uffington (pers.n.), Ufton Nervet (pers.n.), Upton, Wallingtons, *Walton*, Weston (2), Woolstone (pers.n.), Wootton. A common field in Grove is called Norton (earliest form 1268–72), and Sutton in Cookham (surviving in Sutton Lo) may originally have denoted an open field. These ns. may be elliptical, meaning 'field north (or south) of the village'. Otherwise tūn occurs occasionally as a first el. in f.ns., e.g. *Toncroft* (Bray), *Le Townesende* (Brightwalton), *Tounforlong* (Wallingford, etc.). *v.* -ingtūn. Also in charters, 789.

tūnman ME, 'villager'. *Townmannemede* (f.n. Denchworth).

turf OE, 'turf'. Occasionally in f.ns., e.g. *Turveye* (Kennington), Turf House Mdw (Easthampstead).

twicen(e) OE, 'fork of a road, crossroads'. Touchen-end. F.ns. in Brightwalton, Sandhurst, Steventon.

*twī-ford OE, 'double ford', i.e. a place where a road crosses two streams. Twyford; *La Twyvorde* (f.n. Kintbury).

*þæcce OE, 'thatch' (*v.* Pt 1 188). Thatcham. Occasionally in f.ns., e.g. *Thacham* (Hinksey), *Thachmed* (Reading). þæc occurs in a charter-n., 789.

þel, pl. **þelu**, OE 'plank', ? 'plank bridge'. Theale (Mr Gover draws attention to Deal Fm in Greatham Ha, *La Thele* Hy 3, another example).

þēod OE, 'people, tribe, region'. ?Tidmarsh.

þēof OE, 'thief'. *Theofait* (f.n. Hungerford).

þiccett OE, 'thicket'. Leckhampstead Thicket, Maidenhead Thicket. F.ns. in Boxford, Brightwalton, Wargrave.

þistel OE, 'thistle'. Occasionally in f.ns., e.g. *Thistelcroft, Le Thistellcrofte, Le Thistelforlong* (Abingdon, Speen, Wallingford).

þorn OE, 'hawthorn tree'. Crowthorne, Hawthorn Hill, *Nachededorne* Hundred, Thorn Hill (Lambourn), and minor ns. for which only l. forms are available. Occasionally in f.ns., usually as a simplex n. (*Thorne* Pangbourne, etc.) or first el. (e.g. *Thorneham* Goosey, *Thornhanger* Boxford, *Thornhulle* Enborne), but sometimes as second el., e.g. *Childesthorne* (Steventon), *Hegge Thorne* (Denchworth). Cf. also *Thre Thornys* (Earley), *Threthornfurl'* (Ashbury). There may be a collective use in *Le Thorn'* Stratfield M, which is the n. of a wood. Also in charters, 789–90.

þornig OE, 'growing with thorns'. Twice in f.ns. with dūn, *q.v.*

þrēo, þrī, dat. þrim, OE, 'three'. Occasionally in f.ns., twice with þorn, *q.v.* Cf. also *Thremelond* (Steventon), *Threhurn* (Swallowfield). Also in charters, twice with þorn, 790.

þrop OE, 'hamlet, outlying farm'. Colthrop, Thrupp (2), Aston Upthorpe. Lost ns. *Clywaresthrop* (Clewer), *Est-* and *West Thorpe* (Reading).

þrostle OE 'thrush'. *Trostelbedde* (f.n. Abingdon).

þrote OE, 'throat', ?'narrow road-junction'. The Throat.

þwang OE, 'thong', probably 'narrow strip of land'. The Thongs, Thongs, *Thongs Mead* (f.ns. Thatcham, Burghfield, Cumnor).

þȳfel OE, 'bush, thicket'. *Thuuelheker* (f.n. Waltham S.L.). Two instances in charters, 790.

þȳrel OE, 'hole, opening', ?'hollow'. ?Thurle Grange.

þyrne OE, 'thorn bush'. *The Broode Thurne, Lokesthurne* (f.ns. Denchworth, Abingdon). Two instances in charters, 790.

þyrs OE, 'giant, demon'. ?*Thorsdiche* (f.n. Sparsholt).

uferra OE, 'higher, upper'. Occasionally in f.ns., e.g. *Overcroft* (Hurley), *Le Ouergrove, Ouerland* (Reading), *Overmylle* (Moreton), usually in distinction to *Nether-*. Cf. *Fyfhyde Overton* and *Netherton* in Fyfield.

under OE, 'under, below'. *Underore*. Occasionally in f.ns., e.g. *Underdown* (Longworth), *Underhull'* (Steventon).

uppan OE, 'upon'. *Upnor*.

upp(e) OE, 'higher up'. Nuptown, *Upledcombe* (later Letcombe Basset), Upper Lambourn, Upton, (Aston) Upthorpe. Occasionally in f.ns., e.g. *Le Updyche* (Uffington), *Upfeld* (Appleford, etc.), *Upgrove* (Marcham), *Uppegrof* (Streatley), *Up Mede* (Ashbury). *Uppinton'* (Abingdon) is from *upp-in-tūne* '(land) higher up in the estate'.

ūt(e) OE, 'outside, on the outskirts, more distant'. Occasionally in f.ns., e.g. *Outlanglond* (Steventon), *Le Owtemede* (Buckland), Out Close (S. N. Hurst).

vacherie ME from Old French, 'vaccary, dairy-farm'. *La Vacherie* (f.n. Kingston Lisle).

valeie ME from Old French. *La Valeye* (f.n. Windsor).

vinȝerd ME, 'vineyard'. Vine Yard, The Vineyard, *Vyneards* (f.ns. Shellingford, Moulsford, Wallingford). *v.* wīn-geard.

wacen OE, 'watch, vigil', used in p.ns. of a watching-place. *?Le Wakenell* (f.n. Aston T).

wād OE, 'woad'. *Wadeiam* (f.n. Sutton C). Two instances in charters, 790.

*wāden OE, 'growing with woad'. Wadley.

(ge)wæsc OE, 'washing, flood'. Wash Common and Hill; Wash Mead (f.n. Cumnor).

wæsce OE, 'place for washing'. *Maydenwashe* (f.n. E. Hendred).

*wæsse, gen. **wassan**, OE, 'wet place, marsh'. ?Wane Bridge.

wǣt OE, 'wet'. Whatcombe. Occasionally in f.ns., usually with land, e.g. *La Wetelond'* (Newbury). *Le Wetelond* (Steventon), *Wete Lond* (Denchworth), *Wetforlong*, *La Wetelonde* (Brightwell).

wæter OE, 'water'. Blackwater. Fairly *freq.* in f.ns., often with slæd, *q.v.* Cf. also *Le Water Furlong*, *Le Water Mede* (Speen), *Le Water-ɷnd*, *Water Croft* (Sandhurst), *La Brodewater* (Inkpen). Broad Water occurs as a mod. minor n., *v.* Index. Also in charters, twice with slæd, 790.

wagian OE, 'to move, shake'. G. Kristensson, *Namn och Bygd* 61 (1973), 49–54, suggests that a deverbal s-verb from *wagian*, which would be intensive or frequentative in meaning, would be a possible base for the r.n. in -ing[2] which gives the p.n. Wasing.

waite ME from Old French, 'watch, look-out place'. *The Wayte* (f.n. Ashbury).

walu OE, **wale** ME, 'ridge of earth or stone'. ?*Muchel and Litel Wales* (f.n. Swallowfield).

-ware OE, 'dwellers'. Clewer.

Wāse, OE r.n. from wāse 'mud' (v. Pt **1** 15–16). Osse Ditch, *Ouse Ditch*, Woose Hill.

weald OE, 'woodland'. Waltham.

wealh OE, 'foreigner, Welshman, serf'. Wallingtons, *Walton*, Wawcott. One instance in charters, 790.

weall OE 'wall'. *Le Walles, Waldich* (f.ns. Windsor, Wallingford.)

weard OE, 'watch, ward, protection', perhaps 'look-out place'. *Le Warde* (f.n. Clewer).

weg OE, 'way'. Broadway, Broadway Copse, Green Way, Icknield Way, *Londoneweye* (later London Rd Earley), Port Way, Ridge Way, Stileway Rd, Weycock. *Freq.* in f.ns., where the following compounds recur: *Brodewey* (Earley, etc.), *Chircheweye* (Kintbury, etc.), *London Way* (Eaton H, etc.), *Milnewey* (Kintbury, etc.), *Myddelwey* (Ashbury, etc.), *Smaleweye* (Earley, etc.), Cf. also *Blakeway* (Hagbourne), *Butter Waye* (Wootton), *Combeweye* (Inkpen), *Croweye* (Steventon), *Fulwey* (Lambourn), *The Hardweye* (Coxwell), *Haywaye* (East Garston), *Medwey* (Harwell), *Neweweye* (Earley), *Sydweye* (Welford), *Wodeweye* (Childrey). Occasionally as a first el., e.g. *Weyacre* (Sutton C), *Weydic* (Abingdon), *The Weye Forlong* (Hagbourne). *v.* -hǣme-, rād. Also in charters, 790–1.

weg-(ge)lǣte OE, 'road junction'. *Lewdehammesweylet* (*v.* Lendham). One instance in charters, 791.

welig OE, 'willow'. Welford. One instance in charters, 791.

wer, wær OE, 'weir, river-dam, fishing-enclosure in a river'. Warfield, Wargrave. Occasionally in f.ns., e.g. *La Were* (Abingdon), *Were Lands, Le Were Pole* (Faringdon), *Hornedwere* (Windsor), *Wydewere* (Fyfield). Also in charters, 791.

*wering OE, 'a river-dam'. *Werynge* (f.n. Streatley 1484, *La Were* occurs in the same list of ns.).

west OE, 'west'. Westcot, West Down Lane, West Fields, West Meadow, Weston, Westridge, *Westwyk'* (later Sutton Wick). *Freq.* in f.ns., e.g. *Westebrugge, Westhowke* (Ashubry), *Westende* (Steventon), *Westfeld* (Kintbury, etc.), *Westhull'* (Balking), *Westmede* (Kintbury, etc.), *Westmor* (Tidmarsh), *Westrugge* (Kintbury), *Le Westeside* (Buckland), *Westwode* (Brightwalton). Also in charters, 791.

westan OE, 'west, west of'. Westbrook (2), Westwood. Occasionally in f.ns., e.g. *Westetownefurl'* (Ashbury). It is not always possible to distinguish between west and westan.

westerra OE, 'more westerly'. *v.* ēasterra. One instance in charters, 791.

westmest OE, 'most westerly'. *West Mest Furlong* (f.n. Moreton).

weðer OE, 'castrated ram'. *Wetherdowne* (f.n. Uffington).

wewe ME, meaning unknown. *v.* Pt 1 282.

weyour ME from Old French, 'pond'. *Weghezur, Le Weyer Close* (f.ns. Inkpen, Appleford).

wīc OE, 'dwelling, farm, dairy-farm', and in pl. 'hamlet, village' (*v. infra* 942–3 for discussion of various senses). Ardington Wick, Bray Wick, Charney Wick, Furzewick (pers.n.), Fyfield Wick, Gooseywick, Grovewick, *Haslewick*, Henwick, *Hollicks*, Littlewick, Pennyswick, Petwick (pers.n.), Snowswick, Sutton Wick, Tulwick (pers.n.), *Westwyke, Wick* (3), Wickcroft, Wickfield, Wick Hall, Wick Hill (Warfield), Wick Lane, Wick Wd, Wickwood Fm. Occasionally in f.ns., usually as a simplex n. (e.g. *La Wike* Sparsholt, *La Wyke* Basildon, *Wyke* Reading) or first el. (e.g. *Wikelese* Woolstone, *The Wykelond* Challow, *La Wykmede* Lambourn). Cf. also *Cowyk'* (Reading), *Kowyke* (Thatcham), *Lestaneswyk* (Bray, pers.n.), *La Musewik'* (Garford). *v.* wīchām. Two more instances in charters, 791.

wice OE, 'wych-elm'. *Wychemere,* ? *Wikenholt* (f.ns. Winkfield, East Garston).

*****wīchām** OE, 'village associated with a Romano-British settlement'. Wickham, Wickham Bushes.

wīd OE, 'wide, spacious'. Whit Coombe, Widmead, Widemead, Wigmore, Wildridings, Woodhay, *Wydemor*. Occasionally in f.ns., where there are further examples of the compounds with (ge)hæg (Hurley, Wytham) and mæd (Shaw, Steventon, Tidmarsh, Tilehurst). Cf. also *La Wydefeld* (Tilehurst), *Wydefelde, Wydegrove* (Pangbourne), *Wideham* (Sulhamstead), *Widenham* (Reading), *Wydestrod* (Windsor).

wiella OE, 'well, spring, stream, river-source'. Amwell (pers.n.), Barwell, Brightwell, Carswell, *Carswell, Castlewell*, Chilswell (pers.n.), Cholswell, Coxwell (pers.n.), Cresswells, The Durnals, Goldwell, Goswell, Hardwell, Harwell, Lertwell, (?pers.n.), ?Sandleford, Sotwell (pers.n.), Sunningwell, Trunkwell (pers.n.), Wellhouse, Woolstone Wells. *Freq.* in f.ns., c.f e.g. *Adewell* (Burghfield, pers.n.), *Benewell'* (Sulhamstead), *Bilderwell, Maydewell* (Bray), *Blakewelle* (Abingdon, Kintbury), *Clerkenwell* (Coleshill, Reading), *Cronwelle* (Lambourn), *Shadwell* (Pangbourne). The compound with **ceald** (as in Cholswell) recurs in Ashbury, Coxwell, Moreton, and that with **golde** in East Garston. Also in charters, usually in the form **wyll**, 791.

*wigga OE, ?'that which moves'. The n. Wigmore occurs in f.ns. in B. Leigh, Brimpton, Midgham, Sparsholt and Sunningwell, and *Wigmores* occurs in Hungerford. The Midgham n. is *Wygemore* 1248, and this may be the same marsh as the 19th-cent. n. in Brimpton. Wigmore He is derived in DEPN from an OE pers.n. or a Welsh compound in *gwig*, but instances occur in minor ns. and f.ns. in several counties (*v.* Gl **4** 156 and cf. Wigmore Fm on 1″ map in Stratfield Saye Ha), and the compound may be a term descriptive of a marsh. It should be noted, however, that mod. Wigmore is sometimes a corruption of ME *widemore* or *widemere*, cf. **wīd** *supra* and W 401.

*wiht OE, 'bend'. Wytham.

wīl OE, 'wile, trick'. Wyld Fm.

wilde OE, 'wild, desolate'. *Wildmore* (f.n. Englefield), *Le Wildewaye* (f.n. Peasemore), *Wildemede* (f.n. Sandhurst).

wince OE, 'winch'. *Wynchehurste* (f.n. Cholsey), The Winch Mdw (f.n. Remenham), *Winchmeade* (f.n. Cookham).

wind¹ OE, 'wind'. *Windesherde* (f.n. Hamstead M).

*windels OE, 'winding gear, winch, windlass'. Windsor.

*wind-geat OE, 'wind-swept gap or pass'. *La Windgate, Wyndʒate, The Wyndʒate* (f.ns. Hurley, Lambourn, Denchworth).

windmulle ME, 'windmill'. Windmill Fm. F.ns. in Bray, Harwell, Inkpen, Moreton, Wallingford.

wīn-geard OE, 'vineyard'. Vineyard (earlier *Le Wyneyerde*). F.ns. in Harwell, Reading, Speen, Tidmarsh.

*winn¹, *wynn OE, 'pasture'. Winnersh; *Wynnebusshe* (f.n. Finchampstead).

winter¹ OE, 'winter'. Winterbourne, Winterbrook, Winterdown. Occasionally in f.ns., e.g. *Wynterscerde* (Abingdon), Winter Leys (Cumnor). In stream-ns. the reference is to brooks flowing in winter, in other ns. usually to pasture on drier ground to which stock are moved in the winter months. Winterdown is associated with a *Somerdon'* in the early ref. One instance in charters, 791.

wīr OE, 'bog-myrtle'. *La Wirslade* (f.n. Lambourn). One instance in charters, 791.

wisc OE, 'marshy meadow'. Whistley (*v.* Pt **1** 100–1 for a list of instances of this compound in p.ns.; it may have been an appellative).

wīðig OE, 'willow'. White Brook. Fairly *freq.* in mod. minor ns. and f.ns., especially in the compound Withybed. There are several instances of Wergs, a mod. form from the pl. of wīðig, and a 17th-cent. form *Wirge* occurs in Grove and E. Hendred. Occasionally in early f.ns., e.g. *Wythye* (Ashbury), *The Wythye* (Winnersh), *Wythiham* (Windsor), *La Widyelonde* (Hurley), *Wythemedegrove* (Binfield). Cf. also *Wergen Pits* (Draycott M 1770) and Withy Pits (Longcot). Two instances in charters, 791.

wōh OE 'crooked'. Fairly *freq.* in f.ns., usually with land (e.g. *Wowelonde* Brightwalton, *Woolond* Ashbury), and in several instances with furlang (e.g. *Wowefurlong* Windsor, *Woghforlong* Earley). Cf. also *Woacres* (Hamstead M), *Woghacr'* (Inkpen), *Le Wooplote* (Sandhurst). Also in charters, 791.

*wōp, ?OE bird-n. *Wopland* (f.n. Inkpen). One possible instance in charters, 791.

*wōrig OE, 'wandering, winding', perhaps 'turbid', used as a r.n. ?*Le Woore* (f.n. Radley).

worð, weorð, wurð, wyrð OE, 'enclosure'. (*v.* 943 f. for discussion of the various senses). Aldworth (?pers.n.), Bayworth (pers.n.), Chaddleworth (pers.n.), Coworth, Dedworth (pers.n.), Denchworth (pers.n.), Hollingsworth, Littleworth (Faringdon), Longworth, Padworth (pers.n.), Pibworth (pers.n.), Seacourt (pers.n.), Sugworth (pers.n.). *Freq.* in f.ns. As a simplex f.n. in Earley (*La Worthe*), Longworth (*Le Wurth*), Reading, Cumnor and Radley (*Le Worthe*), and Windsor (*Le Worthe*, an open field). With an adj. of position in Easthampstead (*Westworth*), E. Hendred (*The East-worth*) and Windsor (*Estworth, Northworth*, distinct from *Le Worthe*). Other compounds include *Bagworthe* (Woodley), *Brute-wrthe* (Coleshill), *Eldesworth* (Windsor, pers.n.), *Liberworthe* (Harwell), *Mereworth* (Cookham), *Peggesworth* (Bucklebury, pers.n.), *Riwurde* (Shrivenham), *Le Weorthstede* (Steventon), *Worth End Gate* (Cookham). The Worth occurs in TA for Buriton Ha. *v.* worðig, worðign. Also in charters, 792.

worðig, weorðig, wurðig, wyrðig OE, 'enclosure'. This derivative of worð is well evidenced as a simplex f.n., sometimes alternating with worð. *Le Worthy* occurs in Enborne, Hurley, Newbury, Shaw, Speen and Thatcham, *Wordy* in Bucklebury. Lower and Upper Worthy occurs as a mod. f.n. in Cookham. In Cumnor, Newbury and Radley there is interchange between worðig and worð, in Stratfield M between worðig, worð and worðign, *q.v.* Several instances of The Worthy, Worthy Mdw, etc. occur in Ha TAs. One instance in charters, 792.

worðign OE, 'enclosure' (the typical W. Midland form of the group of els. comprising worð, worðig, worðign). Only evidenced in Stratfield M, in the series of forms *Wordia* 12th, *La Wortht* 1321, *Worthine* 1571, *The Worthen* 1620, The Worderls *TA*.

wudu OE, 'wood, forest', also 'timber'. The Forehead, Hayward, Hen Wood, Heywood, Kentwood, Lambwood, Stubwood, Tubney Wood, Westwood, Woodcote, Woodcraft Wd, Woodcroft, Woodhill, Woodley, Wood St, Wootton, Woodspeen. *Freq.* in f.ns., usually as a first el. The compound with croft is common. Cf. also *Wodebere*, *La Wodegrene*, *Wodehawe* (Windsor), *Woodbrech* (Cumnor), *Wodefeld*, *La Wodehouse* (Tilehurst), *Wodefeld*, *Le Wodesyde* (Hurley), *Wodefurlong* (Enborne), *Wodehull* (Earley), *Wodemer* (Brightwalton), *Wodeweye* (Childrey), *Wood Yates* (Hamstead M). Occasionally as a simplex n. (e.g. *Le Wood* Welford), and as a second el., e.g. *Brocwod* (Windsor), *Estwode* (Compton, etc.), *La Hyewode* (Inkpen), *Inwode* (Maidenhead), *Lichtwud'* (Cookham), *Northwode* (Reading, etc.), *Suthwode* (W. Waltham), *Westwode* (Brightwalton). Also in charters, 792.

wudu-land OE, 'woodland'. Lambourn Woodlands; *Woodlande* (f.n. Sonning).

wulf OE, 'wolf'. Woolley (2), Woolvers Barn; *Wlfacre* (f.n. Brightwell), *Wlfhull'* (f.n. Sulhamstead). One more instance in charters, 792.

wyrmsteall OE, 'shelter for cattle' (*v.* Pt 2 318). Wormstall (2).

*yfer OE, 'edge or brow of a hill'. Rivar Copse. One instance in charters, 792.

PERSONAL NAMES IN BERKSHIRE
PLACE-NAMES AND FIELD-NAMES

This list includes personal names incorporated in place-names and field-names, page refs. being given for the latter. In some cases it is not certain that the examples contain the personal name, but they are listed here if there is a possibility that they contain it. The discussions of individual p.ns. in Pts 1 and 2 should be consulted in all cases. Some p.ns. are entered twice in this list, as alternative etymologies involving different pers.ns. are given for them.

Some pers.ns. which are cited in their OE forms continued in use in ME, and it is often impossible to say whether a f.n. or minor n. originated in the earlier or later period. The two lists of ME pers.ns. contain only pers.ns. not likely to have been known in England before the 11th cent.

Names which are not independently attested are marked *, and a discussion of these will usually be found in the articles on the p.ns. in which they are considered to occur.

A. OLD ENGLISH

Ad(d)a (*Adecombe* Pt 2 341, *Adewell* Pt 1 210); *Æbba* (Abingdon); *Ælfhild* fem. (Arborfield Cross); **Æsc* (*Æscesbyrig, Ashdown*); *Æðel* (*Adelystre* Pt 1 50); *Æðelflæd* fem. (Elton); *Æðelhēah* (*Æþelheahingwudu*); *Æðelheard* (*Athelardesford* Pt 1 108); *Æðelmǣr* (*Aylmerestrode* Pt 1 34); *Æðelrǣd* (Ardington); *Æðelweard* (*Ailwardesham* Pt 1 95, *Alwardeslond* Pt 2 421); *Afa* (Avington); **Amma* (Amwell).

Babba (*Babeham* Pt 1 85); *Bacca* (Bagmore); *Bacga* (Bagley); *Bǣga* (Bayworth); *Bēaghild* fem. (*Bihildestr'* Pt 2 307); **Bæssel* (Basildon); **Benna* (Benham); *Beorhtgȳð* fem. (*Brystetherudyngge* Pt 1 26); *Beorhtwald* (Brightwalton); **Bera* (Barwell); **Bĕthere* (Betterton; the vowel quantity of the first el. is uncertain, the n. is incorrectly printed in Pt 2 487); *Bicga* (Bigfrith); **Blæcmund* (*Blakemundeslonde* Pt 2 441); *Bōta* (Botley); *Botta* (*Botney* Pt 2 478); *Bōtwulf* (*Botulphus Puddellez* Pt 1 108); **Bracca* (Bracknell); *Brand* (*Brands Bridge*); *Brūn* (*Bruningmere*); **Brūngifu* fem. (*Brungiveaker* Pt 2 538); *Brȳni* (Brimpton); *Bucca* (*Buckenhull* Pt 1 65); **Bunta* (*Bunting-*

bury); *Burghild* fem. (Bucklebury); *Burgweard* (Buscot); **Byssel* (Bisham).

*Cadel (Katesgrove); **Cāfhere* (Caversham); *Cana* (Kine Croft); **Ceadela* (Chaddleworth, Channy Grove); **Ceawa* (Challow, Chawridge); *Cēn* (*Kenesore* Pt 2 342); *Cēol* (Cholsey); **Cifa* (Chieveley); **Cifel* (Chilswell); *Cille* fem. or **Cilla* (Childrey); **Cobba* (Coppington Down); **Cocc* (Coxwell); **Coccel* (Coscote); *Cǣna* (Kennington); *Coll* (Coleshill, the pers.n. is mistakenly starred Pt 2 357); *Cola* (*Calcot*, Colthrop); **Cūla* (Culham Shaw); **Cuma* (Cumnor); *Cusa* (Curridge); *Cwichelm* (Scutchamer); *Cynewynn* fem. (*Kynwynhegge* Pt 2 461, this pers.n. is recorded in the recently discovered will of Æðelgifu); *Cypping* (*Cuppynggesfryth* Pt 1 219).

*Denic (Denchworth); **Dida* (Diddenham); *Dodda* (*Doddyngly* Pt 1 74); *Dud(d)a* (Didcot, *Dudbroke*); *Duduc* (Duxford); *Dun(n)* (Donnington); *Dunna* (Dunmore Fm); *Dydda* (Dedworth).

Ēadgifu fem. (Eddington); *Ēadmund* (*Edmundeslonde* Pt 1 86); *Ēadwine* (Idstone); *Ēadwulf* (*Eduluesbreche* Pt 2 327); **Eald* (*Eldeswurth'* Pt 1 33); *Ealda* (*Aldeduna* Pt 2 362, Aldworth); *Earda* (Ardington); **Ēarmund* (*Earmundesleah*); *Ēata* (Yattendon); *Ebba* (*Ebbelonde* Pt 2 325); *Ecga* (*Eggle* Hundred); *Ella* (Elcot); **Enna* (Eney, also listed on p. 789); *Eofor* (Everington).

*Fobba (Fobney); **Fōt* (Furzewick); *Franca* (*Franckebrooke* Pt 2 358); **Friðel* (Frilsham); **Friðela* (Frilford); *Fugel* (Fulscot, the pers.n. is incorrectly given as *Fugol* Pt 2 524).

*Gāra (Garford); *Gēat* (Yattendon); **Geofa* (Evendon's Fm); **Gunrǣd* (*Gunredesford* Pt 1 42, also listed on p. 794); *Gydda* (Gidley).

Hacca (Hagbourne); **Hǣgel* (*Heylescumb'* Pt 2 472); **Hagol* (*Haheleshull'* Pt 2 312); *Hǣha* (Hennor Mill); *Headda* (Hadley); **Hēahhild* fem. (*Heihildeberewe* Pt 2 441); *Hengest* (Hinksey); *Hereburh* fem. (Arborfield); **Herel* (*Herlesdun'* Pt 1 263); **Herela* (Arlington); *Hereweald* (Harrowdown Hill); **Hereweard* (*Herewardesle* Pt 1 180, *Herwardeslond* Pt 1 95); *Hild* (*Hildeslowe* Hundred, Ilsley); **Hod* (*Hodeshull'* Pt 1 197); **Hoda* (Hodcott); **Holdmǣr* (*Holdemarescote* Pt 2 441); **Hrōc* (*Rokesham* Pt 1 151); **Hrōca* (Rockley); **Hrodel* (Ruddles Pool); **Hucel* (*Hucleseye* Pt 1 253); **Hund* (Hutchcomb's Fm).

*Ideca (*Idekenhull* Pt 2 472).

*Lēoda (Letcombe); *Lēofede* (Lendham); *Lēofgār* (*Levegares-acre* Pt 1 95); *Lēofmǣr* (*Lemmareshamme* Pt 1 193); *Lēofrūn* fem. (*Leverenecrofte* Pt 2 342); *Lēofstan* (*Lestaneswyk* Pt 1 51); *Lēofwaru* fem.

(Leverton); *Lilla* (Lilley); **Lolla* (Lollingdon); **Lorta* (Lertwell); *Lulla* (Lulle Brook).

*Macca (Mackney); **Māda* (Maiden Hatch); *Mūl* (Moulsford, *Mulesfeld* Pt 1 193, *Mulesdon'* Pt 2 327).

Oda (Odney, Olding Hill); *Ofa* (Ownham); *Ordhēah* (Odstone); *Ōslāc* (*Oselakemere* Pt 1 183).

Pǣga (Paley Street, Pangbourne); *Peada* (Padworth); **Pecg* (*Peggesworth* Pt 1 160); **Pēota* (Petwick); **Pinn* (*Pinneshok* Pt 1 35, Pinsgrove); *Pybba* (Pibworth).

*Rēad(a) (Reading); **Rōt* (Ruscombe).

Sǣmǣr (*Samareslond* Pt 1 66); **Sceaft* (*Shaftsey*); **Scear* (Shellingford); **Sc(e)obba* (Shoppenhanger's, Shovel Spring); **Sc(e)ort* (*Scortescumbe* Pt 2 332); **Scīene* (Shinfield); *Scot(t)* (Shottesbrooke); **Seofoca* (Seacourt); *Snell* (Snelsmore, *Snellesputte* Pt 1 243); **Stīf(a)* (Steventon); *Sucga* (Sugnell, Sugworth); **Sunna* (Sonning, Sunningwell, *Sunenhelve* Pt 2 539); **Sutta* (Sotwell, *Sotenham* Pt 1 184).

*Tættuca (*Tottingestone* Pt 2 381, also listed on p. 794); *Tette* fem. or **Tetta* (Tittenhurst); *Tib(b)a* (Tidney); *Totta* (Tadcomb Pt 1 153, also listed on p. 794); **Trumeca* (Trunkwell); **Tubba* (Tubney, Tubworth); *Tulla* (Tulwick); **Tydda* (*Tydeham* Pt 1 260).

Uffa (Ufton, Uffington); **Ugga* (Hugman's Wd).

Wada (Wadley); **Wæcel* (Watchfield); *Wealh* (Wallingford); **Wearda* (Warnham); **Wendel* (Winslow); **Weohha* (Wokefield); *Wicga* (*Wyggenhill*, *Wygginham* Pt 1 23); *Wīcing* (Wicklesham); *Wigbeald* (Willington's Fm); **Willic* (*Wylchesham* Pt 2 425); **Wineca* (Winkfield); *Witta* (*Witeneie* Pt 2 425, Wittenham); **Wocc* (Wokingham); **Wuduca* (Woodcray); *Wulfgȳð* fem. (*Uluethemed'* Pt 1 211); *Wulflāf* (Woolhampton); *Wulfrīc* (Woolstone, *Wolfricheshamstal* Pt 2 313); *Wulfrūn* fem. (*Wlurone Cothstoe* Pt 1 211); *Wulfwine* (*Woluinesfur'* Pt 1 52).

*Ytting (Titlar Hill).

B. MIDDLE ENGLISH (SCANDINAVIAN)

Esgar (East Garston†, *Esegaresgrave* Pt 2 416).

Grim (*Grymesdon* Pt 2 308); *Gunna* fem. (*Gonnecrofta* Pt 1 22); *Gunnor* (*Gunnoresgrave* Pt 2 502).

Thur (*Thuresweye* Pt 2 384).

† East Garston (listed as Garston) is wrongly shown on O.S. *Britain before the Norman Conquest* (1973) as a "Grimston-Hybrid".

C. MIDDLE ENGLISH AND CONTINENTAL

Annot fem. (*Annotecroft* Pt 2 510).

Beringer (*Beringeresfeld* Pt 1 64); *Bernard* (*Bernardestreth* Pt 1 65).

Clarice fem. (*Clarissemor* Pt 1 227); *Clemence* fem. (*Clemencehulle* Pt 1 64); *Cust* fem. (*Custescroft* Pt 1 65).

Eve fem. (*Dame Evecroft* Pt 2 321).

Gilbert (*Gilibertesbreche* Pt 1 239); *Godfrey* (*Godefreyeslond'* Pt 2 319).

Hugh (*Huwemede* Pt 1 169).

Isabel fem. (*Isabelewode* Pt 2 333).

Jack (*Jackeswere* Pt 2 365); *Julian* fem. (*Julianelond* Pt 1 161).

Laurence (*Laurencesmede* Pt 2 297, *Laurencewey* Pt 2 422); *Lethe-nard* (*Lethennardesyate* Pt 1 111; Professor Cameron has found evidence from Li which suggests that this is a side-form of *Leonard*. John *Lethenard*, assessed in Saxby All Saints 1332 *SR*, is called John *Lyonard* 1327 *SR*.).

Martin (*Martynesaker* Pt 1 51).

Nicholas (*Nicholasforlong* Pt 2 521).

Osanna fem. (*Osannehurne* Pt 1 52).

Reynald (*Reynaldesdoune* Pt 1 66; *Reynaldeslond'* Pt 2 423); *Roger* (*Roggerscherd* Pt 2 520).

Sara fem. (*Belldame Saares Heedland, Dame Sarysakyr'* Pt 2 421); *Selina* fem. (*Selinegrove, Selinecroft* Pt 2 322).

Wigan, Wigeyn (*Wyganescroft, Wyganeslond* Pt 1 23, *Wygayneslond* Pt 1 66); *Winegod* (*Wynegodespol* Pt 1 52).

NOTES ON THE DISTRIBUTION AND USAGE
OF SOME ELEMENTS

bær². The distribution of bær² in Berks is limited to the eastern half of the county, Bere Ct in Pangbourne being a western outlier from a small group in Windsor Forest; *v.* Map VI. The single instance noted in Sr (Beare Green in Capel) is not near Windsor Forest. The el. is not listed in W, Gl, O or Bk, but Mr Gover informs us that there are 10 instances in Ha. As the single Sr instance is in the S. of that county, it appears that the E. Berks ns. represent a small northward extension of the general distribution pattern. The -inga- compound in Billingbear perhaps suggests communal use of swine pasture.

beorg. beorg is used of tumuli more frequently than of natural hills (cf. W 415, 422). In Burghfield and Farnborough it may refer to natural hills, but the sense 'tumulus' is possible here also. The el. is common in charter bounds, *v.* 770.

beretūn. All instances of beretūn are in the western half of Berks.

brōc. brōc is a little commoner than burna in ns. which have survived, but it is not a very frequent el. in settlement-ns. The distribution is fairly even. With the exception of *Dudbroke* (the alternative early n. for R. Blackwater), it is used of very small streams or of branches of a river. There is interchange with burna in OE references to the stream from which Hagbourne is named. It was noted in W (415) that brōc and burna were about equally common, burna being generally used of a larger stream. *v.* burna *infra.*

burh. burh is used in three senses, 'ancient fort', 'manor house' and 'market town'. There are 10 certain instances which refer to prehistoric forts. Only ns. which have burh 'manor house' as final el. have been shown on the distribution map of habitative els. (IV). There are five of these (Bucklebury, *Buntingbury*, Eastbury, Kintbury, Sowberry), and they do not yield a significant distribution pattern. burhtūn occurs once, on the W. boundary of the county, and may be an OE habitative term in this instance, as opposed to a n. for a settlement near an ancient fort or connected with a borough.

burna. burna is well evidenced in surviving ns. In *Auborn*, Lambourn and Pangbourne it is used of larger rivers than brōc, but the distinction is not absolute, as Cranbourne, Enborne, Hagbourne and

Winterbourne refer to very small streams. The el. occurs with similar frequency in Sr and Gl, is more frequent in W, but much less frequent in O and Bk. Mr Gover informs us that there are 24 instances in Ha. In S. central and S.W. England the el. appears to be rather more frequent S. of the Thames.

camp. camp in one major n. and four f.ns. has been plotted on Map II, and the distribution is discussed in Introd.

clif. clif in Clewer (on the E. boundary of Berks) refers to the bank of the Thames. In Cleeve Hill (Lambourn) and Winslow (Ashbury), both in the W. of the county, it refers to escarpments. In O, where the el. is more common than in Berks, it mostly refers to river-banks, as e.g. in Clifton Hampden, where the land by the Thames is exceptionally flat. The only certain use of clif meaning 'steep slope' in O is Swalcliffe, in the N.W. of the county. As the sense 'escarpment' is very well evidenced in Gl and W, it may be that the two meanings are characteristic respectively of eastern and western counties, though there is no absolute territorial division between them.

clop(p), cloppa. This is said in Elements to be probably a WSax rather than an Anglian or K word. It occurs in Sr, W, Gl, but not in O. It is used only as the first el. of compounds, with a limited range of second els., i.e. cot, hām, tūn, hyll.

cot(e). Names in cot(e) are plotted on Map IV. The el. is much commoner in the N.W. than elsewhere in the county. It is rare in the E., and this accords with its rarity in Sr. The 13 instances in the N.W. form part of a distribution pattern which shows the el. to be specially characteristic of N.E. Wilts (W 416) and the adjacent part of O.

Six of the 24 ns. are of the 'geographically related' type, probably indicating dependence on more important settlements. Three are compounded with ceald 'cold'. These indications of humble status are offset, however, by the occurrence of 8 of the 24 places in DB. In addition to these, Circourt was a knight's holding t. William, and Didcot and Longcot, though not recorded till e. 13th, are both modern parishes, as are several of the places surveyed in DB. Most of the TRE assessments of the 8 places in DB are relatively modest – Beckett 5 hides, *Calcot* 3, Clapcot 7, Draycott 10, Fulscot 3, Hodcott two estates of 5 hides each, Southcot 2. Buscot, however, has the remarkable TRE assessment of 40 hides. This is clearly not an instance in which the main centre of the estate has shifted from a settlement with a more dignified name, and it looks as if the establishment belonging either to an official or to an individual named Burgweard really was regarded as a cot.

cumb. cumb is slightly more frequent than denu. Mostly it is used of shorter, shallower, broader valleys than denu, The Coombe in Streatley and the valley of Compton Beauchamp being typical examples. The other Berks Compton probably refers to the small widening of the long valley of the Pang in which the village lies, the main valley probably being the denu of *Ashden*. It may be significant that Farn Combe in Lambourn, which is longer and narrower than most valleys with ns. in cumb, has -dene added to the two 14th-cent. forms.

denu. denu is mostly used of valleys which are long and narrow. The perfect example is the long, twisting valley in Kintbury which gives n. to Hidden. The el. is used in this way also in the Chilterns, where the valley which gives n. to Harpsden O 72–3 is a similar feature.

dūn. Many ns. containing dūn are on the Berkshire Downs (which was *Æscesdūn* in OE), or refer to spurs projecting from the Downs. Where the reference is to a different massif, as in *Æbbandun*, Faringdon, Ogdown, *Snowdon*, Standen, the feature is usually extensive, either flat-topped, or with broad, flat shelves. There are also several dūn ns. on the edges of ridges, e.g. Ryedown, which is on a low ridge between streams, and Hadden. Only in Harrowdown does the el. refer to a small, abrupt, isolated hill, and it is noteworthy that *Hill* has been added to the modern form of this n. Only a small proportion of ns. in dūn are settlement-ns. – Bowden, Bowdown, Evendon's Fm, Faringdon, Sanden, Standon. Abingdon is probably named from the Boar's Hill massif, *v.* Pt. 1 2. Faringdon is a major settlement, and may have been the centre of a very big estate, *v.* Pt 2 366.

ende. There is little trace of ende in the sense 'small hamlet', characteristic of some counties, e.g. Herts, Wa. Southend in Brightwalton may represent this, since it is isolated, not at the southern end of a village and not (like Knollend) in the extreme tip of the parish. Some other instances may occur among mod. minor ns., e.g. Moss End in Warfield.

ersc. ersc is only found in E. Berks, the most western example being a f.n. in Grazeley, S.S.W. of Reading. The distribution in the country is a S.E. one. Elements cites ns. in K, Ess, Sx, Herts and Sr, and one f.n. is noted Mx 198. Mr Gover informs us that there are 4 instances in Ha (excluding f.ns. and charter bounds), and these are in Peters-

field, Dogmersfield and Odiham, all E. of Reading. The only exceptions to this distribution noted so far appears to be two f.ns. in W (W
430), and one in Gl (Gl 4 123). ersc is frequently compounded with
words for crops, as in Beynhurst (bēan) and several compounds with
āte, ryge, hwǣte. This may indicate that it describes land not subject
to normal crop-rotation. The hundred-n. Beynhurst probably refers
to a meeting-place, which is likely to have been on the edges of
cultivated land. A meaning 'intake' might be considered. v. Introd.
837, 840.

fal(o)d. Except for the compound of uncertain meaning found in
Wyfield, *Wyfold'*, Wyvols Ct and Wyfold in S.E. O, fal(o)d is only an
occasional f.n. el. in Berks, as in O. The area (including part of
S. Surrey) in which it is an important p.n. el. lies well to the S. of
Berks.

feld. Ns. in feld have been plotted on Map III except for those, such
as Aldfield, Mousefield, Pitfield, which are clearly not relevant to the
general settlement-pattern. The el. is much more common in E. Berks
and the Chilterns than in the W. A high proportion of the E. Berks
and Chiltern ns. in feld are parish ns., and it seems clear that in this
area the el. has a quasi-habitative significance, perhaps arising from
the feld being an open or cleared area used for cultivation. The group
of parishes W. and S. of Reading – Bradfield, Englefield, Burghfield,
Wokefield, Stratfield, Swallowfield, Arborfield and Shinfield – is
most striking. Here are eight parishes, contiguous except for modern
intrusions like Beech Hill, all but one of which (Arborfield) are
surveyed in DB. As can be seen by comparing Maps III and IV,
habitative terms are very rare in this area. It appears that feld is the
normal term for a settlement here, v. Introd. 835–6, 841.

The group of ns. in feld in Windsor Forest includes three parishes,
Binfield, Warfield and Winkfield. The other members of this group
are Littlefield Green in W. Waltham, Cruchfield in Bray and *Losfeld*
in Clewer. Warfield, Winkfield and *Losfeld* are DB manors, and all the
ns. refer to settlements.

In N.W. Berks only two p.ns. in feld have been plotted on Map III.
Watchfield is a pre-Conquest and a DB estate. Here, and in Clanfield
in the adjacent part of O, the use of feld as a quasi-habitative el. seems
probable. The other N.W. Berks n., Ganfield 'open land of the
sports', refers to the meeting-place of a hundred, and is not a
settlement-n. In S.W. Berks the only instance of feld plotted on Map
III is Wickfield Fm in E. Shefford, which is a minor settlement-n.

Just over the border in W, however, is Froxfield, which is a parish, and was an estate in A.D. 804. It appears that the use of feld as a major settlement term, which is common in E. Berks and The Chilterns, occurs sporadically in W. Berks and the adjacent part of O and W.

The relationship of feld, as a major p.n. el., to woodland would make an interesting study. It may seem paradoxical to regard feld as a term connected with woodland, but land which is 'open' (as the conventional translation has it) is being contrasted with land which is not, and this contrast would be most apparent in or on the edge of forest. The use of feld in p.ns. W. and S. of Reading doubtless refers to the presence of forest to the E. It was noted in O 1–2 that there was an area along the N.W. foot of the Chilterns referred to in OE charter bounds as *on þæne feld*. This use of the term in contrast to the wooded hills is similar to that suggested for the ns. in feld W. of Windsor Forest. The O and Bk settlement-ns. in feld which occur in the Chilterns, however, illustrate another use of the el. Those plotted on Map III are Nuffield O, Greenfield O, *Abfield* (in Stokenchurch) Bk, Turville Bk, Binfield O, Rotherfield O. Of these, Nuffield, Turville, Rotherfield and possibly *Abfield* are major settlement-ns. These places do not adjoin the Chiltern forests; they are some of the villages of the Chiltern plateau, and must have been surrounded by the woods which are assumed to have covered the hills (O xii). In these ns. feld seems to have the same sense as lēah (*q.v.*), referring to open land used (or perhaps made by clearing) for the purpose of settlement in a forest region. This is probably true also of the ns. in Windsor Forest, as O.S. Geological Map Sheet 269 shows them situated in an area of almost unrelieved London Clay.

Ns. in feld are likely to refer obliquely to woodland, whether they lie on the outskirts of it or within the forested area. On the other hand, not all patches of woodland have ns. in feld associated with them. The el. is strikingly absent from Hormer Hundred, and from the area of the cluster of names in lēah which has been tentatively identified with the forest of *Barroc* on Map II. It may be that these anomalies are due to different dates in the change to the English language in these regions, but a country-wide study of the p.n. el. feld would be required in order to assess the course and approximate dating of its sense-development. *v.* Introd. 836 for another possible interpretation of this distribution-pattern.

fenn. This el. is even rarer than in Sr and W, and appreciably rarer than in O.

flēot. This el. is rare, but the examples noted make it clear that as in Sr (104), O (445), W (431) and Ha it refers to a river or a small stream.

ford. ford is an important major p.n. el., and settlement-ns. containing it have been plotted on Map V. There are only two in the E. of the county, Twyford and Sandford, fairly close together on R. Loddon. There are a number of examples in the S.W., Hungerford and Denford on R. Kennet, Sandleford and Shalford on R. Enborne, Stanford on R. Pang, and Shefford and Welford on R. Lambourn. The main concentration of settlement-ns. in ford is in the N.W., Garford, Frilford, Lyford, Hatford, Stanford and Shellingford being parishes on R. Ock or its tributaries, and other instances occurring on both banks of R. Thames. This distribution is discussed in Introd.

fyrhð. This el. is rare, but better represented in the E. of the county than in the W.

grāf. Surviving ns. in grāf for which there are early spellings are plotted on Map IV.

grēne². grēne² refers to a village green in The Green in Holyport, Leckhampstead and Steventon. In Brightwalton Green, however, it refers to a hamlet distinct from the main village. This last use, which appears to be characteristic of some ancient woodland areas, is very well evidenced in E. Berks, cf. e.g. the ns. in -Green listed for the parish of Bray Pt 1 48–9, and such settlements as Pinkney's Green in Maidenhead, Cox Green in W. Waltham. Examples in other wooded areas of Berks include Trash Green in Burghfield, Hunt's Green in Boxford. This semantic development would repay study.

hǣme. hǣme is well evidenced but not as common as in O (O 449), probably because E. Berks formed part of an area, including Bk and Sr, where it was not used.

hām. Ns. in hām are plotted on Map IV. The el. is notably rare in N.W. Berks, the only example being Wytham, near the Thames. It is better evidenced in S.W. Berks, where some examples (as in the adjacent part of W) appear to be closely related to Roman roads and settlements. This aspect of the distribution pattern is discussed in Introd. Sulham, in the centre of the county, is near the Roman road from Silchester to Dorchester. In E. Berks the situation is complicated by the difficulty in distinguishing hām from hamm in p.ns. by the Thames. It is probable that some hām ns. occur near the river. The only ns. in hām in E. Berks away from the Thames are Waltham and Wokingham. Waltham is near a line of Roman remains which are probably related to the presumed Roman road from Silchester to St Albans (*v.* Introd. 804–5). For Wokingham *v.* -inga-.

Of the 10 ns. in the county which seem reasonably certain to contain hām, 7 are ns. of modern parishes. Comparison with surrounding counties is difficult because of the problem of distinguishing hām from hamm. It seems clear, however, that hām is appreciably more common in Sr than in Berks. It is probably slightly less common in Bk and O. It is 'probably a rare el. in Gl' (Gl 4 193). W has 10 probable examples, the same number as Berks, but allowing for the greater size of W this means that hām is less common to the west of Berks.

hamm. Of the 22 Berks ns. which certainly or almost certainly contain hamm, 8 are ns. of parishes. Of these, 7 are mentioned in DB or earlier. Benham, while not a modern parish, is the n. of several DB estates, so should be counted as another major n. in hamm. Of these 9 major p.ns., only Wittenham shows the meaning 'land in a river-bend', which may be the earliest sense of the el. in p.ns. (*v.* M. Gelling, NoB XLVIII, 140–62). This sense may also be found in the minor n. Ham Fields, but the commonest meaning of hamm in Berks, in major and in minor ns., is 'river-meadow'. The late sense 'enclosed plot, probably in marginal land' is well represented; Warnham, Wicklesham, Witnam's Barn contain this, and it occurs in charter boundaries (*v.* 663–4).

Settlement-ns. in hamm are plotted on Map V. The el. is not significantly more frequent in any one part of the county. Comparison with surrounding counties is difficult, for the reason mentioned under hām. It appears likely that hamm is appreciably more common in Gl than in Berks, and rather less common in Bk and O. The frequency is similar in Berks, Sr and W.

hāmstede. hāmstede is a major p.n. el. in all Berks instances, with the possible exception of Bothampstead. (One certain and one possible instance in charter bounds are not counted here.) Of the 8 ns., 5 are recorded in DB and the other 3 occur before 1200. The ns. are plotted on Map IV. They occur in the S.W. and E. of the county, not in the N.W.

Only 3 ns. in hāmstede are listed in Sr, all minor ns., as is the single instance in O (which is plotted on Map IV). Bk has 2 lost ns. (one of which is on Map IV), and a surviving Leckhampstead, identical with the Berks Leckhampstead; all 3 Bk examples are major ns. Mr Gover informs us that in Ha the el. only occurs in charter bounds. One

instance (Grimstead, a parish) is noted in W. Gl has 3 examples, one
a parish, one a DB manor whose n. was supplanted by the French
Miserden, and one a minor n.

In view of this rarity of hāmstede in surrounding counties, the 8
examples in Berks constitute a notable feature of the county's
nomenclature, especially as they are fairly close together. There is a
similar concentration in W. Hrt, *v.* Hrt 245.

hāmtūn. Bockhampton, the single surviving instance of hāmtūn, is a
DB estate of 8 hides TRE, and must be classified as a major p.n., by
contrast with the f.n. *Bechamtone*, mod. Beachampton, in Hurley,
which is the only other instance noted in Berks. The el. is very rare
in Sr and Bk. O has 4 probable examples. Mr Gover informs us that
the el. is more frequent in Ha, with c. 10 instances. In W and Gl, 14
and 9 examples are listed respectively, and even allowing for some
uncertainty in the identification of this el. it seems clear that its
frequency is greater to the S. and W. of Berks. It is commoner still in
Wo. The single surviving instance in Berks is in the W. of the county.
v. Introd. 831.

hlāw. It is probably safe to say that hlāw, hlǣw refer to tumuli or to
mounds of artificial outline (as in Scutchamer). For instances in
charter bounds *v.* 780. The el. is very rare in Sr, and only found in a
few f.ns. in Ha (*ex inf.* Mr Gover). In W it is about as frequent as in
Berks, but it is rather more common in Bk, O and Gl, reflecting a
general increase in use to the N. of Berks. *v.* Introd. 828–9.

hōh. hōh is rare in Berks, as it is in Sr, O, Gl and W. It is appreciably
more common in Ha (*ex inf.* Mr Gover) and Bk. The el. has a patchy
distribution in the country, perhaps governed primarily by topographical considerations.

holt. holt is well represented in Berks, but only once occurs in a major
n. (Sparsholt). It is less common in Sr and Bk, and was not noted at
all in O. Mr Gover informs us that there are 17 examples in Ha, and
26 are noted in Gl. It is rather rare in W, however, so cannot be
assumed to become steadily commoner to the S. and W. of Berks.

hrycg. Of the 13 Berks ns. in hrycg only Curridge, Hartridge and
Irish Hill are DB manors.

hyll. There is a good deal of variety in the topographical application
of hyll, and the senses evidenced in Berks ns. overlap to some extent
with those of dūn, *q.v.* A few instances of hyll – e.g. Gold Hill, South
Hill Pk – could equally well have been ns. in dūn. On the whole,
however, it is evident that hyll is used of smaller features. Beech Hill,

a small eminence defined by the 200' contour, is a good example, and it is probably significant that the hyll of Coleshill, while nearly as high as the dūn of Faringdon, is smaller in area. hyll is used of a slight rise on a road (e.g. Rood Hill), and occasionally of a low ridge (e.g. Wood Hill), but also of a steep escarpment in the Inkpen area. It is sometimes applied to small knobs on a large massif, e.g. Boar's Hill and Thorn Hill, and in this sense there is some overlap with dūn; Boar's Hill is not much different from Lollingdon. As with dūn, only a few ns. in this category refer to settlements – Coleshill, *Hull*, Sunninghill.

hyrst. Ns. in hyrst are plotted on Map VI. Three of the 10 (Sandhurst, S. N. Hurst, Tilehurst) have become parish-ns., but all are late-recorded, and the el. does not appear to have been used in pre-Conquest times in the formation of settlement-ns. in Berks, *v*. Introd. 837. The use in Gl (Gl 4 194) is similar to that in Berks. The el. is much rarer in surviving ns. in Bk and O, somewhat rarer in W. It is a very important p.n. el. in Sr, but most examples are concentrated in the S. and S.E. of that county, and Mr Gover informs us that it is similarly common in S. Hants, but rare in the N.

īeg. īeg is an important el. in settlement-ns. in N.W. Berks, and these are plotted on Map V. Charney, Goosey, Hanney, Pusey, Tubney are parishes on R. Ock or its tributaries; Cholsey and Hinksey are parishes on R. Thames, and Mackney is a hamlet in Brightwell parish, not far from Cholsey. All these ns. are recorded in DB or earlier (Mackney and Hinksey are not in DB, but are in pre-Conquest charters). The parishes are often surrounded by streams, but the occurrence of some of the ns., especially Cholsey and Mackney, as topographical features in charter bounds, and the topography of some other sites such as Tubney, suggest that the characteristic īeg referred to in a settlement-n. in this area was a low hill in marshy ground. Witney is a good example of this usage in the adjacent part of O.

The other surviving ns. in īeg show that it was also used to designate meadowland on an island site. Berry, Borough Fm, Eney, Fobney, Levery, Odney, Shaftsey, Ray Ct, Rowney, Tidney, Towney show this use. In this sense the el. is well represented in E. Berks, but not in the S.W. or N.W. (unless this is considered to be the original sense in Hinksey). There are examples (e.g. Andersey and Otney in Culham) on the O bank of the R. Thames.

The use of īeg as a final el. in early settlement-ns. is seen in O in Witney and possibly in Osney. It occurs in some ns. in N.E. Sr such as Battersea, Bermondsey, Chertsey, and in some major ns. in W where Dauntsey, Oaksey, Patney and Pewsey are parishes. There are 4 parishes in Gl with ns. in -ēg and one (Eyford) in which it is the first el. It seems possible that īeg should be regarded, like feld and lēah, as a quasi-habitative el. in major p.ns., referring to a site suitable for a settlement in marshy country. It is not difficult, in practice, to distinguish ns. in this category from those in which īeg refers to meadowland. *v.* Introd. 819.

-ing². Ns. in -ing² have not been plotted as a separate category on a Distribution Map, but all except Wasing are shown on the maps illustrating the charter bounds, and the surviving ones are plotted with the symbol 't' on Map V. They are all stream-ns. Except for Wasing, all are in the valley of the Ock, and they constitute another strand in the individual character of the toponymy of this region. It is noteworthy that the 5 surviving ns. are all parish-ns. or (in the case of Ginge) DB manors. *v.* Introd. 821–2. Gillian Fellows Jensen considers that ns. in -ing² are the first els. of some compound ns. classified here under -ingtūn, *q.v.*

-ingas. Ns. in -ingas and -inga- are plotted on Map IV. The 2 -ingas ns. are close together (*v. infra*), but the -inga- compounds are scattered over the county and do not form a marked characteristic of any one area, though the type is rather better represented in the E. than in the N.W. or S.W. The *Sunningas* of Sonning were the people of a large province, the settlement called Sonning being on the W. boundary of this, and Sunninghill perhaps on the S. boundary; and the presence of some *Sunningas* in another province gave rise to the n. Sunningwell. It is possible that the *Horningas* of Hormer Hundred (migrants from which are mentioned in a 10th-cent. n. in O) also constituted an ancient province. The *Woccingas* of Wokingham (the only -ingahām n. in Berks) may have been a detached group of settlers from a province round Woking Sr. *Bruningemere* is a parallel formation to Hormer (though possibly with a pers.n., not a topographical term, as first el.), and the forest of that n. stretched at least from Bradfield to Oare; this may contain the n. of another early administrative district named, like Hormer, from the meeting-place of the *Brūningas*. Attempts to weave other -inga- ns., such as Shellingford and Wallingford, into a hypothetical early administrative pattern would be too fanciful to be useful. If nothing had been known of the *Sunningas* except the n. Sonning, we would not have been aware that the p.n. is on the W. boundary of the province. This, and the occurrence of Sunningwell in another area, may indicate the hazards of trying to reconstruct administrative geography from such p.ns., though it is probable that the ns. do relate to administrative units. Stenton (IPN 50) considered that the *Rēadingas* of Reading were the *folc* of a *provincia*, adducing in support of this the great DB manor of Reading, which covered an area at least seven miles wide. Reading is one of the few instances in the country in which an -ingas p.n. bears a close correspondence to the site of early pagan Saxon burials. On the analogy of Sonning, however, the tribal n. *Rēadingas* may have become attached to the settlement at Reading because this was the place which lay near the boundary between *Rēadingas* and *Sunningas*. On this interpretation, the proximity of Reading and Sonning does not indicate that this is the centre of a region of early settlement, but rather that this is the border between two tribal territories.

It is clear that the use of -ingas and -inga- in Berks p.ns., whether added to a pers.n. or a topographical term, does not provide a useful guide to the regions of earliest settlement. The relative frequency of the type in the E. of the county accords with the greater frequency of such ns. in Sr than in W. *v.* Introd. 815.

ingtūn. ingtūn ns. are not numerous in Berks. The p.ns. here considered to fall into this category number 10 certain and 3 possible. All except Ardington have been plotted as -ingtūn on Map III. Eight of them are in the S.W., the other 4 in the N.W. Probably little significance should be attached to the absence of the type in the E. of the county, as tūn is very sparsely represented in that area. The distribution of ingtūn is considered under tūn.

Places with -ingtūn ns. mostly enjoy a fairly high status in Berks. The only ones not in DB are Elton and Everington. Of the remaining 10, the only one with a low TRE assessment (3 hides) is Woolhampton. Steventon was assessed TRE at 20 hides, and Betterton contained two estates of 10 hides each. Avington, Brightwalton and *Ulvritone* were assessed at 10 hides, Donnington and Willington at 8 hides. Brimpton contained 2 estates of 4½ and 3½ hides. Kennington is mentioned in DB, but no hidage is given, and there is none in the 10th-cent. charter for this place.

The classification of -ington ns. usually adopted in EPNS vols has recently been challenged by Gillian Fellows Jensen in *Sydsvenska ortnamnssällskapets årsskrift* (1974). She considers that EPNS editors take the first els. to be pers.ns. more often than they should, and do not allow sufficiently for the addition of tūn to a p.n. or a topographical term in -ing. In Berks, she suggests that Brightwalton,

Brimpton, Donnington, Everington and Steventon are wrongly
analysed as pers.n. +-ingtūn, and her criticism of the etymologies
given for these ns. must be considered in some detail.

For Brightwalton, Dr Fellows Jenson suggests a p.n. *Beorhtwald
'bright wood'. Brightwalton, as can be seen from Map III, is at the
edge of a patch of wooded country, so the etymology is not impossible
on topographical grounds; but the proposed p.n. is not altogether
convincing, as beorht is a rare p.n. el., and weald is only found once
in Berks in the compound Wealtham (modern Waltham), which was
probably an appellative (v. Introd). The proposed p.n. would be an
unusual one, whereas the pers.n. Beorhtweald occupies three columns
in Searle's Onomasticon.

As regards Brimpton and Donnington, Dr Fellows Jensen's case
rests mainly on the recurrence of these p.ns. in a number of counties.
She lists 7 ns. which are identical with Brimpton, and 21 which seem
to be from the compound found in Donnington. She suggests that the
first els. of both ns. are ing² p.ns. formed on appellatives referring to
hilly places. For Brimpton she suggests an -ing formation from 'OE
brūn, *brȳne in the sense "edge brow of hill"', but she does not give
documentation for this supposed el. which is not in Elements. For
Donnington she suggests an -ing formation from dūn. The second
suggestion seems the more convincing, but if an ing² p.n. *Dūning
were in sufficiently common use to father 21 p.ns. in tūn, one might
have expected it to be on record once or twice without the addition
of tūn. There are detailed charter bounds for the hilly area N. of the
Berks Donnington, but such a p.n. does not occur in them. The
pers.n. Dun(n) is well recorded, and it could have been particularly
common at the time when the p.n. type pers.n. +-ingtūn was being
formed, which may have been a restricted period (v. Introd).

Dr Fellows Jensen's discussion of Steventon is open to more
serious objection. She says that the occurrence in charter bounds of
the phrase stifingc hæma ge mære proves 'that the x-ing part of an
ingtūn p.n. has existed in its own right'. This statement is not
consistent with the general use of -hæma- (q.v.) in OE charter-bounds
and ME f.ns. in Berks and O. As can be seen from the examples listed
on pp. 778, 874, -hæma- is added to the first syllable or the first two
syllables of a compound p.n. without much regard for sense and
certainly without implying that the truncated p.n. had an independent
existence. Cf. especially cing hæma gemære in the bounds of Longworth. This refers to the boundary of Kingston, but it does not prove

that *cing* was a p.n. in its own right. Other examples include *Cuceshæma gemære* referring to Cuxham O and *easthæma gemære* referring to Aston O. The later forms for Steventon support the OE forms in suggesting an original **Stīfingtūn* rather than **Stȳfingtūn*, and this does not seem at all likely to have been a wooded area where the clearing of tree-stumps would be necessary, so it is doubtful whether **stȳfing* 'clearing' would be formally or topographically appropriate for this n.

For Everington, Dr Fellows Jensen suggests an -ing derivative of eofor 'boar', rather than *Eofor* pers.n. + -ingtūn. The K n. Evering is a possible parallel, but may be a n. in -ingas. For *Elington* Dr Fellows Jensen's suggestion has been accepted, *v.* 849.

land. The only Berks n. in which land seems likely to mean 'estate' is Speenhamland. Otherwise it means 'cultivated land' or 'strip in an open field'. Only Newland has become a parish. The el. is appreciably commoner in surviving ns. in Sr, Gl and W, but is similarly restricted in sense and found only in minor ns. In Bk and O it is rather less common than in Berks.

lēah. lēah is much less common than in Sr, Ha, W and Gl, but with 54 examples it is nevertheless the commonest el. apart from tūn in surviving ns. in Berks. An attempt has been made to classify these 54 ns. as Major Names (i.e. parishes and/or DB manors), Hamlets or Fms, and Woods.

By far the largest number, about 30, fall into the second category of Hamlets or Fms. There are 14 major ns., including Woodley, which is late-recorded, and there are at least 13 instances in which the n. clearly refers to a wood.

The major ns. in lēah are fairly scattered in and among the areas in which the el. is found. (The distribution in the county is patchy, as can be seen from Map III.) There is no group of adjacent parishes with ns. in lēah, such as occurs, e.g., in N. Warwickshire. In this respect the Berks use of lēah differs from that of feld, *q.v.* There is no area where lēah seems to be a regular term for an important settlement, as does feld in the district S. and W. of Reading.

The meaning 'wood' is particularly well evidenced in Berks. BCS 366 gives the ns. of three woods attached to Wickham in Welford, and two of them, Poughley and *Trindley*, contain lēah. This sense is evident in at least 13 p.ns. in lēah which are referred to as woods in OE or ME refs. For this reason, it is particularly difficult in Berks to distinguish between the senses 'wood' and 'clearing'. The parish ns.

in lēah are mostly in close proximity to other examples in which the el. is most likely to mean 'wood', so 'clearing' cannot automatically be assumed even in a parish n. The late meaning 'meadow' is easier to discern in a few ns. in E. Berks (*infra*), and Radley in Hormer Hundred may also contain the el. in this sense.

Clear instances of lēah in the sense 'meadow' are to be seen in E. Berks in the ns. Lea, Whistley and Woodley (*v.* Pt **1** 146), in a marshy area on the W. boundary of Windsor Forest; and it is possible that this sense should be considered for some ns. S. of Reading, especially Hartley. It is in E. Berks that the later developments of lēah to mean 'open space in woodland' and 'meadow' are most clearly seen. The earliest meaning 'wood' is less well evidenced here, but it does occur in Littlewick, which refers to a wood in OE and ME refs. The major ns. along the Thames – Streatley, Purley, Hurley in Berks, Henley O and Fawley Bk – probably refer to open spaces in woodland.

In Hormer Hundred, where the el. is well represented in contrast to the rest of N.W. Berks, the meaning 'wood' is clearly evidenced in Bagley Wd. Most of the other ns. in this group probably refer to open spaces in woodland, but Chawley, with cealf as first el., may mean 'pasture', and Radley may mean 'meadow'.

The most notable concentration of ns. in lēah occurs in S.W. Berks, and this group may mark the position of the ancient forest of *Barroc* from which the county is named. Some of these ns., e.g. Bradleywood, Eastley, Gidley, Hailey, refer to woods. The group contains 4 major ns., Fawley, Ilsley, Chieveley, Woolley, and here, and in some Fm-ns. such as Henley, the el. may refer to open spaces in woodland used for settlement. No trace has been found in S.W. Berks in surviving ns. of lēah in the sense 'meadow', and this may indicate that the el. went out of use here earlier than it did in E. Berks. The scarcity of other terms for a wood in this part of Berks (*v.* Map VI) suggests that lēah retained the meaning 'wood' for a considerable time here. *v.* Introd. 836–7.

mere. There are 13 Berks ns. in mere, apart from f.ns. Two of these, Hormer and Ripplesmere, are hundred-ns., so refer to pools which marked meeting-places, and it is suggested on p. 932 that *Bruningmere* may also have been a meeting-place. Of the remaining 10, Catmore and Peasemore are DB manors and Stanmore was a pre-Conquest estate. These three settlements lie fairly close together between The Ridgeway and the valley of R. Lambourn, and they probably indicate the importance of ponds for settlement-sites in this hilly area where there are no streams. Dunmore Pond, just W. of Brightwalton, is in this area. A similar concentration of settlement-ns. in mere was noted O 474 in The Chilterns.

mersc. mersc is less common in Berks than mōr, q.v., both in surviving ns. and in f.ns. It is rare in settlement-ns. Tidmarsh has become a parish, but the n. is late-recorded. There is an area N. of Wantage where mersc seems to be used in preference to mōr for marshy land on the tributaries of R. Ock. Broadmarsh, Challowmarsh, Pinmarsh and Smallmarsh occur here. Similar ground to the W. has, however, given rise to the ns. Bagmore and Moor Mill, and the more extensive marshes to the E. are generally referred to by ns. in mōr. mersc is less common than mōr in Ha, Sr, Bk, O and Gl. The two els are more evenly balanced in W, where mersc is appreciably commoner than in Berks.

mōr. mōr is well represented in surviving p.ns. in all parts of Berks in the sense 'marsh', and this is the only sense in charter bounds (v. 785). This is the meaning in Moreton, the only major n. in which the el. occurs. The other, probably later, sense, 'barren upland waste', occurs in Snelsmore and in a string of ns. along the Corallian Ridge between R. Thames and R. Ock, Southmoor being the most easterly of these. Snelsmore, in the S.W. of the county, refers to a raised area now called Snelsmore Common, which is called *lytlan hæþfeld* in charter bounds (653). Snelsmore is first recorded in 1242–3, but Southmoor is recorded as *Mora* t. William, which may indicate that this sense comes in at the end of the OE period, v. Introd. 837.

It would be difficult, perhaps impossible, to isolate any topographical factors which caused some marshes to be designated by the term mōr, and others by mersc, q.v. There does not appear to be a clear sense-distinction between the two els. in Berks, though one has been noted elsewhere; v. H. Maynard, 'The Use of the Place-Name Elements *mōr* and *mersc* in the Avon Valley' (*Transactions of the Birmingham and Warwickshire Arch. Soc.* LXXXVI, 1974, pp. 80–4). Mrs Maynard has established that in Wa mersc is consistently used of more useful land.

ōra. There are 11 ns. in ōra, other than f.ns. (in which the el. is not common). Eight of these, a high proportion, are settlement-ns., and Bagnor, Boxford, Cumnor, Oare and Windsor can be classified as major ns. (i.e. modern parishes and/or DB or pre-Conquest estates). The other three settlement-ns. are lost places in Ripplesmere Hundred, one of which, *Ortone*, is a small DB manor.

The sense of the el. is uncertain in *Ortone*. Of the remaining 10 ns., 4 contain ōra in the sense 'river-bank', and 6 in the sense 'hill-slope'. 'River-bank' is seen in Bagnor, Boxford, *Hennor* and Windsor; and as Cumnor and Oare fall into the 'hill-slope' category, it is clear that both senses were current when major settlement-ns. were being coined in Berks.

The el. is of similar frequency in Sr, but only used in minor ns. Bk has six examples, only one a major n., this being Hedsor, which, like Windsor, is beside the Thames. O, like Berks, has 11 ns. in ōra, and a similarly high proportion of major ns. among them, several in the Chilterns. To the west the el. is less common; W has six examples, Gl has two, and in both counties there is one major n. in ōra. South of Berks, ōra is more common; Mr Gover informs us that there are 25 instances in Ha.

pyll. This el. is used of a small stream in Berks, as in O (O 462).

rīð. rīð, with five surviving examples, is better represented than in the counties to the S., W., and N. The el. is, however, appreciably more common in Sr than in Berks. Three of the five surviving Berks ns. are in E. Berks, but Childrey and Hendred are in the N.W. of the county, and the single possible instance of rīðig is also in the N.W. rīðig is rare or absent in all the surrounding counties.

sceaga. sceaga is represented by two ns., one in the E. and one in the S.W. of the county, the latter being a DB manor. The el. is similarly rare in Bk and Sr, and not represented at all in O. Gl and Ha have five examples each. There are 10 in W, all minor ns.

scēat. The use of scēat as a second el., with development to -*shot*(*t*), is found in one surviving n. and one f.n. in the E. of the county. It is fairly common in N. and N.W. Sr and N.E. Ha. It does not occur in Bk, O, Gl or W, though *scīete is found in W and Gl.

***scīete**. This el., a variant of scēat, is rare, but more widely distributed in the county than scēat (if it be assumed that ME forms *Shete* etc. are likely to derive from *scīete rather than from scēat, *v.* 903). The best-recorded instance is Sheet St in Windsor. The f.n. *Shete* occurs in W. Hanney in the N.W. of the county.

steall. This el. (independently of the compound hāmsteall) is only represented by one f.n. in Newbury. It does not occur in Bk, O, Sr or W. It is better represented in Gl, but still rare.

stede. This el. (apart from hāmstede, *q.v.*) is only represented by three f.ns. None of these is in the E. of the county, so they cannot be associated with the use of the el. in Sr, where there are 17 examples (excluding f.ns. and ns. in hāmstede). Mr Gover informs us that there are 14 examples in Ha. Apart from f.ns. and ns. in hāmstede the el. does not occur in Bk or O. In Gl it is slightly better represented than in Berks, and it is appreciably more common in W. It is clear from the maps in Sandred that the area in which stede is an important el. in p.ns. (apart from such compounds as hāmstede) lies S. and E. of Berks. It is the northern limit which causes Berks to be excluded, rather than the western one. *v.* Introd. 820.

stoc. The total absence of stoc from Berks p.ns. is surprising, as the el. is well represented in Ha, Sr, Bk, O, Gl, W, though less frequent in Sr than in the other counties in this group. Three of the O ns. in stoc are beside the Thames (*v.* Map IV), so only just over the Berks boundary.

stōw. The use of stōw in Berks closely resembles that in O, where it occurs in Godstow and a few f.ns. Gl is the only adjacent county in which it is more common. It does not occur in W, except for one example of Cotstow (f.ns. in cot-stōw have been disregarded in this context). The sense 'meeting-place' is not clearly evidenced in Berks apart from two ns. in pleg-stōw, *q.v.*; this sense occurs in a number of Gl ns., and in the Bk hundred-n. Bunsty.

strōd. This el. is well represented in the E. of the county. Apart from this, there is one example in Hormer Hundred, and several in a small area in the S.W., in the parishes of Greenham, Hamstead M. and Shaw. The el. is fairly common in Sr. Only one instance was noted in Bk, and none in O. It occurs in Gl and W, but less frequently than in Berks. Mr Gover informs us that there are four instances (excluding f.ns.) in Ha. This would appear to be one of the els. which are characteristic of Sr and E. Berks, *v.* Introd 840.

tūn. Exact figures for Berks ns. in tūn are difficult to calculate because of uncertainty as to whether such examples as Bray Town and Netherton should be included. The number is between 45 and 50, however, and with the 13 ns. listed under ingtūn this gives a total of 60+, giving tūn a short lead over lēah as the commonest el. in Berks ns. (apart from f.ns.). Those which seem likely to be pre-Conquest habitative ns. (numbering 50) are plotted on Map III, and the distribution of these is discussed here together with that of the ingtūn ns., also shown on Map III.

The distribution within the county is markedly uneven. Only five symbols occur E. of the Roman road from Dorchester to Silchester. There are 18 in the S.W., and 27 in the N.W. The five ns. marked in

E. Berks are widely scattered, the only suggestion of a pattern being that two are beside the Thames and one by a Roman road. In the S.W., there are three relatively isolated examples between the Icknield Way and the R. Lambourn, but most of the ns. are on the Lambourn or to the S. of it. In the N.W., while some ns. in tūn are by the Thames or by the smaller streams, the el. is mainly characteristic of the line of settlements at the foot of the Downs. It is notably scarce in the vicinity of the Ock and its tributaries.

The two main conclusions to be drawn from the pattern on Map III are that tūn is a very rare el. in E. Berks, and that, with the possible exception of Hormer Hundred, ns. in tūn are rare in areas where other p.n. els. indicate ancient forest. As regards comparison with adjacent counties, the scarcity of tūn in E. Berks accords with its rarity in Sr, which has considerably fewer examples than Berks. Bk has about the same number as Berks, O has appreciably more, but still less than 100. Mr Gover informs us that Ha has c. 140, which means that tūn is more common to the S. of Berks, even allowing for the greater size of Ha; and this is true to the west, where W has rather more ns. in tūn than Ha. In none of these counties, however, does tūn predominate as it does in Gl, where there are over 200 examples.

The significance of the distribution pattern of ns. in tūn in Berks is qualified by our knowledge of the circumstances in which some of the ns. arose. This is a county in which tūn was a living p.n. el. in ME, and Balsdon, Marlston and Templeton are 12th- or 13th-cent. ns. These have not been marked on Map III, however, and more significant in the present context is the fact that Uffington and Woolstone can be shown to have come into existence as ns. for estates rather than settlements in the mid-10th cent., and East Garston in the mid-11th cent. This same process of p.n. formation has been noted in E. Wiltshire, v. Introd. 824–5. The majority of ns. of the 'pers.n. + tūn' or 'pers.n. + ingtūn' type are likely to have arisen before c. 950, but there is a strong possibility that many of them were coined in similar circumstances to Uffington and Woolstone, perhaps between c. 750 and c. 900. Such ns. as Aldermaston, Chilton, Kingston and Knighton may be classed for this purpose with those having a pers.n. as first el. It cannot be proved that none of these ns. goes back to the period when English p.n.s first came into use, but such evidence as we have suggests that they are considerably later, that they arise from an incipient manorialism, and that they may have replaced earlier English p.ns. of a different type. This last can be proved to have

occurred in the case of Uffington and Woolstone, which were parts
of a larger estate called *Æscesbyrig*, and in the case of Kingston Lisle,
which was part of the area called Sparsholt. The meaning of tūn in
these ns. seems to be 'estate', rather than 'farm' or 'village'.

Another category of ns. in tūn which is not likely to date from the
earliest use of English is the 'geographically related' type. Some of
these (e.g. Aston in Remenham, Easton in Welford, Weston in
Buscot) are late-recorded, and could not be classified as major ns.
Aston Tirrold and Upthorpe (considered as a single example of the n.
Aston) has a much more dignified history. There are four estates here
in DB, so it is clear that this Aston throve as an independent settlement, but it seems probable that it was originally named from its
relationship to Blewbury, one of the most impressive of the greater
Anglo-Saxon estates in the county. In so far as such a thing can be
identified, Blewbury should be considered the p.n. in this area which
is most likely to date from the first use of English speech, *v.* 829–30.
Sutton Courtenay, another of these 'geographically related' ns., is a
large and important estate in DB, but the n. probably arises from its
position S. of Abingdon. Milton, the 'middle' farm or estate which
lies between Sutton and Steventon, is also large and important in
1086, but whatever the antiquity of the settlement, the n. can hardly
have come into use until the ns. Steventon and Sutton were established. It is interesting that Sutton is the most northerly of this line
of tūn ns., suggesting that the process of English naming here may
have been triggered off by that estate being named from its relationship to Abingdon. Netherton and Upton can probably be put into the
'geographically related' category (Upton being named from its
relationship to Blewbury), and Eastmanton may be placed here also.

Other ns. in tūn which are likely to have originated at a relatively
late date are Charlton (*v.* Pt 2 475) and Newton. Wallingtons and
Walton may belong with Charlton as ns. referring to a category of
workers on a large estate, but if wealh means 'Briton' they are of
earlier origin.

If it can be accepted that Aldermaston, Aston (2), Charlton (2),
Chilton, Eastmanton, Easton, Kingston (3), Knighton, Milton,
Netherton, Newton, Nuptown, Sutton, Upton, Weston (2) are unlikely to be amongst the earliest English p.n.s, and that there is a
strong possibility that the pers.n. + tūn and pers.n. + ingtūn ns. refer
to 'manorial' owners who were not of the first generations of English
speakers in Berks, then we are left with Clapton, Compton (2),

Drayton, Eaton (2), Hinton (2), Moreton and Wootton, which may be
primary habitative p.ns. Of these 10, 8 can be classified as major ns.,
the exceptions being Clapton in Kintbury and Hinton in S. N. Hurst.
The 10 ns. are fairly widely scattered, and no conclusions can be
drawn from their distribution except that, as already stated, tūn is a
habitative el. of almost negligible importance in E. Berks. Wallingtons
and *Walton* cannot be classified as they may refer to Britons (in which
case the ns. are early) or to serfs, in which case the ns. are in the same
class as Charlton.

þrop. There are four surviving Berks ns. in þrop and two lost ones.
The lost ns. (not marked on Map IV) are in Reading and Clewer, and
if these are included the examples are scattered throughout the county,
and cannot be said to link up with the distribution pattern of the el. in
adjacent counties. Only two instances (one lost) were noted in Sr.
Mr Gover informs us that there are eight in Ha, all but one in the N.
of the county. W has 10, 5 of which are shown on the part of W included on Map IV. There are 25 instances in Gl, 10 in O and 7 in Bk.
In all these counties except Sr the el. shows a tendency to occur in
clusters, which it does not have in Berks. All the Berks instances are
minor ns. and none is recorded early.

weald. The only instance of weald noted in Berks is Waltham,
which may be an appellative, *v.* Introd. The el. does not occur in Sr
or W. It is better represented in Bk and O than in Berks, though still
very rare. Mr Gover informs us that there are five instances in Ha.
Gl has 14 examples (including f.ns.), mostly in the Cotswolds.

wīc. wīc is always a minor p.n. el. in Berks, and the meaning
'dairy-farm' is appropriate for most examples. The *wikae* which
supplied cheese for the refectory are mentioned in Abingdon (II, 287),
and a *wica* which produced 10 weys of cheese is mentioned under
Buckland in DB. Many of the Berks places are first recorded in 12th–
14th cents. as *La Wyk, Wyke, La Wike*, etc., and later had the parish
n. prefixed, as Ardington Wick, Bray Wick, etc. The only example
recorded in an Old English source is *Hollicks*, OE *heal wicum*, named
from its position in a corner of the parish; and similar situations are
occupied by other examples, as e.g. Wickcroft Fm which occupies a
projection on the E. boundary of Englefield. Some of the ns. (particularly Furzewick, Gooseywick, Haslewick, Littlewick, Petwick,
Tulwick) were probably in use well before the Norman Conquest, but
there is no reason to suppose that any of them dates from an early
stage in the use of the English language in Berks.

The el. is most common in the N.W. of the county (*v.* Map IV).
As regards adjacent counties, it is of similar frequency in Ha and Sr,
but less frequent in Bk, and much rarer in O. It is very much more
common in Gl and W. Bk has two ns. (Tetchwick and Tingewick)
which occur in DB and contain -inga-. Some of the Gl ns. in wīc occur
in DB, as do two of the W ones. There is no sign in Berks of this
occasional use of wīc in major ns.

wīchām. For the significance of the two Berks examples of wīchām,
v. Introd. 802–3.

wiella. wiella refers certainly or probably to a spring in Amwell,
Brightwell, Coxwell, The Durnals, Hardwell, Harwell, Lertwell,
Sotwell, Sunningwell, Woolstone Wells. In other ns. it may refer to
the stream rather than the spring from which it rises, but it is only
used of small streams. There are no instances in r.ns. to compare with
Cherwell O. Of the 22 examples (apart from f.ns.), 8 are major ns.
The el. is about equally common in Ha, somewhat less so in Sr and
Bk, appreciably more common in O and W, and much more common
in Gl.

worð. Of the 13 ns. (apart from f.ns.) listed as containing worð, 10
are major ns. (i.e. referring to a parish and/or DB estate), and several
of these are recorded as pre-Conquest estates. Longworth and Littleworth (both originally *Wyrðe*) were assessed at 30 and 31 hides TRE,
and Chaddleworth, Denchworth and Padworth contain more than
one DB estate. This function of worð as a habitative el. applied to
major settlements should be distinguished from its use in f.ns., for
which *v. infra*. In f.ns. it appears, together with worðig and (in one
instance) worðign, as a term for a unit of agricultural land. Hollingsworth should perhaps be considered in this category.

Omitting Hollingsworth, we have 12 Berks settlement-ns. in worð.
Of these, two are in E. Berks, four in the S.W., and six in the N.W. (*v.*
Map IV). Mr Gover informs us that there are 21 such ns. in Ha, and
27 are listed in Sr. For W, 16 ns. in worð and one in worðig are listed.
The three related els. worð, worðig and worðign are all much more
common in Gl. In Bk and O, however, worð is very rare as a habitative el., with two and three examples respectively. In all these counties, as in Berks, there is a high proportion of ns. in worð which have
a pers.n. as first el.

Details of Berks f.ns. containing worð and worðig are given *supra*
917–18. This use of worð in f.ns. was noted in Sr 366–7 and in W (where
worðig also occurs) 450. In Gl (**4** 188–9), worð, worðig and worðign

are well represented in f.ns., and instances occur even in Bk (259) and O (475), where the el. is otherwise rare. Mr Gover's lists of ns. from Ha *TA*s show that such f.ns. as The Worth, The Worthy occur in that county also.

worð and worðig in f.ns. appear to have been regarded in the main as evidence of lost habitation sites, though it has been remarked (Löfvenberg 238, Sr 366–7) that the evidence from surnames and f.ns. shows that worð was in living use in ME, and the Sr discussion suggested that the el. sometimes denoted a very small enclosure. It is unlikely that the Berks f.ns. refer to lost habitation sites, partly because they are too numerous, partly because worð as a habitative el. refers usually to major settlements which, even if they have disappeared now (as Seacourt), had a good chance of being included in DB. It is much more likely that worð and its derivatives had another meaning, separate from the habitative one and remaining in use till a much later date, and that it is usually this sense which is found in f.ns. This would be similar to the use of stede in f.ns. in Ess and Herts, detailed in Sandred chapter VI.

A much more detailed study than is possible here would be necessary in order to form conclusions as to what agricultural institution gave rise to f.ns. in worð. The Laws of Ine (40) say 'Ceorles weorðig sceal beon wintres and sumeres betyned'. This has been translated 'homestead' (*English Historical Documents* I, 368), but it might perhaps be associated with the use of this group of words in f.ns. in Wessex, and taken to refer to a piece of land farmed severally, not necessarily with a dwelling-place. This is not irreconcilable with the occurrence of *Le Worth* as the n. of an open field in Windsor and elsewhere, as the manner of cultivation in different parts of an estate could change over the centuries, or a n. which originated for an enclosed plot farmed by one man could survive as the n. of an open field which either supplanted the enclosed plot or lay beside it. The terms *worth* and *worthine* are on record in ModE dial. for a piece of ground (Gl 4 198, Löfvenberg 238).

wudu. This el. is rather rare in surviving ns. in Berks, as it is in Bk and O. The only major n. in which it occurs is Wootton. It is much more common in Ha, Sr, Gl and W.

PLACE-NAMES WHICH ARE WHOLLY OR PARTLY PRE-ENGLISH

Altwood; Berkshire; ?Cane Lane; Charney; Cherbury; ?Coleshill; Cruchfield; ?Crouch Hill (f.n. Winterbourne); *Humber*; Icknield; ?The Ince (f.n. Cookham); Kennet; Loddon; Ock; Pingewood; Severn; Speen; Thames.

FRENCH PLACE-NAMES

?Beaulieu Ct Fm; *Beaurepir, Beawlewstile, Bewley Lane* (f.ns. Clewer); Beamy's Castle; *Belestre*; Bray; *Deulacresse* (f.n. Clewer); Malpas; Orts Rd.

INDEX

TO THE OLD ENGLISH CHARTER BOUNDARIES
OF BERKSHIRE

Abingdon: E VII, E VIII
  Charter to which bounds are attached,
    719
  Bounds, 732
  Charter, 719
  Bounds, 735
  v. 623, 628, 629, 631, 632, 633
Æscesbyrig, v. Uffington, Woolstone
Appleford: G II
  Charter, 750
  Bounds, 754
  v. 621, 623, 624, 629
Appleton with Eaton: E I
  Charter, 717
  Bounds, 723
  v. 621, 632
Ardington, v. Ginge
Ashampstead, v. Basildon
Ashbury: C VIII
  Charters, 677
  Bounds, 694
  v. 617, 629
Ashdown, v. Ashbury
Aston Tirrold and Upthorpe, v.
  Blewbury
Aston Upthorpe: G XII
  Charter, 752
  Bounds, 766
  v. 621, 624, 630, 631, 632

Balking, v. Kingston Lisle
Barkham: A (b) I
  Charter, 640
  Bounds, 642–3
  v. 617, 618, 624, 628
Basildon (*Bæstlæsford*): G III
  Charter, 750–1
  Bounds, 755
  v. 623, 628, 629, 632
Bayworth, v. Wootton
Beedon, v. Chieveley, Stanmore
Benham: B (b) V
  Charter, 658
  Bounds, 668
  v. 618

Bessels Leigh (*Earmundesleah*): E II
  Charter, 717
  Bounds, 724
  v. 618, 628
Blewbury, with Aston T., Aston U.,
  N. and S. Moreton: G IV
  Charter, 751
  Bounds, 758–9
  v. 618, 621–2, 623, 624, 626, 627, 629,
    630, 631, 632, 633
Boxford: B (b) VI, VII
  Charters, 658
  Bounds, 669
  v. 630
Brightwalton: B (b) I
  Charter, 657
  Bounds, 660
  v. 624, 628, 631, 632
Brightwell, Sotwell and Mackney: G V
  Charter, 751
  Bounds, 761
  v. 619
Brightwell, without Mackney: G VI
  Charter, 751
  Bounds, 763
Brimpton: A (b) II
  Charter, 640
  Bounds, 643
  v. 620, 624, 628, 633
Buckland: D XIV
  Charter, 702
  Bounds, 715
  v. 617, 618, 624
Bucklebury, v. Hawkridge

Cern (? in Pusey): D II
  Charter, 699
  Bounds, 705
  v. 617, 618, 621, 624
Charney Bassett: D I
  Estate, 699
  Bounds, 704
  v. 623, 699
Chieveley and Beedon, parts of:
  B (a) II

[947]

INDEX

TO THE INTRODUCTION TO
'THE PLACE-NAMES OF BERKSHIRE'